MANAGING ADDICTIONS

Managing Addictions

Cognitive, Emotive, and Behavioral Techniques

F. MICHLER BISHOP, Ph.D., CAS

Jason Aronson Inc.
Northvale, New Jersey
London

This book was set in 11 pt. Galliard by Alabama Book Composition of Deatsville, AL and printed and bound by Book-mart Press, Inc. of North Bergen, NJ.

Library of Congress Cataloging-in-Publication Data

Bishop, F. Michler.
    Managing addictions / F. Michler Bishop.
        p.   cm.
    Includes bibliographical references and index.
    ISBN 0-7657-0267-3
    1. Substance abuse—Treatment.   2. Substance abuse—Psychological aspects.
    I. Title.
    RC564 .B576   2000
    616.86'0651—dc21

                                                            00-020329

Printed in the United States of America on acid-free paper. For information and catalog write to Jason Aronson Inc., 230 Livingston Street, Northvale, NJ 07647-1731. Or visit our website: http://www.aronson.com

To Nelun,

Tonya, Manena, David, Anusha, and Arun

CONTENTS

Foreword   ix
    G. Alan Marlatt

Preface   xiii

Acknowledgments   xv

Part I: Key Principles and Techniques

1. The Stages of Change   3

2. Core Techniques   39

3. What Contributes to a Client's Problems?   75

4. Initial and Ongoing Assessment   107

Part II: Helping Clients Manage Their Addiction

5. Keys to Effectively Engage the Client in Treatment   139

6. Should Your Client Stop, or Just Slow Down?   153

7. How to Work on Type I Client Problems   165

8. How to Work on Type II Client Problems   203

9. How to Work on Type III Client Problems   235

Part III: Helping Clients Manage Their Emotional Life

10. Anger and Addictive Behavior   263

11. Depression and Addictive Behavior   303

12. Anxiety and Addictive Behavior   333

13. Shame and Guilt and Addictive Behavior   371

Part IV: Other Issues

14. Working with Clients with Serious Psychological
    Problems   407

15. The Role of Spirituality   427

References   447

Index   469

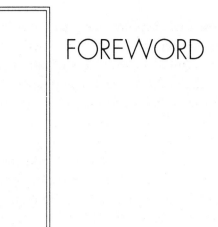

FOREWORD

It gives me great pleasure to write this Foreword for Michler Bishop's superb book. Finally there is a clear exposition of a comprehensive clinical approach to the treatment of addictive behaviors and associated psychological problems. One of the key strengths of this book is that it presents an integrated treatment approach as an overarching model that therapists can use as a guide as they help their clients manage or overcome their addictions. It also provides an integrated approach to the treatment of co-occurring disorders for clients who have both addictions and other psychological problems that are often reciprocally interrelated.

There are several aspects of this book that I particularly like. The integrated treatment model incorporates a number of related clinical techniques and approaches under the general rubric of cognitive-behavioral therapy (CBT), including motivational stages of change, motivational enhancement therapy (MET), rational-emotive behavior therapy (REBT), relapse prevention (RP), and harm reduction (HR). Other treatment approaches are discussed in detail, ranging from self-help groups to pharmacotherapy. Until now, there was no single volume that brought this integrated model together in such a consistently practical and user-friendly manner.

Parts I and II provide an overview of the treatment model. Treatment techniques are matched to the client's motivational stage of change in which the therapist offers help by following the client's own goals for his or her preferred outcome, whether this is abstinence or reduction of harmful consequences of ongoing use. Particularly impressive is the level of scholarship and clinical expertise demonstrated in the author's coverage of diagnosis and assessment procedures (Chapter 4), methods to enhance client engagement and retention in therapy (Chapter 5), choice of client goals between quitting or cutting back (Chapter 6), and clinically matched interventions for clients who are in a specific motivational stage including precontemplation (Chapter 7), contemplation (Chapter 8), or active behavior change (Chapter 9).

Part III and IV target clients who present with problems that are comorbid with addictive behaviors. Again, the treatment approach to these dual disorders is based on an integrative CBT model, thus offering a major advantage to clients who seek to understand the reciprocal interaction between their addictive problems and other psychological or behavioral disorders. The author describes, from his extensive experience, how to integrate treatment for a range of psychological problems including co-occurring problems with anger (Chapter 10), depression (Chapter 11), anxiety (Chapter 12), shame and guilt (Chapter 13), and severe psychological disorders (Chapter 14). The final chapter provides a comprehensive discussion of various spiritual approaches that have been applied in the treatment of addiction problems, ranging from traditional 12-step orientations based on a "Higher Power" or theistic framework to those with a transpersonal (non-Deity) focus, including Buddhism and other Eastern spiritual disciplines.

Numerous case studies throughout the book illustrate how various techniques can be applied with specific clients. Finally, as one who is devoted to the scientist-practitioner model, I was very pleased to see that basic and applied research related to these clinical interventions are given "top billing" in each chapter. Many chapters open with a section entitled, "What Does the Research Show?" in which empirically validated procedures are presented as a justification for including them in the treatment plan. Several highlighted boxes ("Research Note") focus on specific research studies related to the theme of each chapter.

The end result, a balanced blend of scientific and clinical expertise, is a terrific new book that soon will become required reading for anyone—whether student or professional—who wishes to learn and apply this integrated CBT model. The addictive behaviors field owes a debt of gratitude for Dr. Bishop's seminal contribution that represents the cutting edge of the emerging paradigm shift in addiction treatment.

G. Alan Marlatt, Ph.D.
Professor of Psychology and Director of the
Addictive Behaviors Research Center
University of Washington

PREFACE

I have written this book for therapists and counselors who seek more effective methods to help clients manage their addictive behaviors. The general approach of the book is based on what has come to be called cognitive-behavioral therapy (CBT) and its precursor, rational emotive behavioral therapy (REBT). CBT/REBT techniques can help people change, especially when many forces are pushing them in the opposite direction. They can help clients understand *why* they behave as they do and *how* to change.

The book focuses on how to integrate CBT/REBT techniques with Prochaska and DiClemente's (1982) stages of change model. These techniques can work whether addictive behavior is thought of as a disease or as a complex biopsychosocial phenomenon, and practitioners from a variety of therapeutic perspectives can use them. It also addresses the emotional problems that contribute to lapses and relapses. Each chapter focuses on techniques to help clients better manage the cycles of emotional disturbances and addictive behaviors and to reduce the harm they may cause.

I am a scientist-practitioner and trainer, and research guides my work. Most chapters cite relevant research. This information may help clients better understand why they are having difficulty changing, and it may help them to decide what steps they need to take.

Given the complexity of addictive behaviors, practitioners need to be flexible in working with clients. Moreover, despite the pressures of managed care, they need to develop long-term relationships with their clients. Although some clients are able to cut down or stop addictive behaviors relatively quickly, others continue to grapple with lapses and relapse throughout their lives. Clients have other problems as well, and when they encounter difficulties they need to be able to call on the practitioner, knowing that they have an experienced, empathetic person to whom to turn.

To change their behavior for the long-term, clients need to develop ways to withstand and override both the internal and external pressures to maintain the status quo. Being sensitive to the difficulty of changing amid these pressures is critical for both clients and their therapists. In addressing these issues, we come face to face with the fascinating areas of human consciousness, motivation, and intentionality. As we learn more about these topics and gain a better understanding of some of these age-old human mysteries, we will be able to be of greater help to our clients.

ACKNOWLEDGMENTS

I have been fortunate to be able to base my work as a therapist on the excellent research and tireless work of many people, but especially Alan Marlatt, William Miller, Barbara Mc-Crady, Mark Sobell, Linda Sobell, Jim Prochaska, Carlo Di-Clemente, and Reid Hester, and their associates. Their work encouraged me to enter a field that was changing and is continuing to change.

I am grateful for the opportunity to train and work at the Albert Ellis Institute, and especially to Albert Ellis for his advice and many suggestions and to Janet Wolfe for her support and supervision over the years. While working on this book, I continued to see clients at the Institute, and I thank the various members of the staff there for their valuable assistance. At the beginning of my professional life, I had the good fortune to work with the late Caleb Gattegno. I feel his influence throughout this book.

I have been enriched by the friendship and professional association of other people I have met through the Institute including Ray DiGiuseppe, Windy Dryden, Eric Jongman, Catherine Mac-Laren, Manolo Mas Bagà, Ed Nottingham, Didier Pleux, Hank Robb, and Emmett Velten. I thank my professional colleagues in the New York State Psychological Association Division on Addictions who not only have become friends but have added to my own professional growth, including Lisa Director, Scott Kellogg, Robert Lichtman, Debra Rothschild, Andrew Tatarsky, and Alexandra Wood. I have also been fortunate to have met many very helpful and friendly colleagues in Division 50 of the American Psychological Association and the Addictions SIG [Special Interest Group] of the Association for Advancement of Behavior Therapy, including Kim Fromme, Bruce Liese, Fred Rotgers, and Tony Toneatto.

I have benefited from association with SMARTR [Self-Management and Recovery Training], and through SMART I have been grateful for my association with Tom Horvath, Joe Gerstein, Phil Tate, Rich Dowling, Chuck Fritsch, Robert Sarmiento, and especially Shari Allwood, a godsend to the organization.

Over the years, many people at the State University of New York, College at Old Westbury have been of help, but especially my good friends Vicki Wolfe who read many chapters as they were written and Mervyn Keizer who encouraged me to write. I also had the wonderful help and support of my late colleague and friend, Charshee McIntyre.

I have also benefited from the expertise and valuable assistance of the editorial staff at Jason Aronson, including Norma Pomerantz, Anne Marie Dooley, and especially Elaine Lindenblatt.

I am grateful to my many friends over the years, but especially Dexter Coolidge for encouraging me to stretch and grow.

I express my appreciation to Malani Desanayake. Without her kind and dependable help I could not have had the time to write this book.

And, of course, I thank my family—my late parents, especially my mother, who taught me the value of unconditional love; my sister Margi, who taught me how to read and who has always been there for me; and my wonderful sister-in-law and various brothers-in-law, especially Bill, who always showed interest in my progress. I give special thanks to my children Tonya, Manena, and David, for years of love, fun, support, and encouragement, and to Anusha and Arun for bringing new wonder, joy, and laughter into our home and for making it so easy to get up at 7 A.M. and write.

Most of all, I want to thank my wife, Nelun, who has continually provided love, support, and affection. Without her help I would not have written this book. I hope that I am and will always be as much help to her as she has been to me.

I

KEY PRINCIPLES AND TECHNIQUES

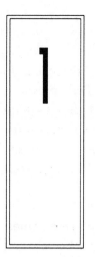

THE STAGES
OF CHANGE

Our life is shaped by our mind; we become what we think.
—The Buddha

STAGES OF CHANGE MODEL

This book is about learning how to change behaviors that are very difficult to change. The Stages of Change Model (Prochaska and DiClemente 1982, Prochaska et al. 1992, 1994) provides a very useful way to conceptualize such change.

Stage I—Precontemplation

In the first stage, the client is not contemplating changing, hence the term, *precontemplation*. The client may be in this stage for many reasons. For example, she may be demoralized. She has tried to change her behavior many times before and always failed. Thus, she does not want to think about trying again. Or she may not think she has a problem. (Chapter 7 focuses on the various reasons the client may not be contemplating change and how to motivate her to consider changing.)

Stage II—Contemplation

After a while, something may happen to cause the client to begin to contemplate changing. This is Stage II. Perhaps she is arrested for driving while intoxicated, or a friend dies of lung cancer, or her husband threatens to leave her unless she gets some help. She begins to think about the pros and cons. Perhaps she would like to change, but it seems too hard. Stage II is characterized primarily by ambivalence.

One of my clients, Sara, had tried to stop drinking several times. Every time she went back to drinking, she felt so angry at herself, and everyone in her family was so disappointed, that she didn't really want to try again. But she was thinking about it, and continued to think about it for two years.

Stage III—Preparation

For most people, changing an addictive behavior is a difficult and complex task, but their likelihood of success increases the more they prepare. The client may begin to look for a counselor or therapist, or she may buy self-help books or tapes. She may attend Alcoholics Anonymous (AA) meetings to see if she can find one she likes.

Stage IV—Action

Finally, the client decides to try to change. She decides what she wants to do, and she starts to do it. She may decide to cut down on the number of cigarettes she is smoking or to stop smoking entirely. She may decide to stop drinking completely or to drink only on the weekends. Such clients come to therapy when they have already started to change but are having difficulty sticking to their plan. Initially, they may not be ambivalent about changing, but they often reexperience the ambivalence of Stage II.

Stage V—Maintenance

After a period of time, the client may be able to think of herself as having moved to the maintenance stage. She finds it easier and easier to stick to her new pattern of behavior. There is no set time for moving from action (Stage IV) to maintenance (Stage V), and some people may recycle back to the precontemplation stage many times before being able to remain at the maintenance stage.

Stage VI—Termination

At the termination stage the client's hard work is over. The new pattern of behavior is firmly implanted, and the client can consider herself "recovered."

AA members never use the term *recovered*, preferring to call themselves "recovering alcoholics." To them, it would be foolish to assume that their problems with alcohol are ever completely over. They know how easy it is to slip back to Stage I or II. Many AA members and some doctors and mental health professionals insist that no one ever recovers from alcohol dependence and that all participants must continue to attend AA meetings regularly for the rest of their lives. However, research now indicates that this is not true for all people (Hester and Miller 1995). For example, for other addictive behaviors, such as smoking, many ex-smokers have no desire whatsoever to smoke again.

ADVANTAGES OF THIS MODEL

This model has four main advantages:

1. **It can help keep the client motivated.** To help clients understand how to think about change, practitioners can address the stages of change and can give them a copy of the descriptions of the stages (Figure 1–1). Clients should be encouraged to think about change as a process with varius stages, and to accept that they may move through this process many times before they reach their treatment goals.

Stage I	Precontemplation	You don't think about it. You are either (a) ignorant (you don't realize that you have a problem) or (b) demoralized (you've given up).
Stage II	Contemplation	You start thinking about it, but you're ambivalent.
Stage III	Preparation	You prepare to change, although you still may feel ambivalent.
Stage IV	Action	You start to change. Ambivalence may continue to be a problem.
Stage V	Maintenance	You try to maintain your change through relapse prevention techniques such as review and rehearsal.
Stage VI	Termination	At some point, you may consider yourself recovered.

Figure 1–1. Prochaska and DiClemente's model of change.

2. **It can help both the therapist and the client accept the possibility that change can stop and even go in reverse.** When the client does lapse or relapse, she can see it as a normal part of the process, although perhaps discouraging and disappointing. Lapses and relapses are common, and the therapist should always be ready to help the client restart the process when the time is right.

3. **It helps determine the therapeutic approach.** Techniques that help the client maintain her change may not work well, and may actually do harm, when she is in the first

three stages of change. Therapists do better, more effective therapy when they select cognitive, emotive, and behavioral techniques based on the client's stage of change.

4. **It helps prevent professional burnout.** To many therapists success in the treatment of addictions requires client abstinence. Anything short of abstinence equals failure. However, no other complex biopsychosocial behavioral pattern or disease labors under such a demanding criterion. Clients are making progress if they move from one stage to the next.

Frank, a young man, was sent for therapy by his aunt. He had been jailed three times for getting into fights while drunk. He had a good job in construction, and his aunt thought that if he could get a handle on his drinking, he could probably live a fairly good life. In the first session, Frank made it clear that he thought therapy was stupid—definitely not something a *man* would do—but "I want to keep my aunt happy," he said. "She's done a lot for me. But she just doesn't understand. All of my buddies drink. I really don't drink too much." He was clearly in Stage I, precontemplation, either because he genuinely did not realize he had a problem, especially given the norms of his fellow construction workers, or because he was in denial, perhaps afraid that if he tried to change he would lose his friends or not succeed and further upset his aunt.

However, by the end of the first session, Frank was beginning to think about the possibility of modifying his drinking behavior. He was not sure that he wanted to do anything, but he acknowledged that he had gotten into a lot of trouble as the result of drinking and that that was not true for the majority of his friends. So perhaps he could learn to drink less and still keep his friends. The idea that his behavior might have anything to do with anger, perhaps at his father who had abandoned him when he was 5, didn't make any sense to him, but he did acknowledge that learning how to drink less might be helpful. Thus, he moved from Stage I to Stage II in one session, and he was contemplating changing some of his behavioral patterns.

With clients who have multiple problems—two or three addictions, posttraumatic stress, anxiety, depression, no job, and few friends—each of the goals in therapy can be conceptualized in terms of the stages of change. Each change will move through a number of stages. Many changes will include hesitant, fitful starts, perhaps many failures, and, eventually, more sustained success. Conceptualizing change as a series of stages and as a recursive process helps therapists work patiently with clients on each of their interlocking and overlapping problems.

THREE TYPES OF CLIENTS

It is often possible within a few minutes and with a few questions to determine what stage of change the client is in for any particular problem. For clinical purposes, three types of clients can be delineated:

- **Type I clients are in Stage I.** They have probably been sent to therapy, rather than coming of their own volition. They do not admit to having a problem.
- **Type II clients are in Stages II and III.** They are usually ambivalent. They often acknowledge that they have a problem, but they are not sure what, if anything, they want to do about it. Part of preparing for changing is being in therapy to explore their options.
- **Type III clients are in Stage IV or V.** They know they want to change. They are not ambivalent. They want help in maintaining the progress they have made so far or in starting again.

This way of conceptualizing clients and their problems helps the therapist determine how to work. However, clients often have more than one problem, and usually they are not in the same stage of change on each problem. For example, the client may be a Type III client regarding his heroin problem. He wants to stop using. But he is a Type I client regarding smoking cigarettes. He has no interest in cutting down or stopping.

THE BASIC ABC MODEL

When Ken, a tall, heavyset man, first entered my office, he looked tired and worn out. After having devoted over 25 years to a large, well-known insurance company, he was laid off at age 52 when the company downsized his department. Since that time he had been drinking during the day and smoking marijuana almost every night. He could not accept being treated so badly by his company after so many years of service. He alternated between rage and depression. He could not see how he could get another job, especially at his income level. His wife was trying to find work, but after many years out of the work force, it was not easy. Their only child was a college student studying to be an accountant. He lived at home and worked as a temp doing word processing, and thus was able to cover his personal and school expenses. Ken helped with tuition.

We will return to Ken shortly. The basic theory underlying all cognitive behavioral theories of psychological behavior, including addictions, is expressed in Ellis's ABC format (Ellis 1962, 1995, Ellis and Dryden 1997, Ellis et al. 1988): A stands for an activating event or adversity, perhaps a potential "trigger"; B stands for the beliefs or thoughts a person has about the A; and C stands for the consequences—what a person feels, thinks, or does as a result of the A and the B's.

Fundamentally, cognitive-behavioral therapy (CBT) and rational emotive behavioral therapy (REBT) assert that, except in some limited circumstances, A's do not cause C's. Human beings, with their beliefs, in effect stand between the A and the C, thinking about, interpreting, and evaluating what is happening, has happened, or might happen. It is these thoughts, the B's—made up of interpretations and evaluations—and not the A's that cause the C's.

According to Ellis's basic model and those of other major

cognitive-behavioral theorists (Beck 1976, Mahoney 1991, Meichenbaum 1977), Ken's company's behavior cannot make him angry or drive him to drink. It may contribute to his anger or his drinking. However, it is what he *thinks* about and how he *evaluates* his company's behavior that determines how he feels and what he does. The problem resides primarily in his underlying pattern of thinking or core beliefs, an idea shared by the Epicureans and Stoics, and to some degree by ancient Eastern thinkers like the Buddha, as well as modern thinkers such as Khrisnamurti (1972, 1989).

According to Ellis's model, thinking is sometimes rational and sometimes irrational. Words like *irrational* and *rational* have specialized meanings in other settings, for example, in philosophical arguments (Dryden and Still 1998). However, in REBT *irrational* means that something does not make sense given the context and a person's goals and values. Such beliefs are also sometimes called "unhelpful," "self-destructive," or "dysfunctional." Consequently, clients' goals and values have a central role in determining if their beliefs are irrational or rational. If two clients have very different goals, the same belief may be rational for one but irrational for the other.

Two students, Liam and Jim, are studying for an exam. Liam likes to gamble, but frequently gets into trouble when he goes to a casino. He stays too long and spends too much. He also often uses gambling as a way to avoid studying. Jim is quite different. He is a bit of a loner and has grappled with low-grade depression (dysthymia) for much of his life. He rarely goes out and studies more than he probably needs to considering that he always gets A's on his exams. In the past, he has often used studying to avoid social interactions even though he realizes that is not in his best interest. He has consistently put his goal of getting good grades ahead of his goals to become a better socializer and to have a fuller, happier life. He now knows that this contributes to his dysthymia, and that his low social skills may interfere also with another of his goals, to become a successful doctor. He has been in therapy to try to become generally happier in his life. As part of that work, he has decided on the following rule: "If I get an invitation to go out, I will never decline it."

One Thursday evening, a friend calls and says, "Hey, I'm going with a bunch of guys to Foxwood Casino. Want to come?" If Liam declines to go, thinking, If I go out, I won't get enough studying done, that may be completely rational (and reasonable). For Jim, however, that is probably irrational, part of Jim's cluster of knee-jerk, automatic beliefs, including, "Socializing makes me uncomfortable, and I don't want to be uncomfortable tonight."

Hidden, Irrational Beliefs

Frequently, clients reveal only the rational parts of their beliefs. Part of the therapist's job is to help clients uncover the hidden, irrational parts, or to give voice to thoughts that they are not aware of and that may never have been expressed in words. These parts may have a powerful, controlling role in the clients' lives. Jim genuinely does feel uncomfortable socializing and he may genuinely not want to feel uncomfortable tonight. But if he declines the invitation—and violates his decision to go out whenever invited—it may be because, without being aware of it, the apparently rational beliefs have two quite powerful irrational beliefs behind them: "Socializing makes me uncomfortable, and I can't stand being uncomfortable when people can see me." The second part is the irrational part. First, of course, he could "stand it." Second, such a belief will undermine his attempts to reach his goals.

Now let's consider: "I don't want to be uncomfortable tonight, and I have to get what I want." The first part is perfectly rational if his goal is to avoid discomfort—a legitimate goal in most cases, but not necessarily for Jim in this situation. However, it is clearly irrational for him to think "I have to get what I want." That is the stereotypical thinking of a 2-year-old.

Let's return to Ken's example. Six months after therapy began,

Ken started working for a group of real estate development lawyers. One lawyer in particular was a difficult person to work with, a fact well known throughout the firm. One late Thursday afternoon, this lawyer could not understand a point Ken was making, and suddenly lashed out at him in front of some of the other men working on the project. In the following ABC layout, it is not assumed that Ken would actually say to himself the beliefs listed. However, it is hypothesized that he thought along those lines. He may not have actually put the thoughts into words or been aware that he was thinking such thoughts, but that is the job of therapy—to help him become more aware of how he thinks in such situations and to give words his underlying beliefs.

The activating event (A) was that the lawyer criticized him in front of his colleagues. Here are some of Ken's possible underlying thoughts/beliefs (B's):

1. I hate it when I get yelled at.
2. It's one of the most humiliating things in the world.
3. I would have liked to have smashed him to pieces right there on the spot.
4. I want a drink.
5. A drink will make me feel better.
6. I have to have a drink.
7. I can't stand being criticized.
8. I have to get out of here.
9. He shouldn't have criticized me in front of my co-workers.
10. When someone yells at me, I never know what to say (like I should).
11. I should get another job.
12. I'm such a jerk.

Here are some possible consequences (C's): rage, anxiety, fear, humiliation, shame, and depression; leaving the office before quitting time; and going to a bar and having a drink.

Some of the B's listed are rational and some irrational. According to the model, irrational beliefs lead to unhelpful feelings and behaviors and rational ones lead to helpful feelings and behaviors. If Ken's plan is to stop drinking, some beliefs will probably undermine that plan but some will not. Which beliefs are rational and which are irrational?

1. "I hate it when I get yelled at" is rational. It states a fact. But Ken probably is really thinking, "I hate when I get yelled at, and getting yelled at is something that shouldn't happen to me. I can't stand getting yelled at. It is intolerable."

2. "It's one of the most humiliating things in the world" may seem rational to Ken but not to other people who would find many other things much more humiliating. It does not have to create problems for Ken unless he adds, "humiliating things should never happen to me" or "I can't stand it."

3. "I would have liked to have smashed him to pieces right there on the spot" is not irrational. It expresses one of the things Ken would have liked to have done. But it will only lead to trouble if he adds, "I have to do what I like. I can't stand doing nothing," and acts on these thoughts.

4. "I want a drink" is not irrational. It reflects Ken's preference for a drink and for relief, which he expects that a drink will provide. But hidden alongside the thought "I want a drink" is probably the thought, "I have to have a drink" or "I want a drink, and I have to have what I want." He probably further angered himself by adding even hotter thoughts, such as "It's not fair" and "I should be able to have what I want when I want it," which make him feel righteous and rebellious.

5. "A drink will make me feel better" is clearly rational because it is true. But he is probably really thinking, "A drink will make me feel better, and I have to feel better. I can't stand how I feel."

6. "I have to have a drink" is not rational. He may *want to* (in the sense of preferring to) have a drink, but he does not *have to* have a drink.

7. "I can't stand being criticized" is clearly irrational. Of course he can stand it. But being criticized was about one of the worst things that could happen to Ken. He *could* stand a lot of things in a lot of different situations, but being criticized, especially in front of other people, was not one of them. It pushed some very old, very sensitive buttons. Thinking "I can't stand it" usually made him feel even more upset—desperate, hopeless, helpless, angry, and anxious.

8. "I have to get out of here" is also irrational, and underlying this belief is probably the equally irrational belief, "I can't stand it here."

9. "He shouldn't have criticized me in front of my co-workers" is a little trickier. If Ken means, "If my boss wants to be considered professional by his subordinates, he shouldn't criticize them in front of each other," then that is a "conditional should." In other words, to achieve one condition, to be perceived as professional by his subordinates, Ken's boss has to behave in a certain way. But if Ken means "he shouldn't" because it's bad and wrong, and bad and wrong things should never happen, that way of thinking is clearly irrational. Ellis calls it Jehovian thinking because he is acting as if he is the Old Testament God Jehovah.

10. "When someone yells at me, I never know what to say" is perhaps correct for Ken. He *is* bad at responding in an effective manner when someone yells at him. But he is probably upsetting himself by adding ". . . like I should." That is, he is really thinking, "When someone yells at me, I never know what to say, like I should." He has escalated a preference—"I would like to be better at arguing back when someone yells at me"—to a demand—"I must be

better." Perhaps Ken grew up in an alcoholic family and his father always intimidated everyone in the family. Ken never learned how to argue back because whenever he tried, he never won. Sometimes he was physically beaten. So now, whenever he gets yelled at, other thoughts go through his mind (although perhaps not in verbal form): "I can't stand being yelled at. I hated it when Dad yelled at me, and especially when he yelled at Mom. I never could stop him. I should have been able to do something. What was wrong with me?" These ideas/beliefs make it even more difficult for Ken to cope with being yelled at as an adult. It is much easier for him to think "I can't stand it" than "I don't like being yelled at, but it's not the end of the world. I don't think bosses should yell at subordinates in front of their co-workers, but I'm not the first person. He has done it to other people before. He will probably do it again. Man, I hate it, but I better keep my mouth shut. I hope I can eventually get a better job."

11. "I should get another job" is not irrational if Ken has a conditional should in mind: "I should get another job if I want to be happier at work. I really don't like working at this kind of firm."

12. "I'm such a jerk" is clearly an overgeneralization. He may have acted like a jerk when he went to the bar, but his actions do not make him a jerk.

According to the model, different beliefs give rise to different emotions. Some of those emotions may be not only negative but also destructive, unhelpful, unhealthy, or dysfunctional; that is, they interfere with Ken's accomplishing his goals. But each of these words will be given meaning (or "construed," to use the current term) by the therapist and the client working together. The client's goals, values, and culture—in interaction with the therapist's goals, values, and culture—ultimately determine how words are given meaning and used in therapy.

ENHANCED MODELS

Innovative therapists and researchers have modified the basic model, suggesting other ways of conceptualizing the B's and focusing on factors that affect the beliefs people hold onto and the way those beliefs may have been implanted or adopted in the first place. Beck (1976, Beck et al. 1993) proposes that "automatic thoughts" create most psychological disturbances. He does not see demandingness or exaggerating the negative (Ellis's "awfulizing") as essentially more damaging than "personalizing" or "all-or-nothing-thinking." Mahoney (1991) suggests that humans "construct" the meaning of events and that it is these constructions that affect what occurs at C. Young (1994, Greenwald and Young 1998) suggests complex "schemas" underlie B's and play a major role in affecting the C's. Linehan's dialectical behavior therapy (DBT) (Linehan 1993ab, Robins 1999) is perhaps the closest to REBT in that both emphasize the importance of working on acceptance of self and the world while at the same time working on developing the skills necessary to better regulate emotions, tolerate "frustration" (Ellis) or "distress" (Linehan), and pursue one's goals. Linehan bases the acceptance part of her approach on Zen Buddhism, while Ellis initially based the acceptance part of his therapeutic approach on Stoicism. However, much of his writing is more akin to Buddhist thinking than to Stoicism. One major difference is that Linehan has made behaviors that interfere or interrupt therapy the second most important focus of her approach.

Keep It Simple

The acronym KISS, standing for "Keep it simple, stupid," was popular in World War II. It was designed to remind officers and strategic planners to keep things simple because, under the pressure of combat, human beings could not think straight. Keeping it simple was the best way to save lives.

In the midst of a crisis or an intense urge, most people cannot think straight. Under these circumstances, clients do not need a wide variety of techniques. In fact, some research suggests that attempting to teach clients too many techniques leads to poorer outomes (Brownell et al. 1986, Project MATCH Research Group 1997a).

Many of the various CBT and CBT-like models have interesting points to make. However, the precise model the therapist uses may not matter much to clients. Ideally, they will learn a few approaches that they can use. These techniques may be very simple, but they may have a large impact, helping clients move forward toward fulfilling their goals. Besides teaching them techniques that may help them better manage their problems, what may be most valuable to and appreciated by clients is that someone is listening. They are not alone in this sometimes terrifying world. There is someone they can turn to for support, advice, and help.

No doubt, the simple ABC model does not completely or accurately portray the complexities of human biopsychosocial life. It is a heuristic tool to help clients make sense of what is happening when they are confused, frustrated, and upset. But it works well. Although many of the newer theories may make insightful additions to the basic model, I think it is the very simplicity of the ABC model that will cause it to endure. It gives many clients a sense of "self-efficacy" (Bandura 1997). It helps them understand what is happening to them and respond more effectively to the A's in their lives. It can also be very helpful to the therapist in working effectively with clients and in handling the inevitable frustrations of doing therapy.

RESEARCH NOTE

The success rate for the treatment of addictions is comparable with that of other chronic illnesses (O'Brien and McLellan 1998), ranging for alcoholism from 40 to 70 percent; for opiate dependence, from 50 to 80 percent; for cocaine dependence, from 50 to 60 percent; and for nicotine dependence, from 20 to 40 percent.

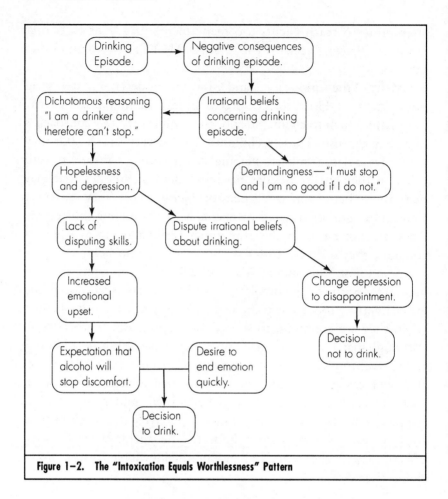

Figure 1–2. The "Intoxication Equals Worthlessness" Pattern

THE MODEL APPLIED TO ADDICTIONS

How the therapist conceptualizes addictive behaviors affects the treatment of his or her clients. It affects what techniques are used and how the therapist views the clients as human beings. Chapter 3 discusses the many possible ways of conceptualizing the factors contributing to addictive behaviors. Below we will consider some models and the way client beliefs play a role.

Ellis and his associates (1988) offer several schemas. Figure 1–2 outlines what may occur if a client believes that drinking makes her a worthless human being. The activating event is a drinking episode. This A is followed by a number of negative consequences, which stimulate various irrational beliefs (B's) concerning the drinking episode: "I must stop and I am no good if I do not." Underlying this demanding belief is the tendency to link her evaluation of her self with her evaluation of her behavior. Drinking is contemptible behavior, so she is contemptible.

In addition, she thinks, "I am a drinker and therefore can't stop." Here she labels herself. Although "I am a drinker" is true, other unstated, even more powerful beliefs often hide just beneath the surface: "That defines who I am and that is *all* I am, and because that is *all* I am"—clearly a cognitive distortion—"I can't stop."

Such beliefs/thoughts easily lead to new C's—hopelessness and depression. Two pathways then exist: According to Ellis and colleagues (1988, p. 34), the client may "dispute [her] irrational beliefs about drinking," which has the effect of changing her depression into only disappointment and leads to her deciding not to drink more. Or the client may lack the skills necessary to effectively cope with her irrational thoughts and feelings of hopelessness and depression. Hence, she becomes more emotionally upset. Then her expectation that alcohol will stop the discomfort kicks in. Coupled with her desire to end the emotional discomfort quickly, she decides to drink.

Discomfort anxiety and low frustration tolerance are central to REBT's theory of addictions. After numerous sessions with clients, Ellis (1978–1979) noticed that many had great difficulty labeling the feeling they experience when (1) they anticipate that they are not going to be able to do what they want to do, or (2) that they are going to have to do something they do not want to do. Anyone who has decided not to drink and then watches others drinking at a wedding or business meeting knows the feeling. Or anyone who has decided not to eat dessert and then sits watching his companion eat a moist slice of chocolate cake knows the feeling. Discomfort anxiety may also manifest itself when we think about forcing ourselves to do something we do not want to do, such as exercising or paying taxes. Discomfort anxiety is often mixed in with guilt, shame, and self-condemnation, all of which may lead to depression.

Some clients in some (or many) situations demonstrate a very low tolerance for frustration, low frustration tolerance (LFT). They may not demonstrate LFT in all settings. They may easily run marathons or take care of an aging parent, both of which require a high tolerance for frustration. But they may convince themselves that they cannot tolerate the frustration and discomfort associated with not having a drink at certain times of the day or in certain settings or given certain circumstances.

Ellis and colleagues (1988) hypothesize that many therapists (and clients) miss the importance of discomfort anxiety and low frustration tolerance for a variety of reasons. First, clients move very quickly to eliminate it. Consequently, they do not report it. Instead, they report that they were very angry over a fight with their wife or that they felt lonely or depressed. They do not notice and do not report the feelings that they experience when they could not get immediate relief. Therapists also often ask clients how they feel. Clients tell them how they feel at that moment, after the lapse or relapse. But discomfort anxiety occurs before the lapse or relapse. To uncover the role of discomfort anxiety, therapists must be careful to focus on what occurs right before a lapse or relapse. In this book, I make a distinction between working on "pre-AB's," the activating events and beliefs *preceding* a lapse or relapse, and on "post-BC's," the beliefs and feelings *after* a lapse or relapse (see Chapter 2).

Figure 1–3 illustrates the role of discomfort anxiety and LFT. Another schema (Figure 1–4) offers what the model suggests may occur if a client has a "sensation-seeking personality."

According to the model, breaking these patterns requires a combination of factors: (1) an increase in a client's know-how (e.g., learning new cognitive, emotive, and behavioral techniques), (2) a change in the client's sense of mastery or control (self-efficacy); and (3) a change in the way the client perceives and interprets lapses and relapses.

Marlatt (1985a) proposes the following model (see p. 22) of

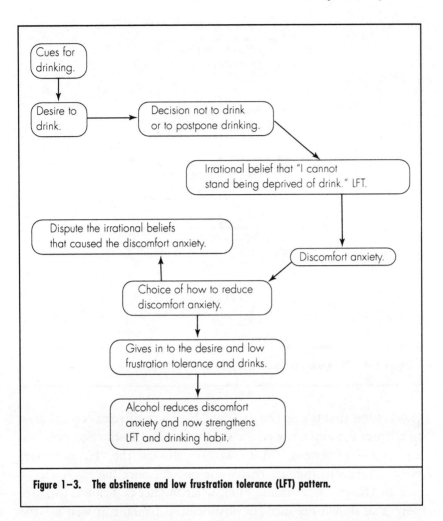

Figure 1–3.   The abstinence and low frustration tolerance (LFT) pattern.

the process leading to a full-blown relapse (Figure 1–5). The client may engage in an effective coping response that will lead to greater self-efficacy, which Marlatt (1985a) defines as "the individual's perception of his or her ability to cope with prospective high-risk situations" (p. 128) and "a person's subjective sense of mastery or control over temptations or urges to engage in the taboo behavior" (p. 132). If the client does not respond with an effective coping response, his decreased sense of self-efficacy coupled with his

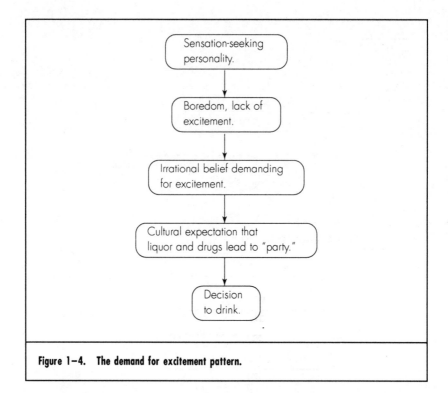

Figure 1–4. The demand for excitement pattern.

expectation that taking the drug will have a positive effect may lead to a lapse, the initial use of the substance. The abstinence violation effect (AVE) (Marlatt 1985a), which I also call the "Häagen Dazs effect," refers to the fact that some people, once having started a pint of Häagen Dazs think, "Oh, what the heck. It doesn't matter now. I've blown my diet [or abstinence]. I might as well eat the whole thing [or drink the whole bottle]." In other words, many people hold an all-or-nothing belief, which contributes to lapses becoming full relapses.

Beck and his associates (1993) offer a model focusing on the various kinds of beliefs—addictive, anticipatory, and facilitating (or permissive)—that contribute to an addictive episode (Figure 1–6). The authors note that "cognitive therapy is aimed at modifying each of the categories of beliefs, anticipatory and permissive, as well as the underlying core beliefs (e.g., 'I am trapped') that potentiate

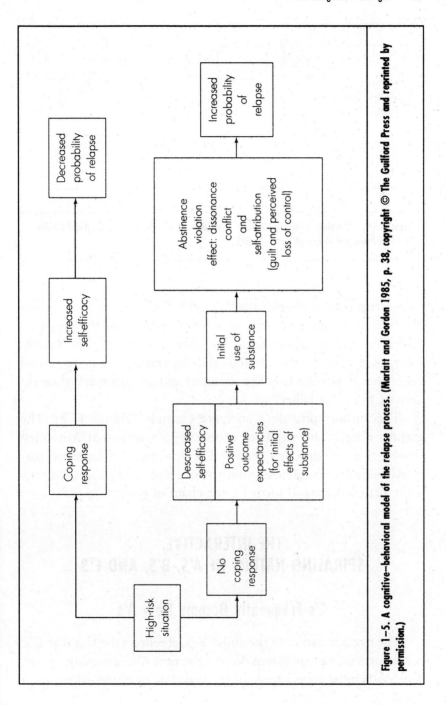

Figure 1–5. A cognitive–behavioral model of the relapse process. (Marlatt and Gordon 1985, p. 38, copyright © The Guilford Press and reprinted by permission.)

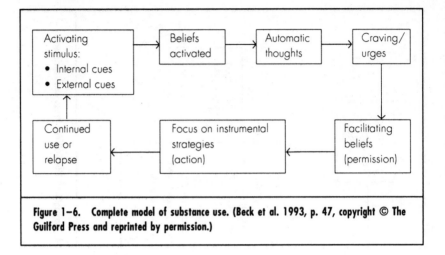

Figure 1–6. Complete model of substance use. (Beck et al. 1993, p. 47, copyright © The Guilford Press and reprinted by permission.)

these drug-related beliefs" (pp. 47–48). They go on to note that "craving . . . seems to arise as a reflex reaction to the stimulus. However, the situation does not directly 'cause' the craving: Interposed between the stimulus and the craving is a drug-related belief that is activated by the situation and an automatic thought derived from this belief" (p. 48).

The authors provide a concrete example (Figure 1–7): The authors note, "The sequence proceeds so rapidly that it is often viewed as a 'conditioned reflex.' The automatic thought, in particular, seems to be almost instantaneous and can be captured only if the patient learns to focus on the chain of events" (p. 48).

THE INTERACTIVE, SPIRALING NATURE OF A'S, B'S, AND C'S

C's Frequently Become New A's

The circular nature of the above model reflects the fact that C's, consequences, can and often do become new A's, activating events. Therapists must have a sense of the time line of events—first, what

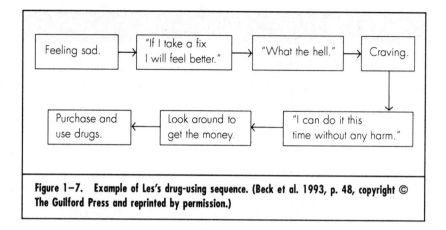

Figure 1–7.   Example of Les's drug-using sequence. (Beck et al. 1993, p. 48, copyright © The Guilford Press and reprinted by permission.)

happened; second, what the client thought; and third, how that affected his subsequent thoughts, feelings, and actions. The following three scenarios may help illustrate this point.

Suppose the client, Fred, goes out, gets drunk, wrecks his car, and gets a DWI summons. In working with him, the therapist discovers that he is damning himself and creating all sorts of feelings of shame and hopelessness, as outlined in Scenario I below. The therapist may then see that the consequences, C1, are becoming a new set of activating events, A2, and that Fred is on the verge of telling himself (and perhaps the therapist) that he can't stand it anymore. He feels completely despairing and helpless about being unable to change his very torturous situation. He is tired of listening to the self-critical voices in his head. If he continues in this pattern, he will drink before the night is out, which, in turn, will become a new activating event, A3.

At some point, Fred may decide to try to stop. He may even resolve never to drink again. But often, after a given amount of time, a new activating event or adversity will come up. And he will probably not be prepared for the discomfort anxiety that immediately develops when he tries to adhere to his decision not to drink.

C3 becomes a new A and the cycle of drinking, self-recriminations, anxiety, rage, and more drinking continues. How-

Scenario I		
A1	**B1**	**C1**
Drinking; car accident; DWI	"What a jerk you are." "Now look what you've got yourself into." "If I drink, I'll feel better." "Nothing will ever change." "I can't stand it anymore." "Life sucks." "Oh, the hell with it."	Depression; self-hatred; shame; anger at the world; anxiety over job; no driver's license; missed work.
A2	**B2**	**C2**
Depression; self-hatred; shame; anger at the world; anxiety over job; no driver's license; missed work.	"I can't stand this anymore." "I'm hopeless." "I'm a hopeless failure." "I'll never get back on track."	Depression about depression. More drinking to cope with negative affect, and to silence self-critical inner voices.
A3	**B3**	**C3**
Depression about depression. More drinking to cope with negative affect, and to silence self-critical inner voices.	"I can't stop now." "It doesn't really matter." "No one cares anyway." "Liquor makes me feel better." "I couldn't stand to stop now." "Maybe tomorrow."	More hopelessness, despair, etc. Drinks even more to cope.

Scenario II		
A1	**B1**	**C1**
Fred loses his job because of lateness and excessive absences.	"Now what am I going to do?" "I'm not going to drink." "It will just make matters worse."	Discomfort anxiety; ego anxiety; shame; anger at the world; anger and depression over the loss of his job.
A2	**B2**	**C2**
Discomfort anxiety; ego anxiety; shame; anger at the world; anger and depression over the loss of his job.	"I can't stand this discomfort." "This is terrible." "I have to have a drink." "I have to get some relief." "I can start over tomorrow." "I am such a loser."	Drinks; self-loathing.
A3	**B3**	**C3**
Drinks; self-loathing	"What a jerk you are." "Now look what you've got yourself into." "If I drink, I'll feel better." "Nothing will ever change." "I can't stand it anymore." "Life sucks. Oh, the hell with it."	Depression; self-hatred; anger at the world; rebelliousness; self-pity; more drinking.

Scenario III		
A1	**B1**	**C1**
Fred loses his job because of lateness and excessive absences.	"Now what am I going to do?" "I'm not going to drink." "It will just make matters worse."	Discomfort anxiety; ego anxiety; shame; anger at the world; anger and depression over the loss of his job.
A2	**B2**	**C2**
Discomfort anxiety; shame; ego anxiety; anger at the world; anger and depression over loss of his job.	"God, I feel awful." "I know a drink would make me feel better." "But if I do that, nothing will ever change." "I want to have a better life." "This will pass." "I don't have to depress myself; this is bad, but not the end of the world."	Feels more hopeful; less out of control; less depressed; less discomfort anxiety; less ego anxiety.
A3	**B3**	**C3**
Feels less out of control; feels more hopeful; feels less depressed; less discomfort anxiety; less ego anxiety.	"This is very hard, but not too hard." "I think I'm going to be okay, but maybe I'll call Sam just in case." "I'm worried, but it won't help to freak out."	More hope; stronger sense of control; no drinking.

ever, in therapy Fred may become aware that discomfort anxiety is a major obstacle and that it accompanies most behavioral change. He may begin to doubt the wisdom or effectiveness of his usual pattern of self-recriminations and self-berating. Thus, scenario II may change to look like the schema in scenario III.

Such a change in thinking is usually not sufficient. Other changes in the environment and in his relationships will also have to occur. However, the fact that he begins to see a way of affecting his thinking, feeling, and behavior may help him make changes in these other aspects of his life as well.

RESEARCH NOTE

Is it stress or how the client *thinks* about stress that contributes to lapses and relapses? In their study, Hutchinson and colleagues (1998) combined irrational thinking, impulsivity, and compulsivity into one scale, the irrational-coping scale. They theorized that impulsive and compulsive behaviors were both forms of self-misregulation and that clients who have alcohol-related problems "encode stressful situations in an irrational fashion and use self-defeating mechanisms (i.e., impulsive and compulsive patterns) to deal with these 'awful' situations" (p. 70). They note that "irrational coping had a substantial impact on alcohol problems, even above the influence of depression. *Stress did not account for an additional amount of significant explained variance*" (p. 69, my emphasis). Hence, as they hypothesize, it may be irrational thinking *about* stress combined with a tendency to use impulsive and compulsive coping behaviors rather than stress by itself that leads to problems with drinking.

OTHER IMPORTANT ISSUES

Frequency, Duration, and Intensity— Another Way to Measure Success

Behavioral change can be looked at in terms of three criteria: frequency, duration, and intensity (FDI). For example, if the client reduces the number of drinking days per month, that is a change in frequency, and that represents progress. If he used to drink for at least five days straight when he relapsed before, but this time stopped after an evening of drinking, that is a change in duration and represents progress of a different kind. If the client reduces the number of drinks consumed in an hour or in a day, that is a change in intensity, and it represents progress as well. Similarly, if the client has less frequent panic attacks, that is progress. If an attack occurs but doesn't last as long, that is progress. If it is only half as intense, that is also progress.

For many clients and their friends and family, success is measured only in terms of abstinence. But this measure does not take into account the complexity of addictive behaviors (and most other human behaviors, as well) or the difficulties inherent in change or the way change usually occurs (slowly and with many movements backward and forward). Researchers do not look at progress in an all-or-nothing manner (Project MATCH Research Group 1997a).

Thinking of change in terms of FDI may keep clients working toward greater positive change without getting demoralized and quitting. They do not have to face an all-or-nothing challenge.

The Why and the How

Working as a therapist involves a combination of science and art. Scientific research over the past fifty years has shown that many techniques work, but learning how to use them effectively with a diverse clientele requires the sensibilities of an artist.

In the past, people went to psychoanalysts in the hope that gaining insight into the functioning of their unconscious and conscious mind would permit them to live happier, fuller lives. Many people found and continue to find psychoanalysis helpful. My clients come for similar reasons, but I see myself as someone who has studied and continues to study *how* to help people change specific behavioral patterns. Understanding *why* is not sufficient. Insight often helps encourage and motivate clients to engage in the process of change, but they also want to know *how*.

After I explain this approach, my clients often give me a look of relief. They want help, and they have been worried that we would have to spend many sessions talking about their mother and their childhood. They didn't think that would help. But they had an idea of what therapy was like, and were resigned to having to go that route. Thus, they are relieved to know that I am not going to spend a great deal of time asking them to think about their past. I am going to focus on learning how to change.

However, I do not believe that searching for the roots of a behavioral pattern is a waste of time. It is true that even if we try to understand the roots of the problem, we may never be able to fathom what really happened or how it had an impact on our lives. Perhaps we were born that way. But my experience suggests that understanding why has tremendous therapeutic and motivational value: Understanding why helps people develop a more compassionate, accepting attitude toward their problems and toward the process of change. Many clients grappling with addictions are racked with guilt, shame, and depression. Their problems are often chronic, and relapses are common. Blaming themselves contributes to longer, more destructive relapses. Understanding stimulates compassion and acceptance, which, in turn, help clients stay the course. Moreover, clients may be more willing to return to therapy when they believe the therapist understands them, helps them feel better, respects the complexity of their problems, and makes it easier for them to accept themselves with their problems and to try again.

Understanding why also may increase clients' motivation to

change. Knowing how to change is not sufficient. They have to *want* to change. Once they better understand the roots of their problems, they may be motivated to transcend those roots. Perhaps this occurs because most people do not like to be controlled, not only by others but also by their conditioning and their past. If a client has a hypothesis about how she "got that way," she may become more motivated to undo what contributes to her misery.

I was recently working with a woman who said she thought she had an inordinate fear of being abandoned. She said she thought everyone had a fear of abandonment, but hers was extraordinary. She also thought that it caused her to get into bad relationships and to use sex and drugs to cope with her constant anxiety. It was our second session, and I already knew that she was the oldest child in the family. "Did your mother lose any children before you?" I asked. She looked at me surprised and then said, "Yes. Before I was born, she had three miscarriages. And there was a daughter before me who died at about six months of age. I think she had diarrhea on and off and never gained weight. Finally, she died. No one has ever talked about it in the family, but I know about it because my godmother told me."

I, too, was surprised. Perhaps my hypothesis, only one of several that I was entertaining at the moment, had merit. "Isn't it possible," I said to her, "but this is only a hypothesis, that when you finally arrived, you were extraordinarily precious, even more so than most babies are to their mother. And your mother was constantly anxious that somehow her tie with you would be severed? Day after day, even when she held you close to her, she had this sense of dread. And you picked that up. A fear that somehow the world was threatening and particularly that there was always a chance you would be separated from your mother. Perhaps it is at the root of your unusually strong fear of abandonment—and your belief that you have to always be with a man and hold on to him no matter what or numb yourself with alcohol and drugs if that is not a possibility."

I looked at her to see if what I had said made any sense. She looked a bit stunned. Of course, my hypothesis could be completely wrong, but it has helped her begin to accept herself *with* her anxiety. In the past, she always looked for a way to get rid of it, even if she knew the way she chose was not really what she wanted to do in the medium and long run. Now the amount of anxiety she feels has decreased, perhaps because she does not evaluate it in such a powerfully negative manner. Helping her understand Why (or at least hypothesize why) appeared to make her more receptive to working with me and to exploring the how.

Caution 1: Some clients, especially those in Stage IV, want help only with the how. They are fully motivated and often want to know how to change without lapses and relapses. In such cases, exploring why may be a waste of their time and money.

Caution 2: Other clients, often those who are ambivalent about changing, will spend the entire session relating one story after another. They love to talk about what happened (the activating events, the A's) but are hesitant to look at what role they themselves may have had in creating the C's, the consequences. If this occurs often, therapists may want to suggest spending half of each session trying to understand the why and half on figuring out how to better cope with what is happening. Clients may want to spend the whole session talking, driven by an underlying belief that the therapist has to understand what happened, and sticking to the agreed time may create more problems than it solves.

People Live in Space and Time

As humans, we are not alone in our ability to analyze situations and change our behavior accordingly. Viruses, dogs, and trees, to name only a few of the organisms on this planet, can all do that. But we are capable of something much more powerful than thinking.

We can think about our thinking. We can reflect on our actions, both past and future. Unlike most other organisms, actions we take are affected by our awareness of our place not only in space but also, and often more importantly, in time. It is in this sense that we can say we live primarily in time. We are always thinking about the future and the past. And we are often more affected by what we think is going to happen and what has happened than what is happening at this very moment: "If I don't take some Valium, I think I'm going to die." "I can't believe how stupidly I behaved. I need a drink." "I hate being alone. What's wrong with me? I'll never find a good boyfriend."

Each time we think about what we have done, we can condemn ourselves for behaving so stupidly, feeling ashamed and humiliated all over again. Or if we remember how someone hurt us, we can feel the anger seethe up inside us all over again. But we do not live just in the past. We can also imagine the way we may behave in the future and fill ourselves with anticipatory shame and humiliation.

Our ability to reflect holds the seeds of great accomplishments as well as of searing self-criticism, doubt, shame, and guilt. We can paint pictures, design buildings, and write books. More importantly, we can reflect on how we behaved in the past and change our behaviors. In sum, we can reflect and envision, rejoice and regret, praise and condemn, inspire and delude ourselves—all because of our ability to think about our thinking, feelings, and behaviors both in the past and in the future.

Changing addictive behaviors is particularly difficult because we are not always clear about what we want most, a better near-term future or a better medium-term and long-term future. Do we want to feel better now (meaning very soon in the future) or later? In addition, we have an immense capacity to delude ourselves, to pretend, and to avoid. We also forget. We not only forget (or pretend to forget) what really happened the last time we gambled or drank or used drugs, but we also forget what we want in the long term, or decide it is not worth it or is unobtainable. Our perceptions, interpretations, and evaluations of what will happen over time become critical as we help clients grapple with addictive behaviors.

Karniol and Ross (1996) present some interesting insights into the very important issue of the perceived impact of consequences over time on human behavior. They note, for example, that "possible futures differ on three major dimensions: positivity (i.e., Does the future hold good or bad outcomes?); controllability (i.e., Can one influence one's future outcomes?); and temporal distance (i.e., How far away is the envisaged future?)" (p. 595).

Wanting and Liking: Are They the Same?

In an experiment, Lamb and associates (1991) put recovered heroin addicts in four experimental conditions. By pushing a lever, they would receive an injection of (1) a saline solution, (2) a weak morphine solution, (3) a moderately strong morphine solution, or (4) a strong morphine solution. The results: It was not surprising that the subjects did not like the saline solution, and, after a while, stopped pressing the lever. It was also not surprising that they liked the intermediate and rich solutions and continued to press the lever in each case. However, surprisingly, even though they said that they did not like the weak solution (they rated it as "empty and worthless" just like the saline solution), they kept pressing the lever—indicating that they still wanted it even though they said they did not like it.

Researchers Kent Berridge and Terry Robinson (1995) at the University of Michigan suggest that "wanting" and "liking" are not represented by the same processes in the brain. In their model, "wanting" results when certain neurobehavioral systems become sensitized, especially in the mesotelencephalic dopamine system.

The functioning of this system, like the functioning of other brain systems, is not directly accessible to us. However, a person's behavior may provide a clue about her processing. We can tell, for example, that she can see something (can process visual input in her brain) by asking her to point at it or touch it. In brief, we can infer something about how her visual processes are operating by watching what she does.

Similarly, we may only be able to tell what her system is

sensitized to—what she wants at some deep level—by watching her behavior. This may explain what is going on when we watch ourselves doing something because we want it, for example, lighting a cigarette, while another part of our brain is wondering, "Why are you doing that?!! You don't even like it anymore."

Could the two words *like* and *want* reflect the fact that two different neurochemical system are operating? Perhaps we learn (by reinforcement outside of our awareness) to want something even though, after a while, we say we don't like it anymore.

THE IMPORTANCE OF RESEARCH

Cognitive-behavioral therapists generally relate to clients as if they are responsible human beings who can make their own choices and decisions. To make choices, however, clients need information. A client may be wondering: "What percentage of people get in trouble with alcohol?" "Can I cut down or do I have to stop?" "Can people learn to moderate their gambling?" "Will naltrexone stop my cravings for cocaine?" Therapists can help by providing the best, up-to-date, research-based information.

We are at an exciting time in the addictions field because we are acquiring more information daily, information that may be of help to clients. However, as with nutritional information over the past twenty years, some of this information may be incorrect. The research may be incomplete or flawed. Of greater importance, what is generally true based on the study of a large group of people may not be true for a specific person. Most people stung by a bee suffer only minor discomfort. Thus we can say that bee stings generally are not dangerous. But a few people die. Similarly, most people can drink alcohol, but some get into trouble of one kind or another because of it.

Providing clients with information that is as accurate as possible will help them make informed decisions regarding which treatment goals to pursue and which strategies and techniques to try. Here is a small sample of the information that I have found useful when working with clients. (Newsletter services, such as DATA, Brown

University Digest of Addiction Theory and Application, review and summarize the most relevant recent research.)

The Problem

- According to the 1994 National Comorbidity Study, substance abuse/dependence is the most prevalent lifetime mental health disorder. Over a lifetime, 27 percent of the population will suffer from substance abuse; the current prevalence rate (the percentage of people who have been suffering from the problem in the past 12 months) is 11 percent. In contrast, 19 percent of the population will suffer from an affective disorder over their lifetime (11 percent currently); 25 percent will grapple with an anxiety disorder (17 percent currently) (Kessler et al. 1994).
- Comorbidity is the norm. 14.6 percent of people with anxiety disorders meet the criteria for lifetime alcohol or drug use disorder; 32 percent of people diagnosed with an affective disorder meet that criteria; rates often exceed 50 percent in acute psychiatric settings (Carey et al. 1999).

Treatment Works

- Twelve months after outpatient treatment, alcohol, marijuana, and cocaine use were all down at least 50 percent (Hubbard et al. 1997, based on the Drug Abuse Outcomes Study [DATOS] of 10,100 clients in over 100 treatment centers around the U.S.).
- Interviews with a subset of participants one year after three months of outpatient treatment found that heroin use was down by 56.2 percent (compared to the preadmission year); cocaine use, down 57.2 percent; marijuana use, down 76.3 percent; and alcohol use, down 65.1 percent. "Sexual behavior risk" and "predatory illegal acts" had also decreased by 53.8 percent and 64.3 percent, respectively (Hubbard et al. 1997).

- Project MATCH participants, regardless of the program they were involved in (twelve-step faciliation, motivational enhancement, or cognitive-behavioral coping skills therapy), showed improvement in number of days drinking and drinks per day. After 12 months, those who had been in inpatient facilities were 90 percent abstinent, compared to 20 percent before treatment (Project MATCH Research Group 1997a).

2 CORE TECHNIQUES

*Psychologists who will be extant in the year 2000 will have to be . . .
enormously more* broadly *trained than the subspecialized people
turned out today.*
—Gardner Murphy, 1969
"Psychology in the Year 2000," in *American Psychology*

It is important to acknowledge that many clients have stumbled
on or discovered techniques that work in the short run even though
they often cause serious problems over the medium and long run.
These "addictive techniques" have four appealing characteristics:

- The results are often very pleasurable in the short-run.
- They are easier and take less practice to learn.
- They work faster than cognitive-behavioral therapy/rational
  emotive behavioral therapy (CBT/REBT) techniques ("Li-
  quor is quicker").
- They almost always work.

Part of the therapist's job is to motivate clients to substitute less
pleasurable, sometimes less effective (in the short run) behaviors for
very pleasurable, effective (in the short run) behaviors.

FIVE KEY CLINICAL TECHNIQUES

Four of the following five basic CBT/REBT techniques are primarily cognitive, but all five affect all three domains (cognitive, emotive, and behavioral):

- Developing a plan
- Teaching the ABC(DE) technique
- Doing a "time effects" analysis
- Role playing (and reverse role playing)
- Brainstorming

Developing a Plan

Ultimately, the most important step in managing addictive problems is developing and testing a plan and then figuring out how to stick to it. A plan describes what the client wants or intends to do over the next week or month. This technique is outlined, step by step, in greater detail in Chapter 8. Initially, the therapist and client decide on a plan for the coming week. The plan may be quite experimental, especially for a client who is not sure what he wants to do. Once they have decided on a plan, the therapist spends additional time exploring and deciding on strategies to help the client maintain the plan.

In future sessions, the therapist reviews how well the client was able to maintain the plan. Which techniques and strategies helped? Which did not? What happened when the client was unable to maintain the plan? What contributed to his breaking his plan? The therapist tries to get a better understanding of how the client derailed himself.

Session time should also be spent preparing and rehearsing for anticipated potential trigger situations. What can the client try to think, feel, and do to help himself maintain his plan?

As I discuss in much greater depth in Chapter 9, Type III clients know what they want to do. They have come to therapy for help in trying to abstain or to moderate their addictive behaviors. They want to reduce the number, duration, and intensity of lapses and relapses. The therapist can help them develop a plan and then test it out between sessions.

Type II clients, however, are unsure about what they want to do. The therapist can develop an experimental plan with them that will help them discover what they want to do. At the same time, they will reveal a great deal about their thinking regarding change, such as what their goals may be, what their beliefs are regarding working on and toward changing, and how much and hard they may be able to work. Figuring out a workable plan functions as a valuable ongoing assessment tool.

Clients with Type I problems are the most difficult to work with because they either do not acknowledge that they have a problem or they are not interested in changing it at this time. However, they may be motivated to work on another problem or to work on someone else's problem. In each case, the stages of change model will help the therapist decide on how to proceed.

In general, the client should set up his plan at a time during the day or week when he is able to think straight. During a session may be a good time. Then the trick is to figure out how to maintain that plan when he is not feeling so rational—when he is tired or hungry or has a very strong urge and cannot think straight. For example, suppose he decides on a Sunday morning not to drink for a week. At 5:30 P.M. Sunday evening, he may not think and feel the way he thought and felt in the morning. What techniques will help him stick to his plan at that time?

Teaching the ABC(DE) Technique

Ellis's famous ABC technique is relatively easy to learn and, as a result, is quite popular, not only with therapists but also with clients. The technique provides clients with a way to untangle the jumble of interacting, overlapping confused thoughts and dysfunctional feelings and behaviors. More importantly, it can help them figure out better ways to respond—instead of just reacting. In what he has called the first preventive, "psychological inoculation" program, Martin Seligman, a past president of the American Psychological Association, has shown that teaching teenagers the ABC technique significantly decreases the number who will get depressed during the two-year follow-up period (Jaycox et al. 1994).

The ABC technique can provide a client suffering from addictive behaviors with the beginnings of a feeling of control. If he gets into a tough situation in the coming week, an effective tool exists—a tool he can carry around in his head and use on the spot. Knowing he can do something other than his standard, addictive response will often begin to motivate him to try to do something differently.

It is very helpful to do ABCs in session and in writing. Then the therapist can give the sheet of paper to the client as he leaves (after making a copy for his files). The client can fill out one or two forms during the week and bring them to the next session (or fax or mail them to the therapist). These forms provide the therapist with a way to do ongoing assessments and a quick and direct way to see how the client thinks. Many of my clients are pleased that I really want to see how they grapple with their problems.

Doing a Generic ABC(DE)

It is not difficult to do an ABC, but clients need help in the beginning.

Step 1

Start at **C** (the **Consequences**). The therapist asks his client:

"What do you want to work on?"

"What would you like to talk about?"

"How are things going?"

"How are you feeling?"

"Bring me up to date. What's been happening?"

Opening with "What do you want to work on?" immediately indicates that therapy is primarily for working on and managing problems. This opening is especially useful for clients who have been trained by other therapists to talk on and on about what has happened during the past week. However, other openings may be more appropriate for some clients, especially if they look as if they are already suffering from various pressures. "What would you like to talk about?" or "How are things going?" clearly is a gentler approach.

The minute my client Shirley walked into the office, I could see that she was depressed and angry. I started by saying, "What happened? You look upset." She told me not only that she had been drinking since Saturday night but that she was very depressed. Thus, she gave me two consequences in the first minute of the session.

Step 2

Explore the **A**'s (the **Activating** events). The therapist tries to determine what the activating events prior to the lapse or relapse were. He could ask: "How did you convince yourself to drink? You also seem angry. Why are you feeling angry? What happened?"

Some clients initially have no idea why they relapsed. It takes considerable skill to figure out what occurred. I like to use the metaphor of a videotape. I want to create a videotape in my head (and in my client's as well) of what occurred minute to minute, hour to hour, and sometimes day to day prior to the moment when she starting drinking or gambling or engaging in unsafe sex.

In Shirley's case, she had spent Christmas with her family and was upset by how negative and critical her mother was, not just to her but to her sister as well. Some further questioning revealed that she had returned to her house "miserable" and had drunk an entire bottle of wine in one go.

Step 3

Uncover the **B**'s (the **Beliefs**). This is the tricky part. The therapist tries to help the client uncover what aspects of her thinking, feeling, and behavior contributed to the consequences. In the beginning of therapy, she probably will simply point to the A's as causing the C's. In this step, the therapist tries to help her begin to see the role of the B's, her beliefs, in what happened.

In Shirley's case, the therapist could ask:

"When you were driving home and just before you downed the bottle of wine, what were you thinking?" (Or "What were you telling yourself?" to use the common CBT/REBT phraseology.)

"How did you convince yourself that drinking was an okay solution?"

"Was there any debate?"

"Did you consider doing anything else?"

As I discussed in the previous chapter, REBT-ers frequently use the term *irrational beliefs* for thoughts that contributed to Shirley's drinking (and to making herself rageful and depressed). Any belief that sabotages Shirley's medium- and long-term goals is "irrational" in REBT terms. The therapist and client can use different terms, as long as the terms are helpful and clear to both of them, such as *destructive beliefs, stinking thinking, unhealthy thoughts, dysfunctional thoughts,* and *unhelpful thoughts.* Cognitive therapists usually use the terms *cognitive distortions* and *automatic thoughts.* (There are theoretical differences in the meaning of these terms, but most clients are not interested.)

Normally, clients think rationally at the same time that they are thinking irrationally. That is, rational and irrational components are mixed together and the therapist will have to listen carefully to help the client untangle them. (As I noted earlier, instead of "rational," the therapist may use other terms, such as *healthy beliefs, sensible beliefs, helpful thoughts,* and *helpful beliefs.*)

Often the unhelpful or irrational part is hidden or the client is not aware of it. "I want a drink" is not irrational or even unhelpful. It may just be true. He wants a drink. But he may secretly be adding something else. The entire thought may be: "I want a drink, and I have to have what I want." It is this combination of a simple, indisputable thought, "I want a drink" with an irrational belief, perhaps held over from early childhood, "I should get what I want when I want it" that may lead to addictive behaviors. The therapist's job is to help clients uncover or discover the irrational or automatic beliefs lurking underneath the seemingly benign overt thoughts. Taken together they contribute to the client's addictive behavior patterns.

Step 4

After identifying some of the beliefs that may be contributing to the client's emotional disturbances and addictive behaviors, it is time to examine, question, challenge, and/or **Dispute** (hence the **D** in the expanded ABCDE model) the validity, helpfulness, rationality, and reasonableness of the various beliefs/feelings/behaviors that contributed to the C's. (See Six Kinds of Disputing, below.)

Step 5

Look for new, more **Effective** (the **E** in the ABCDE model) ways of thinking, feeling, and behaving for the future.

Six Kinds of Disputing

There are more than six kinds of disputing, but we can start with six. In fact, many therapists tend to get stuck using only one or two kinds, and their therapy suffers as a result.

Functional

Functional disputing—perhaps it should be called "practical disputing"—focuses on the practical consequences of continuing to hold onto an irrational belief. The therapist might ask the client: "Given your goals and values, how does thinking that way help?" "If you want to succeed at your job and have been passed over for a promotion, how does repeating 'It's not fair. He's such an asshole' (referring to your boss or perhaps to the person who got the promotion) help? It will get you angrier. Is that in your best interest?"

Philosophical

Philosophical disputing focuses on the worst-case scenarios. If not getting a promotion means the client should look for another job, is that really the end of the world? "And why should your boss behave fairly? If your boss has always acted unfairly, is there any reason he should suddenly act differently? In fact, why should the world be fair? No doubt we would all prefer that unfair things did not happen, but we all know they do."

Empirical

Empirical disputing, like empirical science, focuses on the evidence. "Is there any evidence that not getting promoted means you should look for another job? Perhaps you really are not ready, even though you believe you are. What is the evidence that you are ready for the promotion? What is the evidence that your boss has acted unfairly? If there is good evidence, is there any evidence that things should always go the way you think they should go?"

In the above examples, I have emphasized *Socratic* disputing, giving examples that rely on questioning. With some clients a more direct style may be best. This type of disputing is clearly more like teaching, so it is called *didactic* disputing. However, there is no reason to be confrontative with either style (see Thug Therapy, below). Teachers can be very gentle and understanding as they tell someone who has great difficulty with math how to solve a problem. Or they can sound harsh, irritated, and judgmental. As noted elsewhere, research does not support the old style of confrontation in the treatment of addictions (Miller 1995).

Humor and metaphors are also very effective when therapists help clients explore their beliefs. Humor lightens what can be a difficult and painful process. Metaphors enlighten in ways regular language cannot. We all use metaphors—"asshole," "pig," and much stronger ones—precisely because they are so powerful. For example, the therapist can suggest to the client that she think to herself whenever her boss begins to infuriate her, "He's a giraffe" instead of "He's such an asshole." Of course, giraffe is a much cooler word. That is, it probably triggers much cooler associations in the brain. Giraffes will never change. They will always have long necks and they will always eat leaves off the high branches of trees. And the client's boss is probably going to always behave the way he does. That's it. The client cannot change that. She can try to accept it, but she cannot change it. Thinking of her boss as a giraffe may help her to accept that fact in a cooler, more rational manner.

Thug Therapy

Just because the therapist thinks he sees what is irrational about a client's thinking does not mean that it is therapeutically wise to immediately dispute her belief. Some therapists and counselors—especially men—attracted to CBT and REBT occasionally slip into doing what I call thug therapy. They beat clients over the head disputing their irrational beliefs. If the clients cannot see the crookedness in their thinking, the therapists will show them. Women clients may recognize this as a typical male syndrome: such therapists do not listen very well, they don't empathize, and they get irritated if the client disagrees with them.

Ellis favors the word *dispute*, partly because he believes therapists and clients had better actively and vigorously go after their irrational thinking. *Dispute* is a fine word, but therapists can also examine, question, or evaluate a belief *with* the client. Better yet, therapists can help clients learn to do it on their own.

Finally, some therapists, following an older version of the medical model, may think they have a responsibility to "cure" their patient. They are attracted to CBT and REBT but apply the techniques in an overzealous manner. Others, again mostly men, try to imitate what they see in Ellis's style. But they leave out the subtleties, the sense of humor, and the complete lack of investment in solving a client's problems that characterize Ellis's personal approach.

On the other hand, simply being heard and gaining insight are frequently not sufficient. A client must work on himself to change. That is why CBT and REBT are supplanting Freudian and Rogerian psychotherapy. Freudian and Rogerian therapies helped people change, but they were often very inefficient, especially with addictive behaviors. Miller (1995) suggests that the best therapists exhibit a combination of warmth and firmness and are both supportive and directive. Mechanical, thug therapy is not only arrogant; it dishonors the complexity of a client's problems and his capabilities to learn to solve these problems himself.

D Also Stands for "Do Something"

Disputing is only one cognitive intervention. Some REBT-ers and CBT-ers get stuck on it. There are many other effective behavioral, emotive, and cognitive interventions that may be equally helpful, such as role playing, analysis of the positive and negative effects of various behaviors, rational emotive imagery, and deep diaphragmatic breathing, as discussed below and throughout the book. Ellis (e.g., Ellis 1962, Ellis and Dryden 1997, Ellis and Velten 1992, Ellis et al. 1997) argues that some interventions are only palliative, for example deep diaphragmatic breathing, and that if the client does not change the way he is thinking, he will continually create the same kinds of emotional disturbances. Once he is emotionally upset, he will revert to his favorite form of addictive behavior. However, sometimes the client may be too upset to do any kind of cognitive disputing or questioning. Breathing deeply or meditating may help him calm down. At that point, he can examine and evaluate his thinking. However, he may not need to do so. The breathing on its own may have removed his upset. Of course, Ellis may be correct that it would have been better if he had worked on his thinking and his underlying beliefs, too. Feeling better may be very helpful, but it does not necessarily help him get and do better in the long run. On the other hand, some clients resist learning other kinds of interventions, such as visualization, meditation, and deep breathing. Perhaps they are not open to such techniques because of other beliefs: "It won't help." "It won't work. Not this time." "I couldn't do that." "It'll be too hard."

Where Should the Therapist Begin after a Lapse or Relapse? Pre-AB's or Post-BC's?

When the client has lapsed or relapsed, the therapist has to decide where to begin. Should he focus on the pre-AB's, the activating events and the beliefs *before* the lapse or relapse? Or on the post-BC's, the beliefs and consequences *after* the lapse or relapse, which the client may be experiencing in the therapy session? Is there a best place to start?

It is usually better to explore what triggered the drinking episode in the first place. This is a departure from traditional therapy. If a client says, "I got fired," it is normal to ask about how the client felt after he got the news and how he feels now. The therapist might also ask what he was thinking and is thinking. But when a client has lapsed or relapsed, it is often better to move back in time to look at what occurred before the event. Initially, the client may only identify the activating events that contributed to his lapse or relapse. But with the therapist's help, he can learn to spot what he typically says to himself when bad things happen and how that contributes to what he typically does. Then slowly, he can develop a set of cognitive, emotive, and behavioral skills to break the cycle. As he practices those skills through different situations, sometimes with success but sometimes without it, he will develop more competence and self-efficacy. He will learn to question, dispute, and challenge the rationality, helpfulness, and validity of his beliefs, taking into account his goals. At the same time, he can learn which behaviors help, for example, calling a friend, going to an AA meeting, doing an ABC, distracting himself, or eating something before leaving his office. He can discover which CBT/REBT techniques move him toward getting more pleasure out of life overall without resorting to addictive behaviors.

The therapist should focus on the post-BC's when he senses that another relapse may be imminent as the result of the client's beliefs and consequent feelings. The client may be able to change the way he thinks and feels sufficiently to head it off.

There are also many other books with useful ABC(DE) examples, such as Ellis and Velten's (1992) *When AA Doesn't Work for You*, Tate's (1993) *Alcohol: How to Give It Up and Be Glad You Did*, Ed Nottingham's (1994) *It's Not as Bad as It Seems*, and Edelstein and Steele's (1997) *Three Minute Therapy*.

Doing a Time-Effects Analysis of the Positive and Negative Effects Over Time

Although many medications have unpleasant side effects, clients with addictive problems have a difficult time recognizing the "time effects" of their addictive behaviors. Time effects focus attention on the fact that the positive and negative effects—or the costs and benefits—of any chemical or addictive behavior change over time. In motivating people to consider changing, an analysis over time of the positive and negative effects makes a client more aware of the choices he is making and what may be affecting those choices.

In doing a time-effect analysis, it works better to start listing the positive effects of continuing to drink or use drugs or engage in some other addictive behavior. Clients will be quick to list the negative effects, despite the fact that they are in therapy in part because of the positive effects. They continue engaging in a variety of addictive behaviors because of the benefits, not because of the costs. They may resist listing the benefits, perhaps partly because they are so used to denying the benefits to themselves and beating themselves up about the costs. Or they may think therapy is only for talking about problems. In any case, the therapist should help them make as long and honest a list of the benefits over time as they can. They can fold a piece of paper in half length-wise, and start with the very short-term positive effects over time, for example, in one or two minutes. Then they can move on to the effects that occur in two hours, in a day, in two weeks, in two years, and in twenty years. They can do the same thing for the negative effects. They can carry the list with them, and the therapist should keep a copy for his files.

In brief, the client first makes a list of the benefits and costs of engaging in the activity. Then he considers the gains and losses of cutting down or stopping. (See an example in Chapter 8.)

Role Playing (and Reverse Role Playing)

Much of cognitive-behavioral therapy is based on the notion that how we talk to ourselves and others has a significant effect on how we feel, think, and behave. Especially with clients who already know they want to change their addictive behaviors, helping them learn to talk differently both to themselves and to others is extremely useful. They need practice, and often a lot of it. In session they can do role plays, and reverse role plays. They can also write out role plays (like screenplays) and bring them into session.

Brainstorming

Why should the therapist waste the client's time teaching him new skills if he already knows how to help himself? He may not remember what has helped in the past or he may remember but not be doing it.

The following questions may reveal to the therapist and the client that he already knows what will probably work. Then the therapist can shift the focus to what is preventing the client from doing it.

- "When you cut back or stopped last time, how did you do that? Have you ever tried to stop any other kind of addictive behavior?"
- "What worked?"
- "Have you tried to do the same thing this time?"
- "Why hasn't it worked?"
- "Perhaps you are preventing yourself from doing it now. What do you think you might be telling yourself that's stopping you?"
- "When you listen to your voice in your head, when you think about applying the same techniques that worked in the past, what do you hear?"
- "How do you feel when you think about applying the same techniques that worked in the past?"

"But . . . -ing"

Caution: Clients may engage in extensive "but . . . -ing" when brainstorming degenerates into advice giving. Ellis points out that every problem has two aspects: a practical side and an emotional side. If the therapist helps clients with their emotional problems, many know how to solve their practical problems on their own. On the other hand, some clients will continually pressure the therapist for solutions, and if the therapist attempts to solve each new problem they bring up, they constantly "but" most of the therapist's ideas: "But you don't understand . . ." "But that won't work because . . ." "But I can't do that . . ." The result? The therapist winds up exhausted from trying to solve their many problems, and the clients wind up annoyed at the therapist for not coming up with any solutions that will work. The therapist winds up annoyed at the clients for being dissatisfied and annoyed. And the therapist winds up annoyed at himself for having gotten into this type of interaction in the first place.

There is a time for brainstorming and even for advice giving. But how much of the session has been focused on looking for practical solutions or on advice giving? If the therapist starts feeling frustrated, it is probably because he is working too hard to solve the client's practical problems while the client is sitting there "but . . . -ing."

However, ultimately brainstorming is valuable because clients often already know what works for them, but for a variety of reasons they are not doing it. The ABC technique is especially effective at uncovering what is stopping the client from using what he already knows will help.

KEY ASPECTS OF REBT

Enlightened Hedonism

More than any other therapy, REBT explicitly promotes enlightened hedonism. It encourages people to increase their overall pleasure in life. I think that is what often attracts people to REBT. It asserts that people can learn how to live happier, fuller lives. That is the "carrot" or "hook" that often brings them into therapy. Many REBT-ers use the term *enlightened hedonism* (in contrast to *hedonism*) to stress the point that we are not referring to a self-absorbed, egocentric hedonism. We recognize the importance of taking others into account when pursuing the pleasures of a full life. In fact, there are times when it is clearly in our own best interest to do what someone else wants.

People suffering from addictive behaviors often desperately try to decrease the misery or increase the pleasure in their lives. They feel miserable and want to feel better. Or they feel good and want to feel better. Some clients, in fact, may simply be short-run hedonists. They like the short-run effects and are not so displeased with the medium- and long-run effects to moderate or stop their behavior. Friends and family members may not agree, but that is another matter. (Note: A client may agree that she is just a short-run hedonist. But often this is just another way of beating herself up and blaming herself for her problems. She is in therapy because she is, in fact, not *only* a short-run hedonist.)

Most clients will not be solely short-run hedonists. They may continually use short-run methods to feel better, but they would prefer to live a more balanced life—if only because of the problems caused by their current manner of living. They know that their overall pleasure is low. It is continually being undermined by their attempt to feel better in the short run.

Unconditional Self-Acceptance

Central to REBT is the idea that rating yourself on the basis of a particular behavior creates significant, ongoing psychological problems (Ellis 1962, 1996, 1998, 1999, Ellis and Dryden 1997, Ellis and Harper 1997, Ellis and MacLaren 1998).

A client, Frank, gambled away all of his savings in one night. When I saw him, he was dejected and said he felt "worthless." No doubt he *was* worth less in terms of the accounting concept of net worth. But how did losing his money make him worth less as a human being?

Frank has many friends who like him and think well of him, and he performs many tasks very well. Outside his gambling, he is honest, generous, and very helpful. To accurately assess his overall worth, we would have to assess all of his behaviors and all of his skills and abilities and all of his characteristics in all different situations in all time periods. We would, of course, also have to agree on the rating system we were going to use. Even a super-computer could not do the job. This is especially true because some aspects of Frank's behavior and people's evaluation of him change day to day.

Yet many clients still tend to rate themselves in an overall, global sense. And they cannot unconditionally accept themselves with their problems. No doubt most of us have a tendency to do the same thing—to rate ourselves, our totality, on the basis of whether someone likes us or doesn't like us at the moment or whether we have done well or not. Hauck (1991) refers to it as "the rating game." REBT, however, asserts that this rating, coupled with demandingness to be different, creates much of the anxiety, shame, guilt, anger, and depression—and addictive behaviors—seen in clients. Instead of looking at the total picture, clients link their total worth to a particular behavior or person and then make irrational evaluations of their whole personhood. Consequently, if the client's boss appears to be happy with her work, her feelings about herself—her self-esteem—rises. But if her boss gets angry and criticizes her, her self-esteem sinks. She cannot relax because she is always worried about what her boss will think. She has linked her feelings to someone else's emotional ups and downs. Because she cannot completely control how her boss thinks, feels, and behaves, her feelings about herself are at the mercy of others. She is like a puppet. Except she has put the strings of her emotional life in her boss's hands. No wonder she is so often anxious and feels so helpless and hopeless.

When Frank engages in addictive behaviors, he eventually rates himself based on his behavior, putting himself down, that is, condemning and denigrating his self along with his behavior. REBT maintains that he could learn (and choose) to put his behavior down but not himself. He could choose to give himself unconditional self-acceptance while working on his problems. If he did, he would lessen the likelihood of relapsing.

Like some of my other clients, Frank also has a unique pedagogical philosophy (or educational theory) that he applies only to himself. He beats himself for doing something "stupid" in the belief that beating himself will motivate him to change his behavior and help him learn. He freely admits that he would not apply this approach to anyone else, because he doesn't think it would work or that he or she would deserve it. But he consistently uses it on himself, even though the shame and guilt and depression he creates often lead to more gambling.

REBT Focuses on Four Types of Irrational Thinking

1. **Is the client engaging in "catastrophizing" or "awfulizing," thinking and evaluating activating events in an exaggerated, negative manner?** Many clients have a habit of "awfulizing" and "catastrophizing" about things, making frightening and threatening mountains out of routine and familiar molehills. On a scale of 0 to 10, they consistently evaluate almost everything negatively as an 8 or a 9. By evaluating things in an exaggerated manner, clients fuel their emotional upsets and convince themselves that things are too awful to stand without some kind of chemical or activity to alter the way they are feeling (and thinking and behaving). As noted previously, Shirley, has an especially critical mother. She has been critical and negative since Shirley was a little girl. Shirley "can't stand her" and frequently drinks after talking to her or after a visit. If she could think, "I wish she were different, but she's not" and not evaluate her mother's behavior as so awful, she would not get nearly as upset and might not convince herself that she has to drown her feelings with alcohol.

2. **Is the client making things worse by sneaking in the thought, "I can't stand it"?** Many clients add fuel to the fire by also feeling or thinking: "I can't stand it anymore." Shirley clearly falls into this pattern. She suffers from chronic bouts of discomfort (anxiety, frustration, rebelliousness, anger, and depression) due to low frustration tolerance (LFT). She quickly convinces herself that she cannot stand the discomfort any longer. Sometimes she also engages in "anticipated LFT." She has a drink because she does not think she will be able to stand the discomfort that may come if she doesn't have a drink.

3. **Is the client engaging in demandingness?** Usually the client will not be aware that she is fanning the fires of her upsetness by quietly telling herself various kinds of demanding thoughts: "She should treat us differently. She shouldn't

be so critical. She should be more loving toward both of us."
"I should be different. I shouldn't have been so argumen-
tative. I shouldn't have lost my temper. I should be able to
drink like other people." "The world should be different.
Life shouldn't be so hard. This shouldn't be so hard. It's not
fair (as it should be)."

Substituting "must" for "should" may help the client
see the demanding nature of her thought. "Life must be
fair" immediately sounds irrational. Similarly, "I must not
lose my temper" and "I must be able to drink like other
people" sound equally unreasonable.

When we don't upset ourselves about something, we
usually are thinking something preferential and less god-
like. For example, we are probably saying something like, "I
don't like it that she's critical, but she's always been that way.
I wish she were different, but she's not. It's sad, but I don't
have to depress myself about it. That's the way she's always
been. It probably has nothing to do with me. I'll never like
it, but I can put up with it for one day."

4. **Is the client engaging in some form of global self-
downing?** The client probably puts herself down. She
cannot accept herself as a typical human being with problems. She cannot accept that she is like the millions of other
humans who for thousands of years have had great difficulty
guiding themselves through life without creating problems
for themselves and others. She repeatedly condemns herself
without compassion for her repeated errors, saying to
herself: "How could I have been so stupid?" (Possible
hidden belief: "I should never behave stupidly.") "I'm such
a jerk." (Possible hidden beliefs: "I am my behavior. If I
behave like a jerk, I *am* a jerk. I must never behave jerkily.")
She fails to realize that the works of the Buddha, over 2500
years old, and the Bible, probably older, all clearly indicate
the trials and tribulations of life and our consistent ability to
"sin" and make mistakes.

Being human, we are very good at escalating our emotional reactions by creating a vicious circle of demandingness, awfulizing, LFT, and self-downing (Figure 2–1). In contrast to Ellis's emphasis on the four kinds of thinking outlined above, Beck's (1976) cognitive therapy focuses primarily on a variety of "automatic thoughts" or cognitive distortions. Table 2–1 lists ten kinds of cognitive distortions. The list is similar to one in David Burns's (1981) well-known book *Feeling Good*; however, I have altered the wording a bit to make them more relevant to addictive behaviors. I give it as a handout to clients.

The Role of Emotions

Ellis originally named his therapy "rational therapy." He now acknowledges that had it been the 1970s and not the 1950s, he would have chosen the term *cognitive* instead. He quickly realized that emotions were central to therapeutic problems and amended the name to rational emotive therapy (RET), a term he used for over thirty years. In 1993, Ellis renamed RET rational emotive behavioral therapy (REBT) because he thought the new name better reflected the fact that his approach had always incorporated behavioral techniques and homework assignments.

Some therapists and counselors who come to the institute in New York also seem to want to do only rational therapy (RT). They appear averse to dealing with emotions, preferring to spend hours examining the finer points of different types of disputing. They seem insensitive to how someone might be feeling and how those feelings might be affecting his or her thinking. Less commonly I meet someone who prefers only to do behavior therapy (BT). Many therapists combine RT, really cognitive therapy (CT), with BT, to practice cognitive-behavioral therapy (CBT). However, in my experience they still seem to underappreciate the central importance of emotions, especially in the treatment of addictions.

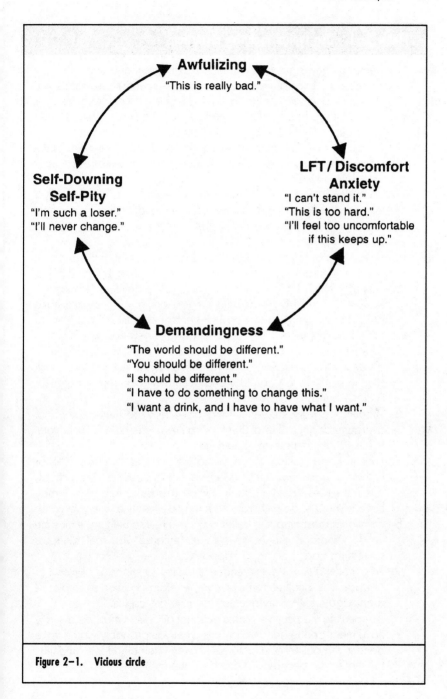

Figure 2–1.   Vicious circle

Table 2–1.   Ten typical cognitive distortions

1. *Demandingness*: Look for "should" statements that sound as if they make sense. Hiding underneath are some unrealistic demands that you, someone else, or the world should be different from the way you or the world *is*. Substitute preference statement: "I would like it if she didn't act that way, but she does."

2. *Negative exaggerations*: "awfulizing" or "catastrophizing" statements. Ask yourself: "Is it really that bad?" or "How bad is it from 1 to 10?"

3. *Low frustration tolerance* (LFT): often related to low discomfort tolerance. Some people have much more difficulty than others tolerating frustration and discomfort. You frequently upset yourself by thinking, "I can't stand it."

4. *Self-downing*: self-criticism, self-condemnation; related to self-pity. It is easy to crank up your emotional disturbance by creating a vicious circle of (1) demandingness, (2) awfulizing, (3) I-can't-stand-it-itis, and (4) self-downing. For example: "I shouldn't have used drugs again. I screwed up—and it's awful." "I can't stand facing my girlfriend." "I'm such a screw-up. I never do what I plan."

5. *Overgeneralizing*: sweeping statements. "I never do what I plan" is an example. Overgeneralizing statements are not true across all situations. Try to talk carefully and accurately about your behavior and the behavior of others.

6. *Labeling*: a very powerful (and potentially destructive) form of overgeneralizing. "I'm a drunk." "You're an asshole." Such statements usually lead to more unhelpful behavior.

7. *Personalizing*: taking things personally that really have little or nothing to do with yourself. When your child does poorly in school, it is not necessarily your fault. When a boss is sarcastic, it may have nothing to do with you. That may be his style with everyone.

8. *Emotional reasoning*: the belief that if you *feel* something, it must be valid. Where is the evidence that because you feel anxious, something bad is going to happen?

9. *All-or-nothing thinking*: the tendency to think of things as all-good or all-bad. It is another form of overgeneralizing. For example: "I drank again. All of my attempts to quite are useless."

10. *Discounting the positive*: statements that discount what you actually have managed to do (and ignores what you probably would have done in the past). For example, "I haven't gambled for six months, but that's only because I didn't have the money."

ISSUES TO KEEP IN MIND

Difficult Clients vs. Clients with Difficult Problems

One of the objectives of this book is to encourage clinicians to think differently about clients suffering from addictive behaviors. Many therapists and counselors shy away from working with addicts, perceiving them as extremely difficult clients.

If therapists feel successful only when they help a client get over his or her problem, then they will perceive such clients as difficult because they have difficult problems, many of which may be chronic. What therapists expect of themselves and of a client—that is, their own underlying belief systems concerning what they should be able to accomplish with a client and what a client should be able to accomplish with their help—will clearly affect how therapists feel at the end of the workday.

In brief, if therapists slip into rating themselves based on the way a client behaves, they will not enjoy working with addicted clients. Earlier in this chapter, I discuss how the stages of change model may help therapists prevent professional burnout by thinking about a client and his problems—and their responsibilities—differently.

Automatized Behavior

Why Do C's Seem to Be Caused by A's?

Much of what we learn, we overlearn. That is, we learn it so well that we can do it without much conscious attention and energy. One way of conceptualizing such behaviors is to think of them as having become "automatized." As such, "automatized behaviors" have many advantages. They allow us to do many things during the day. For example, most of us can drive an automobile and hold a conversation at the same time. Many of us can do this with ease and without fear of an accident. Automatizing behaviors, that is, learning and practicing them until they require only very minimal amounts of attention and energy to function, permit us to learn new behaviors with the freed-up attention and energy.

A person, place, or thing, even a smell or color, may trigger a conditioned response in some people. There is ample evidence now that this is true (Bargh and Chartrand 1999, Gollwitzer 1999, Wegner and Wheatley 1999). The response will probably be both physiological—neurochemical changes in the brain, changes in secretions in the intestine, changes in tension in the abdomen muscles—and psychological—changes in thoughts, in feelings, and in other behaviors. As a result, the client may report, "I suddenly found myself walking into a liquor store."

However, behavior is never totally automaticized. We must use a small amount of consciousness or attention and energy to monitor the running off of the many complex patterns of behavior that we have automaticized during our lifetimes. This is true of even some of the most automatized behaviors, for example, walking and talking. In New York City, if we do not use a little energy and attention as we are walking and talking to monitor our walking, we will not only bump into someone, we will also trip on something.

Why Is This Concept Relevant?

Many aspects of addictive behaviors are automatized, and changing automatized behaviors is often extremely difficult. We have to bring attention and energy back to the behavior, and we must do so consistently for a sufficiently long period of time to undo the overlearning and automatizing that we spent so much time and attention and energy on in the first place. Some readers may object: "I did not spend a lot of attention and energy learning how to smoke pot or drink alcohol," and that may be true. They did not have to spend a lot of attention and energy becoming addicted to gambling or shopping. The behavior patterns involved became automatized rapidly.

RESEARCH NOTE

Automatic evaluations may affect our behavior without our being aware of it. Even as toddlers we push away from us things that we do not like and pull toward us things that we do like. In an experiment with adults, subjects were asked to push a lever away from themselves as quickly as possible when a word was flashed on a screen. They pushed more quickly if the words were negative than if the words were positive. The reverse was also true. Those asked to pull the lever toward themselves did so faster if the word flashed on the screen was positive rather than negative. Subjects were not asked to evaluate the words, just to respond as quickly as possible. Hence, their behavior appears to have been affected by their nonconscious evaluations (feelings) about the word (Chen and Bargh 1999, as cited in Bargh and Chartrand 1999).

Why Is It Difficult to Change Automaticized Behavior?

1. **Triggers are difficult to recognize, and old behavioral patterns start running off, practically automatically, before we are aware of them.** Clients report that they catch themselves in the midst of an addictive behavioral pattern feeling as if they don't know how they got there: "I don't remember what I was thinking. I just went into the bedroom closet and took a swig."

2. **Many triggers may stimulate similar addictive behavior patterns.** Clients may have to learn new responses to a number of different triggers. Since it is usually to our advantage to let such overlearned, automatized behavioral patterns run, it takes a lot of attention and energy and time to substitute and practice new patterns in response to multiple triggers.

3. **Having to change complex behavioral patterns is not common and may not make sense to clients.** Most of the

time, we behave fairly automatically. We are not very mindful, moment to moment, of what we are doing. Most behaviors are not the result of conscious, reflective decisions but occur in reaction to the demands of the situation. The brake lights on the third car ahead of us go on. Without seeming to think about it, we move our foot from the accelerator to the brake pedal. In most situations we are accustomed to letting patterns of behaviors run because we are generally satisfied with the results. To have to bring attention and energy back to a situation may not make sense to clients, even though they have learned many new behaviors and modified many old ones almost as a routine part of life.

4. **Clients may be unmotivated or undermotivated to change.** We start to change a behavioral pattern only when we do not like the results. For the most part, letting behavior patterns run is the norm. Moreover, most clients like the first, short-run results of addictive behaviors. It is only the medium- and long-term results—the hangovers, the lost relationships, the lost money—that they do not like. Consequently, they are often ambivalent about changing.

5. **Changing takes attention and energy and time.** There is that old joke about a visitor to New York who was lost. He stopped someone and asked, "How do I get to Carnegie Hall?" "Practice, practice, practice," the other replied.

And what might be called "mindful" practice takes energy. Even when clients are not ambivalent and are sure they want to change, the automatized nature of such behaviors often makes changing very difficult.

RESEARCH NOTE

Recent studies suggest that you cannot engage in conscious self-regulation frequently during the day. The resources needed for self-regulation appear to get used up very quickly. In eight different experiments, doing a task (such as not eating chocolate chip cookies or not thinking about white bears) made it more difficult to do a later task that also required self-control (for example, not showing signs of amusement while watching a funny videotape or turning off a boring movie) (Baumeister et al. 1998, as cited in Bargh and Chartrand 1999).

How Can a Person Change Automatized Behaviors?

This book is devoted to answering this question. If it were easy to change addictive behaviors, a one-page pamphlet or a one-line slogan—"Just Say No!"—would suffice.

To consciously and willfully regulate one's own behavior, evaluations, decisions, and emotional states requires considerable effort and is relatively slow. Moreover, it appears to require a limited resource that is quickly used up, so conscious self-regulatory acts can only occur sparingly and for a short time. On the other hand, the nonconscious or automatic processes . . . are unintended, effortless, very fast, and many of them can operate at any given time. Most important, they are effortless, continually in gear, guiding the individual safely through the day. [Bargh and Chartrand 1999, p. 476]

As for clients, many of their automatic processes do not guide them "safely through the day."

What About Willpower?

Until about a hundred years ago, the will was thought of as a distinct entity. William James (1958) in critiquing the concept, noted: "All our deeds were considered by the early psychologists to be due to a peculiar faculty called the will, without whose fiat action could not occur. Thoughts and impressions . . . were supposed to produce conduct only after the intermediation of this superior agent" (p. 117).

In my workshops and in doing therapy, in answer to a question about willpower, I ball up a piece of paper and gently throw it at one of the participants. I either choose someone with glasses, because I don't want to risk scratching a cornea, or throw the ball to one side of the person's face. Recently at a workshop I tossed it at a woman sitting in the fifth row. Her hand came up almost instantly and she caught it, but she also flinched and blinked.

"Next time, don't move anything," I told her. I carefully threw the paper ball again. She kept her hands down, but she flinched and blinked again.

"Try not to move anything. You have glasses on, so I can't really hurt you. There's no danger I will really hit your eyes. So try not to even blink."

After waiting a moment, I threw it again. That time she did not move or blink at all.

"How did you do that?" I asked.

"I don't know. I just tried not to blink."

"How?"

"I don't know. I just concentrated on not moving anything?"

"Yes." I said. "I call that concentration 'attention and energy.' Where did you 'concentrate' your attention and energy?"

She didn't understand, so I asked, "Did you put attention and energy on your toes?"

"No," she said.

"Well, where did you put it? Can I throw it again?"

"Yes."

"Okay. But this time watch very carefully what you do and try to tell us."

I threw the ball again, and again she did not move at all.

"Great. What did you do?"

"I put a lot of attention on the muscles around my eyes and I stared at your nose. Keeping my arms still was not a problem."

"Yes. You did not have to use as much attention and energy to keep your arms still because that reaction is not as instinctual as your eye blink. But you overrode your eye blink as well. Correct?"

"Yes."

"But it took quite a bit of attention and energy—and some practice—to do that. Right?"

"Yes."

Many behaviors are so instinctual—we were born with them— or so overlearned that they operate in what seems like an automatic fashion. If we want to change one of these patterns of behavior, then we must bring attention and energy back to the behavior. This is true whether we are trying to learn not to overspend or to use drugs or, conversely, to learn to hit a golf ball differently or drive on the left side of the road in Britain. If we step into a bar—or even think about stepping into a bar—all sorts of scripts, patterns of behavior, and neurochemical changes involving very minimal attention and energy start to run off.

Suppose I asked the woman in my workshop to participate in an experiment. No matter when I threw the ball, she would not catch it or flinch or blink. Let's suppose she was motivated to participate in such an experiment. Even though the woman had learned how to inhibit her behaviors, consider how much attention and energy it would take for her to be watchful throughout the entire workshop. For most clients, changing their addictive behaviors takes a great deal of attention and energy and time.

We know what it is to *put attention on something*. And we know what it is to *put energy into a project*. Thus, these terms make more sense than *willpower*.

I agree with Bateson (1994) that thinking of the problem in terms of "myself" or "my willpower versus alcohol" (or some other addictive behavior) may increase the probability of relapsing. Moreover, when we focus on *not* doing something, we must keep our attention on the very behavior that we don't want to exhibit.

But we know that just thinking about something activates (primes) the brain. So here we set up a situation where we keep attending to a behavior that we don't want to stimulate in the first place. Then, Bateson points out, we have to create another entity, a "self" that is supposed to resist the running off of the behavior.

Where should we put our attention and energy? On our "self"? What does that mean? Where is it? In the situation with the paper ball, people eventually learn to put attention and energy around their eyes and in their arms and to use other strategies (e.g., looking at my nose) that help. Suppose the woman just focused on the ball and said to herself, "I have to resist this temptation to blink with my *self*" and did nothing else. How successful would she be?

In part, the cognitive-behavioral revolution has provided people with better ways to respond when they want to change an addictive behavior. We now have tools that they can learn and use to help themselves change when willpower and resolutions are not enough. (See Chapter 3 for more discussion about willpower.)

A Useful Metaphor: The "Mind" as a Committee

Freud utilized a model of the mind with three aspects: the ego (in German, the word for "I"), the superego (literally, in German, the "above-I"), and the id (in German, the "it"). Most people can easily relate to this model, perhaps partly explaining its enduring popularity. Cartoonists often depict an angel hovering on one side and a devil on the other with the character standing confused in the middle—the hapless ego or self trying to figure out the right path to follow.

It may be more reasonable to think of our mind as made up of more than the three parts proposed by Freud. We now know, from cognitive science, neurochemistry, genetics, cultural anthropology, sociology, economics, and various schools of conditioning and social learning in psychology, that there are many forces affecting the way we think, feel, and act. At various times, each of these may affect whether a person "decides" to engage in or manifest addictive behavior or not. "Decides" must be in quotation marks because there is ample evidence that we sometimes (or often) behave, thinking we have decided to do so when there is little or no evidence of conscious decision making. Research suggests that we act or behave first and then attribute a reason for our actions later (Bargh and Chartrand 1999).

Each of the forces acting on us may be represented, not all at once, but at varying times, by a "voice."

One client told me recently that she had absolutely no intention of drinking when she woke up, no intention at all at lunch, but then "suddenly" at 6:30 P.M., walking home from the office, she decided to stop in her local liquor store.

It is as if another "voice" suddenly took over. Earlier, when she decided she was not going to drink, it is as if those "voices" were not heard. Later, in a session, when she "convened the committee," it "voted" not to drink for the rest of the week. However, two days later, again as she left her office at 6 P.M., other "members" of the committee raised their voices demanding that the committee reconvene. It did, and the vote, not surprisingly, was in favor of stopping in the liquor store.

When we are very ambivalent about something, having a very hard time deciding what we want to do and not do, various ideas go through our heads, or various voices can be heard. One voice may have developed over many years of childhood saying, "I always get the short end of the stick in life. I deserve better. Life sucks," and accompanied by a feeling of being down and full of self-pity. Another voice may counter, "That kind of thinking is not going to help. That's just 'old' thinking. I have to try to think more long-term for a change." Still another, fueled by physiologic changes, may introduce, "I'm really tired and achy. I can't stand it anymore. I have to have a little tonight."

During a session, the therapist can encourage the "committee" to meet and the therapist and the client can listen to the various voices. One voice may be sure the client should stop for a week. Another voice may assert that that is much too ambitious and will only lead to disappointment. Another voice may be heard saying, "This is all too confusing. I can't do this. It's too hard," while still another says, "Get a grip. Stop being so immature." The therapist and client can explore the voices of the various constituencies in her head vying for attention. Eventually, the client will decide what she wants to try to do. In essence, the committee "votes." Perhaps it votes to abstain completely. Or perhaps it votes to drink only four times a week and never to have more than one drink an hour or more than three per session of drinking. This book discusses ways to help the client decide what she wants to do. But equally difficult, she has to learn how to carry out her decision in the face of myriad environmental cues and numerous internal, often unconscious, highly automatized mechanisms underlying her behavioral patterns. That is the essence of the therapy work: uncovering what contributes to her addictive behaviors and then developing techniques to withstand and ultimately override those forces.

"Voices" vs. "What are you telling yourself?" or "What are you thinking?"

The question "What are you telling yourself?" suggests that *you* are doing something active. You have a part in it. That implies that you can take some responsibility for what you say to yourself. Cognitive-behavioral therapy has its foundation in the fact that we all talk to ourselves and to some extent guide and monitor what we are doing and what we are going to do (or have the illusion that we are doing) (Bargh and Chartrand 1999). Ellis (1962, Ellis et al. 1988) appears to emphasize the active role more than Beck (1976, Beck et al. 1993), whose term *automatic thoughts* clearly suggests that the thoughts simply occur.

My clinical experiences suggest that different clients respond better to different phrasings of the question. "What are you telling yourself?" works better with some clients than "What are you thinking?" or "Listen to your voices." But the reverse is true for others. "What do the voices say to you when you listen?" may get at their inner self-talk more effectively. Naturally, therapists should be careful using the term *voices* with some clients. They may not understand the metaphor. They may really think that there are separate voices in their heads telling them what and what not to do. However, some people have found it beneficial, especially at the beginning of their recovery process, to create some distance between their healthy self and their *addictive voice*, a term Jack Trimpey (1992) coined in 1988. Some choose to think of that voice as the voice of their "lizard" or "baby" or "salesman" or "Beast." They actively engage in a kind of splitting because it helps them to make a distinction. Their addictive voice always cunningly, creatively, persistently, pushes for drugs or alcohol or whatever it craves, according to Trimpey and those who follow this model. Their healthy self has to learn to recognize this voice and how to ignore it.

RESEARCH NOTE

Recent experiments provide empirical evidence that much of how we think and feel and behave may and can be influenced by cues in the environment that we are completely unaware of. For example, people in one experiment were primed (unbeknownst to them) with a list loaded with words related to stereotypes of the elderly ("Florida," "stroke," "wrinkle," etc.) while others were shown another, unloaded list. The primed subjects later exhibited qualities associated with the elderly. They could not remember as many aspects of the room where they studied the lists as could those who had not been primed. More amazingly, they even walked down the hall more slowly upon leaving the experiment.

In another experiment, subjects were primed with a list of words related to rudeness or politeness. Rudeness-primed subjects interrupted 65 percent of the time, while politeness-primed subjects interrupted only 16 percent of the time. Controls, primed for neither rudeness nor politeness, interrupted 38 percent of the time. In interviews later, none of the subjects reported being aware of being primed (Bargh et al. 1996, as cited in Bargh and Chartrand 1999).

A Useful Metaphor:
"Anchors" and "Spin Doctors"

Television news anchors often come on the screen after a presidential speech and interpret and evaluate the speech for us. In effect, they often tell us, or at least suggest, how and what we should think and feel about what the president said.

Because these interpretations are so important, each political party now employs "spin doctors" to tell the reporters and anchors what they have just seen. They interpret and evaluate the speech for the interpreters—the reporters and anchors. They naturally attempt to give a positive spin to anything the president may have said or done and a negative spin to anything his opponents may have said or done.

As humans, we are always watching how we behave, think, and feel, commenting to ourselves about what we observe. It is as if we have a little anchor or spin doctor hovering over our shoulder, analyzing, interpreting, and, more importantly, evaluating everything we say, feel and do. Unfortunately, many clients have only negative spin doctors and anchors in their heads.

Brian, a 32-year-old client of mine, is struggling to finish his law school degree and uses coke on occasion to "chill out." He continually gives a negative spin to his life: "I'm too late. Everybody else has already gotten a good career. Look at Jim. He's already vice president at Merrill Lynch. And John. He's already married and has two children. What do I have? Nothing." His internal spin doctor, instead of giving a positive spin to what he has said and done and felt, continually gives a negative spin to everything. The interpretations are almost always critical and evaluations almost always negative. These interpretations and the evaluations reflect his underlying beliefs, some of which have deep roots in his childhood: "I absolutely have to succeed. If I don't succeed, I'm doomed." But if he succeeds, he may alienate the rest of his family, none of whom have been successful in life.

Another client, Betty, has been married to John for over twenty years. Both she and John have had problems with alcohol throughout most of their marriage, but Betty is trying to stop drinking. While they used to spend a lot of time together, John now often sits in their basement rec room, drinking and watching TV. Betty then begins to feel a mix of rage, humiliation, and depression, the effect of comments by the persistently critical spin doctor in her head: "You're never going to change. He's never going to change, either. Our marriage is a hopeless failure. How did I get in this mess? There's no way out. He's impossible." These thoughts often lead her to start drinking as well.

The client's anchor and spin doctor may also have a significant effect on what occurs after a lapse or relapse. Before contemplating changing, the client may say, "What a night," and think nothing more about it. But if the client is already beginning to try to change, he may say to himself something negative—"Wow, what a jerk. How could you have let him get to you so much? You always screw up"—or something more positive—"That was a mistake. Oh, I feel wretched. No more."

Many clients may have been beating themselves up for so long that they may say in therapy, "I understand what you are telling me, but it just doesn't feel right." They are so accustomed to their normal way of interpreting and evaluating that it is difficult to consider another way. It will take time, effort, and practice to change. First, the therapist must help them acknowledge that they do have a very negative anchorperson or spin doctor in their heads, and that it is not helping them. In fact, it may be the main factor behind their lapses and relapse. The therapist must help them learn to interpret and evaluate events in a more balanced manner.

Caution: As the therapist works at helping clients observe how negatively they evaluate everything they have done, are doing, and expect to do, he must be sure that they understand that he is not suggesting putting a bright face on a bad relapse. The problem is that their inner reporting is way out of balance—all negative. Betty rarely, if ever, has something good to say about her behaviors, thoughts, or feelings. Even when she thinks about her behavior in the future, she envisions berating herself for her usual screw-ups. We want equal time for both negative and positive spin doctors.

3 | WHAT CONTRIBUTES TO A CLIENT'S PROBLEMS?

For every complex problem, there is a solution that is simple, neat, and wrong.

—H. L. Mencken

Clients want to know why. Why are they behaving the way they are behaving? They also want to know how to change. This chapter explores some of the factors that may contribute to the "Why?" The remainder of the book suggests how to deal with or overcome the problem.

Some clinicians refer to addictions as complex biopsychosocial problems, but in fact, even more factors may be involved. Clinically, the way therapists think about this problem affects how they treat clients. What are their beliefs regarding addictions? Do they have sufficient evidence to back up those beliefs or are they basing them on just a feeling or in some cases on their own experiences as a recovering addict? Assuming that addictive problems are due to only one factor, for example, brain chemistry or irrational beliefs or not attending AA meetings, will probably lead to a form of arrogant, insensitive, and ineffective therapy. Such assumptions are often a result of the belief that "the way I got cured is the only way," and may reveal more about a therapist's own rigidly held beliefs than anything else.

It is very common for people to believe many things based on their experiences, but unfortunately our own personal experiences can often bias us in wrong directions. To take one example, for centuries people believed that the sun went around the earth. In fact, evidence to prove that this belief is correct can still be collected. You can watch the sun rise in the east and then go around the earth. The evidence can even be collected again and again—a repeated measure! It is so obvious that only an idiot would deny it, but it is still wrong. What anyone can see with his or her own eyes can mislead almost everyone into a set of beliefs that are fallacious.

Even more important than the therapist's beliefs are the client's beliefs. How does he conceptualize his problem or problems? How do his beliefs about the causes of his problem affect his efforts to change?

Therapists must consider many factors when they are working with clients who are grappling with serious addictive problems. If there are various contributing factors, the solution may have to be varied as well. We must consider many possible contributing factors, asking ourselves, "How might this factor affect the way we work together? How might it affect my client's efforts to change? What can we do to increase (if it is having a positive effect) or decrease (if it is having a negative effect) its impact?

DOES THE CLIENT THINK SHE HAS A DISEASE?

"You're not bad, you're sick. It's in the book." Over 300 disorders are described in the current *Diagnostic and Statistical Manual* (American Psychiatric Association 1994) (*DSM-IV*); eighteen years ago, only 108 were listed (Sharkey 1997).

To what extent is the client's problem a medical problem? Is an addiction a kind of disease? This topic has been widely debated over the past ten years. If one raises this question on the Web, he will set off a storm of messages and counter-messages that will continue for weeks. The more people think of their addiction as a disease, the less they blame themselves and the less others blame them for their behavior. If it is a disease, it is not their fault. Labeling alcoholism a disease has stopped people from thinking of it as a moral disorder. But, of course, just because one has a disease does not remove all of the responsibility for taking care of oneself and for managing one's disease.

According to Alan Leshner (1997), director of the National Institute for Drug Abuse, "Addiction must be approached more like other chronic illnesses—such as diabetes and chronic hypertension—than like an acute illness, such as a bacterial infection or a broken bone. . . . That makes a reasonable standard for treatment success—as is the case for other chronic illnesses—the management of the illness, not a cure" (p. 46).

However, it should be clear that not all diseases are the same. Some are caused more by agents that invade our systems and sicken us and some are caused more by our own lifestyle choices.

Consider the various types of afflictions from which humans suffer and the role of personal responsibility in each:

Type I

Type I afflictions are all caused by an outside agent, for example, a virus or a bacteria that attacks us and makes us ill. It may overwhelm our defenses and cause our death. Modern Western medicine is highly respected around the world because it has developed ways to help us defeat these agents and increase the length of our lives. Type I afflictions can be divided into two subtypes depending on how preventable they are. For example, we could keep our children home to try to prevent them from getting measles or strep throat, but not for long. We accept that there is little we can do to prevent them from getting these diseases in terms of changing their lifestyles. However, with some care, we can avoid getting cholera and malaria. In addition, we can greatly reduce the chances of contracting HIV by always engaging in safe sex, by limiting the number of sexual partners, and by using rubber gloves if we work in medical settings.

Type I	Type II	Type III	Type IV	Type V	Type VI
Influenza	Asthma	Drug abuse	Gambling	A broken hip	Wars
Mumps	Diabetes	Drug dependence	Compulsive sex	A ripped meniscus	Earthquakes
Measles	Hypertension	Alcohol abuse	Compulsive shopping	A back injury	Floods
Cholera		Alcohol dependence			Hurricanes
Malaria		Nicotine addictions	Computer addictions		
HIV		Heart and brain attacks			

Figure 3–1.

Type II

Outside agents play a lesser role in Type II afflictions. Genetics and lifestyles play a more important role, as we have discovered increasingly over the past fifty years. Diabetes and asthma appear to run in families. We inherit a predisposition to be afflicted with one of them. Outside agents may exacerbate diabetes, that is, cultural and economic forces (e.g., marketing) may induce us to eat too much sugar. As a result, we may worsen our state, but the original condition is probably inherited. Most people who have diabetes "relapse" to old habits of eating and drinking. Only about 30 percent follow their doctor's instructions.

Type III

Type III afflictions are caused to some extent by the agents we put into our bodies. Genetics probably affect how much an individual may want to introduce those agents, but environmental cues, social context, and lifestyles play a critical role. It is what we put in our mouths during many, many meals that eventually clogs up our arteries and does the damage. Similarly, smoking cigarettes eventually damages our lungs and stimulates the growth of cancer cells. We can decrease the likelihood of having heart attacks or strokes (now referred to as brain attacks) by eating less fatty foods, but many cultural, economic, and social factors encourage us to eat more. The reverse is also true. Fewer people develop problems with alcohol in countries where alcohol consumption is forbidden and severely punished.

Type IV

Agents appear to play no role in the development of Type IV afflictions, such as gambling and compulsive sex. However, other kinds of "agents," such as advertising, radically alter our surrounding environmental cues. Advertisers spend hundreds of millions of dollars each year to affect our behavior, to convince us to shop, smoke, drink, and gamble, and they associate sex with practically every product imaginable.

The majority of the disorders listed in the *DSM-IV* do not involve an agent and thus would fit into this Type IV category. However, perhaps anxiety disorders should be categorized as a Type II affliction as there is probably a genetic component or a Type III affliction because caffeine may be a major contributory factor. Depression probably also has a genetic component, but it may be more affected by our everyday behaviors and our thinking than by an agent. (It is possible, however, that we will someday discover that depression is kicked off by a viral-like agent.)

Type V

Trucks may hit us and trees branches may fall on our heads, but many "accidents" are not just accidents. Lifestyles choices often contribute to how often and how severely we injure ourselves. An automobile accident may be unavoidable, but if we couldn't be bothered to put on our seat belt ("We're only going a short way"), our injuries could be much more severe. At the gym, if we fail to warm up sufficiently ("I don't have time; it's too much trouble"), we increase the probability of injuring ourselves. It is even worse if we simply cannot get around to going to the gym at all ("I don't have time." "I'll go to the gym tomorrow."). If we suddenly decide to go skiing, our previous avoidant behavior may contribute to, if not cause, an injury.

Since many addictions are often varieties of avoidant behaviors, the injuries that clients suffer both physically (falls, liver damage, as well as possible changes in the brain), socially (lost relationships), and economically (lost jobs) resemble type V afflictions.

Type VI

Lifestyle choices may even affect type VI afflictions. People have been injured or have died in coastal areas because they failed to leave the area when a hurricane was approaching or, worse, went down to watch the waves and got swept away. Economic and social factors may force poor people to build houses in areas where mud slides and floods put them in constant risk of injury or death.

*   *   *

In brief, addictions are on a continuum. They are a variety of human afflictions that are affected by lifestyle choices, by an agent that is introduced in the body by our own actions (e.g., alcohol, nicotine, heroin, etc.), and by environmental "agents" in the form of advertising, cultural norms, and other social and environmental cues. Labeling them a "disease" suggests to some people that a factor outside of their control is the major contributing factor. Such a conceptualization removes the moral stigma from the problem. However, lifestyle choices (e.g., diet and exercise) often affect whether we get or do not get a disease. Lifestyle choices also have a major impact on how we manage the disease and on the frequency, duration, and severity of its recurrence.

If the client believes that her problem is medical, not much can be gained by disputing this belief. Rather, it is important to understand how her beliefs affect her efforts to change.

RESEARCH NOTE

The alcohol industry has reasons to support the disease model. It would like consumers to believe that if they don't have the disease, they can drink without any problems. But many people who do not meet the *DSM-IV* criteria for abuse or dependence can and do have problems—sometimes with serious consequences—after consuming alcohol. For example, among over 6,000 college students surveyed, one in four women reported having been raped or having been a victim of an attempted rape, and 12% of men reported having committed acts that met the legal definition of rape or attempted rape; 55% of the women and 75% of the men reported having used alcohol and/or other drugs before the assault (Koss et al. 1987, as cited in Dimeth et al. 1999).

Beliefs that May Impede Treatment

"The doctor is responsible. The doctor will fix my problem. I hope (think) there must be a pill I can take that will help me overcome my problem."

Many people still turn to a doctor for a cure. In the medical model, the doctor diagnoses our problem and takes responsibility for our cure. Our sole responsibility is to comply with the doctor's instructions. However, increasingly doctors are recognizing that lifestyle factors play a significant role in heart attacks, strokes, asthma, and many other diseases.

The client may be unaware that she is functioning within a medical model. She may be unaware that she is waiting for someone to cure her problem. She may have gone to three hospitals for inpatient treatment, but nothing has worked. Unfortunately, such a belief system does not appear to work very effectively for overcoming or managing addictions. Clients must take more responsibility for resolving their problems, and lifestyle changes are almost always required.

It may help to find out how the client thinks about another medical problem that she may have, such as asthma or acid reflux. What does she do for that? To what extent does she believe that the doctor will cure her or that a pill will remove the symptoms? To what extent does she accept or resist the notion that she could make some lifestyle changes that might ameliorate or eliminate her problem?

Sometimes it works better to explore how other people in her family respond to medical problems. If someone in her family has a sore throat, what does he or she do? Is there anyone in her family who is bad at taking care of herself (or himself)? For example, when her mother is given medication, does she refuse to take it or consistently forget? Is there anyone who seems to get sick a lot partly because she doesn't take care of herself? Such questions will help the therapist explore what the client thinks she should do when *she* has a disease. What is her role and responsibility?

E. Fuller Torrey (1986) in his *Witchdoctors and Psychiatrists* suggests that all healers around the world use the same techniques although they may not look similar. He calls one of the four techniques the principle of Rumpelstiltskin. Torrey asserts that simply naming the affliction has great curative power. Labeling an addiction a disease may, in fact, stimulate the client's psychological (and perhaps biological) autoimmune system. That is, it may motivate her to do what she needs to do to get over her "illness" or to manage it better. AA may have tapped into this technique by encouraging its members to admit that they are alcoholics, effectively naming the problem. But as most members of AA know, that is not sufficient. They must "work the steps."

IS THE CLIENT'S PROBLEM A "BRAIN DISEASE"?

In 1997, Leshner entitled his article in *Science*, "Addiction Is a Brain Disease, and It Matters." He makes two assertions: First, brain chemistry in people who have addictive disorders is different from those who do not. Leshner acknowledges that we do not know whether or not this was true before their addictive behaviors developed. Second, the use of certain chemicals to the point where one becomes addicted alters the brain. At that point, Leshner asserts, the user cannot control his behavior (relevant to that chemical) without "treatment strategies that include biological, behavioral, and social-context elements" (p. 46). Leshner is also quite clear that "the major goal of treatment must be either to reverse or compensate for those brain changes" and that "these goals can be accomplished through either medication or behavioral treatment" (p. 46). According to Leshner, addiction is a brain disease that manifests itself depending on the social context and environmental cues. As evidence, he cites the example of soldiers who became addicted to heroin in Vietnam, but on coming home to a completely different social context and environment, they were able to permanently quit.

How is this relevant for therapy? It is certainly possible that some people are born with invisible (to date) structural and/or chemical abnormalities in the brain. (Magnetic resonance imaging [MRI] and positron emission tomography [PET] scans are helping us understand some functioning in the brain, but much is still invisible to us.) As a result, they may be more prone to engaging in what we call addictive behaviors in an attempt to help themselves compensate for or cope with these abnormalities. They are self-medicating (Khantzian 1985). It is also fairly obvious that brain chemistry differs from one individual to the next. Many of us drink tea or coffee to affect the way we think, feel, and behave. But some people cannot tolerate caffeinated beverages, and different antidepressant medications affect different people differently. Most clients have a drug of choice. They may use several drugs, but they generally gravitate toward one. This also may be due to brain chemistry differences.

Both dopamine and serotonin now appear to have major roles in how we feel and how motivated we are to act. Situations or thoughts about situations that will lead to more rewarding conditions appear to stimulate an upsurge of dopamine in the medial forebrain bundle. Imagine dopamine floating around and helping people feel more like taking action. Continually, over time, dopamine is reabsorbed by other cells in the brain. However, if the client snorts cocaine, the cocaine will block this reabsorption. More dopamine will continue to slosh around the system, making the client feel better and feel like doing things. Similarly, nicotine appears to slow down the way an enzyme, monoamine oxidase (MAO) B, breaks down and eliminates dopamine. Hence, more is left in the system. Antidepressant MAO inhibitors work in a similar way, making them an effective treatment of depression for some clients. Amphetamines act in a different manner. They increase the release of dopamine into the system.

We are only beginning to understand the chemistry involved. The next fifty years should provide fascinating data and food for thought for physiologists, biologists, neurologists, psychologists, and philosophers, as well as for the general public.

We now know that some people are born with the ability to sprint much faster than others, and others have an unusual genetic ability to run long distances. We would have to train a great deal to beat them, that is, to overcome their genetic advantage. In a similar fashion, we may discover that the dopamine system (or other, interrelated systems) of some people makes it far more difficult for them to behave responsibly—to stick to a task, to do what is in their medium- and long-term best interest, not just what is in their short-term best interest—to take care of themselves. We may conclude that the more responsible person is not necessarily more "mature," but is blessed with a different brain chemistry. It is easier for them to think and behave in a manner that we consider responsible. But this is clearly a very slippery slope. We have already seen in Nazi Germany what may happen if a country's population begins to think that a group of people are genetically different. Moreover, it is politically easier to think that the problem resides in the brain of individuals than to think that the problem may be the result of the political, social, and economic (and spiritual?) systems those individuals live in.

George Albee (1982, 1996) has presented the most clearly articulated arguments outlining the effects of a disease orientation to mental and emotional disorders. He states,

> The *DSM-IV* discrete disease model sends investigators on a search inside the body of the suffering person looking for genetic, biochemical, and other physical defects, and into the environment for causes that trigger these internal defects. On the other hand, the stress-learning model focuses the search on environmental factors such as poverty, exploitation, and prejudice that produce augmented stress. This latter model accepts efforts to strengthen resistance to stress, such as social competency training, improving self-esteem and self-confidence, and providing support systems. [1996, p. 1131]

On the other hand, what if the brain disease hypothesis is partly correct? What if, for a combination of genetic and environmental reasons, some individuals are chemically disabled? What kind of impact could this have on therapy? First, if someone is genuinely disabled, either by a structural or chemical abnormality in the brain, then certainly empathy and compassion are in order. On the other hand, just as we expect some kinds of responsibility from other people who are disabled, where do we draw the line? Do we mean that addictions affect a person's ability to make decisions in general or only about a certain chemical (or activity) and only in a certain social and environmental setting?

As we gain a better understanding of brain chemistry differences and their impact on behavior, our conceptualization of responsibility will probably have to change. But at this date, except in the case of severe psychological disturbances, we will still hold people responsible for their behavior. However, it is clear that environmental cues and social contexts dramatically affect brain function, consciousness, and behavior. In some circumstances, judging from a person's behavior, we might decide that he or she cannot live in a particular environment or be in certain social contexts without relapsing. But most of us already believe that. We do not think a person who has a serious problem with alcohol can remain in a bar for long without finally having a drink. If someone who has had a problem with heroin continues to live with other people who are using heroin or cocaine, it is likely that he will eventually use.

Ultimately, we arrive at a position that is probably true for many of the other problems therapists help people with, such as depression and excessive anxiety. It is useful to remember that people differ in the way their brains and entire nervous systems function. Some of these differences probably affect the extent to which they are motivated to do almost anything, including changing various behaviors. In addition, some of these differences probably also affect the degree to which they can make responsible decisions. If some people are operating at what we might also call a "chemical disadvantage," the therapist's role is to help them accept that reality and to learn what environmental conditions help them function best. The ultimate goal, as with any disability, is to help them live as full a life as possible, while doing as little harm to themselves and others. Because of brain chemistry and brain structure differences, some people may find it much more difficult to change than others. But even quite disturbed people can change.

We know that significant structural changes occur in the brain with continued and intense use of a chemical. But this is probably true of all activities, whether it is playing the piano or smoking pot. However, unlike piano playing, some behaviors may become addictive by causing changes in the very parts of the brain that affect motivation and decision making. It is clear that the chemicals that are routinely abused have this impact. Alzheimer's disease (the causes of which are not understood yet) appears to have a similar impact, as well as an adverse effect on memory. But Alzheimer's does not push us to continue to do what is creating the brain changes.

Are these changes reversible? There is clearly some research that shows that they are. But we do not know whether all of the changes can be undone or what helps reverse the damage. Nevertheless, we do know that we can continue to function sometimes remarkably well, even after sustaining serious injuries to the brain. Even if structures in the brain are changed, we may be able to compensate for the changes without significant or noticeable alterations in our thinking, behavior, or the way we feel. Moreover, recent research (Noble 1998) provides conclusive evidence of brain cell growth in humans. We have known for a long time that two other organs, the skin and the liver, can regenerate. However, it was accepted that we could not and did not grow brain cells. Now we know that is incorrect. In mice, the growth rate is astounding, approximately 20,000 per hour in one area of their brain. Monkeys also appear to have a similar capacity. So there may be hope that even serious damage to the brain can be repaired over time.

Beliefs that May Impede Treatment

They say it is a brain disease. There's nothing I can do about my brain.

Just because the brain is an organ inside our head does not

mean that we cannot change its functioning. We ingest chemicals (e.g., caffeine, nicotine, sugar, and salt), jog, talk to our friends, and daydream, all of which alter brain functioning and brain chemistry. *It's not fair that other people can enjoy this chemical, but I can't.* This is correct. It is not fair. And, as I point out elsewhere, believing that we are a victim of unfairness can create intense destructive feelings, such as rage and self-pity. It is healthy to want to do what others do if we also want to, but it becomes a problem when we slip into thinking that we should (must) be able to do whatever we want.

I should be able to function even if I use. I should be able to control this chemical, that is, I should be able to stay in control even after ingesting some of this chemical.

These are interesting beliefs, and more common than one might think. Young people wonder "How much I can hold?" Almost everyone who has or has had a problem with one chemical or another has gone through the period of testing.

CASE VIGNETTE

Recently, a client of mine said she had taken the drug Ecstasy even though she did not like its effect. She wanted to prove to herself that she could control her behavior even after taking the drug. "Why?" I asked her. "Some people appear to have become immune to the chemicals injected by rattlesnakes. Are you interested in finding out whether you, too, can 'control' the effect of rattlesnake venom and keep on behaving as if you hadn't been bitten?"

She seemed surprised. "No," she said.

"Then why do you want to prove that you still want to dance and can still dance after you have taken Ecstasy?"

"I don't know."

"Perhaps you have a hidden belief that you should be able to maintain control of your behaviors even under very adverse conditions. When I was 14, I had two glasses of wine on the sly on

Thanksgiving. Then my mother asked me to fill the water glass on the table. They were glasses with stems, so they could tip over easily. I remember trying to see if I could pour the water without spilling one drop. And I did. And I felt very good. I had proved I could feel tipsy but still control my behavior. Is that kind of what you are doing?"

"Yes, I think so."

"So you are kind of thinking, 'If I can do this, I am a better person.'"

"Well, no. That sounds silly. It doesn't make me a better person."

"But it seems to have been an attempt to raise your self-esteem—how you felt about yourself as a person."

"Yes, maybe it is. I want to see if I can do it."

"Did you take into account that some people are more sensitive than others to a chemical or a mix of chemicals?"

"What do you mean?"

"Well, it is always curious to me. We all seem to accept that we are very different physically. You could certainly run faster than I could, and probably dance longer into the night. But we don't seem to accept that we are very different chemically, despite the fact that there is plenty of evidence that we are. Most people can enjoy strawberries, but some can't. They will have a terrible allergic reaction. Some people can eat spicy food with no ill effects. Others get diarrhea. Why? Because they are different chemical 'factories.' They process foods differently. Does it make Sally a better, stronger person, if she can 'will' her body not to respond to the chemicals in Ecstasy?"

"Well, no."

"I'm not sure you believe that. I think maybe you believe a person who cannot be affected by a drug is a stronger person. Is that right?"

"Well, a little bit."

"And if they can't stave off an allergic reaction to strawberries, are they a weaker person?"

"No."

"Well, this is an interesting belief that you have. Many people share it. They should be able to control their use of alcohol or heroin.

Some realize that these chemicals directly affect parts of the brain that seem to be active when motivation and judgment and self-regulation (control) are involved. I wonder if it has something to do with your feeling that you could never do what you wanted in your household because your mother was such a domineering, controlling person?"

We continued along these lines in an attempt to examine not only her belief that she should be able to maintain her control even after ingesting various chemicals but also to help her accept that even though others might be able to do so, she cannot.

If a client believes "When I'm drunk, I am completely out of it. When I'm high on cocaine there is no way I am going to use a condom," does he really believe that he could not alter his behavior, even for a moment, if offered $100,000 on the spot or if someone threatened him with a gun? If he has a brain disease but could stop, even for one minute, it tells us that environmental cues outside his brain—in this case, the anticipated reward/penalty—still can affect his brain's functioning. Is *he* doing it or the anticipated reward/penalty doing it? This is a question for philosophers and cognitive scientists to ponder. What is relevant for us is that the interior brain never functions totally independently of what is exterior to it.

RESEARCH NOTE

According to the National Institute on Drug Abuse (1999), "One study found that only four out of more than 12,000 patients who were given opioids for acute pain actually became addicted to the drugs. Even long-term therapy has limited potential for addiction. In a study of 38 chronic pain patients, most of whom received opioids for 4 to 7 years, only 2 patients actually became addicted, and both had a history of drug abuse" (p. 2).

DOES THE CLIENT BELIEVE
HIS PROBLEM IS DUE TO GENETICS?

After years of the nature vs. nurture debate, most people accept that both nature and nurture contribute to the way we think, feel, and behave, and that they affect each other (e.g., Anthenelli and Schuckit 1998, McGue 1999). We may inherit a predisposition to be very musical and wind up being an accomplished pianist. We may also inherit a predisposition to become addicted to heroin. However, the environment plays a major role in determining whether either one of these predispositions manifests itself in piano playing or heroin addiction.

Unfortunately, the media often take research findings and simplify them to the point where they are no longer correct, and it is this misinformation that may be remembered. The NIAAA is currently funding the Collaborative Study on the Genetics of Alcoholism (COGA) as part of the attempt to map the entire human genome. Not surprisingly, preliminary data suggest that several genes play a role in predisposing a person to have problems with alcohol.

In sum, genes do not determine behavior; however, many different kinds of genetic predispositions interacting with a variety of environments may make it more difficult for a particular person to change an addictive pattern of behavior.

Beliefs that May Impede Treatment

If it's genetic, maybe I can't help it.

Almost everything we do, think, and feel is affected by our genetic wiring. But diabetics learn to handle their condition. Congenitally blind people learn to function almost as fully as sighted people and may function even better in many areas.

Is there a secondary gain for holding on to this belief? If someone is demoralized after many attempts to stop drinking, does holding on to the belief that it is genetic help him cope? Rationalization as a defense mechanism is not always bad; it may help him survive until he believes he has the resources to tackle the problem again.

It's not fair.

As noted elsewhere, this is one of the hardest beliefs to work on, especially because it is often true. Life is unfair. Some people are attractive, bright, confident, good athletes, socially adept, and rich. The reverse is also true. But it is a very difficult reality to accept and one that clients can get stuck on. It may be especially difficult in this culture to accept that we cannot do anything about something that is unfair.

My father smoked all his life, and he lived to 85.

At times, this is a variation of the "fairness" issue. If Dad could get away with it, I should be able to, too. Many of us also look for some shred of evidence that we can get away it, without changing the way we behave. As I discuss in Chapter 7, we refuse to acknowledge that the proverbial stick may finally hit us.

DOES YOUR CLIENT BELIEVE HER PROBLEM IS DUE TO A LACK OF WILLPOWER?

The client may believe that she has not been successful because she lacks sufficient willpower. As Rollo May (1969), in his careful analysis of will has pointed out, " 'Willpower' was conceived by our nineteenth-century forefathers as the faculty by which they made resolutions and then purportedly directed their lives down the rational and moral road that the culture said they should go" (p. 180). It is this view of willpower that most of people appear to subscribe to. It is some kind of faculty, somewhere within themselves that is weak.

May (1969) states: "One of Freud's great contributions—if not his greatest—lay in his cutting through the futility and self-deceit in Victorian 'will power.' " He goes on to note, however, that "the image that emerged was of man as determined—not *driving* any more, but *driven*" (p. 180, May's emphasis). Over the past fifty years, this notion of being determined or driven has been reinforced by behaviorism and by numerous studies that suggest that many of our behaviors run off automatically, often as a result of factors outside of our awareness (Bargh and Chartrand 1999). May asserts that we either have to "retreat before this destruction of our vaunted 'willpower' or push on to the integration of consciousness on new levels" (p. 181).

Lack of willpower and a related concept, lack of discipline, arise as explanations when two criteria are met. First, we employ these phrases when we are trying to do something that is counter to our normal pattern of behavior and are not succeeding. We do not admire a person's willpower to eat his salad. If he declines dessert, that's another matter. Then we may admire his willpower. The term is used when we go against our natural tendency to do something, when we override our automaticity.

Second, we use the term when we have to endure some discomfort to do what we set out to do. For example, it is difficult and in some ways uncomfortable to sit at a dinner and not eat any dessert. We do not say it takes willpower for an American to stay in the left lane when driving in England. To do that takes concentration, which is to say we have to focus our attention on the road, on not misunderstanding the signs, and we may tell our passengers that we cannot talk and drive at the same time, even though we can in the States. We do not say it takes willpower to learn a new way to swing a baseball bat. It takes practice and concentration.

It is only when we eat a dessert or take a drink when we had previously decided not to do so that we say we lack willpower. It is only when we are not studying and we think we should be studying that we say we lack discipline. In each case, we attribute our failure to change to the fact that we could not muster the courage or find the energy or endure the discomfort that would have been required to go against our normal, automaticized behavior. It is for that reason that we think of ourselves as weak.

But Freud and modern cognitive science suggest that that reason (our attributing our failure to willpower) may be only partly correct, if at all. Many other factors affect our desire or lack of desire, our willingness or unwillingness, our ability or inability to override our normal pattern of behavior.

Conversely, if we do manage not to drink or use or gamble (that is, to change our ingrained behavior) in spite of or in the face of some or all of those factors, we might attribute that to our willpower. In reality, our change may be more correctly attributed to many other factors, including our beliefs that change is worth it; our beliefs that not changing would cause us too much pain; our beliefs that we can do it (self-efficacy); learning techniques to help us do it (know-how); practicing those techniques (which, in turn, is affected by our beliefs that it is worth it, etc.); changes in brain chemistry due to pharmacological interventions or meditation or exercise; getting together with people who can help us; environmental cues and social situations that support our efforts to change; and insight into the factors that consistently derail us.

Because each client is so unique physically, chemically, and psychologically (and lives in a specific social context as well), each one will have to figure what she/he has to do to change the behavior she/he wants to change. For a variety of reasons, some clients find it easier to change than others. A few will not have to do very much more than to decide to change. However, the client may find changing very difficult. Consequently, she may need to do some or all of the following:

- Learn techniques to help her better manage (regulate) her emotional life, for example, the ABC(DE)'s, since emotional upsets often cause her to derail herself (to "throw in the towel," "fall of the wagon," etc.).
- Practice those techniques on a daily basis.
- Join AA or an alternative self-help group such as SMART [Self Management and Recovery Training] to connect with other people who are grappling with a similar problem.
- Meet individually with a therapist to help her uncover some of the reasons (conscious and unconscious) that may contribute to her derailing herself, and to learn other techniques

to help her reduce the frequency, duration, and intensity of lapses and relapses.

- In group or individual therapy, figure out and practice what she could say in difficult situations to help herself.
- Move from the city where all of the environmental cues stimulate urges in her to use cocaine and where cocaine is readily available.
- Learn techniques to help her resist urges and cravings.
- Get pharmacological help with her chronic low-grade depression (dysthymia) or her chronic anxiety.
- Read self-help books as well as books about larger issues in life, such as Kasl's *Many Roads, One Journey: Moving Beyond the Twelve Steps* (1992).
- End her relationship with a person who is continuing to use.
- Get out of a job that she thinks contributes to her use (for example, because other people in her workplace use cocaine or because her job contributes so much stress to her life).
- Increase the time she spends exercising.
- Begin to meditate or do t'ai chi.
- Be more careful about getting enough sleep at regular times.
- Eat more regularly and rely less on junk food.
- Purposely do things to increase her tolerance for discomfort and frustration, such as refusing to smoke the usual cigarette after lunch; sitting for an hour at sun-up to meditate; making a speech that she would have avoided in the past; calling someone to have dinner that previously she would have not dared to call; speaking up when someone in her family behaves obnoxiously; fasting for a day once per week or per month.

Each of the above behaviors may make it easier for the client to make the changes she says she wants to make. And if she accepts that many factors may make it more difficult to change, she may be less prone to pin her difficulties on the simplistic, outdated concept of weak willpower. Recognizing the difficulty and complexity of changing addictive behavioral patterns, she may take the actions (engage in the behaviors) that will increase the probability of initiating and maintaining a change.

RESEARCH NOTE

Peter Gollwitzer (1999) calls the actions we take in order to reach a desired goal "implementation intentions." He has shown in a number of studies that teachers can increase, for example, the number of students who hand in an assignment on time by asking them, in advance, to specify exactly when and where they intend to write the required report. In another study, women who indicate a strong intention to perform a breast self-examination did so during the next month 100 percent of the time if they were also asked to form implementation intentions (again, exactly where and when they would do it). Only 53 percent of the those not asked to specify their implementation intentions performed the exam. Addictive behavioral patterns are clearly more complex. Consequently, the client may have to do many things in order to eventually effect the desired change in her behavior.

Although research indicates that many of our behaviors may be triggered by environmental cues completely outside our awareness, we have the feeling that, as our goals and purposes in life change, it is possible for us to decide to reprogram ourselves or override (transcend) our conditioning. As Jerome Bruner (1983) has noted in his book *In Search of Mind: Essays in Autobiography*, "Once we 'intend,' once we set a course for ourselves, we no longer go it alone. We commit ourselves to institutions and traditions and 'tool kits' which, if our stars read right, will both amplify our powers and lock us in our path" (pp. 3–4). In later chapters I outline ways in which therapists and counselors can help people, especially those troubled by addictive behaviors, to develop the tools in their "tool kit" so as to live happier, more fulfilling lives.

OTHER FACTORS TO KEEP IN MIND

Unconscious Processes

Numerous experiments (Bargh and Chartrand 1999, Gollwit-zer 1999, Wegner and Wheatley 1999) demonstrate that at least some of the time we behave in response to stimuli that we are simply not aware of (or, more correctly, to stimuli that we are not aware that we are aware of). Many clients are even unaware that they are trying to alter the way they feel when they drink alcohol. They come to therapy because their drinking mystifies them: "Why do I keep doing something that I think I want to stop?" Many of the techniques in this book are designed to help people bring to awareness ways of thinking that they may have been unaware of but that affect how they behave.

Was one of my clients, Mary, so unable to change her drinking habits because she unconsciously believed that she should never be in a "bitchy" mood? Or was it because her father had secretly continued to drink (despite telling the family that he had stopped) until his death? She had not gotten along very well with her father. They shared practically nothing in terms of likes and dislikes. Did she continue drinking to bond with him, albeit posthumously?

Another client of mine, Nancy, an attractive, young executive in the cosmetics business, not only thought she drank too much, but also reported having one disastrous affair after another. She frequently went home with a man on the first date, only to loathe herself later. Every one of her longer term relationships was with a very heavy drinker, and many of her one-night stands were with similar men. In therapy, it turned out that her alcoholic father had always been cold to her or berated her. Was she unconsciously trying to make one of these heavy drinking men love her as her father had not? Was she trying to show herself that this time she would get it right? When she was younger, all her attempts to win her father's love had failed.

She had always been rebuffed. But this time she would be so perfect that her boyfriend would love her as she had always deserved. Or was a nondrinking, more stable man unconsciously too threatening to her, considering her own chronic low self-esteem? As we worked together, we came up with several possible beliefs: "I must prove that I am lovable." "If a man makes loves to me, I'm okay." "I can't stand waiting to see if I am loved." "If I don't find the right man soon, I may be doomed to a lonely, miserable life (so I better not take time to find out what kind of person I'm going to bed with)." "A nice guy wouldn't like me." "If he's 'sicker' than I am, he won't leave me."

Developmental Factors

When asked how old they were when they first drank or first had a panic attack or first felt depressed, many people answer "Twelve." Clearly, the huge chemical changes that occur in puberty lead to vast changes in the way people look, behave, feel, and think. As a rational emotive behavioral REBT therapist, I have noticed that many people seem to change from trying to do what they think their parents think they should do to trying to do what *they* think they should do. They have to fit in. If parents suggest that they do not have to fit in, this is taken as further evidence that the parents just don't understand them.

If a 70-year-old man loses his wife of fifty years and starts to go to a casino every day, this is also, in my opinion, a developmental problem, because adjusting to the loss of a lifelong partner and to the other realities of becoming older are developmental issues. A recent study of gambling found prevalence levels for pathological and problem gambling of 1.6 percent and 3.85 percent respectively, in the general population (Shaffer et al. 1997). What percent of these people are over 70? When a man over 70 loses his life's savings, he cannot recover as can a man in his twenties or thirties. If the average age of becoming dependent on alcohol among Harvard graduates was 40 (Vaillant 1996), what is the average age of developing critical problems as the result of addictive gambling?

Unfortunately, we do not have normative data on the development and resolution (or lack of resolution) of most addictive disorders.

As is well known, men (and many women, especially professional women) may hit difficult developmental waters around 45, the famous mid-life crisis. They may be thinking: "It's not fair." "I'll never succeed, and without succeeding, how can I be a man? I must succeed." "It's too late. I never made it." "Everybody else is succeeding. What is wrong with me?"

In contrast, only a few young people in their early twenties think this way. Generally, 20-year-olds, although similarly troubled by fears of failing, of humiliating themselves, and of disappointing their parents, have their life ahead of them and can always think, "I can do better. I can fix this." They frequently do not agree that they are addicted. And the idea of abstaining, especially for life, does not make sense to them. They have not had enough bad events—there is not enough evidence—to convince them that change, let alone abstention, is necessary.

RESEARCH NOTE

Alcohol use among college students is involved in 67 percent of the cases of residential hall damage, 65 percent of violent incidents, and 29 percent of student attrition, and suspected in 41 percent of cases of lowered academic performance. The strongest predictor of heavy drinking among college students is the belief that "alcohol makes it easier to act out sexually" (Dimeff et al. 1999, p. 12, citing Larimer et al. 1997, a study of college drinking among college fraternity and sorority members).

Gender

There is still a great deal to be learned about the impact of gender on addictive behaviors. There is some research evidence to support the hypothesis that men and women differ in what causes addictive behaviors and what causes relapse (Anthenelli and Schuckit 1998, Blume 1998, Pettinati et al. 1997, Wilsnack et al. 1997). The belief systems of women and men are inevitably different, influenced by age and by biological, cultural, and other factors. For example, a 38-year-old woman will probably not have the same concerns as a 38-year-old man. If she wants children, her biological clock is ticking. Even if she has children, she must begin to work at accepting that these are the only children she is going to have. She is not going to meet another man, marry, and have another family with him. This may be very difficult for some women to accept. Men and women who have opted for a career and decided not to have children may be especially affected by what they have accomplished or not accomplished when they are approximately 45 years old. However, if a woman has not been successful, this reality may be especially hard to accept. She chose to pursue a different route from most of her peers. Moreover, such a decision was often made in the face of enormous pressure from her family and her environment. So it can become very easy for her to begin to doubt everything that she has ever believed or decided and to feel hopeless, helpless, and trapped.

RESEARCH NOTE

Dimeff and her associates (1999) provide a wealth of useful information for a practitioner in their manual for the BASICS (Brief Alcohol and Screening and Intervention for College Students) program:

- In general, men metabolize alcohol at a rate 30 percent slower than women. They also tend to weigh more, so if a woman tries to keep up with a man, drink for drink, she will probably become twice as intoxicated.

- The more water in the body, the more the impact of alcohol gets diluted; 55 to 65 percent of a man's body is water, but only 45 to 55 percent of a woman's.

- Hormonal changes and oral contraceptives may cause the level of alcohol in a woman's blood to remain for a longer time period, especially 1 week before and 1 week after menstruating.

Temperament

Interest in temperament has been increasing over the past few years, although pioneering work was done in the 1960s by Thomas and his colleagues (1968). From the very first day, children exhibit markedly different temperaments. Some infants sleep through the night from the first day; others awake frequently and are difficult to quiet down. One child tries to climb on anything and everything, despite frequent slips and falls, while another most often is content to sit quietly, examining bottle tops, spoons, and pieces of puzzles. Environmental factors, especially traumatic events, may cause changes in these basic temperamental styles, but often they remain constant through life. Is there a connection between risk-taking at 18 months and risk-taking, including experimenting with drugs, gambling, and sex at 18 years of age? If there is, does such a liking for risk predispose one also to addictions? Experimenting with various risky behaviors may not necessarily lead to an addictive level of activity.

Why is this relevant? It may help a client accept that he is wrestling with something that he did not ask for—a predisposition to become addicted to certain activities or substances. If he chooses to then throw up his hands and conclude that there is nothing he can do about it and thus give himself an easy excuse, that is a choice. But he may also choose to accept that he has been dealt certain temperamental predispositions. Now it is his responsibility to figure out how to best plan and accommodate his life to that reality.

Familial Factors

To what extent is one doomed to be an alcoholic if one's father and mother were alcoholics? No doubt, family factors have an influence on how we behave. Some of that influence is probably due to genes and some of it to the family environment that we grow up in. For example, genetics may cause some children in a family to be especially anxious. But at the same time, being raised by a very anxious mother or father will probably also have an impact. Moreover, if the family solution to constant anxiety is drinking, it stands to reason that a child may adopt that solution as well. But many children of alcoholic parents do not. In fact, the majority do not (cf. Anthenelli and Schuckit 1998, Robitschek and Kashubeck 1999, Schuckit and Smith 1996).

Spiritual or Existential

Living in New York, I have the opportunity to work with Christians, past-life believers, Orthodox Jews, Muslims, and people from many very different cultures. It is critical to understand what they believe. Does what is happening to them have a meaning within a larger framework? Do they believe there is a god who will help them? If so, do they pray? Or is there something else they think they should be doing to obtain help? Or do they think they should solve their addictive problems on their own? In which case, why? What are they telling themselves? How does it affect their ideas about how they may overcome their problems?

People in AA and many others argue that deep psychological change cannot occur without a concurrent spiritual change. AA's third step states, "We made a decision to turn our will and our lives over to the care of God as we understood him." However, there are many Christians and Muslims who are troubled by what they perceive to be a too literal interpretation of those ideas. Although it is not in the New Testament, many Christians believe God helps those who help themselves. In a similar fashion, Muslims have the saying: "Trust in Allah but tie your camel first."

May (1969) and other psychologists who see themselves as primarily existential therapists believe that our human capacity to question everything, including the meaning of life, forces us to confront the frightening fact that we must choose what to do with our lives. Is it possible that the client finds the necessity of choosing and of taking responsibility overwhelming and resorts to various addictive activities as a means of escape? Fully "working the program" for many members of AA means developing completely new reasons to live, including new life goals and values and a new community of friends.

Behind the client's problem may lie larger existential and spiritual issues. Therapists do not want to spend session after session discussing such issues, but to ignore them completely is foolish.

Cultural and Ethnic Factors

Social factors affect whether we start smoking or drinking or engaging in other addictive behaviors and at what age (Castro et al. 1999, Hays 1995). It is hard to imagine a wedding without champagne or a Christmas party without alcohol. Construction workers have traditionally been heavy drinkers. The Irish spend much of their recreational time in pubs, which are part community centers and part bars.

Many people in France drink wine at a leisurely pace with a leisurely meal, and usually twice a day, and French children traditionally in many areas drank water with a little wine, although increasingly they are now given some kind of soda. Spanish young people traditionally drink as a part of socializing, while American young people often drink to get drunk. In China, gambling is widespread but is not seen as a societal problem, and pathological gambling was recently dropped altogether from the Chinese Classification of Mental Disorders (Lee 1996, as cited in *The Wager* 1997b). In this country, Asian players account for 80 percent of the revenue from high-stakes games in major Las Vegas hotel casinos (Shaffer 1996 as cited in *The Wager* 1997b). Thus, there is plenty of evidence that the customs of different ethnic groups have an impact on the way addictive behaviors develop and how those who engage in addictive behaviors are treated. However, it is also true that there are tremendous variations within as well as between ethnic groups (Castro et al. 1999). Therapists and counselors are beginning to understand that they cannot simply apply standard therapeutic techniques and expect them to work on everyone.

However, at the same times as there may be considerable cultural differences in the way we think and behave, there may be widespread similarities. Many people, especially those living in developed, technologically advanced portions of their societies may share many similarities in the way they think, feel, and behave. Hence, many therapeutic techniques may make sense and work with some people in all cultures.

Social and Economic Factors

Although there has been considerable discussion in the past few years concerning the significance of diversity issues and multiculturalism in research and treatment, class is rarely discussed. This may be partly because American society is more used to grappling with the problems of race and ethnicity. However, socioeconomic status has an impact on the development of addictions and how they are treated. For example, persons with good health insurance coverage have access to more and better care. In one study the better their coverage was, the more people availed themselves of smoking cessation programs (Curry et al. 1998). On the other extreme of the spectrum, from 40 percent to 53 percent of the dually diagnosed Supplemental Security Income/Social Security disability income (SSI/SSDI) recipients who appealed their denial of recertification lost. Older, white persons with more severe psychiatric problems were more likely to appeal, and older, white recipients were more likely to win their appeals (Watkins et al. 1999).

Dr. Hallan Hurt, chairman of the Division of Neonatology at

the Albert Einstein Medical Center in Philadelphia, notes that "a decade ago, the cocaine-exposed child was stereotyped as being neurologically crippled—trembling in a corner and irreparably damaged. But this is unequivocally not the case. And furthermore, the inner-city child who has had no drug exposure at all is doing no better than the child labeled a 'crack-baby'" (Mozes 1999).

Political Factors

Politics are involved in numerous ways. We have legislated which chemicals are legal, such as Valium, Ativan, Ritalin, and Prozac, and which are not, such as heroin and marijuana. No other kind of psychological disorder or medical disease can cause one to be arrested and mandated into treatment. The fact that addictive behaviors affect aspects of the nervous system involved in judgment lead many people to condemn "addicts" on moral grounds and to attempt to change their behavior through the justice system rather than the health care system.

Methadone helps people previously addicted to heroin function, and Prozac, Zoloft, and the other antidepressants help people afflicted with depressive disorders function. People using methadone may not be more dependent on it than depressed people are dependent on their medications. But methadone is the only medication that cannot be prescribed by a psychiatrist or an internist. A very few programs accommodate professionals who want to use methadone, but most clients must go to clinics each morning to get their medication. Most professionals are not going to risk going to the same location each morning. In addition, regardless of whether they should or should not think this way, they may not want to rub elbows with unemployed "street people." They cannot take a job that requires travel because they must be able to get their dose every day (except weekends, and some programs make other exceptions). Needless to say, they cannot go on vacation, unless they save a little methadone each day and store it up or buy it illegally on the street. Traveling out of the country is even more difficult.

These policies are the result of political decisions. I do not want to argue the merits of these decisions here, but they clearly have an impact on therapists' ability to help a professional client get off of heroin and stay off. In addition, the political aspect itself has an impact on the client's thinking about himself, unless he is an exceptionally independent thinker!

4

INITIAL AND ONGOING ASSESSMENT

Many techniques and strategies considered to be specific to substance abuse assessment and treatment are actually special cases, or logical extensions, of more generic clinical skills. [Carey et al. 1999]

When a therapist meets with a client for the first time, it is useful to keep in mind a number of different goals, such as determining the client's stage of change, finding out how the client wants to proceed, and understanding how an addictive episode occurs. As I have suggested in preceding chapters, a client's goals and his stage of change strongly influence how the therapist decides to work.

Some clients may want the therapist to diagnose their problem much as they seek a medical diagnosis from a doctor. Torrey (1986) has pointed out that naming a person's problem may have curative powers in and of itself. That may be why AA members so strongly believe that saying publicly, "Hi, I'm Jack, and I'm an alcoholic," is a critical step in the recovery process. Similarly, someone who has tried desperately for years to feel less depressed may experience a great sense of relief in being told that he is suffering from dysthymia. It may also have a significant motivational impact. Giving a problem a name makes it more real and may motivate clients to figure out what to do about it or how to manage it.

Approximately ninety years ago, behaviorists began to focus on behavioral patterns. What happens first? What reinforces it? Then what happens? They called this a "functional analysis." They were most interested in understanding how environmental cues and, more recently, inner behaviors such as cognitions and emotional and physical states contribute to a behavioral pattern. Therapists are most interested in helping clients change behavioral patterns. Properly identifying the problem and accurately assessing the seriousness of the problem are important, but helping clients figure out how to change this pattern (or manage it better) is the ultimate goal. In an attempt to do this, what may be more important than anything else is the client's readiness to change. On the other hand, naming the problem and discussing its seriousness may affect his readiness.

DEFINITIONS

Some clients want to know "Am I an alcoholic?" But that is the wrong question. It comes from the medical model, not a biopsychosocial model. It is like asking a doctor: "Do I have measles?" Regarding problems with alcohol, not only is the term *alcoholic* not used in the *DSM-IV*, but it is not possible to answer that question with a clear yes or no. However, it is possible to assess the extent to which any addictive behavior has become a problem for a particular client. Even doctors have had to take a less than all-or-nothing stance regarding AIDS; some people carry the virus but show no symptoms. They are HIV positive but do they have AIDS?

Webster's 1828 dictionary defined addiction as "the act of devoting to or giving up in practice" and "the state of being devoted." Among Romans, it meant the "assignment of debtors in service to their creditors." Webster's *Third New International Dictionary* (1969) defines an addiction as "the quality or state of being addicted; specifically, the compulsive uncontrolled use of habit forming drugs beyond the period of medical need or under conditions harmful to society."

Chapter 3 discusses many possible contributing factors to addictive behaviors. It may help to think of an addiction as (1) a behavioral pattern that changes the way the client feels, thinks, and behaves, (2) that he or she likes in the short-run, (3) but not in the medium- and long-run, and (4) that is very difficult to change. This definition is designed to help clinicians help clients, but what really counts are the consequences for the client over time. The definition does not specify who is to decide whether the medium- and long-run consequences are negative, and who is to say whether or not it is a difficult behavior pattern to change. Ultimately, it is for the client to decide.

However, a client may change because the consequences or potential consequences change. Society may make it very difficult to get his favorite substance and may incarcerate him if he gets caught with it. Or he may lose his driving license as the result of a DWI. His boss may threaten to fire him. His wife may threaten to leave him. His teenage son may refuse to talk to him when he is drinking. In fact, if the medium- and long-run real and imagined consequences are not sufficiently negative, he may never change his behavior.

The *DSM-IV* devotes almost one hundred pages to substance-related addictive behaviors, in addition to fourteen pages to impulse-control disorders not elsewhere classified, including pathological gambling, and eleven pages to eating disorders. If the therapist is asked or required to make a diagnosis, he or she will have to determine whether the client meets the criteria for abuse or dependence. A client may have several problems, some substance-related and some not. He may be dependent on alcohol and abusing cocaine, and he may meet the criteria for dysthymia and social anxiety.

Caution: If the client wants insurance reimbursement, it may be better for him to find out exactly how much he will receive before he submits a claim with a diagnosis for some sort of substance abuse or dependence on it. In some cases, a $500 deductible must be met first; then the managed care company will only pay 50 percent of what it considers reasonable and customary. At the same time, that diagnosis goes into the client's company's computer. If his company is bought by another company, the computer files may be merged, and the diagnosis will follow him. It is supposed to be confidential, but I know of one case where the forms (with the diagnoses) went to the human resources department where my client worked. Fortunately, he was the human resources manager, so he quickly made that piece of paper disappear. It comes down to a simple question: Is it worth the risk, given the continued stigmatization of substance abuse and other mental disorders by the general public? If the managed care company pays what it considers reasonable and customary, that may mean about $35 a session. The client will probably save that much (or more) by not buying alcohol or drugs. A second question to consider: Will a precise diagnosis help the client help himself? The profession's (or state's) code of ethics may require that the therapist make a diagnosis and have it in his files. But if it does not, is it in the client's best interest to do so? To what extent does a precise diagnosis help in choosing ways to work during a therapy session?

DSM-IV CRITERIA FOR SUBSTANCE ABUSE[1]

The diagnosis of substance abuse (in contrast to dependence) focuses on the harmful consequences of repeated use. Abuse is defined as:

A. A maladaptive pattern of substance use leading to clinically significant impairment or distress, as manifested by one (or more) of the following, occurring within a 12-month period:
    (1) recurrent substance use resulting in a failure to

---

1. The following *DSM-IV* criteria for Substance Abuse and Substance Dependence are reprinted with permission from the *Diagnostic and Statistical Manual of Mental Disorders, Fourth Edition*, copyright © 1994 American Psychiatric Association.

fulfill major role obligations at work, school, or home (e.g., repeated absences or poor work performance related to substance use; substance-related absences, suspensions, or expulsions from school; neglect of children or household).

(2) recurrent substance use in situations in which it is physically hazardous (e.g., driving an automobile or operating a machine when impaired by substance use).

(3) recurrent substance-related legal problems (e.g., arrests for substance-related disorderly conduct).

(4) continued substance use despite having persistent or recurrent social or interpersonal problems caused or exacerbated by the effects of the substance (e.g., arguments with spouse about consequences of intoxication, physical fights).

B. The symptoms have never met the criteria for Substance Dependence for this class of substance. [APA 1994, pp. 182–183]

DSM-IV CRITERIA FOR SUBSTANCE DEPENDENCE

In contrast, the criteria for dependence focus on tolerance, withdrawal, and compulsive use. Dependence involves:

A maladaptive pattern of substance use, leading to clinically significant impairment or distress, as manifested by three (or more) of the following, occurring at any time in the same 12-month period:

(1) tolerance, as defined by either of the following:

(a) a need for markedly increased amounts of the substance to achieve intoxication or desired effect

(b) markedly diminished effect with continued use of the same amount of the substance

(2) withdrawal, as manifested by either of the following:

(a) the characteristic withdrawal syndrome for the substance (refer to Criteria A and B of the criteria sets for Withdrawal for the specific substances)

(b) the same (or closely related) substance is taken to relieve or avoid withdrawal symptoms

(3) the substance is often taken in larger amounts or over a longer period than was intended

(4) there is a persistent desire or unsuccessful efforts to cut down or control substance use

(5) a great deal of time is spent in activities necessary to obtain the substance (e.g., visiting multiple doctors or driving long distances), use the substance (e.g., chain-smoking), or recover from its effects

(6) important social, occupational, or recreational activities are given up or reduced because of substance use

(7) the substance use is continued despite knowledge of having a persistent or recurrent physical or psychological problem that is likely to have been caused or exacerbated by the substance (e.g., current cocaine use despite recognition of cocaine-related depression, or continued drinking despite recognition that an ulcer was made worse by alcohol consumption)

[Note: There are a variety of specifiers included on pp. 180–181 in *DSM-IV* that have not been included here.]

[APA 1994, pp. 180–181]

A few additional points:

- According to the *DSM-IV*, a large number of people who are dependent on alcohol never experience withdrawal symptoms. Thus, just because the client does not have withdrawal symptoms does not mean that he is not in serious trouble. (Only about 5 percent of those dependent on alcohol ever experience severe complications of withdrawal, e.g., delirium, grand mal seizures.)
- Dependence can apply to all substances except caffeine.
- Abuse can apply to all substances except nicotine and caffeine.

- Several researchers have suggested that impulsive control disorders (ICDs) should be thought of as forms of addictive disorders or behavioral addictions (McElroy et al. 1998). Substance abuse disorders are considered forms of ICDs in the *DSM-IV*.
- ICDs, however, do not have a formal category in the *DSM-IV*. They are listed in a residual category and include ICDs not elsewhere classified (intermittent explosive disorder, kleptomania, pathological gambling, pyromania, trichotillomania) and ICDs not otherwise specified (compulsive buying or shopping, nonparaphilic sexual addictions, sexual compulsions, and eating disorders).

RESEARCH NOTE

Of 140 patients meeting the criteria for pathological gambling, 47 percent met the criteria for lifetime substance abuse or dependence; in three studies of compulsive shoppers, 33 percent met the criteria for lifetime substance use disorder; in a study of thirty-six sexually compulsive men recruited by newspaper ads, 64 percent met the criteria for a lifetime history of substance use disorder (McElroy et al. 1998).

Clients in therapy who do not meet the criteria for either abuse or dependence may still be in danger of seriously harming themselves or someone else. For example, they may sometimes drink excessively and then drive home or get into a physical fight but not often enough to be considered to have the recurrent social or interpersonal problems required by the criteria.

Other Addictive Behaviors

As I noted above, the *DSM-IV* devotes only three pages to pathological gambling. A recent book on addictive behaviors omits gambling and eating disorders completely. Are eating disorders a form of addictive behavior? Shoplifting? Overspending? Overspending is particularly problematic. At least when a client gives up a substance, she usually has some extra money at the end of the week to treat herself to something. But if she has spent herself into $35,000 worth of debt on a $21,000-per-year salary, what does she have to look forward to, not just at the end of the week, but for the many years to come? The working definition I have included above defines such problems as addictive behaviors.

PRIMARY GOALS FOR THE FIRST SESSION

1. **Determine if the therapist can be of help to the client.** In a large city, where there are many resources available (although not necessarily many CBT programs), the therapist may decide that seeing a client on an individual basis will not help. Some kind of adjunctive therapy, for example, a group or a program that runs for half a day or all day, is necessary. However, if it is clear that the client cannot or will not attend such groups or programs, then what? Perhaps the therapist cannot get such a client to stop but may be able to help him reduce the risks he is taking and the harm he may do to himself and others. On the other hand, the therapist may simply be colluding with him in putting off the day of reckoning when he has to do what he does not want to do or thinks he cannot do (see Chapter 5).

2. **Motivate the Client to Schedule a Second Session.** The real goal is to establish a good working relationship. But that won't happen in only one session. (One exception: a brief intervention, often by internists and emergency room staff, has turned out to be remarkably effective in some cases [Bien et al. 1993, Finney and Moos 1998, Fleming et al. 1997, Zweben and Fleming 1999]. Getting the client involved in treatment may be important for two reasons: the client may have taken years to make the decision to call a

professional for help, and he or she may wait many months or even years before seeking out another professional for help.

As many addictions are chronic problems, the client may benefit from establishing a relationship with a mental health professional so that over the years he has someone to help him when his own resources are not sufficient. This does not mean keeping him in treatment past what is helpful, a charge levied against some analysts. But the client may have many false starts and many lapses and relapses, and may follow a long, difficult, frustrating path. Therapy and working toward change will ultimately help him.

3. **Move the client from one stage to the next.** Doing so in the first session is not at all impossible. For example, a client may announce, "I really don't want to be here, but my boss thinks I have this alcohol problem—which is not true—but he somehow got it into his thick head, and now I gotta see you." He sounds as if he is a Stage I client. However, if by the end of the session he says, "Well, I agree. I seem to have got myself in a mess," this may mean that he has moved to Stage II, contemplation.

The Third Mode of Psychotherapy

I advocate of what I call the third mode of psychotherapy. The first, psychoanalysis, was very intensive and often lasted years. The second, under managed care, expects problems to be solved in x number of sessions or less. In the third mode, the therapist tries to build a relationship with the client that will last over a long period of time. The client may not see the therapist often and not for numerous sessions. But when he lapses or relapses, which may or may not happen throughout his lifetime, he can call on the therapist for help. Many of my clients have an internist, a lawyer, and an accountant or tax advisor. I want them to call me when they run into psychological problems.

ACCURATELY ASSESSING THE CLIENT'S PROBLEMS

What Is the Client's Stage of Change?

After some chatting, Adele began her first session by saying, "I'm not sure I have a problem. I think I may be an alcoholic, but I'm not sure." In contrast, Bill started with: "I'm just here because my wife thinks I have a problem. I don't think so, but I decided to get her off my back by humoring her." Adele is in Stage II, contemplation, and Bill is in Stage I, precontemplation. In addition, because many clients have more than one problem, a Type I client regarding the use of alcohol may be a Type III regarding depression. In other words, clients may not be ready to acknowledge that their alcohol consumption is a problem, but they may want help for their depression.

What Are the Client's Goals?

Rogers's (1961) client-centered therapy represented one of the first serious breaks with psychoanalysis. Originally, all psychoanalysts were physicians and they took their medical model with them into therapy. They were responsible for the diagnosis and for the cure. Moreover, because a client's problems were assumed to be in the subconscious and defended against, a client could not know what he needed to work on. In fact, the presenting problem, the problem that the client said he wanted to work on, was assumed not to be the problem.

Rogers argued forcefully and effectively against such an approach in psychotherapy, and many cognitive-behavioral psychotherapists and counselors have followed his lead. For them, the key question is: What does my client want to work on?

I may think very strongly that it would be better for a client to quit using heroin, but I still consider that his choice. This is not because I think he has a right to choose or that he is free to do what he wants. These are political questions. I take such a position because I do not want to become one more voice (another part of the superego) telling him what he should do. Once I am in that position, he may begin to lie to me and to resist my efforts to help him.

If a client asks me what I think, I try to give a straight answer while continuing to maintain my consultant role. For example, if someone were to ask, "Do you think I should stop drinking?" I might answer something like this: "Well, I think that is for you to decide. But based on what you have told me, I think you would get more overall pleasure in life if you quit drinking alcohol. But it is your life. We can work together to help you decide what you want to do, but ultimately you choose the goals."

The question "What do you want to do?" and its opposite, "What do you want not to do?" are key to the first session as well as to subsequent sessions. It brings time, that all-important element, immediately to the forefront.

Most clients are ambivalent. They do not know what they want to do. That is one reason they have come to therapy—to try to figure out what to do and to explore their options. Some clients are too depressed or too confused by substances to know what they want to do, but the question clearly indicates who is in the driver's seat. When the client is making little progress and lapses and relapses are common, the question "What do you want to do?" is a powerful intervention. It is his life and his responsibility to figure out how to manage his life.

When helping clients figure out what they want to do and are interested in doing, I avoid the word *negotiate*. Negotiating always involves two sides, for example, a union and a company, trying to obtain as much of what they want as possible. To use the word in therapy suggests that I have my agenda and the client has his and we have to find a middle ground. I prefer to help my client uncover or discover what he wants to do and how he is stopping himself from doing it.

How Serious Is the Client's Problem?

The therapist and client need to explore the medium- and long-term problems that result from the addictive behaviors.

Recent History

When was the last time the client used (drank, gambled, etc.)? The therapist can do a pre-AB (see Chapter 2) to examine in detail what happened immediately prior to the lapse or relapse, during, and after. The therapist wants to be able to visualize where the client was, what he was doing, and what he did, and to hear what he was saying to himself and to others—especially how he contributed to his lapse or relapse. The therapist wants a sense of how he was feeling physically and emotionally. A complete time-effect analysis will provide further valuable information.

Past History

When did the client start? When did it become a problem? For how long has it been a problem? Why does he think it became a problem?

What? How Much? When?

What does the client prefer to drink? use? do? How much? How fast? To get a more accurate sense of what my client may be using or drinking, I usually exaggerate what I think may be the answer. For example, if I think my client may be drinking about 6 to 8 beers a night, I ask: "How many beers do you drink in the evening? Two six packs?" The answer often is, "Oh, no. Never. I never drink more than six or seven cans, maybe eight, but that is unusual." Had I asked "How many beers do you drink?" I think I would have been told a lower number. This is not because most clients routinely lie, and the research does not suggest that. Even clients are not mandated into treatment may put a slightly positive spin on bad news. I use the same technique for coffee and colas, often finding out that my client is ingesting large amounts (600 to 1,000 mg) of caffeine per day.

What Are the Problems?

Here the focus is on behavioral consequences. Does the client slur his words? Fall down? Drive home drunk? Has he ever injured himself as a result of his addictive behaviors? For many young clients, drinking and drugging are not problems. Getting arrested and having to be in therapy are problems. However, there may be other problems (in essence, consequences of the addictive behaviors) that they don't like. For example, perhaps they totaled their car. Or perhaps they broke an arm or a leg. Or they got thrown out of school or lost their right to housing on their college campus.

Other Addictive Behaviors

What other drugs does the client use or addictive behaviors does he engage in? Are they a problem, as well? How did they become problems? Why does he think they became problems?

Other Medications

Is the client taking antidepressants? Valium? Xanax? How do they work? Are there any side effects? Who is prescribing them? An internist or a psychiatrist?

Other Chemicals

Caffeine? Colas?

Other Problems

Diagnosing psychological problems is not easy because they may be the result of the addictive behaviors or the cause or both.

There is often a complex interaction. Stopping drinking may affect other disorders; thus, assessment must be ongoing. Every session provides an opportunity to reassess and reevaluate the client's problems.

Can the Therapist Treat This Client?

Can the therapist provide the level of care that the client needs? Will individual sessions be sufficient? Does the client need to be hospitalized? Is he suicidal? Does he need to be detoxed? Does he need to be evaluated for medication?

Given the shame, sense of hopelessness and despair, and degree of self-loathing that many clients afflicted with addictive disorders have, it is important to do a good suicide assessment and to keep notes of what was done as the result of the assessment (Figure 4–1). If the therapist cannot provide the level of care required at this time, he must refer the client to an inpatient or outpatient facility or to a psychiatrist. Unfortunately, many psychiatrists still do not want to treat people who are actively using drugs or drinking, even if the depression the client is suffering from may not be the result of the chemical abuse. This is very frustrating, especially in a small community. Cultivating a good relationship with a psychiatrist who is willing to work with users is definitely worth the time and effort. In addition, it may be very useful to have a second professional available to help work through the layers of problems some clients have.

What Happens in the Behavior Pattern?

Because CBT/REBT sees addictive behaviors as behavior patterns, it is very important to try to understand how those patterns play out. What happens, moment to moment? What are the A's and B's (the Pre-AB's) that preceded the C, the lapse or relapse? We want to be able to visualize the setting, to know who the people were, and to hear what the client said to himself and to the others in the scene. What contributed to his lapse or relapse?

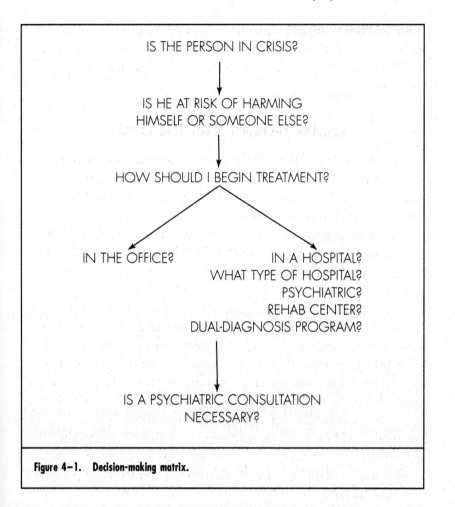

Figure 4–1.   Decision-making matrix.

Primary and Secondary Triggers

Marlatt (1985a) reports finding eight reasons for relapse which were quite similar across five different addictive behaviors: gambling, heroin use, problem drinking, smoking, and overeating. Moreover, three factors contributed to three-quarters of the relapses: negative emotional states (35 percent), interpersonal conflict (16 percent), and social pressure (20 percent).

Potential Primary Triggers

Internal

- Unpleasant emotions
- Pleasant emotions
- Physical discomfort and/or pain
- Urges and cravings
- Testing personal control

External

- Conflict with others
- Pressure from others
- Socializing

The therapist can use this list to obtain a more accurate idea of the factors that contribute to the client's lapses and relapses. For each item the client can rate how strong it is as a trigger. The therapist asks, "How often do you drink (or use drugs, etc.) because you are experiencing unpleasant emotions? For example, how often do you think you drink because you are anxious or angry or depressed or bored?" If the client indicates that unpleasant emotions may be a factor, "How strong a potential trigger is experiencing unpleasant emotions, from 0 to 10 where 0 means unpleasant emotions are never a trigger and 10 means they are very often a powerful trigger?" For pleasant emotions: "Some clients drink because they feel good but they want to feel better. Most champagne advertisements and some beer advertisements are based on this idea. It is time to celebrate. We feel good. Alcohol will make us feel better! Between 0 and 10, how strong a trigger is feeling good and wanting to feel even better to you? Between 0 and 10?"

Some clients report high numbers for practically all of the potential triggers listed above. Others may report that they drink only because they have physical pain, and that alcohol helps. Still others may maintain that they smoke marijuana five or six times a day because they have always done that. Nothing, in particular, triggers off their behavior, from their perspective.

I do not usually go through the complete list in a formulaic fashion, but it is a useful guideline to keep in mind when working with a client.

Potential Secondary Triggers

Early in his writings about general psychological problems, Ellis (1962) discussed the importance of secondary problems, problems about the problem. The client may have been drinking for the past two weeks, and that is a problem. But he may have problems about that problem—he is ashamed and depressed about his return to drinking. One of the most frequent and powerful secondary triggers is what Ellis (1978–1979) has called discomfort anxiety. When a client tries to cut down or stop, he will almost always begin to feel uncomfortable, a kind of anxiety about not doing what he is accustomed (and may still want) to do.

With nonaddictive disorders it may be better to attend first to the secondary problem, for example, the depression about the depression or the anxiety about the anxiety. Otherwise the client may continue to be vulnerable to making himself depressed or anxious or both. However, as I noted in Chapter 2 , with addictive behaviors the reverse may be true. Unless the therapist thinks the secondary problems, for example, the discomfort anxiety or the shame and depression about drinking, are going to trigger another relapse right after the session, he should first focus on the pre-AB's, the activating events and beliefs that lead up to an addictive episode, and then on the post-BC's, the beliefs and consequences (depression, shame, anxiety, etc.) that follow and that will very likely contribute to a new relapse.

Focusing on the pre-AB's facilitates discovering how an addictive episode unfolds. What kind of urges, images, physical feelings, and emotions does the client feel before he starts to convince himself to act?

What Does the Client Already Know?

The therapist should work with the client's strengths. She may already know how to solve her problem but not realize that she knows. Or she knows that she knows, but she needs some help getting started again. Or she may know that she has a better chance of succeeding if she is in therapy. Many forms of short-term therapy take advantage of the fact that many clients have the necessary resources and know-how to resolve their problems. They may have overcome their addictive problems in the past. They may be in therapy because they relapsed or to work on a different addictive problem. The following questions may help:

1. **Have you ever stopped or cut down before?** If the answer is yes, what has the client learned from the experiences?

2. **What worked? How did you help yourself stop or cut down last time?** If the client stopped smoking or drinking or gambling before, how did he manage to do that? What techniques did he use? Did he take a course, such as Smoke-enders? Did she go to AA or Gamblers Anonymous (GA)? After many attempts, one of my clients stopped smoking by continually visualizing a photograph he had seen in a hospital of a lung blackened by years of smoking. Evoking that image helped him resist his urge for a cigarette.

3. **What have you tried this time? How has it worked?** How successful have you been? Through these discussions, the therapist can note the way the client perceives and thinks about successes and failures. Does she evaluate any failure in a self-derogatory manner? Does she blame herself or others? How does she conceptualize addictions? Does she think of them as indications of weak willpower? a disease? a bad habit? a genetic problem? How much does she blame herself for the problem or for not having solved her problem?

4. **Why isn't it working as well as it did last time? What is different? What is similar?** The client may have tried the same technique, and although it worked in the past, it is not working now. In working with Bob, I learned that in the previous year, after attending only two AA meetings, he had thrown out all of his liquor and had stopped drinking. He had stayed sober for nine months and reported never feeling better. He could not understand why the same technique had not worked for him again. He had tried going to AA meetings and they had "just annoyed me," he reported. He was furious that he was beginning to wreck his life all over again. Later, it turned out that he had been going with a friend the first time. She had stopped drinking with AA's help but recently had started drinking again and had not returned to AA. Although they were not romantically involved, her relapse appeared to have completely undermined not only his reason to quit but also his faith in AA.

5. **What have you tried to change before?** Although the client may not have stopped or changed an addictive behavior before, she may have changed some other type of behavior. Has she dieted? What has she learned about dieting? If she has not worked on an addictive behavior before, can she identify any behaviors she has changed? Perhaps she has changed the way she asserts herself in relationships or the way she swings a tennis racket. Or perhaps she has rented a car in London or somewhere else where she has had to drive on the opposite side of the road—a major change in behavior! What did she learn from the experience that might apply with an addictive behavior? What is not applicable?

6. **What do you think would help now?** Some clients will answer, "I don't know." However, many have an idea. Therapy, going to AA, doing t'ai chi, and starting to meditate again are all answers I have heard. Once a client has said what might help, the therapist can focus on how

he is stopping himself from returning to those behaviors or activities. The therapist can focus on getting him restarted again, with that being part of his homework.

7. **How can I help you?** If a client seems clueless (and is not there because he was forced to come to therapy), the therapist may find the best approach is to simply ask, which signals to the client that he ultimately is in charge of how therapy progresses.

8. **What have you learned from past therapists or counselors?** The therapist may discover that the client has learned many things that may be useful in the future. Unfortunately, however, the answer may be "Nothing." Is this because the previous therapist was not helpful? Or is this an indication that the client often blames others for his problems? Or perhaps the client tends to take a very passive role in therapy, unaware that the responsibility for change resides in him.

9. **Have medications helped?** Although members of the AA community are much less critical of psychopharmacological drugs than they used to be, there are still many people who think they must get off all drugs. However, with the increasing awareness that many clients suffer from multiple afflictions, for example, alcohol dependence, gambling, depression, and social anxiety, many professionals see the value of including various medications with psychotherapy. The client may have taken Prozac or Xanax in the past, but stopped, only to start drinking or gambling or shoplifting again.

10. **What other things have helped or hurt?** Clients may know things that have helped in the past—often simple things like going fishing or to a baseball game or getting to bed earlier or eating more regularly—but they have neglected these aspects of their life. Perhaps they have become too depressed to do them. What is preventing them from starting to do these things that they like again? The therapist may be able to help them get started again by

taking a professional approach, not the approach of a mother, father, or spouse. The stages of change are just as relevant to recreational activities as they are to gambling.

What Are the Client's Other Resources?

Employment

Is he employed? Has he been employed at the same place for a long time or has he had many jobs? Has he ever lost a job because of drug use or alcohol abuse? Does he like his job? What does he earn? (It is somewhat amusing that clients are often more willing to answer questions about their intimate sexual behavior than they are about their earnings. However, it is often an important piece of information.)

Friends and Family

Is he married? How does he get along with his wife? Does she know about his problem? Everything about it? Does he have friends? Does he get together with them often? Do they also know about his problem? Do they share it with him? Do they think it is a problem? Has any of his friends ever quit or slowed down? How does he get along with his family members? If he doesn't get along well with them, why not?

These questions may reveal a very demanding side to the client. People never do as he thinks they should! He may also have an overly critical nature, and a tendency to think that he would never behave that way. People never live up to his standards.

Spiritual and/or Religious Beliefs

Does he have any spiritual beliefs? Is he religious? Does he worship at any particular place? If so, has he talked with someone in his place of worship? What happened? Did it help? If not this time, why not? Does he think it would help? Does he want to agree to do that during the coming week? Does he pray? If so, what does he pray for? Help? Forgiveness? To take away the problem? Does just sitting in a place of worship help? If he believes in God's will and that everything is a manifestation of God's will, what is his responsibility or role?

Sex

Does he have an active sex life? Is it satisfying? Does he use a condom? If not, how does he convince himself that nothing is going to happen? How long since he has had an AIDS test?

Hobbies and Recreational Activities

Does he have any other pleasures in life or have addictive behaviors become his sole pleasure? What did he used to enjoy? Basketball? Movies? Yoga? Does he do anything to keep himself feeling healthier? Does it help? How? How often does he do it?

What Is the Riskiest Part of the Client's Addictive Pattern?

What is your client doing that is the riskiest aspect of his addictive behavior pattern? Going to a dangerous part of town to purchase drugs? Driving home from a local bar? Binge drinking with his fraternity brothers? Shoplifting? Unprotected sex with a prostitute after using cocaine? It is often true that the client is not going to be able to stop his addictive behavior immediately, and perhaps never totally. It is important to discuss with him how to reduce the harm that he might do to himself or to others.

Unfortunately, *harm reduction* as a term has been linked in some people's minds with legalization of drugs. This may partly be due to the fact that many people in the harm reduction movement do not focus on reducing the addictive behavior. For example, Wodak (1995) defined harm reduction as "those policies and programs which are designed to reduce the adverse consequences of mood altering substances without necessarily reducing their consumption" (p. 340). In addition, another focus of harm reduction programs, especially when they started in the Netherlands and in Britain, was an effort to treat substance abuse more as a public health issue than as a criminal issue. Needle exchange programs became the most common example of harm reduction programs, and many politicians joined others in denouncing such programs as helping or encouraging people to use drugs.

In my practice, harm reduction or minimization focuses on helping clients reduce the harm they may do to themselves and/or to others while they are working to change their addictive behavior. How does that translate into practice? If I am fairly sure that a client may go to his local bar on Saturday night and drink heavily, is there any way I can help him get home without driving? Can he walk home? Would that be less safe than driving, even though he couldn't kill someone else? Can he take a cab? If so, what can we do to ensure that he *does* take a cab? Certainly, he will not be thinking straight when he leaves the bar. If he has the keys, he will more than likely drive home. But if he walks to the bar, perhaps a safe enough thing to do, he won't have the keys when he leaves. Is he willing to do that? How sure is he that he will stick to that plan?

If the most dangerous thing your client does is to have unprotected sex with a prostitute after he buys and uses coke at a bar, how can you help him reduce the risk of this behavior? Does he think he can give up the sex altogether? If not, does he always have a condom? Can he still rely on himself to use it? How does he convince himself that he can get away with it? Does his spouse know? Has he been tested for HIV?

Once we begin to consider some forms of addictive behaviors as chronic, lifelong problems, the issues of risk and harm reduction become more central to treatment.

What Might Help?

To help review with my client what might help, I often give him a copy of "Trying to Change a Behavior? Seven Points to Keep in Mind" (Table 4–1).

What Does the Client Seem Willing to Do This Week?

The answer to this question will depend on the type of client, Type I, II, or III. But because CBT and REBT are both focused on helping the client change, it is important to explore with her what she might like to work on between sessions. The therapist can tailor what she might do to her stage of change.

Homework

Homework is probably not the best word, and some clients really hate it, in which case the therapist can simply not use it. But some clients may like to be assigned something to do, such as keeping a drinking log, filling out one or two ABC forms, or making an appointment with a doctor.

The homework should be practical. But it can be difficult, such as not drinking for a whole week, calling for an interview, or going to a party without the benefit of drugs. Even if the client is not able to do it, the therapist and client have the opportunity to do a pre-AB on the assigned behavior and to understand better what happened. If the client is a chronic self-downer, the therapist will also have an opportunity to help him process his failure so that he does not feel himself to be a failure. He can begin to give up linking his constant assessment of his behavior with his assessment of himself as a person.

ASSESSMENT INSTRUMENTS

Many clients will tell the therapist their problems and what they want to work on. This is fortunate, because for practitioners who

Table 4–1.   Trying to change behavior? Seven points to keep in mind.

1. Goals:
   Pick a goal. Make it specific and achievable. It may not be your final goal. Later, you may decide it is not the right goal for you. But you have to start somewhere!

2. Motivation:
   What will be the positive and negative effects for you over time?
   Is there a way you can "sweeten the carrot"?
   Can you make the "stick" more threatening? Would that help or hurt?
   Do you need to better balance your conflicting wants?

3. Connections:
   Are you connected with other people who can help you?
   Do other people know your goal?

4. Know-how and practice:
   Do you know what to do?
   Do you know how to do it?
   Can you accept the discomfort that goes along with practice?
   What are you going to do? When? Be as concrete and specific as possible (day? time? place? how much? how many?)

5. Failures:
   What do you do when you fail? Beat yourself up? Call yourself names? Convince yourself that practicing is too hard? Convince yourself that the goal is not worth it?

6. Successes:
   Savor your successes. Feel pleased that you did what you set out to do. Reward yourself if you think that will help.

7. Reevaluate your progress:
   Should you adjust your goal?
   How can you increase your motivation?
   Would more connections help?
   How are you stopping yourself from practicing?
   Are you learning from your failures?
   Are you savoring your successes?
   What do you want? What are you doing? Do you like it?
   (Glasser 1989)

may see clients with a wide variety of addictive problems, there are really not that many assessment instruments with good validity available, except for alcohol use. Most assessment instruments were developed by researchers for research purposes. (For more information on assessment instruments, see ASAM 1998, Dimeff et al. 1999, Donovan 1999.) For a thorough assessment, the SUDDS (Substance Use Disorder Diagnosis Schedule; Harrison and Hoffman, 1989) is probably the best choice. However, the SUDDS takes 45–60 minutes, and if time is limited, consider one of the following:

Alcohol Use Disorders Identification Test (AUDIT)

AUDIT contains ten yes or no questions. Eight or more yes answers indicates that the person probably has alcohol use problems. AUDIT was developed by the World Health Organization to be used in a wide variety of health care settings. It appears to be useful for identifying people in primary care offices who are problem drinkers but do not meet the criteria for abuse or dependence (Bohn et al. 1995).

CAGE

CAGE contains only four questions:

1. Have you ever felt you should Cut down on your drinking?
2. Have people Annoyed you by criticizing your drinking?
3. Have you ever felt Guilty about your drinking?
4. Have you ever had a drink first thing in the morning (an Eye-opener) to steady your nerves or get rid of a hangover?

Two or more yes answers indicates the likelihood of a problem with alcohol. One yes suggests the need for further evaluation. CAGE is frequently used in emergency rooms as a quick assessment tool.

The Michigan Alcoholism Screening Test (MAST)

The MAST consists of twenty-five questions. (It is also available in briefer forms, but the twenty-five-question form does not take much time.) Jacobson (1989) suggests the following grading scale: zero to four questions answered yes, probably the client does not have a problem with alcohol; five to nine, possible problems; ten to eleven, probably problems; twelve or more, likely problems. Jacobson has warned that the traditional cutoff of five causes too many people to be labeled as having problems who do not have problems.

SPECIFIC INSTRUMENTS TO ASSESS PROBLEMS (VS. USE)

The Rutgers Alcohol Problems Inventory

Using twenty-three items, this questionnaire may help therapists work with Type I and II clients because the focus is on the problems resulting from drinking, not on use/abuse/dependence. Time required: 5 minutes.

Drinker's Inventory of Consequences

This is a fifty-item self-administered test designed to assess consequences over a person's lifetime as well as during the past three months. It looks at five areas of possible problems: intrapersonal, physical, social, impulsive, and interpersonal. Time required: 10 minutes.

Brief Sexual Behaviors Survey (BSBS)

The BSBS was developed by the authors (Dimeff et al. 1999) of BASICS (Brief Alcohol Screening and Intervention for College Students), a harm reduction program designed to help reduce college drinking. It is designed to collect information about sexual partners, condom use, and the use of alcohol and drugs during sexual encounters. Time required: 3 minutes.

SPECIFIC INSTRUMENTS
FOR ASSESSING THE STAGE OF CHANGE

The University of Rhode Island Change Assessment (URICA)

Using thirty-two items, four stages of change are assessed with this item: precontemplation, contemplation, action, and maintenance. Time required: 8 minutes.

Self-Assessment

Prochaska and colleagues (1994) suggest four simple statements for the self-assessment of the stage of change:

1. I solved my problem more than six months ago.
2. I have taken action on my problem within the past six months.
3. I am intending to take action in the next month.
4. I am intending to take action in the next six months.

The stage of change is determined as follows:

Precontemplation: "No" to all four statements.

Contemplation: "Yes" to item 4; "no" to 1, 2, and 3.

Preparation: "Yes" to 3 and 4.

Action: "Yes" to 2; "no" to 1.

Maintenance: "Yes" to 1.

There are fewer instruments to assess other forms of addictive behavior, although various stage of change assessment instruments have been used in research into a variety of other health-threatening behavior, especially smoking. The therapist should not assume the client will bring up potentially embarrassing behaviors, such as problems with eating, sexual behavior, shoplifting, and overspending. Arnold Lazarus (1981, 1997), founder of multimodal therapy, has created a very good guide for doing a thorough general assessment, including an assessment of problems with drugs. He uses a mnemonic device—BASIC-ID—to ensure that he covers all aspects of a client's possible problems: behaviors, affect, sensations, imagery, cognitions, interpersonal relations, and drugs.

SESSION GUIDE:
A STRATEGY FOR THE FIRST SESSION—
TEN KEY QUESTIONS

1. What stage of change is the client in?
2. What are his goals? What is he interested in doing?
3. How serious is the client's problem?
4. What does the client already know? Past attempts? Successes? Failures?

   a. What happens when he drinks? uses? overeats? How does it occur? (Do a Pre-AB.)

   b. What is stopping him from changing? How is he derailing himself?
5. Internal resources? External resources?
6. Can the therapist treat this client?
7. What is the greatest risk?
8. What might be the most effective interventions? Cognitive? Emotive? Behavioral?
9. What does the client seem willing to do this week?
10. Homework?

II

HELPING CLIENTS MANAGE THEIR ADDICTION

5 KEYS TO EFFECTIVELY ENGAGE THE CLIENT IN TREATMENT

Whatever is worthwhile is difficult.
—Ovid

PRACTICING UNCONDITIONAL ACCEPTANCE: RATING THE BEHAVIOR, NOT THE "BEHAVER"

Both rational emotive behavioral therapy (REBT) and DBT dialectical behavior therapy focus on acceptance. Ellis (1998, 1999) has created two mnemonic acronyms, USA and UOA, as teaching devices. USA stands for unconditional self-acceptance and UOA for unconditional other acceptance.

Many clients condemn themselves for their behavior. There is little evidence that their beating themselves up motivates them to change. In fact, the reverse is usually true: The more they beat themselves up or even anticipate doing so, the more they drink or drug or continue some other addictive behavior. They cannot accept themselves while at the same time acknowledging their behavior. If they acknowledge that they drink or gamble too much, they know they will put themselves down. Consequently, to protect their (probably already fragile) sense of self, they deny the seriousness of their behavior.

If therapists practice rating only the client's behavior and not him as a person, they will inevitably begin to cultivate a nonjudgmental attitude toward him. Such an attitude is useful in encouraging clients to talk honestly about their problems and about their lapses and relapses. They will also be less likely to lie. But suppose a client who drove drunk and killed someone does not appear to feel any remorse. What does it mean to accept such a person? What does it mean to accept his behavior? What is the best therapeutic outcome? Would it be best for the client to work toward being able to say: "Well, it happened, I cannot turn the clock back, and it won't do any good to condemn my entire self; it was bad behavior, but it is now time for me to get on with my life and do the best I can"? But what does "do the best I can" mean? What are the client's responsibilities to the victim's family? These are complex, difficult questions. If therapists adopt a philosophy (and technique) of acceptance, specifically extending unconditional acceptance to a client regardless of his behavior, then they must be careful about how it is understood. That is, as they practice unconditional acceptance (because it is therapeutic), they must be careful not to appear to condone, approve, or absolve behavior that has hurt other people (and the client).

Then what is the therapist's job? To help the client learn patterns of thinking, feeling, and behaving that reduce the chance that he will ever drive drunk again? To help him develop a greater consciousness of the consequences of his actions and more empathy for those he may hurt? To help him make amends as a therapeutic exercise? If we answer yes to these questions, the therapist may still be faced with the challenge of motivating the client to make changes, based on where he is in terms of the stages of change.

Therapists may be able to help a client work toward a balance between not being crippled by past events and learning from them, and accepting responsibility for those he may have injured, including himself, without condemning his totality, thereby further disabling himself.

TREATING CLIENTS WITH RESPECT

When we respect someone, we usually have high regard for the way he lives, how he behaves, and the values that are reflected in his behaviors. But even though therapists believe it is important to treat a client with respect, they may not respect the way the client has lived, the choices he has made, and the values that have guided his behavior. When therapists treat someone with respect (whose behavior they do not respect), they may be doing it for a variety of reasons. First, it may facilitate therapy, from a practical standpoint. Second, they respect the complexity and mystery of life sufficiently to know that they are not in a position to judge or to disrespect. Third, they will never fully know what caused the behavior that they do not respect.

It is not always easy to maintain such a stance, as it is not always easy to extend unconditional acceptance to some clients. It is much easier to use our own standards and to judge others accordingly.

BEING EMPATHETIC AND SUPPORTIVE

I practice "supportive REBT." I try to be supportive while I work actively with my clients. Most clients, although they may not show it, are in various states of misery. They may act cocky and arrogant, but even if they are mandated to be in therapy, they are often miserable. The therapist can more rapidly engage the client by listening to their side of things, and even taking their side initially: "That must be very difficult to have your wife nagging at you. I'm sure that's not what you wanted your married life to be when you got engaged?" Later (see below) therapists can do an ABC on the client's problem as a way of introducing him to another way of thinking and responding to his problem.

REDUCING THE HARM

What is the most risky behavior the client is engaging in? That is always the most important question in every session. Clients often know that what they are doing is risky and they may not want to tell even their therapist, but if the therapist demonstrates empathy, respect, and unconditional acceptance, there is a greater likelihood that the client will report what behaviors she is engaging in that are potentially harmful, such as unprotected sex, parasuicidal behavior, or driving drunk. As several authors (Marlatt 1998, Tatarsky 1998, Wodak 1998) have shown, harm reduction addresses the harm that people may do to themselves and others as they attempt to better manage their addictive behaviors.

BEING AN EFFECTIVE THERAPIST

Being an effective therapist can include the following:

1. **Teaching practical, useful skills.** A client may like the ABC technique because she can use it immediately to help herself and thus feel better. She has found a therapist who gives her something useful to do right in the first session, and she has the feeling that she may be able to master her problems. Teaching a very anxious client relaxation techniques may also be very useful. She will quickly realize that the therapist is interested not only in the roots of her behaviors (the "why") but also in providing practical help (the "how").
2. **Giving the client useful information.** See the research notes for information that may be helpful to clients.
3. **Giving the client a useful homework assignment.** (See subsequent chapters for suggestions.)

Sharing Information

Traditionally, psychoanalysts in training were taught never to share information from their lives, despite the fact that Freud's records clearly indicate that he often did so. Sharing may take several forms. Therapists may share something about their own efforts to change various behaviors, or something about an interest they have in common with the client. Revealing an interest shows the therapist's enthusiasm and strongly signals that he is a healthy human being who has likes and dislikes. But therapists should not share information that they later might regret sharing, such as where they live. Obviously, sexual likes and dislikes should not be shared with a client.

Guidelines for Sharing Information

Suppose therapists share something with a client that they later think may have been a mistake. They can use the following techniques to determine if they have made a mistake:

The three-peers technique: The therapist imagines explaining what he did and his reasons for doing so to three peers he respects or three imaginary people. If they listen and then say, "Well, we might not have done that, but we can see why you did and it doesn't sound unethical or unprofessional or stupid to us," then the therapist can probably assume that he did not make a mistake. However, if they look puzzled or frown, the therapist probably erred. Discussing the problem with the client will probably only make it worse. The therapist should talk to a colleague or supervisor.

The mirror-in-the-morning technique: If the therapist looks himself in the mirror in the morning, will he be able to say, "What I did may not have been wise, but it was not a terrible error?" Or "What I did made sense at the time. Things did not turn out as I expected, but I behaved professionally at each step along the way." If not, it is probably wise for him to discuss the situation with a colleague or supervisor. If things turn out badly, he will be glad that he sought out the advice of another professional.

Robert J. Sternberg (1986), in his triangular theory of love, proposed that all relationships could be described along three dimensions: intimacy, passion, and commitment. Intimacy has to do with how much people in the relationship share their thoughts, feelings, and dreams with each other. Passion reflects how much a person wants to be with another person. Commitment indicates how strongly a person has decided to remain in the relationship. Sternberg measured the characteristics of any given relationship by asking the participants to rate, from 0 to 10, the strength of their intimacy, passion, and commitment in the relationship. He also arrived at terms for eight varieties of love. For example, "infatuated love" involves high passion but practically no intimacy or commitment. "Romantic love" is defined by high passion and intimacy but low commitment. "Consummate love" is high in all three. Some relationships produced quite congruent triangles. That is, both members felt similarly about their involvement in the relationship. Other triangles did not overlap at all.

A good psychotherapy relationship also reflects the same three dimensions, but the therapist and client, as in nontherapeutic relationships, will feel differently about the relationship. They both may feel committed to the relationship. The therapist may look forward to working with some clients as much as they look forward to working with the therapist. On the other hand, although some clients may be very eager to see the therapist, he may not feel the same way, and the opposite may be true, especially in mandated cases. Obviously, the biggest difference in a psychotherapeutic relationship involves intimacy. Given the professional nature of the relationship, the therapist will probably share only selected, limited information about his life. In contrast, the client will probably share a great deal, perhaps more with the therapist than with any other person in his life.

REMAINING CLIENT-CENTERED

Carl Rogers (1961) was one of the first to overthrow the medical model in therapy. He strongly argued that clients knew best what they were ready to work on. Doctors might know best how to treat measles, but therapists should let clients tell them what they want to do and when. In the area of alcohol treatment, several studies suggest that letting clients choose their treatment leads to better outcomes (Hester and Miller 1995).

SPECIAL PROBLEMS THE THERAPIST MAY ENCOUNTER

I have watched quite a few counselors and therapists work, and it is clear that some, even though they are in a helping profession, have no respect for some of their clients. They feel their clients are less than human and beneath contempt. They may try to hide it, but I can hear it in the tone of their remarks and see it in their body language. Of course, their clients can hear and see it, too. How likely are such therapists and counselors to be of any help, if they clearly disrespect their clients?

I do not know if it is possible for some of these therapists and counselors to change their beliefs and attitudes. Perhaps they should find another job working with another kind of population. If they do not work to change their attitude, they will probably be of little or no help and may, in fact, do harm.

What Therapists Can Do When They Have Strong Negative Emotions Toward a Client

Apply the Stages of Change Model to Their Own Problem

Are they a little like one of their mandated clients? They can't admit they have a problem in this area or they are ambivalent. They wish they could feel differently, but they can't. What might help them move from one stage to the next? What might help maintain that change?

Look at One's Underlying Philosophy

One answer to the problem may lie in the philosophical position central to REBT: Just because the client's behavior is bad, lazy, horrible, or heinous does not make him entirely bad, lazy, horrible, or heinous. Of course, this philosophy flies in the face of the way must of us were raised to think. If someone lies, we call them a liar, and we think ill of them. But a more accepting philosophy (accepting of the person but not necessarily of the behavior) may not be as foreign or alien to our way of thinking as we may imagine. Would we return to a doctor who showed by his tone and attitude that he thought we were jerks because we were not following his recommendations to exercise, to cut down on our fat intake, or to take the medicine he prescribed? We may expect and tolerate his disapproval of our behavior. But we would not accept his disapproval of us as a person. We would then probably find another doctor.

Similarly, it is critical that therapists focus on helping the client change his behavior, without labeling him. Labels can help us decide how to respond, but they can also blind us to other possibilities. *DSM-IV* labels may help therapists think about a client, but may also limit their ability to relate to them in a fresh and creative manner.

Do an ABC on One's Own Thinking

Step 1

Get at the C's (the consequences). How are you feeling (and behaving) that you think is a problem? Contemptuous? Hateful? Afraid? Depressed? Hopeless?

Step 2

Try to uncover your beliefs, your thinking, that is contributing to your feelings and your actions. What are you telling yourself about the client? About having to work with such clients? For example: "He scares me. I hate working with people like that. He isn't interested in changing his behavior. This job is a joke. He's such a loser. She's such a manipulator. She lies to me and actually thinks I'm going to believe it. What kind of jerk does she take me for?"

Step 3

Look at your thinking. What is rational about what you are thinking and what is irrational (or helpful and unhelpful)? Examine, question, challenge, and, when appropriate, dispute the irrational parts of your thinking. How does it make you feel when you label someone? How does it make you feel about working with him or her? How does it make you feel about working in general?

How does labeling help? How does it hurt?

What are you thinking to yourself that contributes to your fear? Perhaps it is not irrational. Perhaps there are precautions you should be taking that you are not taking.

Are you similarly contemptuous of yourself when you are avoidant? Act stupidly? Deny that you have a problem? Lie? Procrastinate?

Where is the evidence that just because someone does something stupid or bad that makes them stupid or bad? When are semantic shortcuts okay, perhaps even useful?

Step 4

What could you tell yourself that might help you change? What else could you do to help yourself? How could you try to feel instead of trapped, hopeless, angry, afraid, etc.?

Talk to a Supervisor, Colleague, or Lawyer and Document These Conversations

Therapists at times have a client they have an intense feeling about. Countertransference would not be such an important topic among psychodynamically trained therapists if this were not true. Therapists should have a supervisor or colleague they can talk to so as to help them work through such problems. With some clients a lawyer or the state's ethics committee should be consulted. Notes should be kept about these consultations.

Lying and Denial

Clients may lie about their drug use because they have developed a habit of avoiding and dissembling, perhaps in order to preserve their minimal sense of self-respect or ego strength, or because they have been mandated to be in therapy. The therapist may have to report clients' behavior to someone in authority. If that is the case, it may be in their best interest to lie. Telling the truth may get them thrown out of a program that is helping them.

To handle these clients, the therapist should repeatedly indicate that what the clients choose to work on is up to them. Even if the treatment facility has strict guidelines, it is still the client's life. I tell people that I am an expert in helping people change. But what they decide to change or not to change is their business; this applies to adolescent mandated clients, too. If the therapist has to report to parents or to a parole office, then the likelihood of the client's lying increases significantly.

Some agencies require abstinence as the therapeutic goal, so therapy works toward maintaining abstinence. The client is supposedly choosing to accept that goal, if only temporarily to stay in the program. But even if he does not accept that treatment goal, he may be willing to work on other problems (see Chapter 7 on mandated clients).

A client may lie because he himself cannot stand hearing the truth from his own mouth. Learning to say what is real, what is true, especially to people outside his circle of friends, represents a profound change. As a result, the stages of change model and everything that the therapist knows about helping people change will apply to the client's problem of learning to tell the truth. It will also most probably involve the client's relapsing to precontemplation and contemplation even after some time in the action stage. How the therapist responds to lies and relapses in drug use or some other addictive behavior will affect how change occurs in the client.

The therapist should not take lying personally. If a client lies, it is not a personal affront or offense. It is an indication of his beliefs about how the therapist might act in the future if he told the truth.

Professional Enabling

Therapists may see a client who has been sent to therapy by someone else who has paid for the sessions. If such a client continues to engage in addictive behavior(s) despite claiming to want to cut down or stop, what should the therapist do? If the therapist becomes enmeshed in the client's elaborate network of enablers, it may be best to refer the client to someone else.

I always tell clients with whom I am not making any progress that someone else will ask questions differently, suggest different techniques, and have a different sense of humor—all of which may help him do better. Of course, sharing such feelings and thoughts with the client may help him get unstuck, but that is not always the case. The therapist should then decide on the number of sessions until termination, and give the client, in writing, the names of three other professionals. If he agrees, the therapist should get permission in writing to talk to each of them in the event that he goes to see one or more of them.

Multiple Diagnoses

Most clients suffer from other psychological problems in addition to addiction. In the past ten years, people became more aware of this reality and started dual-diagnosis programs. The term *dual* recognizes that many clients had both an addiction and another psychological problem. However, the term is a misnomer because many clients have more than one psychological disorder, including multiple addictions. They may be dependent on alcohol but abuse marijuana, or may abuse alcohol and marijuana and have problems with gambling. In addition, they may suffer from dysthymia and social anxiety. Other information may suggest posttraumatic stress disorder or attention deficit hyperactivity disorder (ADHD).

When a client has many interacting problems, the Stages of Change model becomes even more valuable. It helps the client to think of being at different stages of change on different problems. It also helps the client accept the often frustrating nature of change, especially when there are many problems, and it helps the professional keep from suffering burnout. Accurately identifying the variety of problems the client is grappling with may also help the therapist obtain more services for the client from managed care. However, therapists should be careful about overpathologizing clients.

Working with Clients
Who Are Still Drinking or Using Drugs

The fact that many psychologists and psychiatrists will not treat clients who are actively using drugs is puzzling. If they think addictive problems are manifestations of a disease, why are they refusing to see such people? If they think drinking and drugging are manifestations of a biopsychosocial problem, who better to help people with such problems than mental health professionals? However, it is still common that psychiatrists and psychologists will refuse to see addicted clients. Often this seems to be the result of old stereotypical beliefs about the "alcoholic" or "addict." Unfortunately, many well-dressed, well-behaved, middle-class, highly verbal clients are also suffering from addictions.

"But they won't remember anything from the session," is a comment I frequently hear. Of course, if the client is nodding off, it is impossible to work with her. But this occurs rarely, unless the person really doesn't want to be in therapy. Some clients, if they come to therapy "high," have used only a small amount of their favorite chemical, often because they felt too tense to come to therapy without it. They are not much different from people who have taken a Xanax or a Valium before an important meeting. Using also provides an opportunity for the therapist to address the target behavior. Why did she use before coming to see you? What was she telling herself? What would happen if she didn't use?

ADDICTIVE BEHAVIORS
ARE OFTEN DIFFICULT TO CHANGE

If addictive behaviors were not so difficult to change, they would not be called addictions. But most therapists do not get impatient when someone continues to suffer anxiety attacks or depressive episodes. Why do they react to lapses and relapses differently? Perhaps because they think that engaging in addictive behaviors involves more conscious intentionality than depression or anxiety? Perhaps without knowing it, they have fallen back on the moral model of addictions. They are thinking, "If he had more willpower and was a better person, he wouldn't behave this way." Perhaps they do not think that people can do anything about depression or anxiety attacks, so they judge a relapse into depression or an increase in panic attacks less harshly. In fact, they would not even call them relapses. The difference may be explained by the fact that addictive behaviors often have a large impact on many other people beside the client. For example, his wife and children may suffer from his abusive behavior when he is drunk. Or he may spend all of the family's income gambling. However, many addictive behaviors are ongoing, chronic problems, therapists need to find ways to work with such clients without becoming discouraged and demoralized themselves.

6

SHOULD YOUR CLIENT STOP, OR JUST SLOW DOWN?

> *I can resist everything except temptation.*
> —*Oscar Wilde, Lady Windermere's Fan*

Most clients are ambivalent. They would like to continue to engage in their favorite addictive behavior if they could, but the problems continue to mount or the risks begin to seem more real to them. They start looking for ways to change. But do they have to stop completely? That is the question that most clients grapple with, sometimes throughout their lives. This is the most contentious issue in the field (Heather et al. 1991, Hester 1995, Marlatt 1985b, Rosenberg 1994, Sanchez-Craig et al. 1984). For an excellent review of the history of this controversy, see "Harm Reduction for Alcohol Problems: Moving Beyond the Controlled Drinking Controversy" by Marlatt and his associates (1993).

Research findings may help, but each person is biologically unique, has a unique developmental history, and lives in a unique environment. As a result, it is a question that each individual has to answer for himself or herself.

WHAT DOES THE RESEARCH SUGGEST?

- In Vaillant's (1996) long-term follow-up study (over fifty years) of a group of Harvard undergraduates and a group of Boston inner-city adolescents, mostly white and of Irish descent, at last contact or at death, 19 percent of the Harvard group and 37 percent of the inner city group were abstinent, 10 percent and 14 percent had returned to controlled drinking, 12 percent and 6 percent had been reclassified as social drinkers, and 60 percent and 43 percent were still abusing alcohol.
- During the last twenty years of the study, most of the Harvard subjects alternated between periods of controlled drinking and periods of abuse.
- Between 3 percent and 7 percent of people in the United States develop serious problems with alcohol (become dependent, to use the *DSM-IV* term). The numbers vary depending on who is making the estimate. Approximately 15 percent to 35 percent may be labeled "problem drinkers." They experience some problems during their lifetime (Emrick 1994). Although only occasional, some problems may be severe. The person may run into a tree when driving drunk or may kill someone.
- A recent review of 40 studies (Sobell, Ellingstad, & Sobell, 2000) found that approximately 40 percent of recovery outcomes were limited drinking and approximately 14 percent were limited drug use. Two large scale surveys in Canada of 11,634 and 1034 respondents found that 77.5 percent and 77.7 percent of those reporting a recovery in excess of one year did so on their own without treatment; 38 percent and 63 percent reported drinking moderately (Sobell et al. 1996).
- King & Tucker (2000), in a study of previously alcohol dependent people who resolved their problems without treat-

ment, found three patterns of problem resolution: immediate and stable abstinence; abstinence followed by moderation; gradual cutting down, resulting in stable moderation. Those who ultimately became abstinent made an average of 41 attempts at moderation; in contrast, those who ultimately resolved their problems by drinking moderately, made an average of only five attempts.

- Fillmore (1988, cited in Dimeff et al. 1999) asserts that drinking poses the greatest risk for adults in their early twenties, but by their late twenties, two-thirds have "matured out," that is, resolved their heavy drinking problems without treatment.

- A study by Miller and his associates (1992), who were intentionally selected from opposite sides of the controlled-drinking controversy—"keeping each other honest," according to the authors—looked at the impact of four programs specifically designed to teach moderation to not severely dependent or ill clients (as opposed to looking at how often people moderated successfully who were treated in traditional programs). Long-term follow-up varied from 3.5 to 8 years. Of the original 140 subjects, 99 were found for follow-up. The authors report that 23 percent had been abstinent for periods between 14 and 99 months, 14 percent were "asymptomatic" in that they were drinking without symptoms of dependence or impairment, 22 percent were "improved but impaired," and 35 percent were categorized as unremitted. *Caution:* 41 of the subjects were not found for follow-up, and, as noted above, severely dependent and ill subjects were excluded from the study.

Many patients seen at treatment facilities are not only abusing alcohol or drugs, they are very dependent on alcohol or drugs, and frequently both. The counselors working in facilities are recovering users, so they themselves know the seductive allure of moderation, have tried it more than once, and have always failed. They have also been successful at abstaining. Thus, it is understandable that when they are given the responsibility of helping people recover, they base their judgments on their own experience. Research over the past ten years (e.g., Hester and Miller 1995), however, shows quite clearly that what was true for them may not be true for all of their clients.

From their long experience, the professionals in such facilities observed that the chance that such a patient could engage in some form of controlled or moderated drinking or use was extremely slim, so that permitting the patient to entertain such a treatment goal seemed to go against their ethics. Increasingly, however, professionals working in the field are acknowledging that the chance that such people can abstain is also slim. Thus, the field is changing, and strategies to reduce the frequency, duration, and intensity of an addictive behavior while reducing the risk (and potential) harm users may do to themselves and others are increasing in popularity (MacCoun 1998, Marlatt 1998, Tatarsky 1998, Wodak 1998).

RESEARCH NOTE

For problems with alcohol, acceptance of a goal *other than abstinence* varies widely from country to country. Below are the percentages of inpatient and outpatient facilities in three countries that will accept a goal other than abstinence:

	Inpatient	Outpatient
Norway	90%	59%
Britain	91%	25–91%
United States	47%	5%

However, most treatment professionals in Norway and Britain thought that such a goal was appropriate for only approximately 25% of their treatment population (Rosenberg and Davis 1993, 1994).

Research regarding the manner in which people moderate and/or abstain from other forms of addictive behavior over long periods of time is growing (cf. Oppenheimer et al. 1994, Strang et al. 1997, Toneatto et al. 1999, Tucker and King 1999, Zinberg and Jacobson 1976) but still quite limited. In New York one hears of people using heroin without problems, but none of my clients (nor I) have ever met one. I know and some of my clients know a few people who, on an occasional basis, use cocaine without seeming to develop problems. However, many people run into very serious problems. The same appears true for Ecstasy. In contrast, some people appear to be able to continue to smoke marijuana throughout their lives and never develop serious problems.

Anyone doubting the critical importance of environmental cues on addictive behaviors need look no further than smoking. Laws and office rules have been enacted that made smoking much more difficult to engage in, and smoking and lung cancer have both decreased significantly over the last 35 years. Some smokers have significantly moderated their use of nicotine in the face of these new environmental constraints. Such people are now smoking many fewer cigarettes a day, sometimes as few as two or three. Whether they will eventually abstain is unclear. However, we do know that many people who abstain never return to moderate or heavy use.

There is also a paucity of long-term research into the manner in which people manage nonchemical types of addictive behaviors over a lifetime. As they age, many people stop engaging in or reduce the number of times they engage in unsafe sex, but we know very little about why and how they make such changes. The treatment of gambling and the attitudes toward controlled gambling versus total abstinence are almost identical to those in the alcohol and substance abuse field. This is true even though a one-treatment-fits-all approach is no more supported by research than it is in other areas of addictions treatment. Research, especially in Australia, indicates that programs designed to specifically teach gambling work with some people (Rosencrance 1989, as cited in McCurrin 1992).

Despite the myth that few people who overeat ever successfully keep the weight off, new research shows that many people are quite successful. The 2,500 people included in the National Weight Loss Registry, on average, have maintained a 67-pound weight loss for five years. Between 12 percent and 14 percent have maintained a weight loss of over 100 pounds (to be included in the registry, a person had to have lost over 30 pounds and have kept it off for at least one year; Fritsch 1999). Cognitive-behavioral therapy has been successfully used to reduce binge eating and purging, and long-term maintenance is reasonably good (Wilson and Fairburn 1998).

PREDICTORS OF SUCCESS AT MODERATING

Rosenberg (1993) found that "no single personal characteristic has been consistently predictive," but lower severity of dependence and a "persuasion that controlled drinking is possible" are associated with better outcomes (p. 129).

Miller and his associates (1992) found:

- The more severe the problem, the less likely it is that the client will be successful.
- Those clients who refuse the "alcoholic" label and who have less history of alcoholism in their family are more likely to succeed.
- The first three to twelve months of treatment are strong indicators of what to expect over the long-term; those who managed to moderate in the first months of treatment did better over the long run.
- Asymptomatic drinkers and unremitted drinkers rejected the label of "alcoholic."
- Age, gender, intake MAST (Michigan Alcohol Screening Test) score, intake rating of self-efficacy, family history of depression, and a measure of alcohol life problems were not related to success.

WHAT IF THE CLIENT WANTS TO TRY MODERATION?

The Therapist Should Let the Client Answer His Own Question

What does the client want to do? Does he want to investigate what is best for him while he is in therapy? Then he can decide for himself whether moderating is a good idea. How many experiments has he already run? What do the results suggest?

Occasionally someone asks me about the possibility of moderately using heroin or cocaine. Many of my clients are very skeptical about research studies, especially those funded by the government. I acknowledge that I have heard that some people are managing to use occasionally for long periods of time and are doing well professionally and personally. But I also acknowledge that I have never met such people. Have they? To date, no one (client or nonclient) has.

In contrast, my clients almost always know people who have used alcohol and marijuana for very long periods of time without apparent problems. Hence, I tell them I think there is evidence that heroin and cocaine are different chemicals. Perhaps no one can use them extensively in a moderate fashion and no one can escape the negative consequences. Of course, I still meet clients who would like to try to see if they are the exception. In that case, I focus on reducing the risk of their behavior, while at the same time helping them learn other techniques that may be of use to them.

The Therapist Should Keep the Focus on What the Client Wants

Glasser's (1965, 1989) reality therapy focused on variations of three questions: What do you want? What are you doing? How do you like it (the results)? If the client does not like what is happening to him, the therapist can ask "What were you doing?" and then follow up with "What did you say you want?" Ellis is very direct in telling people, "Look, you can go on wasting your life away, that's up to you, but what do you *really* want to do? Wouldn't it make you happier overall if you slowed down or quit drinking?" Motivational interviewing (Miller and Rollnick 1991) frequently points out discrepancies between what a person says he wants to do and what he is doing. By keeping the focus on what the client wants, the therapist avoids being seen as just one more person who is telling him what he should do. (The effect of such a stance is discussed at greater length in Chapter 7.)

On the other hand, some clients do better when told what to do. For many years teachers debated what was best for elementary school children—discovery learning or direct teaching. Most teachers now realize that some children benefit from a lot of freedom while others need structure. The trick is to figure out what suits which child best. Similarly, while many therapists and counselors may have a bias toward the notion that it is better for people to figure out what is best for them, that may not be the best approach with every client. Some clients have not developed the ego strength or maturity or a sense of what they want, and thus cannot make very good decisions. As Howard Young (1984) has so pointed out, some clients prefer to go to an expert and be told what to do. They know that that will work best for them, and they are often right. They will do better when someone tells them what to do and what not to do.

Some counselors and therapists who lean toward a more humanistic approach may object: Telling them what you think may simply keep them in a state of undevelopment. They need to find out what is good for them and what is not, what makes them happy and what does not. These may be valid points. However, what about the harm they might do to themselves and to others if the therapist takes a less direct approach? No doubt there will be many other opportunities for them to develop their sense of self in other areas.

Caution: In most cases, the client has been told by many people to stop or cut down. He is in therapy because he has not taken that advice or he has tried and been unable to do so. Consequently, the therapist may quickly become one more authority figure who is telling the client what to do. From a Freudian perspective, the therapist may become identified with an internalized parent or with the client's superego. Then he (or his id) may act out against his superego. He may begin to relate to the therapist as one more person who wants him to get better. He may then feel ashamed when he has disappointed the therapist by relapsing, and begin to lie about his use. All of these developments will have a very negative effect on therapy, and the therapist may be rendered ineffectual.

The Therapist Should Help the Client Develop a Specific Plan

All programs designed to help people control drinking focus on setting up very specific guidelines. (See Chapter 8 for more on this topic.)

The Therapist Should Help the Client Reduce the Harm

Some people will be able to stop their addictive behaviors. But many people will continue, on and off, throughout their lives. Even a normally non-problem drinker may get in the car after a Christmas office party, convince himself that he can drive, and on the way home, do considerable harm to himself or others. I advocate that therapists build an ongoing helping relationship with clients, a relationship that may span many years. During that time, despite occasional lapses and relapses into addictive behaviors, clients can learn how to reduce the risk of their behavior if the therapist focuses on it and not solely on helping them to stop.

CONCLUSIONS

The controversy surrounding abstinence vs. controlled drinking, moderation, or social drinking has centered primarily on the treatment of alcohol abuse and dependence, to a lesser degree on the treatment of substance abuse and dependence, and to an even lesser degree on other addictive behaviors, for example, gambling, overspending, and compulsive sexual behavior.

Many people who develop severe problems with alcohol will not be able to totally abstain for long periods of time. Many people who develop severe problems with alcohol will not be able to engage in moderate drinking for long periods of time. Consequently, it makes sense to use an approach that encourages them to establish a relationship with a counselor or therapist who can help them when they fall back into trouble. It also makes sense to help them learn how to reduce the risk of their behavior.

Abstaining is probably the safest approach when people develop addictive patterns of behavior with alcohol, drugs (including nicotine and caffeine), gambling, unsafe sex, and spending. However, even if abstinence may be the safest choice for almost all forms of addictive behaviors (except eating), most people who develop addictive behavioral patterns of work, sex, Internet usage, and exercising will not abstain. They want help to learn to reduce the risks and problems associated with their behavior, such as AIDS and venereal diseases due to unprotected sex, missed work and/or classes due to excessive Internet use, destroyed relationships due to workaholism, ruined credit ratings due to overspending. Even users of alcohol, marijuana, and caffeine usually only want to rid themselves of the problems associated with their use of those chemicals. They do not want to stop using them. People do pretty much what they want to do, constrained mostly by their cultural, social, economic, and political realities.

SUGGESTED RESOURCES

Therapists and their clients who want to try moderating may find the following helpful:

- Behavioral Self-Control Program for Windows. The client version and therapist version are available from Behavior Therapy Associates (505-345-6100) or www.behaviortherapy.com

(see Hester and Delaney 1997, for a research report related to this program).

- A self-help group, Moderation Management Network, Inc., 810-788-8040, P. O. Box 6005, Ann Arbor, MI 48106.
- The books *Moderate Drinking* (Kishline 1994), *How to Control Your Drinking* (Miller and Munoz 1982), *Saying When* (Sanchez-Craig 1993), and *Problem Drinkers* (Sobell and Sobell 1993).

7 HOW TO WORK ON TYPE I CLIENT PROBLEMS

Difficulties strengthen the man as labor does the body.
—Seneca

"What problem? I don't have a problem." The most difficult clients to work with are those who do not think or acknowledge that they have a problem: the client who has been arrested for driving while intoxicated and has been ordered by the court to undergo psychological evaluation and/or counseling; the client who is ordered by his employer to go for counseling or risk losing his job; the client whose wife has made seeing a counselor a condition for staying in the marriage. The old light bulb joke captures the essence of the problem. How many counselors (therapists, psychologists, social workers) does it take to change a light bulb? Just one, but the light bulb has to want to change. All of the techniques outlined in this chapter focus on the problem of motivating people to want to try to work on their problems.

Motivation is an aspect of counseling that has been somewhat ignored by many cognitive behavioral therapists. They have focused more on techniques and less on whether or not a client is ready or motivated to change. This may be partly explained by the fact that cognitive-behavioral therapy (CBT) initially focused on depression and anxiety. In most cases, clients want to get rid of both. They are often motivated to learn ways to manage such problems. In contrast, clients grappling with an addictive problem are not always so motivated to change. They may realize that they have a number of problems, and they may want to figure out ways to handle those problems, but that may not include changing their additive behaviors. They may be primarily interested in getting rid of the problems that result from their addictive behaviors—a nagging wife, financial problems, or worried employers.

In contrast to many CBT and REBT counselors and therapists, for the past twenty years, Miller and his associates have specifically focused on the factors that affect a client's motivation to change. In 1991, Miller and Rollnick published their book *Motivational Interviewing*, and Motivational Enhancement Therapy (MET) (Miller et al. 1992) later became one of the three therapeutic interventions included in Project MATCH (1997a).

Initially, Miller and his associates developed motivational interviewing specifically to motivate problem drinkers to change their drinking patterns. MET consists of four basic techniques. Practitioners are urged to adopt a supportive, empathetic style and taught how to (1) develop discrepancy, (2) avoid argumentation, (3) roll with the resistance, and (4) support self-efficacy. Motivation to change is assumed to occur "when people perceive a discrepancy between where they are and where they want to be" (Project MATCH 1997a, p. 8). Based on an extensive intake interview, feedback is used to raise a client's awareness of the riskiness of her behavior and to highlight the seeming discrepancy between what the client seems to want and what she is doing. A client is given clear advice to change, but, at the same time, she is given a number of treatment options. The therapist strives to "support self-efficacy, in essence, the belief that one can perform a particular behavior or accomplish a particular task" (p. 11).

According to the manual, "[MET] assumes that the key element for lasting change is a motivational shift that instigates a decision and commitment to change. . . . Once such a shift has occurred, however, people's ordinary resources and their natural relationships may well suffice" (p. 11). MET "relies on the client's own natural change processes and resources" (p. 10). Reflective listening is central to MET, but not in a traditional Rogerian fashion. Rather, MET uses reflections to "systematically direct the client toward motivation for change" (p. 11). In the MATCH study, clients were given an extensive (seven to eight hours) battery of assessment instruments, and then provided with computer-generated feedback about their drinking.

The MATCH Motivational Enhancement Therapy Manual explicitly states that "clients are not taught 'how to'" (p. 10). In contrast, this book advocates a both/and strategy. Some clients need only to be helped in motivating themselves. Once they have formulated a plan, they already know enough to carry it out. Other clients, however, may need help developing the necessary motivation and learning new techniques to help themselves change. Most often, they need to learn how to stop derailing themselves. Clients often report that they have been motivated and they have resolved to change, but eventually their plans always seem to go awry. They also frequently need to learn how to handle the negative emotions that they have normally managed with various addictive behaviors. This chapter focuses both on techniques to motivate clients and to help them better manage their lives.

The MATCH manual also notes that CBT "seeks to identify and modify maladaptive cognitions" while MET "explores and reflects client perceptions without labeling or 'correcting them'" (p. 10). A good CBT-er or REBT-er may help a client learn how to dispute his or her irrational beliefs, but it is not a therapist's responsibility to correct those beliefs (see the section on Thug Therapy, Chapter 2). In fact, in a manner similar to MET, it is the client's own goals and values that determine which beliefs are identified as unhelpful.

MET also includes "no training, modeling, or practice" (p. 10). However, my experience suggests that although some people, once motivated, know what to do and how to do it, others do not. They need not only suggestions but also practice in session and between sessions. The MATCH manual states that "the therapist's role is a blend of supportive companion and knowledgeable consultant" (p. 7). This is a good definition, but a knowledgeable consultant, like a good basketball coach or ski instructor, usually suggests specific techniques, may model those techniques, and may even oversee and supervise the practice.

DOES CONFRONTATION WORK?

During the past fifty years, it has not been uncommon in the addictions treatment field for counselors or therapists to take a very confrontative, almost aggressive approach. In contrast, most therapists and counselors in other treatment areas, trained in either psychodynamic or Rogerian approaches, believe in a nonconfrontative approach.

Being empathetic, avoiding argumentation, "rolling" with the resistance, and supporting self-efficacy may seem like normal ways of working to these psychotherapists. Again, this difference is partly due to the fact that many nonaddicted clients seemed to be interested in change. In reality, many clients are addicted to various forms of avoidant behavior and may not be as motivated to change as the therapist may assume. Depressed and anxious clients may procrastinate for months in the face of taking any actions that might lead to real change. Nevertheless, the primary components of motivational interviewing represent a revolution in the treatment of addictions. Moreover, the technique of highlighting discrepancies between what a client seems to want to do and what he is doing is often key to change. Miller and his associates (Hester and Miller 1995) have established that a confrontative approach does not necessarily work as well as had been thought. In videotapes of therapists and clients, there was a direct negative correlation between confrontation and relapse. Therapist confrontations increased the probability of relapses.

WHAT DOES THE RESEARCH SUGGEST?

In reviewing the research related to motivation, Miller (1985, 1995) reports a number of points that may be extremely valuable to practitioners:

- Clients who perceive their therapists as helpful and optimistic stay in treatment longer and are more receptive to change (Thomas et al. 1955, cited in Miller 1985).
- Clients of therapists who demonstrate more empathy have better long-term outcomes (Miller 1995).
- A telephone call or letter may significantly increase the therapist's effectiveness. After a single visit to an alcoholism clinic, clients who were sent a letter ("I'm glad you came in. I think you do have a problem to work on, and I am concerned about you. I hope you will come back, and we'll be glad to work with you if you do.") returned 50 percent of the time versus 31 percent of the time for those who did not receive a letter (Koumans and Muller 1965, cited in Miller 1995). The dropout rate decreased from 51 percent to 28 percent when a similar letter was sent after a missed appointment (Panepinto and Higgins 1965, cited in Miller 1995). A single telephone call increased the percentage of people who returned after an evaluation from 8 percent to 44 percent (Koumans et al. 1967, cited in Miller 1995).

SELECTED CLINICAL STRATEGIES

Session Goals

The session goals for Type I clients are as follows:

1. To get a second session. That is, to engage the client in some aspect of therapy or counseling, when that is appropriate.
2. To move the client from Stage I to Stage II, from precontemplation to contemplation, from "I don't have a problem" to "Maybe I do," when that is appropriate.

Type I or Type II Problem?

Therapists should not assume that a mandated client does not believe he has a problem. He may be very ambivalent, knowing he has a problem but not knowing what to do, and too scared or worried to reveal that. Or he may think he has a problem but doesn't think he can change. Or he may know he has a problem but thinks he can handle the consequences. Initially, he may overtly deny that he has a problem—"I just came to get my wife off my back." But with empathy and a little probing, by the end of the session, he may think that he has a problem or he may report another problem that he would like some help with. As the therapist progresses with the ongoing assessment, he will have many opportunities to develop a number of hypotheses about the client's thinking and to test them out. (See Chapter 4 on assessment.)

Exploring the Reasons for the Client's Resistance

If the therapist empathetically listens to the client, he may be able to uncover why the client does not want to be in therapy. In working with this kind of client, keep in mind some of the possible reasons someone might not want to change (or might be resistant to change). In addition, although rare, the possibility exists that a client does not have the problem the referring party claims he has. If after a careful assessment that appears to be the case, the therapist should get permission in writing, witnessed by a receptionist or secretary, to talk to the referring person. Even if the client has already signed a release form for his insurance or employee-assistance program (EAP), the therapist should have a signed permission letter in his own file in case he is sued.

There are many reasons someone might not be motivated to change, including the following beliefs:

It's not worth it.

I can quit any time.

I can't stand the pain and discomfort of cutting down or stopping.

It's too humiliating to admit that I have a problem.

I don't know how.

I can't.

It's an unfair world.

It's great.

It's exciting.

I can get away with it.

I'll start tomorrow.

I intend to quit later, after a few years, or if it becomes a problem.

I shouldn't have to work so hard to get what I want.

I like being "bad."

Life sucks. What's the point? No one cares anyway.

Fuck it. It doesn't matter.

There are other possible unstated or hidden beliefs, including:

Shrinks are all alike. They just pry into people's private business.

This therapist thinks she can understand me, but she can't. I'm much too complex for that.

When I feel down and hopeless, I feel I *am* down and hopeless. When I feel high, I feel better. I *am* better. It's the only way I can feel better about myself.

When I use cocaine, I know how I am going to feel. That's about the only thing I *can* control in my life.

If I change, I'll no longer be me.

The therapist's own beliefs may impede treatment:

This guy's a jerk. (as he mustn't be; I can't stand jerks.)

I shouldn't have to work with such manipulative, hostile, resistant clients.

This person will never change. He's a bum and will always be a bum (and I can't stand working with such clients. Why do I have such a rotten job anyway?).

Even with all her problems, she still can't even admit she has a problem (as she should). Look at her sitting there. She just wants her subway pass, and then she's back to the streets.

What a hostile little . . . He'll never change. He's just looking for a free ride.

Looking for a Hook

In the first session, especially with a mandated client, I am always looking for a "hook," a way to get my client to think it might be worthwhile working with me.

Find Some Common Ground

If the client has to be in therapy, he is probably not very happy about it. Maybe there is something the therapist and client could talk about that they both share. I've worked on oil wells in Montana and tow boats on the Mississippi, so if my client is a laborer and feels awkward being in a shrink's office, I try to let him know that I haven't been a Ph.D. all my life. One client who was in a particularly bad mood started to talk about how everyone was always trying to "screw workers." I knew he was in the electricians' union, so I shared that I have been a union member all my life, adding that I started as a longshoreman when I was 16. He immediately took more interest in talking to me. It is important to find some way to connect with a client. (However, note the cautions about sharing in Chapter 5.)

What Is Important To the Client?

What does the client care about? For example, he may have wanted to be a particular kind of man, but, in his mind, he is not. He may have wanted to be successful, and he is not. He may have wanted to be responsible or be the head of his family, and he is not. Or he may have wanted a fancy car and fancy clothes, and he does not have them. Or he may like to go camping and hunting, but he is currently in jail. The therapist looks for something the client cares about in order to find a way to motivate him. Ellis spends a lot of time on ABC's and Rational Emotive Imagery (REI), but at various times during his demonstrations, he almost always says something like, "Well, it's up to you. You can go do whatever you want with your life, but if you'd like to be happier, maybe you better try to figure out how you're screwing up your life so much." The "if you want to be happier" is the hook, the thing that moves people to work more with him. (Of course, there are other hooks, as well. Ellis always insists that they can talk themselves out of their enormous difficulties, despite what seems true to them, and that he has tools that they can learn and use. These meta-messages also give clients hope, another critical ingredient in change.)

RESEARCH NOTE

In one study, counselors were told that "certain alcoholics were likely to show remarkable recovery during counseling on the basis of their personality test profiles." Later, therapists rated those clients "more motivated to accept treatment, more punctual and cooperative . . . and [as making] more effort" (Leake and King 1977, cited in Miller 1985, p. 85). Remarkably, even peer clients rated those clients as "more liked and improved." According to Miller, they "showed significantly fewer absences and premature terminations from the program, had more sober days and fewer slips at 1-year follow-up, and

---

were more likely than their comparable peers to have had and held a job" (p. 85). However, the "certain alcoholics" had been chosen at random. They never had the personality test profiles they were purported to have. So it would seem that because the counselors thought the clients were going to do better, they did do better, even in the long run!

Sharing Information with the Client

Each person reacts differently to various activities, such as sex, gambling, and shopping. In a similar fashion, one client may try Prozac and like the result, while another feels as if he is going to go through the roof, and a third reports that it seems to have no effect at all. Similarly, the fact that some people are born with a very sensitive nervous system may help a particular client understand why she has always been nervous and upsettable, and why she has been drawn to some form of addictive behavior or chemical for help. This may not be the whole explanation (and may even be totally wrong), but it may help a client become more interested in working toward resolving her problems.

On the other hand, someone who does not think he has a problem may only become irritated if the therapist starts spouting information. It will only confirm in him a belief that the therapist has an agenda and thus is not prepared to listen.

Discussing the Client's Conflicting Wants

People frequently have conflicting wants, goals, and objectives. In fact, the client may have conflicting wants right at that moment: He wants to "get better," so he wants to be in therapy, but he also wants to get out of the situation (and away from the anxiety and discomfort), so he also wants to use heroin or have a drink. The trick is learning how to balance these conflicting wants. Many of my clients do not seem to be fully aware of how conflicted they are over their various wants and desires. And they do not see that they often must make conscious decisions about how they are going to use their time. This is especially true when they are trying to alter ingrained, perhaps over-learned or deeply conditioned behavior. They are not aware of the attention and energy they will have to bring to the task.

Mary was very embarrassed that the principal of the school where she taught had insisted that she seek counseling. She did not think she drank that much and she could not imagine how someone at the school could have smelled alcohol on her breath, because she swore she never drank in the morning. Mary lived alone, and when she was at home at night she always wound up drinking one drink after the other until she finally fell asleep. After working with her for a while, it became obvious to me that she was not happy with many aspects of her life, but each night she coped by drinking herself into oblivion. She knew she did not really like where she was teaching, although she said she loved children. She thought that she had to do something about finding a new job and developing more friend-ships, but she never got around to it. She also had always wanted to start a baking business, but she didn't bake during the week and only rarely on the weekends. During the week she was too tired, and during the weekends she usually didn't feel in the mood. Because she reported having difficulties getting herself to do things even as a teenager before she started drinking, I hypothesized that she had suffered from dysthymia (chronic, low-grade depression) for many years and was trying to medicate her problem with alcohol. Her drinking only made the problem worse.

Mary was full of conflicting wants. She wanted to feel better overall but consistently medicated away her tiredness and lonely feelings in the evening with alcohol. Her continual use of alcohol also undercut all of her other plans to improve her life. The fact that she had graduated from college, obtained a master's degree, and was a teacher indicated that she did not always sacrifice the medium and long run for the short run. However, perhaps as a result of her dysthymia, she was not very good at cultivating medium- and long-term pleasures. Typical of many women, she was better at taking good care of other people, for example, her students, than she was of herself.

When we started talking about what she wanted in life, she seemed to have completely given up. She went to work, fulfilled her responsibilities as a teacher, took care of some of her chores, went home, and fed herself and drank until she fell asleep watching TV. She hated every aspect of her life. It took many weeks to help her begin to identify what she wanted to be doing in the short run, the medium run, and the long run—and what she did *not* want.

For young people, the conflict is often between what they want to do, for example, continue to drink or smoke, and the negative consequences, such as DWIs, wrecked cars, and lost jobs. They do not really want to give up their drinking or their smoking. They want to find a way to get rid of the consequences and then resume their smoking and drinking. Most young people have to be pushed a little to be serious about the consequences. Seriously and explicitly talking about what they want over time and how they might best get what they want, often helps.

Exploring Ways to Help the Client

The therapist is a facilitator of change, not an adversary. Once he has a tentative idea about what may be causing the client to remain in Stage I, how can he motivate him to begin to contemplate change? That is, what might move him from Stage I to Stage II? The therapist should work carefully, showing concern and a genuine interest in understanding, while at the same time looking for a way to be helpful and to effect some change.

Let's consider each of the possible irrational beliefs listed earlier in this chapter. What approach might the therapist take?

1. "It's not worth it." The client may not think that the proverbial carrot is big enough to warrant putting all the time and effort into changing. It may help to explore what might "sweeten" the carrot. If the client were offered $10,000 per month to stop her addictive behavior, could she? Why? What does that say about her addiction? How confident is she that that is true? Of course, in the real world, there are usually no such clear rewards. What else might help? If she does not think the overall improvement in her life will offset what she has to give up, doing a time-effects analysis may help (see Chapter 3). How the client evaluates what he will get and what he will have to go through to get it will have a great impact on his motivation.

2. **"I can quit any time."** The client may genuinely think he doesn't have a problem. He may also be thinking (and really believe) "I don't drink as much as lots of my friends." "My wife (or boss) is just overreacting." Although unlikely, both statements may be true. For example, the client may work with a bunch of construction workers, all of whom drink a lot, and his wife or boss may be overreacting. But that is not the point. For some reason, he is upset enough to demand to, or be required to, see a counselor, and he has agreed. Arguing with him about the "facts" clearly won't get the therapist very far and certainly won't help achieve the main goal: getting another session. Do an ABC on his wife's problem (see below).

3. **"I can't stand the pain and discomfort of cutting down or stopping."** The client may think she might have a problem (without acknowledging that to anyone) but she can't stand the thought of stopping or even cutting down. She may be thinking: "I couldn't stand the pain of cutting down or stopping." "It's too much trouble." "I can't be bothered." "If I admitted I had a problem, then my husband would really make a federal case out of it. I'd never hear the end of it. I couldn't cope with that."

If she does not think she can stand the discomfort of changing, it may be her low frustration tolerance (LFT) that is getting in her way. But how does the therapist discuss the client's possible LFT without sounding like he is simply labeling her "lazy"? He may sense that that client wants him to be direct and frank. Many of my clients have expressed great appreciation that someone finally told them what they had suspected all along: they were consistently derailing their lives by often avoiding frustration and discomfort. It was like finally talking about a dark secret after years of denial, and they could now decide, first, whether or not to work on their LFT, and second, whether to work with me. Moreover, some clients have a lot of high frustration tolerance (HFT) in some situations but not in others. This is often especially true when it involves themselves.

Betsy not only worked at an investment banking firm where most of the other employees were male, she also took care of her aging mother. She had given me anecdote after anecdote that clearly illustrated that she would push herself through all sorts of frustration and discomfort to complete assignments for her team at work and to make sure that her mother was adequately taken care of. However, she had missed something when it came to herself. She had never realized that she would sometimes also have to push herself through frustration and discomfort when she was working on something that was solely important for herself. Hence, it was initially hard for her to alter her late-night drinking and unsafe sexual encounters. She simply was not as motivated to work hard to do things for herself as she was to work hard to do things for others.

Initially, I began my discussions about the possible role of LFT in Betsy's life by asking her if there were other areas in her life where she demonstrated high tolerance for frustration and/or discomfort. How or why did she put up with the stress, frustration, and discomfort in those situations?

The therapist can ask the client if he has ever done anything in the past that required a high tolerance for discomfort, for example, giving up smoking. Or perhaps he has been in active duty in the military. If he has, what helped him stand the discomfort? What causes him now to think he cannot stand the discomfort or frustrations involved in quitting or cutting down? Is he exaggerating the anticipated discomfort? How can he test out the discomfort he might feel if he were to cut down or abstain? How can he set up situations so he can help himself?

The client may also be engaged in exaggerated, negative evaluations—awfulizing and catastrophizing. His distorted evaluations of a situation will often increase the frustration and discomfort he thinks he will have to tolerate. That is, he exaggerates the difficulty of what he has to do and the obstacles that he has to overcome. Hence, he sets himself up for thinking: "This is too much. I can't stand this." In reality, the hills he has to go over are not mountains, but he has so exaggerated their difficulty in his mind that he thinks he will have to tolerate great amounts of frustration in order to succeed. So it may be that the client does not have such low tolerance for frustration and discomfort. The real problem is in how he consistently perceives the mountain.

4. "It's too humiliating to admit that I have a problem." The client may be too ashamed to admit that he has lost control, that he cannot stop. Strong social stigma is still associated with any form of mental illness, and especially with alcohol and drug abuse, excessive gambling, and other addictions. Clients with addictive problems are often as stigmatizing of themselves as the general public is. As a result, many clients cannot bring themselves to admit that they have a problem. It would make them feel shameful and humiliated—two very strong emotions that most people try to avoid. The client may be saying to himself: "I cannot accept that I have a problem (like this one)." "If I admitted that I had a problem, I would feel really, really bad, and I feel bad enough already." "If I admitted that I had a problem, other members of my family or people at work might find out, and I couldn't stand that. (It would be too humiliating.)" Or he may subscribe to what I call the "John Wayne syndrome": A real man can figure it out by himself. His underlying belief may be, "I cannot accept that I have a problem that I cannot solve on my own (to do so would be humiliating)."

Chapter 12 discusses the impact of shame in greater detail and how to help the client work to reduce its impact.

5. "I don't know how." The client may not believe that she has the competency to change. She may lack the necessary know-how and a feeling of confidence or self-efficacy. Some clients are terrified of trying to change. Having more know-how, the client might entertain changing. She may be thinking, "I would like to change, but I don't know how." "If I admit I have a problem, he will try to make me stop. But I don't think I can stop."

Much of this book focuses on ways to help a client develop know-how. Increasing know-how and self-efficacy can also increase motivation. The more she feels she knows how to change, the more motivated she may be to try.

If she seems to think that she lacks the necessary know-how, is there any evidence in her past that suggests she *does* know how? Has she ever successfully stopped or cut down in the past? How did she do that? What helped? Will it help to try to convince her that the therapist may have the necessary know-how and may be able to teach it to her?

6. "I can't." Even though the client appears to have the know-how or it seems as if he could learn it, he may continue to think that change in this particular area of his life is impossible. Perhaps he has tried many times in the past and failed every time. As a result, he may not want to even discuss the possibility of having a problem or of changing. It is too painful and demoralizing to do so. He may be thinking, "It's pointless. It's impossible. I'll never change." "Every time when I tried in the past, I failed, so what's so different about this time?" "I wish I could, but I can't." "I do not want to start and then fail. That would make me feel worse, and I feel bad enough as it is." "If I work on it and fail, that will be one more reason for my boss to fire me. Then I'd really be in a mess."

If he has given up any hope of ever changing, what has led him to this point? What happened in the past? How did he get derailed or derail himself? What other evidence suggests that he cannot change? Is there anything he and the therapist, working together, could do differently to increase the odds that his efforts will pay off?

Overcoming a feeling of helplessness and pointlessness is extremely difficult. Moreover, a client may have developed a vested interest in maintaining such a position. If he showed any ability to change, others around him might suddenly begin to expect more of him—like going to work or taking on more responsibilities around the house. He may not be prepared to do so or he may be too scared or too addicted to his current lifestyle. Helping a client move out of such an entrenched position requires a delicate balance between supportive, empathetic listening and careful questioning about the client's longer terms goals and values. Everyone stuck in such a situation knows that his life is slipping away. Is this the way he wants to spend it? Perhaps the answer is yes, but perhaps it is not. A few of the many techniques the therapist can use to explore a client's goals and values are described later in this chapter.

7. **"It's an unfair world."** The client may not believe she will really get the "carrot" even if she works for it. She may have several beliefs, perhaps based on real-life experiences. She may be thinking, "Don't trust people. If they say they will give you something if you do what they want, they usually screw you in the end. No matter what I do, they'll still figure a way to discriminate against me."

She may feel that race or class factors have consistently undermined her attempts to improve her life. While clients may appear to hold such views, they frequently will not articulate them, perhaps in the belief that the therapist will not understand. Some therapists in fact pay practically no attention to political, gender, racial, or class factors that may be having an impact on a client's life. Discussing such factors openly will no doubt bring to light feelings and beliefs that may be critical to the problem.

The client may think that the social and economic system are against her, that no matter what she does, she will never get any real "carrots," and that if she does, they'll probably be full of holes or rotten. If this is the case, what in life has taught her this? Is there anything that she can do to change that? Can the therapist help her increase her belief or confidence or faith that her efforts will pay off and be worth it in the future?

8. **"It's great."** The client may like the positive effects of what he is doing so much that it never occurs to him to think about changing. He may also be thinking, "Whenever I get stoned (high, drunk) I have a great time." There may be nothing irrational about this. It is probably true. In fact, when I listen to some people describing their experiences while drunk or high on cocaine or while gambling, it sounds as if they feel, at that moment, as if they

were in paradise. Other people have very different reactions and continue to use or drink or gamble, but it is clear that for some people the effects *are* extremely positive—better than anything else that they experience in life. So for them even to contemplate cutting those experiences out of their lives is difficult and often terrifying.

The client may also be thinking, "I've made a lot of really good friends drinking. Some of my best friends are old drinking buddies." "A baseball game without beer would be . . . like nothing." All of these statements are true for many people. Having good friends is a sign of good psychological health. However, after he has gotten drunk with his buddies, what happens then? Does he drive home drunk? Does he miss all of his classes or fail to show up at his job the next day?

Even if he really likes what he is doing, why is he ignoring the negative consequences of his behavior? Is using marijuana the only way he knows of relaxing? Is alcohol the only thing that he has found that will quiet his ever-critical voices? What is it he loves about gambling? Smoking? Risky sexual encounters? What is it about his behavior that other people object to so much?

9. "It's exciting." The client may know that what he is doing is frowned on by society and may have negative consequences for him, but he loves the excitement too much to give it up. Perhaps his 9 to 5 life is fairly boring. His favorite addictive behavior provides a welcome antidote. So he may be thinking, "I like excitement in my life. What's wrong with that?" There is nothing irrational or necessarily unhealthy about the first statement. But his challenging question goes to the core of the matter. Does the kind of exciting activity he chooses foul up the rest of his life? Is the trade-off between short-term pleasures and medium- and long-term pains worth it? "I've always liked excitement. I can't stand being bored." This first statement is not irrational either. He is just stating what he likes. But he may get into trouble because he is really thinking (although usually not aware of it), "I've always liked excitement and I have to have what I like when I like it. I can't stand it when I don't get what I like." And the belief "I can't stand being bored" may further worsen the problem. It is really the demandingness and LFT hiding behind his seemingly innocuous statements that create the trouble.

If he likes the excitement, what else is he doing in his life that is exciting? Is there a way of getting a similar "high" legally? Risky behavior leads to altered states of consciousness and many people like that. The therapist may be able to help the client find legal ways to fulfill his need for excitement even as he works at a boring job.

The therapist may also want to explore what prevents him from finding a less boring job or from making his job less boring. There may be real economic and social factors that are preventing him. On the other hand, he may be refusing to take risks in his career despite the fact that he takes risks in other areas of his life. He may feel he can control the risk involved in drug use. In contrast, the risks involved in trying to develop a more interesting way to earn a living are too threatening and long term. In addition, he may be exaggerating the negative, boring aspects of his job, and there are ways he can make his job less boring.

10. "I can get away with it." The client may not think the proverbial "stick" is very large or that it will ever really hit him. That is, he may consistently miscalculate the negative consequences of his actions or the probability that he will suffer those negative consequences. He may be thinking, "I don't think that will happen to me." If he has a consistent pattern of miscalculating risk, does he agree with that hypothesis? How have his calculations worked out in the past? Has he liked the results? Is there anything he wants now that might cause him to consider looking more carefully at how he calculates risk?

11. "I'll start tomorrow." Many clients with addictive problems procrastinate and engage in other forms of avoidant behavior. It may help to ask the client if she procrastinates in other areas of her life. If so, how has that affected her life? While she is working on the more difficult addictive problems, the therapist may be able to demonstrate how to work on easier problems, such as by doing a pre-AB (see Chapter 2) on one of her procrastinating behaviors.

12. "I intend to quit later after a few years, or if it becomes a problem." The client may know that what she is doing may have negative consequences for her, but she thinks she can change her behavior later. The current positive effects are good, so she is not interested in thinking about changing now. For example, most young people know that smoking is bad for them, but they smoke because it helps them bond with their circle of friends. Some young men take up cigar smoking. They enjoy not only the smoking itself, but also the camaraderie they experience smoking with their friends and the networking and business contacts they think it helps facilitate.

If the client acknowledges that what she is doing will hurt her in the long run but figures she can change later, is she correctly assessing the risks? Why do others seem to think differently? The therapist can do an ABC on their hypothesized problem.

13. "I shouldn't have to work so hard to get what I want." The client may not accept (or understand) that change almost always creates discomfort, especially in the initial stages, and that he has to work hard on changing. He may also be saying to himself, "Things should be easier for me. Other people don't have it so hard." "If I admit I have a problem, then I'll have to work on it. That would be a pain, and I couldn't stand the discomfort." "Life is too hard." "I work hard but I like to take it easy (and I must have what I like). My wife shouldn't hassle me so much." "I am not like everyone else. Some people may be able to accept being average. I cannot."

If the client appears to harbor these beliefs, it is also likely that he not only has multiple problems but also is very angry as well. At first, it may be almost impossible for him to acknowledge how he is contributing to his problems. Empathetic, client-centered therapy excels with such a client because he is usually not initially open to suggestions from the therapist, who may be able to make some progress by using variations of Glasser's (1965, 1989) questions: "What do you want? What are you doing? How do you like the results?" Such clients also like the ABCs when they can see that it helps them. This is especially true if the therapist can show them how doing ABCs or identifying their "crooked thinking" may help them with the various difficult people in their lives.

14. "I like being 'bad.'" The client may know that what he is doing is frowned on by society and may have negative consequences for him, for example, going to jail, but he likes being "bad." He may even agree that balance in life is important, including the balance between the good and bad, but at least occasionally he prefers "being on the dark side of the force," as one of my clients put it.

If he likes thinking of himself as being on the bad or evil side, as rejecting ordinary societal values, what does this do for him? How does he benefit? The therapist may not gain much in terms of building a working relationship if he probes too much too soon. But the client may have other problems he is interested in working on.

With clients who think in a very antisocial way, the therapist should be especially careful to observe his own feeling and thinking about what the client is saying. As Kellogg and Triffleman (1998) point out, most therapists normally frame problems as being the result of poor upbringing, traumatic events, chemical imbalances, or distorted thinking. But once they start to think that their client is bad or evil as opposed to upset or disturbed, they have little in their training to fall back on.

15. "Life sucks. What's the point? No one cares anyway." Most mandated clients will probably not admit to such thoughts or feelings, especially in the initial session. But when a client who has been working hard relapses and becomes demoralized and depressed, she may begin to think this way. Standard CBT approaches questioning the validity of each belief may help move a client to Stage II, III, or IV.

16. "Fuck it. It doesn't matter." This is a common thought, especially just before a relapse. How does the client feel at the moment that she thinks or utters such a remark? Probably relief, because she knows she is finally going to drink or use or engage in some other form of addictive behavior.

Doing an ABC(DE) on Someone Else's Problem

Everyone has problems, even a mandated client who doesn't want to be in therapy. Therefore, if the client doesn't want to talk about why he was sent to therapy, he may appreciate the therapist's help in dealing with some other problem. Or he may be interested in working on someone else's problem. In that way, the therapist may be able to demonstrate several significant characteristics about the way he or she works:

1. The therapist has a practical focus, primarily on *how to*.
2. The therapist can listen and empathize, but then wants to help the client figure out how he might help himself over the next week.
3. The therapist is nonjudgmental about the client but not necessarily about his or her behavior. The behavior may be helpful or unhelpful (or even ethical or unethical).

I recently started working with Allen. His wife, Christina, was upset by the amount he was drinking, but he did not see it as much of a problem. Most of his friends drank a lot, he said. Every day after work, he went to a local bar. He is a member of the electrical workers' union. We talked about various union issues, how working conditions were changing in New York, and specifically what kind of work he did. Then I said, "Well, how do you think I can help you?"

He shrugged and then said, "Jeez, I really don't know. I don't think I drink too much, but my wife keeps getting on my case about it."

Of course, I realized that the fact that he was in my office said something. Perhaps he wanted to have a better relationship with his wife or perhaps he had just come to appease her. However, he might think he had a problem but did not want to admit it to his wife or to me. Or perhaps he was suffering from dysthymia (low-grade depression) and although he didn't know exactly what was wrong, he knew something was wrong. Maybe there was some other reason that I had not even guessed at.

"That must not be very pleasant."

"Yes. It's a pain in the ass."

"What do you think she's telling herself to make herself so upset?"

"What?"

"What is she thinking to make herself so upset at you? You are telling me that you don't think you drink so much. But obviously she thinks differently. What do you think she is thinking to make herself so upset?"

"I don't know. I think she just likes to bitch about something. She's become a real nag. I can't believe it. I can't even sit in my own house and relax."

"That does sound like a pain in the ass. Maybe you're right. She just has to have something to worry about and nag you about. Let's assume you're right for a moment. Why would she do that? You look like a bright guy. Why don't you psychoanalyze her a bit. Not like Freud, but, you know, try to analyze what's making her tick. Why is she so upset?"

"I really don't know, but I know she's changed."

"What was she like when you first married her?"

"She was really sweet. And we had a lot of fun together. But not now, brother!"

"How many beers do you drink a night now, two six packs?"

"No! Never that much, and I only drink light beers."

"Well, how many? Eight? Ten?"

"Well, about that. No, six or seven. Sometimes eight, I guess."

"When you and Christina were first together, and you were having a great time together, did you used to do that?"

"Yeah. She used to drink a lot, too. We all hung out at a local bar and she drank almost as much as I did. The next morning she couldn't even remember what we had said the night before."

"And that was okay with you? That didn't bother you?"

"Well, not much. Sometimes I got worried. Her father's a drunk, you know."

"No, I didn't know. But when you first got married and were home, did you drink a lot then, too?"

"No. Only when we went out. When we were home, she would have one or two and I'd have two or three. That's all."

"So what's changed in the past four years? You said you had been married for four years, right?"

"Yeah. I don't know. I guess we just weren't having as much fun, and I just started to have a few more."

"That's too bad, I mean, that you weren't having fun with her anymore. Do you ever have fun together these days?"

"Not often. She just always seems angry at me, and to tell you the truth, I'm not so happy with her, either."

"So maybe you've substituted rum for a relationship?"

"What?"

"It's just an old saying. Some people substitute rum, you know, alcohol, for a relationship. They're not happy and they can't seem to figure out how to be happy in their relationship anymore, so they have another drink, which does make them feel better, at least in the short run. But, of course, it doesn't bring their happy marriage back. Maybe Christina is as miserable as you are—because you do sound miserable. Maybe she's as miserable as you are and she also doesn't know what to do. But she doesn't drink because she's afraid of becoming like her father. In fact, maybe she's worried *you're* going to become like her father. She's going to live her father's and mother's relationship all over again. That would scare the wits out of any sane person. Maybe that's what's making her nag you so much. Do you think that's possible?"

"Maybe."

"Earlier I asked you what she might be telling herself or thinking to make herself so unhappy and to make her nag you so much. Maybe she's thinking: 'Oh, my God. Allen is going to become just like my father. What am I going to do?' "

"Yeah. Maybe."

"Well, what would you do if she drank herself to sleep every night?"

"I don't know."

"Well, think about it. What would you do if she drank herself into a stupor every night and couldn't remember what happened the night before?"

"But I don't do that."

"No. I didn't say you did. But I'm trying to get you to think what you would do or think or feel if *she* did?"

"I don't know."

"I think you'd be scared out of your mind, and pissed, and depressed, because you'd be saying something to yourself like: 'Oh, my God. How did I get into this mess? What am I going to do?'"

"I'm already saying that to myself and she's not even doing that!" he said, laughing a bit nervously.

"Yeah. I'm not surprised. You do seem in a bad place. So Christina may be thinking the same thing to herself, 'Oh, my God. What am I going to do?' She might even be thinking, 'I really love Allen, and I know I'm losing him to the bottle.' She may be really very sad and scared, because what she really, really wanted, a loving, close relationship with you, is going down the drain. Do you think she still loves you?"

"Yes."

"And when you're not mad at her—and, remember, whatever you say here has to stay here. If I repeat it, you can sue me, and take away my license. Is that clear?"

"Yes."

"Okay. When you're not mad at her, do you think you still love her?"

"Yes."

"So this is very sad, isn't it. Neither of you is getting what you want, what you had hoped for. I wonder what we could do to help. How does drinking another beer help?"

"Well, I don't know, it makes me feel better. And, as you said, this is a mess."

"Yes, I know. But the fact that you think she still loves you and that you still love her makes it pretty likely that you can do something to get back on the right track. If you and she were happy, do you think you would drink what you used to drink, two or three a night?"

"Yes. I think so. I mean, now it's no fun to be there. I got nothing to do except watch TV and drink beer."

"So could you agree to no more than three beers a night? Because if you did and you stuck to it, I think several good things would happen. One, Christina might stop freaking out. I can't guarantee it, but if she still nagged you as much, at least I could ask her why. I could really ask her why she was so upset if you were sticking to your agreement. So, one, she would stop nagging you as much. Two, alcohol is a depressant. Do you know that?"

"What do you mean?"

"Well, it's the only legal fast-acting antidepressant and antianxiety drug on the market, but it stinks as a medication because it has a dual personality. First it undepresses you and then two hours later it depresses you. That may be adding to some of your misery. Do other members of your family drink a lot?"

"No. My family's not like Christina's. Everybody drinks in her family."

"So, if you were to cut back, first, I think you might be able to get back some of the fun that's disappeared from your relationship with Christina, and, two, you wouldn't be taking large doses of a depressant every night. I think you would feel better in general, about life and about your wife. Does that make sense to you?"

"Yes. So what should I tell Christina?"

"Well, why don't you ask her to come in with you next time?"

"Okay. But in the meantime, what should I do?"

"That's up to you. What is it that you don't want? Nagging, right? So you could discuss an agreement with Christina. You will never drink more than three beers a night and she won't nag you. How many do you usually have with your buddies after work before you come home, five or six?" [Again, I'm using exaggerated questioning in order to get a more accurate picture of the actual use.]

"No. Usually two or three."

"Well, what are you going to do about that? Do you always want to go with your buddies?"

"No. Not really. But everybody does."

"Everybody? What do you mean by 'everybody'? How many work with you?"

"Six."

"Do all six go?"

"No, Fred has kids, so he has to go right home. Jim likes to hang out but he usually only goes with us on Friday."

"So four of you go."

"Well, no. Only Frankie and Dick."

"So, three of you go. Is that something you really love doing?"

"No. Not exactly. I just kinda got into the habit."

"Well, perhaps that was because it wasn't fun to be with Christina anymore."

"Yeah, maybe."

"Well, we don't have any more time to discuss this. Maybe you better wait until you come back in with Christina to talk about any agreements. Is there anything you could do with Christina that might be fun, to try to get back on the right track?"

"Yeah. We haven't been to the movies, and I used to like to go bowling."

"Well, why don't you ask her out on a date? Court her again. Can you do that?"

"Yeah, maybe."

"Well, only do it if it makes sense to you. Okay?"

"Okay."

Doing an ABC on Another Problem

Even if someone who does not want to be in therapy does not want to work on his alleged problem, he may be interested in help with another problem.

After listening to Allen for a while, it became obvious that he was unhappy with a number of areas in his life, and that he had been for a long time. As is typical with people who suffer from dysthymia, he had tried various ways to manage it. He did not start drinking when he was ten or twelve as seems to be true for many clients, but by fifteen he had discovered that beer made him feel better. It also seemed to make him more socially relaxed, and he always seemed to have more fun when he was drinking than when he was doing anything else. He had never had many hobbies and in high school had participated only on the cross-country track team. He didn't like to fish, hike, cook, work on cars, or ski. He watched a lot of movies on TV and liked to go to the movies, but beyond that, he involved himself in few activities that lifted his spirits. Meeting, dating, and marrying Christina had lifted his spirits, but eventually he had fallen back into a slump.

I think he saw that I recognized his unhappiness, and while we worked on helping him drink more moderately and have a happier life with his wife, I also took time each session to educate him about dysthymia. I tried to help him see that a person with a chronic tendency for low-grade depression had to be more purposeful and planful about adding and keeping activities in his life that he truly enjoyed and that would lift his spirits. In addition, I discussed trying one of the SSRI medications, but I could tell from the expression on his face that he was not going to accept that idea, at least not soon. The idea of being on antidepressants did not fit into his image of himself as a man.

Using the ABCs, I tried to help him see how he made minor depressive feelings worse by saying things to himself like, "I'm going to have a lousy day today" and sneaking in, without being aware of it, "I don't know what's wrong with me. Life sucks. Even Christina doesn't seem to love me anymore." No doubt he had more blue days than some other people he knew, but his drinking and his thoughts about his confusion, helplessness, and hopelessness made his negative feelings much more intense. He then relapsed to the only ways that he knew to make himself feel better—watching TV and more beer.

Mandated clients and other clients who do not think they have a problem always have other problems in their lives, such as difficult bosses, teenage sons, critical parents, and, as with Allen, nagging spouses. Once they see that the therapist is interested in working to find solutions and not in just talking, they may be more motivated.

Of course, initially they may think they can get away with "supervision"—the therapist will help them learn how to therapize the people who are giving them difficulty. But in the end, they will have an opportunity to discover ways to work on their own contributions to these difficult relationships.

Exploring the Client's Goals and Values

What really matters to the client? I always assume until convinced otherwise that every client I am working with wants a fuller, happier life. However, I cannot know what such a life would look like. Does my client really care about his son even though he hasn't contacted him recently? Is his pride as a man very important? Is his religion very important? What does it mean to him to be a Muslim? What impact does that have on his goals and values? Given my client's strong belief in God, what are his responsibilities? What is his role? What did he dream of doing in terms of work? How does being unemployed and having a criminal record affect his outlook on life?

A client may not want to talk about her problems with crack, but that does not mean that she does not want to be a better mother. Since she has such difficulty helping herself, can we help her help herself by focusing on helping her kids (with her recovery a by-product)? What is preventing her from doing that?

Even if the evidence suggests otherwise, I always find it useful to give clients the benefit of the doubt. Most people (but probably not all) seem to have an innate drive to lead as full and meaningful a life as they can. Some readers may think of the term *self-actualize* in this context, but many of my clients are so self-absorbed that I hesitate to use such a term with them. It may only increase their self-absorption. I sometimes have a client who declares adamantly, "My recovery comes first," meaning that the concerns of all other people come second, sometimes a distant second. No doubt recovering is paramount, but his recovery may be dependent on his relationships with other people. Again, the core of the issue is balance. A woman who gives and gives and gives and never thinks of her own needs is liable to become resentful and depressed and drink. But a client who continually puts himself first—even if his recovery is very important—may so alienate his friends and family that he will wind up feeling more alone and miserable than ever.

What does the client value in life and what are his goals? While talking with Allen, it became clear that he very much wanted a loving relationship with Christina. Like many men, he wanted to be supported and loved, not nagged at. He also did not like being so miserable. So instead of working immediately on his drinking, which he did not initially acknowledge as being a problem, I focused instead on how I might help him with his relationship and with his overall unhappiness. That led us back to his consumption of alcohol, which he then admitted he had increased in order to cope with his unhappy marriage. Of course, that increased his wife's distress and her nagging, but without help, he could not see another way to manage.

Value Clarification Exercises

Approximately forty years ago, as a result of the self-actualization movement of the late 1960s, exercises were created to help people clarify what they wanted in life (Simon et al. 1972). In one (illustrated below), participants are asked what they would do if they won a large lottery prize. The idea is to get people to articulate what they would do if money were not an issue. Often people list things that they could do without winning millions of dollars. In another exercise, they are asked to write their obituary, that is, what they would like it to say. (Note: This exercise frightens some people, especially those who are superstitious.)

John and I had seen each other only twice before. He was sitting in my office in his normal work attire: faded jeans, an equally faded plaid flannel shirt, and scuffed, dusty construction boots. John was fortunate because his boss was a fatherly kind of person and had taken a liking to him. He wanted to help him straighten out his life, so he told him he would pay for ten sessions of therapy and that John had to go or lose his job. He had been working for four years as a back-hoe operator, except when he was in jail for assault.

As you might expect, John was not particularly happy sitting in a shrink's office, but he was not openly hostile or contemptuous. He looked more bored and impatient. He admitted that he got drunk and into fights. He said he was not drinking, but he was clear that he did not expect to abstain forever. He had just gotten in trouble again, and he knew he needed to "cool it" for a while. Given his age and considering that many construction workers routinely go to a bar after work for some beers, I wondered what he valued enough to motivate him to reduce the amount he drank and the frequency.

John told me that generally he went straight from work to a bar. Although he lived in upstate New York, he didn't fish or hunt or hike. He hadn't any hobbies. He just worked and drank, and, on occasion, got into fights. We had already starting working on how to better control his anger, so that session I asked him what he would do if he hit the lottery for $40 million. I wanted to try to get him to put aside the everyday worries about money and how to make it and to uncover what he might be dreaming about doing. His answers were quite typical in one respect. Everything was doable if he did not spend so much money on beer and if he kept his job.

"So, suppose you won the $40 million lottery. What would you do then?" I asked.

"I'd like to go to Colorado," he said. "I've seen pictures of the mountains in Colorado. I'd really like to go there myself."

"And what else would you do?"

"Go to the Caribbean. That would be nice. And I'd like to own my own place."

"And what else?"

"I don't know."

"Well, think about it for a minute. You have all of this money and since you don't have to work, you have a lot of time. What would you like to do? How would you like to spend your time?"

"I'd like to take flying lessons. I think that would be really great to be able to fly my own plane."

"Great. Anything else?"

"No. I can't think of anything."

"Well, you know, if you didn't keep losing your job and winding up in jail, and if you stopped drinking and spending so much money on beer, you could certainly save enough to take a vacation to either Colorado or the Caribbean in two months. And you could probably save enough money for a house in four to five years. And, in fact, you could start taking flying lessons in a month or two, as well. I know you make good money operating bulldozers and other kinds of heavy equipment, right? How much did you say you made an hour?

"$28."

"That's what I thought. So if you work 40 hours per week, you make about $1,000 per week, and you have practically no living expenses, right?"

"Yup."

"So you could do these things, right? But maybe it's too scary. It would take too much courage to do those things. Is there anything stopping you from doing those things if you had the money?"

"No."

"But beer drinking is quicker and easier and cheaper in the short run. And you get that good feeling and you get to hang out with all of your buddies. Maybe you like that better than a vacation in the Caribbean?"

"Yeah, maybe. But I think I've had enough of that."

"Do you understand my point?"

"Yeah, I think so."

"But it's your life, right? You have to choose what you do. That's up to you. I'm not going to sit here and judge you if you want to drink beer. I'll admit that I think you'll have a happier life if you don't just drink beer, but that's for you to figure out. Okay?"

"Yeah."

"So you have four goals. Which one do you think you'll try to do first? Colorado or the Caribbean?"

"The Caribbean."

In subsequent sessions we talked further about his learning to drive his life like he drives his heavy equipment. It was clear that no one had given John much advice in life or had cared very much what he did, one way or another. I suggested that he had been living his life like sitting in the back seat of car. He kind of just went where someone else happened to drive, and that he shouldn't complain about it if he didn't want to get in the driver's seat himself. It was up to him.

There are many other approaches and exercises therapists can use to explore a client's medium- and long-term goals. This is important work because without long-term goals, some clients will not be sufficiently inspired and motivated to pass up the short-term pleasures that have gotten them into therapy. AA also puts an emphasis on time with several sayings, for example, "One day at a time." But that means that a person has to take care of today in order not to ruin tomorrow. That is one way of ensuring that life will be different tomorrow compared to what used to be true.

PROBLEMS THERAPISTS MAY ENCOUNTER

The Client Does Not Want to Work with the Therapist

When clients are mandated to see therapists, it is clearly a difficult situation, and therapists can easily make mistakes to worsen the situation. For example, if they work from the medical model and see themselves as the doctor, they may quickly become frustrated with what they perceive as difficult, noncompliant, and resistant patients. In contrast, if their primary goal is to get the client to be at least somewhat interested in working with them, they may feel very differently about working with such clients. The therapist's first job is to move a client from precontemplation—in this case, from not thinking about working with the therapist, to contemplation, that is, to being ambivalent about working with the therapist instead of downright opposed. Everything that I discuss in this chapter and the next on helping clients move from Stage I to II or from Stages II and III to IV applies to motivating a client. If the client is ambivalent about working with the therapist, the therapist has a choice. He can think of the client's ambivalence as a positive sign—at least she is considering the pros and cons of working with him—or he can see it as further evidence that she really is a so-called "difficult" client.

To review, three key elements seem crucial: respect, compassion, and know-how. If the client sees that the therapist treats her respectfully and appreciates the difficulties inherent in a human life (that is, he has compassion), he will at least have set the foundation for possible future work. Then if she sees that the therapist has know-how, that he can be of practical value, she may be willing to dare to try to change. She may have met many other therapists in the past who did not respect her or who seemed unduly interested in probing her private inner life or who appeared to have little appreciation for the difficulties of her life. Why should she trust the therapist now? In fact, a psychologically healthy person would approach such a situation—having to work on very personal problems with a therapist that she has not chosen—with considerable caution.

Developmental Issues

Few teenagers and young adults decide to abstain, especially for the rest of their lives, from the use of alcohol. The same may be true for nicotine and marijuana. It may be true that those who experiment with marijuana and alcohol early in life also wind up using cocaine or heroin or both, but this may simply mean that they experimented with many activities, including sex and gambling, that cause mild or major altered states of consciousness, help them bond with their peers, rebel, and so forth. Bonding and taking some risks is part of growing up, but, unfortunately, some people take much larger risks than others.

The underlying beliefs of a teenager or young college student are probably not going to be similar to those of a 45- or 55-year-old client. So it is critical to take into account the age and developmental stage of the client. What is he trying to work on at this moment in time and how do the behaviors that he may be addicted to seem to help? What would help him reduce the harm he may do to himself or others (see, for example, the BASICS [Brief Alcohol Screening and Intervention for College Students] Program [Dimeff et al. 1999]).

Institutional Issues

If therapists work in a facility that demands abstinence of its clients, they must, of course, adhere to its policies. But if the facility's outcome data suggest that the program is not working very well, therapists may want to reevaluate their ways of working. The concept of reducing the harm a client may do to himself or others is sound (Marlatt 1998, Tatarsky 1998). Moreover, Valliant's (1996) study suggests that alcohol abuse and dependence are chronic problems for many people. They oscillate between periods of abstinence, attempts at controlled drinking, and abuse/dependence throughout their lives. During that time, treatment facilities and counselors and therapists may be able to do a great deal to reduce the problems that these clients create. For example, although a client may return to heavy drinking at times, the therapist may be able to get him to change some of his other behaviors.

Above all, the therapist and the facility will want to try to ensure that a client feels comfortable calling when she is having problems again, and that she will call sooner rather than later. This is an important outcome of therapy. If a client makes a call after three days of drinking rather than after three months or three years, that greatly reduces the risk that she will seriously harm herself or others.

FIVE HOMEWORK ASSIGNMENTS

The purpose of homework assignments is to further the goals of the first session, in this case to get another session, and to move the client from Stage I to II, from precontemplation (perhaps denial) to contemplation, from "I don't have a problem" to "Maybe I do." Here are five suggestions:

✓ **Autobiographies.** The client can write about the worst five years of his life, or the best five years, or the best experience in his life. Most people like to tell their story, and they are sometimes pleased that the therapist is interested.

✓ **A drinking log.** The client keeps a log, on a piece of paper, of how much he is drinking. This assignment is more appropriate for Type II clients, but some Type I clients may be interested in doing it (see Chapter 8).

✓ **Recreation.** Many clients who engage in addictive behaviors do not know how to relax and have fun, to do something recreational, without their favorite substance or addictive activity. At the end of one session, Allen's assignment was to do something fun both by himself and with his wife. The therapist should help the client decide what he is going to do and when. It should be very specific. In Allen's case, when I asked him what he thought he might do, he said, "Well, I still haven't finished painting the bathroom and Christina has been nagging me about that for two months now."

I looked at him dumbfounded. "I don't think you understood the assignment," I said. "You are supposed to do something that you would enjoy, that would be fun! Painting is a chore. I admit that it would probably make Christina happy, but we are looking for something that would make you happy! What can you think of?"

It took him five minutes to finally say that he thought he would go get new strings for his guitar. He had always enjoyed playing the guitar and Christina liked it, too. He thought he would enjoy doing that. I was not sure, because he did not sound very enthused, but I decided to wait until the next session to see whether or not he had actually had fun doing it. Then we discussed what he could do with Christina that he would enjoy, and that led into a discussion regarding how he might have more fun with her making love.

✓ **Prayer.** As I discuss in greater detail in Chapter 15, if the client is religious and usually prays, the therapist can suggest that he might pray for clarification in this situation. Even if he believes in "God's will be done" and the Lord's prayer, what is his role? What can he do to help with this situation? Is there a passage in the Bible or a psalm that he thinks relates to his situation? The therapist can ask him to find it and bring it in. As noted above, even if he resents having to be in therapy, he still probably has plenty of problems in his life, and the therapist may gain insight into those problems by getting him to discuss them from his religious point of view.

✓ **Dreams.** Sometimes when I ask people if they have had any dreams or if they have had any especially troubling dreams lately, they respond, "I didn't think you people talked about dreams!" But, of course, dreams often reveal new things about how a client thinks and often helps him start to talk about what is troubling him. Fritz Perls (1969) developed a number of effective ways to work with people using their dreams that can fairly easily be dovetailed with CBT techniques. The client can try to remember one of his dreams and bring it in to a session. Here again, however, with some clients, such a request from the therapist will just be seen as prying and it will work against the therapy.

With a mandated client, sensitivity and creativity are essential if the therapist wants to increase the chances that the client will think therapy is not a waste of time.

MEDICATIONS

Although not acknowledging or agreeing that he has an addictive behavior, the client may be visibly suffering from some other form of psychological disturbance, such as dysthymia (low-grade, chronic depression) or social anxiety. If he is not interested in therapy, he may still be interested in visiting a doctor, preferably a psychiatrist, but if he is unwilling or cannot afford to do that, a visit to his internist might be better than nothing. If he looks unhealthy or seems disturbed, the therapist can say, "I will be happy to work with you, but first you will have to have an internist [if the problem looks physical, or psychiatrist if the problem appears psychological] examine you." I have never had a client reject that. Clients seem glad that I am concerned enough to push them to see a medical doctor even if it meant I would not see them again if they refused.

Mentioning medication to some clients simply alienates them, because they do not acknowledge that they have a problem. But with other clients, like Allen, suggesting medication, especially if one's tone demonstrates genuine concern, may be a clear indication that the therapist is interested in helping and does not want to spend session after session just talking.

RESOURCES

- The MATCH Manual, *Motivational Enhancement Therapy Manual* (Miller et al. 1992), is full of helpful suggestions, including specific questions to ask to enhance a client's motivation to change. It is available for free by contacting the National Institute on Alcohol Abuse and Alcoholism, 5600 Fishers Lane, Rockville, MD 20857. The manual also contains the handouts given to clients. These include useful information regarding the effects of blood alcohol levels and the numbers of hours alcohol remains in a person's body given different number of drinks; for example, on average, alcohol remains for 6.5 hours in a man weighing 160 pounds after he has consumed five drinks. Alcohol remains for 10.5 hours in a woman of the same weight after five drinks.
- A videotape, "Motivational Interviewing," can be obtained from William R. Miller, Department of Psychology, University of New Mexico, Albuquerque, NM 87131-1161. Miller and his associates also run workshops on motivational interviewing.

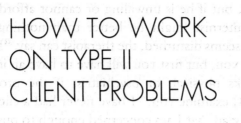

8 HOW TO WORK ON TYPE II CLIENT PROBLEMS

Heaven never helps the man who will not act.
—Sophocles

"I'm not sure I have a problem."

"I think I have a problem but I don't know what to do. What are my options?"

Clients who are ambivalent about changing are the norm in psychotherapy. Even clients suffering from panic attacks, agoraphobia, and/or depression may be ambivalent. They may hate the symptoms, but they may be very ambivalent about doing what will help eliminate them. Medications may help agoraphobia, but the best approach appears to be cognitive-behavioral therapy (CBT), perhaps in combination with medication. However, the CBT approach entails taking small, consistent steps, each of which involves some discomfort.

But ambivalence about changing is not limited to psychological problems. People suffering from back pain want something to eliminate the pain. They may be very willing to take a pill, but they are often much less enthusiastic and consistent about doing all of the other things that may help, for example, losing weight, doing stretching and relaxation exercises, thinking differently about problems in their lives, and simply getting up and moving around. Only about 30 percent of people suffering from hypertension do what they are supposed to do, including taking their medication (O'Brien and McLellan 1998). So clients who are ambivalent about changing are the norm, not the exception, when we consider many human afflictions, not just addictions.

Most of my clients have a number of different problems and are in different stages with respect to each problem.

When I first began treating Cecilia, she was very clear that she wanted to stop using cocaine. Cocaine was a Type III problem for her, and, in fact, she stopped relatively quickly. She also knew she wanted to stop using heroin, but she could not bring herself to the point of deciding what to do. She went back and forth between snorting and injecting and using less and using more until she finally decided to go to a methadone clinic. Thus, for a long time, her heroin problem was a Type II problem, and we spent a great deal of time exploring her ambivalence and considering various treatment options. Her ongoing anger toward herself and toward practically everyone in her life and life in general was a Type I problem. That is, she did not see it as a problem—at least, that is what she said—and she was totally uninterested in working on it, even though I thought it was a continuing source of trouble that contributed to a lot of her other problems.

Cecilia is not unusual, even among a nonclinical population. Most of us have a number of problems that we are working on. Some of them are Type III problems and we are making quite conscious attempts to change our behaviors. Others are Type II problems. We are quite inconsistent in working on them. Some weeks we are in the action phase and are quite determined to change, and then we slide back to the contemplation stage and do not work on changing at all for weeks or months. Is this not the case with eating and exercising, as well as with other activities we may want to engage in or not engage in, such as writing, doing more research, and paying our bills in a more timely fashion? And there are still other problems that we are only dimly aware of and are not actively thinking about changing.

SELECTED CLINICAL STRATEGIES

Session Goals

The session goals for Type II clients are as follows:

1. To move the client from contemplation to action, from Stage II, through Stage III, to Stage IV.
2. To explore possible plans with the client.

Exploring the Problem

Here are some typical beliefs of clients that therapists should watch for:

"I want to change, but I can't."

"If I don't smoke, I'm like a witch—and no one can stand me—I'll lose the few friends I have. You wouldn't believe how mean I am."

"When I use heroin, I know how I am going to feel. That's about the only thing I *can* control in my life (so I have to continue using. It is scary and makes me uncomfortable to even think of getting through life without heroin.)."

"It's just too hard. I've tried before and I've failed every time. (I couldn't stand failing again.)"

"I can't be bothered, at least, not right now."

Some other possible unstated, hidden beliefs include:

"When I feel bad—hopeless, down, helpless—I also feel bad about myself, like *I'm* a failure, a total screw-up. But when I'm high, I feel better about myself. It seems like the only way I can feel better about myself."

"There's no point. Life sucks. Nothing I ever do turns out right."

"I can't change."

"If I change, I'll no longer be me."

The therapist's own beliefs may impede treatment, such as:

"What is the matter with this person? How much evidence does he need? He's never going to make any real effort to change. He's just jerking my cord."

"What a jerk! He keeps screwing up his life but he never learns."

When therapists get frustrated with a client who seems to stay forever in Stage II, a "chronic ambivalater," they should remember the extensive research showing that most people take quite a while to change.

Showing Respect

As I discussed in Chapter 5, if therapists begin to lose respect for a client, they will probably also cease to be effective because they may fall back into traditional, stereotypical thinking about so-called alcoholics and addicts. If a client is really frustrating, perhaps the therapist has invested too much in her changing, thinking, "After all my time and work, she's still doing the same thing. She's impossible." Freud identified repetitive patterns of behavior as the most difficult problems for patients to work on. Thus, the therapist should be thinking, "She and I have worked for a long time. It would be nice if she could see the advantages to changing or how to overcome her fear of changing, but evidently she can't, yet. Maybe I can find another way to help her." Continuing to maintain a professional, scientific interest in the problem will also help.

Showing Empathy, Support, and Compassion

The client probably does not enjoy watching herself remain stuck. Having the therapist and perhaps her family and friends watching as well doesn't make her feel any better. Many people know what it is like to find oneself falling back into the same old patterns again and again. That is perhaps why some recovering (and recovered) individuals think, "You have to be one to treat one." They find that some therapists do not understand the struggle.

Finding Some Common Ground

If therapists have had an addictive problem that they have resolved, they may be able to use that experience to their advantage in working clients. However, there are two potential pitfalls:

1. They may think that what was true for them will be or should be true for everyone else. "That is the way I recovered," they may think. "Why can't he get it? It worked for me." "He's just in denial." Unfortunately, everyone is not the same and what worked for one person may have no meaning or usefulness for someone else. That is the problem with some of the more zealous twelve-step enthusiasts. They cannot grasp that what makes so much sense to them, what has helped them so immensely in changing their lives, makes no sense to some people. Such people are not necessarily in denial. They just look at life and their problems differently.

2. They may share too much. Their desire to help may cause them to say too much about their life and struggles (see Chapter 5).

Waiting for More Information

If therapists need more information from the client, they can explore an area that has not been explored before. Lazarus's (1981, 1997) mnemonic BASIC-ID (Chapter 4) helps in checking all areas that might be relevant. Thus, therapists may discover an aspect of the client's thinking that is contributing to her difficulty in changing.

Exploring Possible Historical Roots

If a client wants to change, the therapist may not need to probe deeply into his inner psychological makeup to help him. However, if a client seems stuck, or moves into the action phase only to move right back to the contemplative stage, it may be necessary to better understand the possible historical roots of this pattern of behavior. On the other hand, the therapist can quickly become mired in traditional therapy, losing the balance between working on the addictive behavior during a portion of every session and exploring the roots.

Discuss the Reality of Conflicting Wants

Everyone has conflicting wants. A client who is ambivalent about changing one or more addictive behaviors is almost always struggling with two issues: balance and time. How does he want to balance short-, medium-, and long-term pleasures? How does he want to use his time? What we do in the short run always has an impact on how we feel and think and what we do (and can do) in the medium and long run. Addictive behaviors always have a positive impact in the short run and a negative impact in the medium and long run. In fact, one reason a young person may disagree with an older person about whether or not he is addicted is that in his mind the medium- and long-run effects are, on balance, positive. Even though he may acknowledge that he missed too many classes and thus got kicked out of school, he may perceive his all-night binges as the reason he now has a group of friends.

My client Carrie knows that drinking at night is ruining her life. However, she is so ambivalent about changing that she has continued to drink almost nightly. Yet she wants to go to work tomorrow feeling physically more alert and less tired and rundown, and she wants to have more activities in her life. She wants to have a long-term relationship with someone. She wants to start sailing in the summers. She wants to start cooking more. But instead, she keeps just getting up, going to work, coming home, and drinking white wine. In other words, at 6 P.M. every day she jettisons her medium- and long-term goals and satisfies her short-term goals: relief, a little pleasure, and then, best of all, oblivion.

"I want to stop drinking, but every night I just start all over again," Elissa says. She can't understand why she keeps opting for her short-run wants over her medium- and long-run wants. I pointed out that that is not true. At 6:30 A.M. she opts to do what will satisfy her medium- and long-term wants. At 6:30 A.M., like most of us, she probably wants to stay in her nice, warm bed. But if she does, at 9:30 she will be twisting and turning, on one level wishing she had gone to work because she is now having to call in sick and lie, and she knows that if she calls in sick too many times she may lose her job, jeopardizing her entire lifestyle—apartment, car, vacations. So she gets up and, shivering, goes to the bathroom to start the day—that is, to try to fulfill her medium- and long-term objectives. So she does not always fulfill her short-term wants at the expense of her medium- and long-term wants.

Carrie is a very good worker. All of her colleagues tell her that. In fact, she works very hard. She rarely if ever takes lunch. She is the one in the office whom everyone can count on. She is the one who is given the extra project that someone else has messed up. At times, it may be gratifying for her to come up with creative solutions to the immediate problems in the office. But if she thinks about whether she would rather be sailing or sitting in an office, there is no question what the answer is. However, she stays put and does her work. Unlike some of her colleagues, she rarely avoids grappling with difficult problems. She clearly has a high tolerance for frustration at work.

But when she comes home, she behaves differently. Why? As Marlatt (1985a) has suggested, her lifestyle is out of balance. She does too many of the things she thinks she *should* do and not enough of the things she *wants* to do. In brief, in the evening, she is tired, hungry, and angry, and it is much easier to reach for a chemical—in this case, ethanol in white wine—to change her mood and feelings than it would be to go to a sailing class or even to read. In essence, she is a different person at 7:00 P.M. and in a different setting, so the way she balances the gratification of her wants changes.

It is not that she does not know how to delay gratification. Anyone watching her during the day can see easily that she knows very well how to delay gratification. But when she comes home, she makes other decisions that make it appear as if she will not delay gratification any longer.

Many clients do not seem to be fully aware of how conflicted they are over their various wants and desires. They keep opting for short-run wants, undermining their medium- and long-run pleasures.

Discuss an Experimental Plan

Clients who are ambivalent are trying to figure out what they want to do. When they seem ready, the therapist can explore what might work for them—a plan that they can try out between sessions. Gollwitzer (1999) suggests that the more the therapist can get the client to specify how she plans to carry out her intentions, the better the chances are that she will do what she plans. For that reason, when helping a client develop a plan (even an experimental plan), the therapist should spend considerable time helping her spell out precisely what she wants to do and how she intends to do it.

Steps to Forming a Plan

Ask Specifying Questions

The therapist should ask questions that help to specify both what the problem is and what plan the client is willing to try to adopt.

A few years ago a professional-looking young woman walked into my office. After we had chatted a while, Carol said, "I don't know if I have a problem, but I think I do."

"What's the problem."

"I drink a lot of wine."

"How much?"

"A bottle a night."

Carol looked as if she weighed about 110 pounds, so I immediately thought that she probably did have a problem, but I continued, "Every night?"

"Yes."

"Do you always finish the bottle?"

"No. I buy those half gallon jugs, so I drink about half every night."

"That's a lot of alcohol. Have you had a general checkup lately?"

"Yes. Everything's okay. Of course, I didn't tell him I was drinking every night."

"Hmmm. Well, what would you like to do?"

"I think maybe I should cut down."

Working with an ambivalent, Type II client, the therapist first has to try to help her decide what she would like to try to do. Would she like to stop drinking for three weeks? a week? every other day? Does she want to cut down to half a bottle of wine per night, every night? Including Fridays and Saturdays? In brief: What is she willing or able to do at this point in time? What kind of plan would help her get what she wants?

When Carol indicated that she wanted to cut down, I responded by saying, "Usually when someone wants to moderate her drinking, I suggest that she stop for a month, and then we can see what to do next."

She looked at me as if I had suggested she cut off her legs.

"A month seems too long?" I asked.

"Yes."

"What about a week?"

She looked dismayed.

"Do you think you could not drink for a week?"

"Do I have to?" she asked.

"No. You don't have to do anything. What do you *want* to do?"

"I don't know."

"Well, now what would you like to do? What about drinking every other night? How does that sound?"

"Yes. Maybe. That sounds okay." But then she half smiled and half frowned. "Does that mean both Friday and Saturday night?"

"Yes, I think it does," I smiled back. "Which would you prefer? Today's Tuesday. So do you want to not drink on Tuesday, Thursday, and Saturday, or not drink on Wednesday, Friday, and Sunday?"

She thought for a while. Of course, by this time, my assessment—and perhaps her own—had proceeded quite far. But I always think it is preferable for the client to decide how serious the problem is. It is for her to decide in light of the other things she wants in her life.

Ask Implementation Questions

Gollwitzer (1999) calls the client's specific plans for how she intends to carry out her plan "implementation intentions." They help her implement her plans. The therapist should help the client specify exactly when and how she is going to do whatever she plans to do. For example, if her goal is to not drink for one week, the therapist can help her increase the odds that she will manage to do that by getting her to plan very carefully what she is going to do instead at those moments when she would normally drink.

Working with Carol, I knew that not only would it help to get her to specify how she was going to carry out her plan but that it was also important to try to increase her motivation. So I continued by saying, "You know that's a lot of wine to drink every night, given your size. I certainly couldn't do that and function the next day. How do you feel the next day?"

"Well, in the morning, pretty awful. And I don't seem to be doing anything else with my life."

I wasn't surprised by that answer. "If you drank less, you know," I said, "you'd feel a lot better the next day. What about if you bought half bottles and only drank one?"

"But they're too expensive," she said, again with a smile.

"Not really, because you would be drinking less. Those jugs cost about $7.99. Right?"

"Yes. That's what they cost."

"And you buy three or four per week. Right?"

"Yup."

"Well, if you buy three half bottles, they'll cost about the same. Of course, they'll probably be better wine. Do you think you would be willing to do that?"

"Yes. Maybe that's a good idea."

"Well, I think you'd certainly feel better. You're putting a lot of ethanol into your body every night. Alcohol is a wonderful, fast-acting antidepressant and antianxiety medication, but is has a dual personality. Later, it's a depressant. Instead of taking Prozac every-day, you're taking 'anti-Prozac.' I'm not surprised you're not doing much else with your life besides work. Drinking a half a bottle would definitely help."

Caution: The therapist must stay on track when trying to help a client come up with a workable, possible plan. She may start to talk about other problems she is grappling with because she is afraid to really develop a plan, which would mean changing. Or, based on her experience in other therapy sessions, she may be more accustomed to talking about the *why* than focusing on the *how*. She may be used to talking about the past in therapy and may wander off to say more about what she thinks are the roots or causes of her problems. Generally, I try to gently guide the discussion back to setting up the plan. Occasionally, it becomes clear that the client wants to talk a bit more about the causes of her behavior before moving on to actually working on changing it, so I listen before proceeding.

I chose to listen to Carol for a few minutes because we were making good progress, there was plenty of time left in the session, and I was also interested in the roots of her problems. I knew that without understanding some of the underlying psychodynamic factors, I might not be able to effectively help her avoid relapses.

Is the plan reasonable?

I set up a plan for going to the gym for Betty, a young, fit woman. She had gotten into the habit of smoking pot every evening at home after work, and as part of trying to stop completely (her plan for her marijuana use), she thought going to the gym would help. But she initially suggested going every night. I thought that that was crazy, perhaps because I hate going to the gym. It seemed totally unreasonable to expect that she would stick to such a plan—and perhaps it was not even healthy. However, it turned out she had loved being at the gym when she went in the past. She liked hanging out there. She liked flirting with some of the trainers. So then it became clear that what would be unreasonable for many people was reasonable for her.

Ask Commitment Questions

Once a reasonable experimental plan has been worked out, the therapist should determine how committed the client is to it.

As for Carol, her plan seemed reasonable. She was a professional woman and had always worked very hard, and I thought that the chances that she could cut her drinking in half and drink every other day seemed reasonable. But when I asked her, "How committed are you to this plan?" she made a face indicating not only some doubt but also some displeasure at the idea.

Ask Likelihood Questions

It is always important to try to gauge to what extent the client may be just going along with the therapist. Even if the client is committed, how likely does the client think it is that she will actually do the plan?

Ask Derailing Questions

No matter how confident the client is and how committed, the therapist should explore how her best intentions might become undone.

I asked Carol, "How do you think you might derail your plan?"

"I don't know. I think I can do it."

"Well, think a little. You didn't look very pleased by the idea when I asked you a moment ago. For example, what about Saturday? You aren't supposed to drink on Saturday. What happens if you get invited to a party?"

"Couldn't I change my plan?"

"Well, usually if you start wiggling around making changes for this reason and making changes for that reason, your plan will look like Swiss cheese before long. If you're going to change it, it would be better to change it right here, when you can think straight. We could revise it—to every other day, except Friday and Saturday. In other words, you would start off not drinking on Tuesdays, Thursdays, and Sundays. But on Fridays and Saturdays, you would drink. Does that sound more reasonable? We want to figure out a plan that you will stick to."

"Yes, I like that better."

"But on Saturday night, you can't bring a half bottle to a party, so what are you going to do?"

"That's not a problem. I never drink too much when I'm with people."

"Never?"

"No, really. I don't get in trouble when I'm with people. I usually only have two drinks, maybe three, but never more."

"Okay. So that won't be a problem. By the way, how will you get to the party. Drive?"

"Well, yes."

"Have you ever gotten a DWI?"

"No. No, I never drink when I'm going to have to drive."

"I thought you said you were going to drive to the party?"

"Well, yes, I mean, no. My friend Frank is going to take me."

"Oh. Okay. You just don't drink if you are driving?"

"Yes."

"That's your plan?"

"Yes."

"Good."

"Now let's go back and review what you have decided and I will write it down and make a Xerox copy and give it to you when you leave. Okay?"

"Yes."

"So what have you decided on?"

"I'm not going to drink on Tuesdays, Thursdays, and Sundays."

"And what else?"

"Oh, that's right," she said with a smile. "I'm going to buy half bottles."

"Do you think you'll open two half bottles in an evening?"

"No. I don't think I'd be that bad."

"Well, it's not really a question of being 'bad,' but we can talk about that another time. How confident are you that you can stick to this plan?"

"Pretty."

"How much is 'pretty'? What percent? 75? 50? 95?"

"75 percent? I think."

Ask Questions that Increase the Likelihood of Success

The therapist should explore with the client what she might do to increase the likelihood that she will succeed. Often clients know what has helped in the past.

"You seem pretty unsure," I said to Carol. "What could you do to increase the odds that you will follow your plan? What about telling your boyfriend about your plan? Wouldn't that help?"

"Yes, I guess so. I know he worries that I drink too much."

"Well, do you want to do that?"

"Yes."

We then spent some time exploring what she was going to drink instead of wine on Tuesdays, Thursdays, and Sundays. Because she was not overweight, we discussed other nice things she could enjoy on those days instead of alcohol, like a nice dessert, going shopping for a new outfit, and so on.

Ask Summarizing Questions

The therapist should have the client summarize the plan she is agreeing to try. Carol and I did not have time during that first session to go through the seven points, outlined in Table 4–1 in Chapter 4, but when she came in the next session, I intended to do so whether she had successfully followed her plan or not.

Reviewing Successes and Failures: Doing Pre-AB's and Post-BC's

Reviewing Successes

In the next session, the therapist can begin by asking, "How did the week go? Did you succeed in maintaining your plan?" If the answer if yes, the therapist should continue to explore what happened in some depth. Clients often downplay the importance of their successes. They think of a therapy session as a time to talk about problems, not successes. But in learning new behavioral patterns, examining how and when we have succeeded may be even more important than examining how and when we failed. It is important for the therapist to get clients to review how they succeeded in maintaining their plan. The therapist can ask:

"What did you do to help maintain your plan?"

"What did you say to yourself that was helpful?"

"What did you say to other people?"

"How did you feel?"

"What did you do that was helpful?"

Reviewing Failures

The therapist should discuss with the client that failing to do something does not make him a failure, and that failing does not have to have a negative impact on his self-esteem. However, it is natural to feel annoyed and disappointed if one does not get what one wants. And if he has hurt himself or, worse, someone else by failing to maintain his plan, it is natural to feel even stronger negative emotions.

When to Explore Pre-AB's

If the client has not successfully maintained her plan, the therapist can explore what happened, that is, the pre-AB's, the activating events and beliefs/thoughts that contributed to (that came before) the lapse or relapse.

The therapist should try to visualize what seems to have occurred and what the client said to herself to convince herself to break her plan. This may require going quite far back in time to get at the beginnings of the lapse or relapse.

When to Explore Post-BC's

If the client seems upset about what has happened, the therapist can explore the post-BC's, what she is telling herself and how she is feeling now, after the lapse or relapse. The therapist can focus on post-BC's if he is concerned that the client may start another lapse or relapse unless she changes the way she is feeling and thinking. In other words, it seems likely she will use or drink or gamble more quite soon to cope with her negative feelings and thoughts.

When Carol came into my office the following Tuesday, I asked her, "How did it go? How did it work out?"

She looked at me with a kind of sick expression on her face.

"What happened?" I asked gently.

"I didn't stick to it."

"Really? What happened?"

"I drank every night."

From the sick, despairing look on her face, I knew that at least she now knew she had a problem, and a serious one at that. She was no longer ambivalent and that was a plus. I started to ask her about the week, proceeding gently and compassionately. I knew she was very upset about what had happened.

"What happened Tuesday night?" I asked.

"Well, a half a bottle is not very much, you know, and I just wanted more, and I had a jug in the house left over, so I opened it. I think I drank about a third more."

"Then what happened on Wednesday?"

She looked even more sheepish, although I could not help but note an impish little smile as she said, "Well, you know, Marlina came over and I haven't seen her in over a year, and we just felt like celebrating, and it was Wednesday night."

"Yes, but you had decided to stick to half a bottle when you drank."

"Yes, I know. But it didn't seem to matter. And we always had such a good time together. In fact, we had a good time again."

"And Friday?"

"I was good on Friday. I just drank one of the half bottles I had bought like you suggested, and it *was* better wine, as you also suggested," she added, with a twinkle in her eye. She seemed to have had a fun week and to be enjoying telling me about it.

"And on Saturday."

"I went to that party, remember, so I just stuck to my two drinks. It wasn't hard. I told you, parties are not a problem."

"And on Sunday."

"I don't know. It just didn't seem to matter, and it was in the house, and I was feeling blue—I always get blue Sunday nights—I guess because I don't really like my job, and I just had what was left in the jug."

"About a bottle?"

"No, less, I think."

As I mentioned above, I had noted that mixed in with her misery seemed to be some pleasure at telling me about her "slips," but I decided to take that up in later in the session. Instead, I asked, "Well, what do you want to do?"

"Well, I guess I really have a problem, don't I?"

"Yes, I guess you do. So what do you want to do?"

"Well, I think I want to stop, but I don't seem to be doing a very good job of it."

"Yes, that's true. In fact, you may find that you can't do it all by yourself. You may find that you have so conditioned yourself or that your chemistry has changed—we really do not know which—but something may be so strong that you cannot do this by yourself. You may have to join a group or work with more people than just me."

"Really? I don't want to do that."

"Yes, I hear you. But you may finally decide, because you want something else even more that you will have to do something else if you are going to overcome your problems with alcohol."

"Do you think I have to give it up completely?"

"I don't know for sure, of course. I haven't got a crystal ball, unfortunately. But you may not be able to drink when you are alone. That is when you lose control. When you feel alone and down, nothing seems to matter anymore. When you are drunk, you can't think straight because you are drunk. When you are lonely and depressed, you can't think straight either, so I think it's highly unlikely you can drink while you're at home and alone—or even have alcohol in the house. But we can see. Perhaps I am being too negative. You can see for yourself over the next few weeks and months."

Coping with Urges

A client is going to be less likely to dare to try changing if he thinks he may be unable to cope with the urges he expects will come. Clients have many reasons for not taking steps to change, but they are especially concerned with their inability to cope and with failing. I give clients the instruction sheet "Coping with Urges" (Table 8–1) as a reminder.

Table 8–1.   Coping with urges

1. Keep a log. Urges only seem to "come out of the blue." As much as possible, get to know the stimuli that trigger them. For example:
   5:30 P.M. upon leaving work
   home alone at 10 P.M.
   when my husband leaves
   after a fight with my wife
   at a business cocktail party
   at dinner with some friends
   at a wedding
   on a particular street corner
   a smell
2. Watch out for apparently irrelevant decisions (Marlatt 1985a). Get to know the ways you convince yourself to repeat your old pattern of behavior.
3. Anticipate and have your policy or strategy worked out in advance.
4. Learn what helps you stick to your policy.
   Don't let the "committee" convince you to reconsider the question.
   What is happening is the result of combination of factors: psychological, neurochemical, social, developmental, etc. Don't get into a debate with another aspect of your self.
   You can reset your policy at another time, when you are thinking straighter.
5. Have a "to do" list of projects, chores, and recreational activities that you want and need to do.
6. Use the HALT acronym:
   Try to avoid becoming overly Hungry.
   Try to avoid getting Angry (practice ABC's).
   Try to avoid getting Lonely.
   Try to avoid getting Tired.
7. Occupy your mind with something else (distract yourself)
   Go to a meeting.
   Talk to or call a helpful friend.
   Eat something.
8. Focus on what you do want—in the medium and long run.
9. Don't focus only on what you don't want. (That's like telling yourself: "Don't think of a pink elephant." You will only stimulate your urges.) A negative goal—"I don't want to drink"—usually won't be sufficient.
10. Learn how to take better care of yourself. Take more responsibility for your emotional and physical life.

When Should the Client Use a Coping Tactic and When Should He Use the ABC(DE)'s?

If the client can think straight, he should work on his thinking. That is, it would probably be helpful for him to use the ABC(DE) technique and try to get at what is "stinking" about his thinking. But what if he cannot think straight? Let's suppose it's 5:30 P.M., and he is walking out of his office building. The sun is setting, and he is tired after a long day of work. He used to have a drink at a nearby bar. If he has an urge to do so now, it is not very likely he can count on himself to think straight. His fatigue, plus feeling hungry, plus the long day, plus all of the environmental cues around him may have an unacknowledged impact on his thinking. He had better select—in advance, when he can think straight—some tactics that he is going to use on the spot without thinking about it in any analytical kind of way. If he is seduced into reconvening the committee (see Chapter 1), he can almost always count on what the committee will vote to do.

The client's tactics may be as simple as saying to himself, "Oh, no. I'm not listening to any of that bullshit. I know where that leads." Other clients may benefit from using a dissociative technique (as a tactic), acting *as if* the part of them that wants to have a drink or get drugs or smoke or gamble is, in fact, not a part of them. It is their "lizard" or the "liquor salesman" or their "inner child" or "the whiner." Acting *as if* the urge is coming from something that is not part of them helps them, especially at the beginning, to get in touch with the various "committee" voices that desperately want to continue the addictive behavior. The technique also helps them accept themselves with thoughts, feelings, and behaviors without instantly and consistently damning their selves.

Do a Time-Effect Analysis

Chapter 4 gives an example of a time-effect analysis. As Marlatt (1985a) pointed out, clients benefit from examining the positive and negative effects of an additive behavior over time. Hence, Marlatt suggests looking at the positive and negative consequences in the short run and in the long run. I find it more valuable to consider more time periods, for example, two minutes, two hours, twenty-four hours, two months, two years, twenty years. In the example on pages 224–25, I was trying to help a client better understand the effects of using and of not using cocaine over time.

Explore the Client's Life Goals and Values

When I am working with a client in precontemplation or contemplation, I am wondering to myself, "What would motivate this person to change?" and this causes me to wonder, "What matters to this person? What kind of person does she want to be or did she want to be before she got into so much trouble that she gave up all of her dreams?" REBT/CBT techniques may help the therapist uncover what has prevented the client (or how the client has prevented herself) from developing into the kind of person she says she would like to be. What beliefs as well as real obstacles have hindered her?

SPECIAL PROBLEMS THE THERAPIST MAY ENCOUNTER

The Client Remains Ambivalent (in Stage II) for Months

In Chapter 7, I suggested the reasons why a client might not consider changing. Similar but not identical reasons may explain why a client keeps thinking about changing but rarely, if ever, takes any meaningful action:

1. **The benefits over time don't seem sufficient to justify the time and effort required.** She may be thinking, *It's too much trouble. I can't be bothered. At least, not right now.* Doing (or reviewing) a time effects analysis may help her decide what she wants to do and when.

If I *use* cocaine tonight:		
Time period	**Positive effects**	**Negative effects**
2 minutes	I feel more aroused, sexually. I feel euphoric. Finally, I feel as if nothing matters. I can zone out, be oblivious.	I lose the opportunity to practice standing the discomfort and seeing that I am not going to die. I lose the opportunity to get better at abstaining for one night. Maybe I'll have a heart attack from an overdose.
2 hours	I still feel good. I feel oblivious but turned on.	I start to feel incredibly paranoid.
2 months	I can't think of any positive effects.	My circle of friends continues to shrink; becoming seriously depressed; my life is going to hell in a basket.
2 years	Nothing.	My life hasn't changed; I feel more alone and lonely; I'll feel even more helpless and hopeless.
20 years		I'll never survive twenty years at this rate.

If I *don't* use tonight		
Time period	**Positive effects**	**Negative effects**
2 minutes	I'll get better at resisting my impulses. I'll get more practice living without it for a night.	I'll get tense. I'll get depressed. I'll feel more lonely and miserable.
2 hours	I won't feel paranoid. I can call friends. I can read.	I may feel very lonely; I always start beating up on myself. I can't stop criticizing myself.
2 months	I won't be so out of control. Maybe I'll be seeing more friends. Maybe I'll finally join a gym. I've been wanting to join. Maybe I won't feel so depressed and unmotivated.	I can't think of any.
2 years	More of the above. I would like to take at least one two-week vacation each year. I would like to go to Europe.	Ditto.
20 years	Maybe I won't be living alone and drinking myself to sleep every night. I would like to get a different job. I would like to find a man—maybe even have children.	Ditto.

2. **She likes the positive effects too much to change.** Again, a time-effect analysis may clarify the issues. If she really likes what she is doing so much, why is she ambivalent? What would tip the scale and cause her to change?

Reframing the Debate

Most of my clients frame the debates in their head as pleasure vs. pain: Which should I do? Work through the discomfort of my anxiety, which will take time and will require that I stand some pain, or drink a beer? The therapist should help the client reframe the debate to pleasure versus pleasure, more specifically, short-term pleasure versus overall (short- and long-) term pleasure. If the client thinks, "Should I have some beers with my friends?" or "Should I do that science assignment?" the pleasure principle will win every time. But this is really the short-term pleasure principle. If the client wants to get the maximum overall pleasure in life, the debate can be reframed: pleasure right now versus greater pleasure over time. It is important to help the client personalize the debate: "Relief and the buzz I get right now versus having a driver's license, going out on dates in my own car, and feeling better about myself." It is also important to emphasize that it his choice, his life.

When John told me that he loved staying up all night in jazz clubs and drinking, I asked, "What's wrong with that?"

"Well, I don't get to work on time."

"Oh. Anything else?"

"No. Well, I'm usually pretty blurry most of the morning, and I don't like that."

In continuing to talk to him, it seemed that he was firmly in Stage I. Finally, I said: "Well, it's up to you. How do you want to run your life. There's nothing inherently wrong with being a pure short-term hedonist. I wouldn't like it, but that's up to you."

Six months later, he showed up in my office again.

He started off the session by saying, "I really remembered what you said."

I'm always curious about what someone remembers from a session, and I had no idea what he might say. "What in particular?" I asked.

"Well, first, you said I was a 'short-term hedonist.' I had never thought of my problems in that way. Then you said it was all right to be a short-term hedonist. It was up to me. I could do what I wanted with my life. I didn't have to beat up on myself. So I went out and, boy, did I enjoy myself. No more self-beatings. I just went to jazz clubs and drank and had a good time."

I smiled. "That's sounds like fun. How did it work out?" He was in my office, so I assumed something was not as great as it seemed.

"Well, it was fun," he answered, but it was clear from his facial expression that he was not happy. "But I really don't like what's happening in my job. I may lose my job if I'm not careful. And do you remember that there were other goals I put on my intake form?"

"Yes, you wanted to find a woman to love and you wanted to stop procrastinating so much."

"Yes. Well, I would like to work on those things."

"That might mean giving up some short-run pleasure."

"Well, that might be okay," he said, somewhat haltingly.

"Okay, let's see what we can do."

3. **The client may consistently miscalculate the costs to him over time.** Is there any evidence that this is true? Is she doing what she wants to do with her life? Is she reasonably happy?

4. **The client does not know how to change or how to function if she changed.** What know-how or skill does he think he is lacking? Could role playing help? What kind of graduated homework assignment might help?

5. **She can't stand the discomfort that often accompanies change.** Even thinking about it may make her uncomfortable. What kind of graduated cognitive-behavioral program might help her? Is she exaggerating the discomfort?

6. **She's given up.** She has tried so many times and failed that he doesn't even want to think about it, let alone talk

about it. In other words, he has slipped back to Stage I, precontemplation. The therapist can do some post-BC analyses to try to determine how this happened and how to get him back on track.

7. **He doesn't trust that her efforts will pay off.** Too many times in the past, "life" has seemed to screw him, even when he is trying her best. What has convinced him? What is the evidence now that his efforts won't pay off? What kind of homework assignment (perhaps graduated, that is, small steps each week) could he do to help her think in a more positive, hopeful manner?

8. **He intends changing some time later in life—tomorrow, next week, next year.** If so, what are his goals in therapy now? Does he just want someone to talk to? What would he like to work on?

9. **She likes being "bad."** Have her goals changed? Has she moved back to Stage I thinking? If so, why? What does it mean to be "bad"? Why does she enjoy that feeling? Was she a "good little girl" for too much of her life and now just wants to rebel? How does that help her? Is that what she wants to do? How does she like what she gets?

10. **He likes the excitement.** How else might he take risks and enjoy the excitement? What else is he doing in his life that is exciting? If very little or nothing, why? The therapist can do Pre-AB's to understand how the client is stopping himself from taking risks in nonaddictive areas of his life.

The Client Misunderstands What the Therapist Has Said About Relapses

The client may be saying to his spouse or partner, "My therapist said it was okay for me to relapse. Most people relapse a lot. So stop getting so upset." What the therapist says does not always get heard the way it was intended. The meaning somehow gets distorted. Some clients want to find a loophole. With them, it may be best to be very explicit: "I am not suggesting you have a license to relapse. It is true that many people do, but many people do not, as well. It may be like a fall when you are skiing. But it could be far more serious—like running into a tree headfirst. As you know, people who relapse may also drive and may kill themselves or someone else. However, *if* you relapse, how does convincing yourself that you are a failure because you failed help? And relapsing may be an opportunity to learn what *not* to do next time."

The client may say to his spouse or partner, "Just because I relapse does not mean I am a bad person, so stop getting so upset." From the philosophical position underlying REBT, one act or even a series of acts cannot make the client a bad person. However, society may judge that what he did was bad and punish him accordingly. For example, if he drank and killed a child when he drove his car off the road, society would hold him accountable. Even if he argued that it was the disease that made him do it, not many people would accept that argument. REBT-ers might argue that he should not be condemned as a horrible human being, but they would not disagree that he should be held accountable for his behavior.

Unlike people who suffer from Lupus, asthma, and muscular dystrophy, people who suffer from addictions such as alcohol and drug abuse or pathological gambling often wind up hurting the people around them. While we as a society may become increasingly compassionate concerning their affliction, we will continue to hold people accountable for their behavior.

ISSUES TO KEEP IN MIND

Is Dysthymia the Underlying Problem?

Perhaps the client suffers from dysthymia—chronic, low-grade depression. Every time he stops drinking or using cocaine (or gambling or overshopping), he feels low, tired, unmotivated, or uninspired. Of course, the effects of drinking or using drugs may be the cause. But the dysthymia may have preceded the addiction. Initially, drinking, drugging, or gambling may have been a way to deal with the unrecognized dysthymia. Because ethanol first acts as an antidepressant before it turns into a depressant, the client may like its effects. Everything seems gray and uninteresting when he is not high. He may have always wanted something more from life, but his depression undermined any consistent efforts he made.

Is Boredom (or a Fear of Boredom) the Underlying Problem?

The client may believe that boredom is the worst possible psychological state to find himself in. He may be thinking, "I should never be bored." "I can't stand being bored." "It's awful to be bored." "I have a boring life. Only jerks have a boring life. What's wrong with me?" Feeling bored produces tension, anxiety, and other forms of discomfort. Having nothing to do may cause the client to notice how little he has in his life. As a result, he uses addictive behaviors to escape (or to avoid in advance) boredom. He may not have realized that boredom is the problem. He may engage in an addictive behavior so quickly, in order to either to stop being bored or to prevent being bored, that he rarely experiences what he is avoiding. In fact, he avoids it so effectively that he does not know what it is that he is avoiding.

Is a Fear of Risk Taking the Underlying Problem?

How did the client wind up with such a boring life? Often, to motivate a client, the therapist can offer to help him change some of the A's in his life in addition to helping him learn to think differently about the A's. To do this, the therapist needs to back up in terms of an ABC analysis and try to uncover how the client derails himself in his attempts to create a fuller, less boring, more enjoyable life. He may be too afraid to take any meaningful risks. He may risk arrest to get drugs, but whenever he thinks his ego or image in on the line, he stops himself.

From birth on, taking risk is essential for physical and psychological growth. However, the client may think that others somehow get ahead and create a life for themselves without enduring the tension and anxiety that come with risk taking. He may be thinking to himself (although he may not be aware that he is doing so), "If I take risks, I might fail and I couldn't stand that. I have already screwed up my life enough. I don't need to add anything new."

The client may not realize that carefully avoiding taking any meaningful risks in life is *very risky behavior*. Ultimately, if the client consistently avoids risks, he may become more and more convinced that taking risks, even small ones, is really terrifying. Then his life may begin to shrink until it consists of little else besides himself and a bottle. Motivating a client to take risks will require all of the skills outlined in Chapter 7 and perhaps some of the techniques to be discussed in Chapter 15.

Is Love of Risk the Underlying Problem?

Conversely, some people get in trouble with addictive behaviors such as gambling and taking various drugs because they think life should always be lived on the edge. There is nothing inherently wrong with this philosophy as long as the client does not mind the consequences of living a risky life. That is the issue. What kind of balance, or lack of balance, does he want in his life? The fact that he is in therapy, even if mandated, suggests that there are at least some problems with his choices. No doubt, some people like the feelings that go along with taking risks, so the therapist can help someone incorporate more legal risk-taking behaviors into his or her life.

Is a Love of Pleasure the Underlying Problem?

Many clients use addictive behaviors to cope with the pains of life, but not all. Some feel good but they want to feel better, and they often convince themselves that they should or have to feel better. So they spend much or all of their time pursuing pleasure. The Miller beer advertising campaign is focused on people who drink to celebrate. You're a construction worker and it's 4 P.M.: "It's Miller time!!" Time to go out with your buddies and celebrate the end of the day.

Wanting to feel better is not a problem unless the client turns his preference into a demand and unless he chooses a technique for feeling better that eventually creates serious problems. Again, the client is confronted with a philosophical (and to some, a spiritual) question. How does your client want to spend his life?

Is a Preference for Altered States of Consciousness the Underlying Problem?

Staring out the window, drinking, having an orgasm, gambling, getting completely absorbed in a book, losing oneself in the Internet, sleeping, and getting high all constitute different states of consciousness. They are altered states in that they are different from a previous state of consciousness or a more frequent state of consciousness. People who get into trouble with sex often love the way concentrating on getting sex (and ultimately having an orgasm) focuses their consciousness. One drink of alcohol for many people shuts up the critical voice in their head. An artist client of mine asserts that pot helps him focus and do the long, tedious work that is sometimes required in his particular form of art. In his normal state of consciousness, he cannot stay at such a tedious task as long. But, he claims, with a little marijuana, he can. Over a million children in the United States now take Ritalin to alter their state of consciousness. In the altered state, they reportedly perform better on academic tasks.

If the client stays in Stage II, it may be because he cannot envision living without the altered state (although he might not call it that) that he gets when he smokes a joint or snorts heroin or drinks alcohol. Changing a favorite addictive behavior may be like asking him to never experience the altered state that accompanies an orgasm or a good night's sleep. Again, the issue involves choices. Does the client have to give up (or moderate) a behavior that is very pleasurable or helpful to him in order to live a better life? If he wants to change, then the question becomes how to manage such a change and how to manage maintaining it.

RESEARCH NOTE

How often do people think they win at gambling? A review of three studies reported in *The Wager* (1997a) provided an intriguing answer: 74.4 percent of adolescents surveyed believed that they had won more often than they had lost. College students were not much more realistic: 66 percent thought they had won more than lost. Even 19.9 percent of adults shared this belief. The report notes: "This . . . 'memory bias' may be one explanation for the persistence of gambling activity despite consistent losses" (p. 1).

FIVE HOMEWORK ASSIGNMENTS

✓ **A drinking log:** The client keeps a record of what she drinks (or smokes or gambles or spends shopping). The therapist should tell her that she is not being asked to cut down. She almost always will cut down by virtue of monitoring her behavior, but that is not the point of the exercise. Some clients may see such an assignment as an attempt to gain evidence to use against them. So the therapist should try to sense if it will help build a working relationship with the client or will have the opposite effect.

✓ **Loss list:** The client makes a list of all of the things she may have lost as a result of her addictive behavior, such as a job, a good relationship with her family, and so on.

✓ **Like/don't like list:** The client makes a list of the things that he likes and does not like in life. He may focus on what he likes to do and does not like to do or simply on what he likes and dislikes. If he is employed, he can list what he likes doing on his job and what he does not like doing. The therapist may be able to help the client live a happier, fuller life by helping him intentionally do as much as he can of what he likes and as little as he can of what he doesn't like. Life is more enjoyable when one does chores and does things that one enjoys, besides addictive behaviors. Marlatt (1985b) has discussed this at length.

✓ **The three-columns technique:** The purpose is to help the client achieve a better balance between what he has to do, what he does for his own self-development (perhaps a novel concept), and what he does for fun. This is discussed in Chapter 11.

✓ **Value clarification exercises:** The client does value clarification exercises (see Chapter 7) to help him take action.

9

HOW TO WORK ON TYPE III CLIENT PROBLEMS

"I want to change. Can you help?"

This chapter focuses on Type III clients, those who have decided they want to quit and are in therapy because they are having more difficulty than they thought they would. They have lapsed or relapsed several times. Primarily in the action stage of change, they may have quit several times in the past. They may have even moved into the maintenance stage, but they have slid back for a variety of reasons.

Some therapists are not especially accustomed to working on a behavioral problem, such as "I am drinking too much and I want to stop," "I procrastinate a lot and it is having a bad effect on my enjoyment of life," or "I know I should exercise, but I don't." They are more accustomed to helping people with a "feeling" problem: "I feel very depressed (and I want to feel undepressed)" or "I'm feeling so anxious I can't concentrate at work." They do not always know where to start with a behavioral problem. I have noticed in observing therapist role playing situations that many therapists start with: "How do you feel about that?" or "Tell me more about your drinking behavior" or "What does that mean to you?" They are trained to help people feel better and to help them understand, in the belief that gaining insight helps people change and being listened to by an empathetic, nonjudgmental person is therapeutic, and they are probably correct. But they are often not very efficient in helping clients make concrete changes in their behavior, especially addictive behaviors.

A client with a Type III problem knows what he wants to do. And he wants help. Later, if he relapses, he may become ambivalent again, slipping back, becoming a Type II client and requiring different approaches, but now he knows what he wants to change. At times, the therapist may find it important to delve more deeply into the roots or causes of the client's behavior because without doing so, the likelihood of a lapse or a relapse may remain high. However, there are times when this is not necessary. No matter how fascinating someone's intrapsychic workings may be, the therapist is wasting the client's time and money exploring issues that are not relevant to accomplishing his goals.

Not too long ago, it was practically forbidden to discuss the possibility that the client would relapse on his way toward achieving his treatment goals. Discussing relapse might provoke a relapse, many people asserted, and was tantamount to giving people a license to relapse. Fortunately, Alan Marlatt's and Judith Gordon's book *Relapse Prevention* has helped change the way therapists think about relapse. No matter whether therapists think of addictions as manifestations of a disease or of overlearned behaviors, they now accept that relapses almost always occur. Moreover, relapses are not seen as a catastrophe, signaling the failure of treatment, but as part of the recovery process. In fact, they may provide the catalyst for clients to rethink their goals and to commit themselves more strongly to attaining those goals. They can also be used to learn better strategies and techniques, and they can provide inoculations against other, more destructive relapses.

WHAT IS THE DIFFERENCE BETWEEN A LAPSE AND A RELAPSE?

A lapse occurs when the client engages in the problem behavior or an aspect of the problem behavior once but does not return to his whole addictive pattern of behaviors (Marlatt 1985a).

When Ben first came into my office, he had been drinking steadily for ten weeks, every day, practically all day. A year later, he bought a bottle of vodka and drank on a Saturday night. But he called me the following Monday. He had stopped drinking and wanted to make an appointment. That time, he had had a lapse. He wanted to figure out what had happened because he realized that if he repeated it, he might not stop at one night of drinking.

Recently, Sara, after a year on methadone and hanging around with some friends who are still using, used some heroin herself. Unlike in the past, she was not completely devastated. She did not use the next day nor for the next six months. No doubt the methadone prevented her from feeling a real high, but her using also reinforced her conviction that she does not want to use anymore. She has changed, and wants to maintain her change. In contrast, whenever she had lapsed or relapsed previously, she had spent days beating herself up and using more to cope her with her despair.

Thomas à Kempis (c. 1413), a German monk, writing about temptation, had this to say in *The Imitation of Christ*:

We must be watchful, especially in the beginning of temptation, because the enemy is easier overcome if he is not suffered to come in at all at the door of the mind, but is kept out at the first knock.

Whence a certain man said: Withstand the beginning, after the sickness has taken vigor from long delay, the remedies come too late.

For first a simple thought comes to the mind, then a strong imagination, afterwards delight, and evil motion and consent.

And thus, little by little, the wicked enemy gains full entrance when he is not resisted in the beginning.

And the longer a man is negligent in resisting, so much weaker does he daily become in himself and the enemy becomes stronger against him. [p. 40]

Notice à Kempis's five stages to an addictive episode: (1) simple thought, (2) strong imagination, (3) delight, (4) evil motion, and (5) consent. He concludes, "The enemy is easier overcome if he is not suffered to come in at all at the door of the mind, but is kept out at the first knock." A more modern way of talking might put it as follows: "Once we start to excite (light up) parts of our brain by thinking about engaging in an addictive behavior, it becomes more difficult to prevent a lapse or relapse." One approach, discussed below, is to establish a clear plan and then figure out what helps to stick to it.

WHAT DOES THE RESEARCH SUGGEST?

- "Rather than progressing, chronic alcohol abuse often appears merely to fluctuate in severity," according to the follow-up study by Vaillant (1996) of a group of Harvard undergraduates through age 70 and a group of Boston inner city, nondelinquent males through age 60 (p. 248). Many participants who abused alcohol spent the last twenty years alternating between controlled drinking and abuse. If this is correct for other groups of people (that is, other than white males), it provides more reason to work in a way that recognizes the fact that many people do not achieve permanent abstinence. Instead, they are faced with managing a chronic problem and we can be there to help them as they move back and forth from one stage to the other.
- The same study found that most people who tried controlled drinking either relapsed or became stable abstainers; if they abstained for five to six years, relapse was very rare.
- On average, the Harvard undergraduates did not begin to abuse alcohol until age 40; the inner city adolescents started at age 29. However, both groups had twice the rate of heart disease and cancer.
- Relapse is the norm, not the exception. According to a

Hazelden study (1998), smokers try to quit cigarettes 10.8 times before they succeed. And it takes them on average 18.6 years to stop completely (that is, between the time they first think about stopping and the time they do). Twenty-nine percent of the sample said "stress/nerves/pressure" was the factor that prevented them from stopping; 12 percent said the cravings were too strong; 12 percent said they liked it too much. Only 5.4 percent said they were concerned about weight gain.

SELECTED CLINICAL STRATEGIES

Session Goals

The goals for Type III clients are as follows:

1. To help your client figure out a plan that will work.
2. To figure out what will help the client maintain the plan and to reduce the frequency, duration, and intensity (FDI) of lapses and relapses.

Deciding on a Plan

Type III clients know what they want to do but they do not always know how they want to do it. One client knows he wants to stop smoking, but is not sure what kind of plan would work best. Another client knows she wants to stop smoking marijuana, and she also knows that she wants to stop immediately. Some clients may start out intending to stop or to moderate and then change their plans. The therapist can follow the steps outlined in the previous chapter.

I worked for only a few sessions with Carlos. His case was quite simple because I soon realized that, to him, a man's word was more important than practically anything else.

Carlos's wife had insisted that he see a counselor because he had arrived drunk at a family function. He admitted that he had been a heavy drinker since the age of 16 over the strong objections of his very religious parents, but he was adamant that he would never get drunk again. He was now 58 and had decided that he was too old to be behaving this way. He had had a responsible position with a local company for over twenty years. He very strongly identified with his Hispanic background. Considering how he talked and carried himself, I said to him, "I get the impression that, to you, a man's word is extremely important. What you say you will do, you will do. Is that correct?"

"Yes. I have always drunk a lot. That is true. But that is because I have always loved to party and to have a good time. But unlike a lot of other men, I have never cheated on my wife."

I assumed that his last remark was designed to indicate to me that when he made a vow, he stuck to it. But I did not respond directly to this remark. Instead I said, "So if you say you are going to do something or not do something, then anyone can count on that. Is that correct?"

"Yes. People know me. If I say I am going to help them, I do."

"But does that apply to drinking? You have drunk for a very long time. I am not saying you cannot stop now, all at once, because some people do. But is that what you are telling me: 'I am not going to drink anymore and that is that'? That is your word."

"No. I said I was never going to get drunk again, and I am not going to drink every day like I used to. But I am still going to have a glass or two on holidays, and I am going to go out sometimes with my coworkers because I like to do that with them. But I will not have more than two. You will see. That is what I am going to do."

"So that is your word. Why don't you tell your wife? She must know you by now. You are a man of your word."

"Yes. But I think she has had enough. And she is right. I behaved very badly. I felt very embarrassed. I am too old to act like that."

"So should we have her in here and you can tell her?"

"No. I can tell her. I already told her, but I will tell her again."

"And then after a while she will see that you mean it."

"Yes."

"But I am worried about your going out to a bar on Fridays and about your drinking at weddings. Do you really think you can do that?"

"Yes. You will see. I will come here every two weeks because that is what my wife wants me to do, and you will see."

"Okay."

And that is what he did. Once we had made it a question of his word, then he felt totally committed to sticking to what he had said. This client is unusual, but not rare. While he was sent to therapy by his wife, he had already made a commitment to change. He was a Type III client, not a Type I.

In private practice, almost every case is unusual, and finding what is meaningful in a client's life provides the "hook" that the therapist needs to motivate someone to change his addictive behavior. Is he religious? Is he a father? Is she a mother? What are the values that she holds dear? A client's underlying goals and values are especially important when he or she does not want to come for therapy.

Reviewing Successes and Failures: Doing Pre-AB's and Post-BC's

Review Successes

As discussed in the previous chapter, even if the client was successful in sticking to his plan, it is important to explore what worked and how she managed to do it. Hearing herself will also reinforce what worked. This is especially important if the client has had to attend a function where sticking to her plan would have been difficult. Many of my clients have routinely used alcohol or some form of drugs, so being able to cope with the everyday hassles of life without falling back on their normal addictive behavior usually provides plenty to talk about.

Reviewing Failures

Clients often have great difficulty sticking to their intentions and resolutions. Failures can be discussed, as in Chapter 8. The therapist should remember, in most cases, to start with the Pre-AB's. Most therapists are very good at exploring how a client thinks and feels about something bad that has happened in her life. A client who has lapsed or relapsed may feel miserable. The therapist's tendency to want to help someone feel better may be so strong that she may immediately start to work on the client's postrelapse beliefs and consequences (the post-BC's). But unless she thinks that the client is probably going to relapse or is still drinking or using and will go right on after the session, it is better to focus on the pre-AB's instead, that is, on what happened *before* the relapse. The client wants to learn how *not* to do Y when he intends to do X. She wants to learn how to behave differently in a similar situation, and to examine what contributed to breaking the plan (see Chapter 8).

Preparing for Future Trigger Situations: Role Plays and Reverse Role Plays

Many clients do not know what to say when they are in a social situation and someone suggests that they have a drink, or do a line, or gamble. Role playing is better than discussing what the client might say because it gives the client practice. By reverse role playing, the therapist can demonstrate how to sound (in terms of tone) as well as what to say.

Role plays may also help clients learn how to debate in their own heads, although there are times that they should probably learn *not* to debate, such as the times when they cannot think straight. At such times, they will probably lose any kind of debate they might start, and other techniques, especially behavioral, will probably work better.

At a workshop, I asked someone to volunteer to do a role play with me. The person who volunteered, Maria, was trying to cut down on her smoking. We worked together for ten minutes and she agreed to give up her after-lunch cigarette. I started by asking her, "Can you see yourself sitting at the table? You have just finished your dessert, a piece of strawberry cheesecake—do you like strawberry cheesecake?"

"Yes."

"Good. I can see you sitting back from the table and getting ready to get up to go out and have your cigarette after lunch, but then you remember the homework assignment you have decided on here. So let me begin. Remember, I'm the cigarette-wanting voice: 'Boy, a cigarette will feel good right now.'"

"Right. You're right. It will."

"Wait a minute. I thought you we're going to play the other side?" I said.

"Yes, but it sounded so good, I couldn't help agreeing with you," she responded, laughing.

"Okay, but let's try again. 'Boy, a cigarette is going to be just perfect right now.'"

"Yes, but you decided not to smoke one because you are doing a homework assignment," she responded.

"Who cares about that assignment. That's his problem. I just had to agree because I was sitting up there. Let's have that cigarette," I role-played.

"Yes, let's!"

"Well, that was fast," I said. "You caved right in. Boom!"

"Well, I know I'm really going to want that cigarette," Maria answered.

"Yes, that's probably true. Do you want to go on? It doesn't sound like your 'healthy voice' is very strong. Maybe, like Popeye, it needs some spinach. Do you have a can in your back pocket?"

"No."

"Um, well, too bad. Shall we try one more time even without the spinach?"

"Okay," she said.

"Forget the homework assignment. I need a smoke," I said, as we started to role play again.

"Yes, but you don't *need* it. You just want it."

"Oh, cut out that REBT stuff," I responded. "Need, want. It's all just semantics. You *need* a smoke right now. Stop the BS."

"Yeah, well, I do *feel* like I *need* it," she countered, "but I'm not going to die if I don't have one."

"Look, you're going to feel very unhappy and crabby if you don't have one," I added.

"You're right. I will," she said.

"Shot down again! Why don't we switch roles. You play your addictive voice since you seem to know it so well. Your addictive voice reminds me of Johnny Cochran, the famous defense attorney. It is extremely well practiced. Up against it, your healthy voice doesn't have a chance. So let me try to play your healthy voice. Okay?"

"Sure," Maria said.

We switched chairs. This is not necessary, but it provides an added touch of drama (and humor) to the role play, and it gets the therapist and client up and moving.

"Okay. You start," I said.

"Let's have a smoke," she said.

"No. I decided that I wasn't going to have a cigarette after lunch."

"Don't be ridiculous. You want a smoke," she said.

"Yes, I *do* want a smoke," I answered. "But I don't always have to have what I want. That's like a 2-year-old: 'I want what I want when I want it.' I don't always have to have what I want."

"Oh, come one. This is a stupid exercise," she said. "What is not smoking one cigarette going to do?"

"A lot. It will help me reprogram my midbrain or wherever my conditioning is stored. I won't believe I can stand it until I see for myself that I don't die."

"Look, one cigarette won't matter. You can do this exercise later."

"Yes, you're right, one more cigarette won't kill me, but then I'll miss the opportunity to watch myself and learn and practice. Ultimately, I want to give up smoking, so I need to practice."

"How much practice can one cigarette give you," she said. "You need to stop kidding yourself. You need to stop completely, set a date like you did last time."

"Yes, that's a good idea. I did do that before, and if I hadn't thought I couldn't get hooked again, I'd have never taken another puff. But now I know what can happen," I put in.

"Okay, so let's set a stop date—and then go have a cigarette."

"No. I know I won't die if I don't smoke, and I think I'll talk to my friends here to get my mind off of it," I answered.

We stopped there. Had we had time, we would have reversed seats again and then again so as to help Maria learn how not to convince herself that it was too hard or pointless to not have one cigarette.

Another client may find that what helps her best is not to get into a debate at all. She may have discovered that if she starts, she always loses. So her role play may sound like this:

Urge voice: God, I need a cigarette.

Committed voice: Forget it.

Urge voice: But it would help.

Committed voice, amused: You won't quit, will you? I'm not discussing it. So that's that. What do I need to do now? Who was I about to call?

Urge voice: Oh, come on . . .

Committed voice: No. I've got things to do. And I'm not having this discussion anymore. Forget it.

The therapist's role is to help the client discover what techniques and what circumstances help him to maintain his plan. Some may find that they can do it quickly as illustrated above, provided that they get involved and their minds are on something else.

Others, at the other end of the spectrum, or in early recovery, perhaps cannot depend on their ability to maintain their plan if they are alone.

Encouraging the Client to
Cultivate a More Balanced Lifestyle

There is a value judgment implicit in the term *balanced lifestyle*. But many clients will not remain motivated to better manage their problems without developing a more meaningful, fuller, and richer life.

Marlatt (1985b) gives lifestyle balance a central role in relapse prevention. In his view, a person who develops a healthy lifestyle finds a balance between doing what she wants and doing what she should. Someone who consistently does mostly what she thinks she should do is open to feeling resentful and to lapses and relapses.

Ellis argues for a different kind of balance, one between short- and long-run pleasures. He explicitly states that "REBT strives for Epicurean hedonism" (Kwee and Ellis 1998, p. 15). Hedonists believe that the highest good in life is to be found in the pursuit of pleasure. However, Epicurus and his followers believed in controlling one's desire with reason and in the absence of pain as the greatest pleasure. As a result, he advised against sexual intercourse, led a simple life, ate mostly bread and water with the exception of some cheese on festival days, and declared that "the greatest good of all is prudence" (quoted in Russell 1945, p. 244).

It is true that some of the original followers of hedonism believed in gratifying all sensual desires, one source of hedonism's negative reputation. Ellis (1962) has noted,

> It has been found through the ages that the short-range hedonistic philosophy of "Drink, eat, and be merry, for tomorrow you may die," is unrealistic: because most of the time you don't die tomorrow, but are much more likely to live and rue the consequences of too much drinking, eating

and merrymaking today. . . . Instead of being encouraged to do things the "easy way," clients are encouraged to do them the more rewarding ways—which, in the short run, is often more difficult. REBT, while embracing neither the extreme views of the Epicureans nor those of the Stoics, strives for a more moderate synthesis of both these ways of life. [p. 292]

Franklin, a client, uses alcohol and marijuana to get through the day. To find out what other activities he might have in his life that he enjoyed, I asked him, "If you took some time off tomorrow, what would you do to just enjoy yourself?"

"Well, I still haven't finished stripping the windows in the living room. They've been sitting there for months. I guess I could do those. And the garage is a wreck. I have been wanting to clean it up for months."

I responded with a puzzled look and equally puzzled tone. "I don't think you understood me," I said. "What could you do to enjoy yourself—to take some time off? I can't think of anything more aggravating than stripping paint. What could you do to enjoy yourself?" I repeated.

"I don't know. I really don't know. I could have a drink," he said with a smile.

As we talked more, it became clear that he, like other clients I have worked with, could not really relax without some kind of chemical. It was as if his "shoulds" haunted and taunted him whenever he tried. There was always a voice in his head and a feeling that he should be doing something—something productive, something other than just enjoying himself.

It is for this reason that I discussed the concept of conflicting wants in Chapter 2. Someone like Franklin cannot get at what he wants to do. He wants to cool out but he also wants to get the window frames done. Depressed clients often want to stay in bed or shut off their critical voice, but they also want to have gone to work.

The Three-Column Technique

To help clients become more aware of their choices in life, I use a triple-column technique. I fold a piece of paper into three columns and label the first column "Self-maintenance," the second "Self-development," and the third "Fun."

Self-maintenance activities are often chores. They are necessary to keep one's life moving ahead. Brushing teeth, doing laundry, and paying bills and taxes are examples. Usually such activities are not inherently enjoyable. Self-development activities further our development as persons. Such activities might include learning how to use a new computer program or going on a religious retreat. "Fun" activities are simply enjoyable—watching television, skiing, eating out, hobbies. Many activities, such as cooking or going to the gym, may be in one person's fun column but in another person's self-maintenance column.

One's job, especially if it is part of a career, may be in all three columns. Some work involves self-development. But some aspects of work are chores. We hope that work sometimes is also fun.

The client can fill in the form in therapy or as homework. Many clients have a distinctly unbalanced lifestyle. Their self-maintenance column may have four or five entries, but the self-development and fun columns may have no entries at all. They may focus only on what they feel they "should" do, making everything in life a chore. As a result, they may wind up feeling resentful and trapped and resort to addictive behaviors as an escape.

Many clients ignore self-development completely. A client may have given up trying to learn the guitar and has never added anything to replace it. Many clients, especially those suffering from even mild depression (perhaps an underlying preexisting condition or chemically induced), have never realized that they may have to intentionally cultivate interests. For years, other people may have planned activities for them. They were put in after-school programs, sent to karate classes on Saturdays, and shipped off to camp for more planned activities during the summer. So they have had little experience in guiding their own recreational lives. They tend to choose the easiest distractions—watching television, taking drugs, hanging out. The activities that lead to a fuller, more meaningful, ultimately more joyful life (another value judgment, no doubt) have never been started or have been dropped.

The therapist can make two copies of the form for his files and give the original to the client. The client can fill in more things as he thinks of them and bring the form to the next session. If he forgets, the therapist has a second copy. The techniques outlined in Chapter 7 facilitate motivating the client to add activities that he likes or to try out new ones. This may require as much (or more) work as helping him manage his addictions. But one affects the other. Without other pleasurable activities, he is very unlikely to give up the one activity that he knows gives him pleasure (or solace). And without stopping or slowing down his addictive activities, he may remain too depressed to take any action toward increasing the overall pleasure in his life.

Suppose a client cannot figure out what he wants to do? Research indicates that people are as happy when they avoid having to do or having to endure what they do not like as when they get what they think they want. In fact, people who win lotteries are usually found to be no happier six months later. So even if the client does not know what he wants, he may know what he does not want, such as being homeless or unemployed, and that may be sufficiently motivating. It may also be possible that initially he may be too confused or too anxious to figure out what he wants.

The Role of Low Frustration Tolerance

Many addictive behaviors yield pleasant results much faster and with much less work than other activities in life. Thus, one obstacle to the client developing new activities, even fun activities, may be low frustration tolerance (LFT). To practice, to learn, to engage in other activities that might provide very pleasurable results in the medium and long run (and even in the short run once they are learned) requires spending time and energy and enduring discomfort. The client may want pleasure easily and quickly. Most people would also make the same choice if the consequences were not negative. What Yochelson and Samenow (1986) argue about criminals may be true for other clients: they have always enjoyed "getting by," fooling the world. It has always gotten them what they wanted with less effort and discomfort compared to the paths other people follow.

The Role of Therapist-Avoidance Behavior

Ellis quite forcefully and directly points out his client's LFT. Therapists may find that it works better to be gentler and more accepting in doing so. However, therapists may have a tendency to avoid doing so altogether, fearing alienating or inadvertently "downing" (criticizing and thus depressing) the client. But if a tendency to avoid frustration and discomfort in life has consistently derailed the client, avoiding this issue won't help. It is possible to be empathetic and compassionate—and honest and direct at the same time. But it takes practice. It is a behavioral change like all other behavioral changes.

As the client gets older and watches his peers become more competent and obtain better jobs, develop good relationships, and have families, he may begin to not like the consequences of his short-term hedonistic life. At that point, he may start to consider changing. However, although he may be in therapy because he wants something, he may be still unwilling to do what it takes to get it. And he cannot accept that others have often worked hard to get to where they are in life. Helping him acknowledge the effects of LFT on his overall happiness may be very important in helping him change. It will also be crucial to help him learn to accept his past errors, stop his chronic self-downing (despite a typical facade of well-being and high self-esteem), and move on.

LFT is not a fixed trait, but it may be a pervasive behavioral style. Figuring out how to motivate him to change such a behavioral style may take a lot of ingenuity and professional finesse (see Chapter 7).

SPECIAL PROBLEMS THE THERAPIST MAY ENCOUNTER

Clients Who Have Slipped Back to Stage I

After a lapse or relapse, clients may have slipped all the way back into precontemplation (Stage I) as the result of damning and demoralizing themselves. They may be thinking; "I can't stand it anymore." "It's just too hard." "I can't ever get anything right." "I was a jerk to think I could change." "I'll never change." This is a problem about a problem, and should be dealt with that way. The client has one problem. He has lapsed or relapsed. He does not need a second problem—being completely devastated and feeling hopeless and helpless because he lapsed/relapsed. Such a response is especially common if a client has been in therapy for only a short time. He may not share the therapist's attitude or philosophy toward relapse. He may believe that he should damn and punish himself and feel guilty and ashamed. He may believe that the therapist thinks the same way, despite what she (the therapist) may have said in previous sessions.

He will probably be watching closely to see if the therapist really believes in this new philosophy that he is expounding. Is she really not irritated, annoyed, disapproving, or disappointed? Is she really interested in figuring out what can be learned from the experience and then building on it? She will have the opportunity to demonstrate that she is by focusing on her post-BC's and asking:

"What are you telling yourself right now about your relapse?"

"What do you think I'm thinking?"

"What are *you* thinking? What are you feeling right now?"

"What do you think I'm feeling?"

"How does that help?"

"What else could you think? Let's assume ten people very much like you relapsed this past week (like you). Do you think they would all be thinking and feeling like you do? What do you think at least some of them would be thinking and feeling?"

"What could you think or do or feel instead that might help you get back on track?"

"Have you ever tried to work on something before and failed? What did you do then? What did you think? What did you feel?"

Clients Who Have Slipped Back to Stage II

It is more common for clients to slip back into Stage II and be ambivalent and unsure about what they want to do. They may be telling themselves:

I don't know if this therapy is going to work.
Maybe I should wait until after the holidays.
This is harder than I expected.
I never seem to succeed. I know relapses are common, but perhaps I just don't have the willpower to do it.

A client in Stage II needs to review her reasons for change and the plan that she has decided upon. If she filled out a time-effects sheet, this is a good time to review it. Perhaps she needs to increase her motivation. Or perhaps she needs to tell more people about her plan, or join a group or go to a meeting.

Clients Still in Stage IV or V

Some clients will still be in Stage IV or V. They are committed to change. However, they may still be saying very negative, destructive things to themselves. Negative, globalizing, catastrophizing self-talk heightens the chances of another lapse and perhaps a full-blown relapse. They may be telling themselves:

"I'm a real jerk." "I know exactly what I want to do, and I keep sabotaging myself." "What's wrong with me?" "How can I be so self-destructive?" "I feel hopeless." "I don't think I'll ever change." "I hate myself for having failed." "I'm a failure." "I'm weak. I don't have enough willpower." "Why can other people do it and I can't?"

Note that some of these beliefs are as strongly negative as those held by people who have slipped all the way back to Stage I. But the client may be clear about her goal. It is very easy, however, for her to slip back into her old patterns of global rating and negative feelings. The more the therapist can help her examine and change her chronically negative self-talk, the more he may be able to help her prevent future problems.

OTHER ISSUES TO KEEP IN MIND

Frequency, Duration, and Intensity

Most people do not stop or moderate addictive behaviors overnight. Any change in frequency, duration, or intensity toward what the client wants to do represents change.

Apparently Irrelevant Decisions

Marlatt (1985a) has pointed out the impact of a series of seemingly irrelevant decisions that, taken as a whole, lead to a lapse or a relapse.

Bart, a client, recently called a friend on Thursday to decline his friend's invitation to go to a basketball game Friday evening. Bart's reason was that he had worked very late both Wednesday and Thursday nights at the office to catch up on some work (which he had decided the previous weekend he could finish during the week instead of on Sunday as he had planned, and rather than working, he had watched TV). So Friday night he was tired, had nothing to do, and was alone in his apartment. Finally, being miserable (he had broken up with his girlfriend three months before), he went to a bar, had a few drinks, and then did a few lines of cocaine in the bathroom. At 3 A.M. he ended up having unsafe sex with a prostitute he had met in the bar.
Working backward, we could see how his seemingly irrelevant

decision to procrastinate a bit longer on catching up on his work (on Sunday) had led to two long nights at work, to fatigue, and to deciding to back out of his plans to spend Friday evening with his friends at the game. Had he, at some level, planned his relapse all along, starting as far back as the week before when he watched TV on Sunday instead of working, thereby falling behind in his work? That is always a question to ponder and explore. Are there patterns that get repeated over and over? If so, what at the beginning of treatment may appear to be apparently irrelevant decisions may come to seem much more planful as time goes on.

Abstinence Violation Effect (AVE)

Marlatt (1985a) also coined the term *abstinence violation effect*. When clients break their plan, they turn a lapse into a full-blown relapse. Recently Emily, having been moderating her diet for three weeks, broke down and decided to order a steak with béarnaise sauce and a baked potato with sour cream. Having thus broken her diet, she then concluded that all was lost and ordered dessert as well. I don't think we have to discuss at length the secondary gains from such (deliciously convenient) distorted thinking!

FIVE POSSIBLE HOMEWORK ASSIGNMENTS

✓ **The plan:** Any plan the therapist may develop with the client constitutes the primary homework.

✓ **Fun:** The client should have some fun—naturally, without engaging in an addictive behavior. For many clients, this is not easy.

✓ **Go to a self-help meeting,** such as a twelve-step meeting, SMART® recovery, or some other kind (Bishop 1995, Gerstein 1998). If they can't find one in their community, perhaps they should consider starting one or attending an on-line meeting.

✓ **Do something nice for someone:** Some clients become very caught up in their own recovery. It is another example of their self-absorption. Doing something nice for another person may help them see that they achieve greater overall happiness by doing what someone else wants.

✓ **High frustration tolerance (HFT) exercise:** The client can do something that helps him develop a greater ability to stand, meet, and overcome challenges and to stand frustration and discomfort. Various kinds of recreational activities such as camping, mountain climbing, motorcycle racing, rebuilding an old car, or learning a new skill will provide opportunities.

Many clients who have quit before know what has helped in terms of exercise, meditation, music, and recreational activities. The therapist should explore with them what worked in the past and what might help now. It is especially important to help the client work on adding activities to her life that she will enjoy, either because they are simply fun or because they give life more meaning. She needs reasons to continue to manage her addictions and create a fuller, happier, richer life.

MEDICATIONS

Fortunately, there are now a few medications that may help people maintain whatever plan they decide on. (For more information consult www.phrma.org and click on New Medicines.) Therapy versus medication is a both/and issue. We know that many health problems, such as asthma, diabetes, hypertension, malaria, cancer, and heart and brain attacks, are influenced by lifestyle choices, but that does not mean we do not use all sorts of medications, chemotherapies, radiotherapy, and surgeries to help ourselves deal with such afflictions. Addictive behaviors often have a direct impact on our ability to think rationally and to make good choices, and various medications may help us in our efforts to manage our problems.

I currently have a client who has been diagnosed with ADHD who is trying to stop using cocaine, but each week he slips from the action stage back to the precontemplation stage, ambivalating for the umpteenth time. One study (Levin et al. 1998) suggests that if he tried Ritalin, he might experience fewer cravings. If he put together more weeks without cocaine, I think he would have a better chance of resolving his problems. True, once off the medication he might relapse, but by then he might have learned a lot about taking more risks as a part of developing a more challenging and rewarding life.

Because everyone responds differently to each of these drugs and each, in certain individuals, may have unpredictable side effects, I urge clients to get a prescription from a psychiatrist, not an internist or general practitioner. A psychiatrist has more experience with side effects. This is especially true when the client is taking two or more medications.

Naltrexone

Naltrexone prevents people from feeling high. Thus, there is less reason to drink. But that is also the problem with naltrexone. Clients often do not use it because they want to feel high. In addition, some people, for example a few artists that I have worked with, insist that they cannot work while on it. But for some clients it may add that necessary grain of sand to the scales, tipping the balance against lapses and relapses. One study (O'Malley et al. 1996) found that during a twelve-week study fewer subjects drank who received naltrexone compared to a placebo (45 percent vs. 78 percent), and they were also less likely to have a heavy drinking day (25 percent vs. 60 percent). However, the results disappeared within six months of treatment. A new medication, acamprosate, may have similar problems, that is, high dropout rates.

Naltrexone has helped clients stay off of heroin for the same reason. In some cases, a month's time-release medication is implanted under the skin after rapid detox from heroin. The long-term effectiveness of such treatment, however, has not been determined.

Six-month outcomes using naltrexone were good (61 percent remained heroin free) with more stable addicts (with no psychiatric disorders or alcohol use problems) in Israel. Those who did better tended to be married, have fulfilled their military service, and have full-time jobs. Five years later only three of the forty-four who successfully completed the study had relapsed (three others could not be found) (Lerner et al. 1997).

Antabuse

Antabuse makes people vomit if they ingest alcohol. As a result, Antabuse adds one further reason for not drinking. When a client cannot think very clearly, for example, when she is alone on a Friday night, the knowledge that she is going to get violently ill is usually sufficient to keep her from trying to get high on alcohol. Clients refuse to take Antabuse or quit taking it for the same reason. But for a client who clearly wants to stop and is having difficulty, Antabuse may be a very valuable resource. Moreover, it appears to have very few side effects.

Methadone

Many studies have demonstrated the efficacy of methadone. There are people who argue that if the client were to switch from heroin to methadone, he would just be trading one addiction for another. But the fact is that he will probably be able to function better on methadone. Moreover, he will not risk death as the result of an overdose or bad drugs, and he will not have to risk arrest as well. Unfortunately, even in New York, it is difficult to obtain methadone without going to a clinic almost every day of the week. Many professionals do not want to risk being observed going to the same location every day and cannot travel without hoarding a supply. In other words, we still have a long way to go in making this medication more readily available to people who would like to use it. When we read (Goode 2000) that prescriptions of Ritalin to very young children (age two to four) more than doubled between 1991 to 1995 despite no testing as to how such a chemical may affect a developing brain, the stigma still attached to methadone becomes clearer (3.2 of every 1000 Medicaid preschoolers in one midwest area were being prescribed antidepressants).

Smoking Cessation Aids

According to Hughes and his associates (1999), there are now many ways for clients to help themselves prevent relapses when they are trying to stop smoking:

Nicotine patches: Rates of quitting using only the patch are still low (5 to 11 percent), but improve with counseling. They also exceed quit rates with a placebo.

Nicotine gum: Rates are also low, 13 to 15 percent, without counseling.

Nicotine nasal sprays: Here the rates are better: 26 to 35 percent. Some ex-smokers prefer the spray because they can give themselves nicotine when they want it, in contrast to the patch where it seeps into their system on a steady basis.

Nicotine inhaler: This device looks like a cigarette and the nicotine is absorbed through the mucous membranes of the mouth and throat. Early studies suggest a quit rate of 6 to 21 percent.

Bupropion: This antidepressant medication has reportedly improved quit rates to 27 to 28 percent. In another study (Jorenby et al. 1999), subjects in the bupropion plus nicotine patch condition gained significantly less weight. Continuous 12-month abstinence rates were 9.8 percent with the patch alone, 18.4 percent with bupropion alone, and 22.5 percent with bupropion and the patch. It may be especially helpful to clients who have a tendency to suffer dysthymia or depression.

RESOURCES

In addition to the materials listed in Chapter 6 designed to help clients who want to moderate their drinking, the following self-help materials may be useful for clients who are either unsure of what they want to do or already committed to changing:

- Ellis and Velten's *When AA Doesn't Work for You: Rational Steps to Quitting Alcohol* (1992).
- Horvath's *Sex, Drugs, Gambling, and Chocolate* (1998).
- Tate's *Alcohol: How to Give It Up and Be Glad You Did* (1993).
- My cassette tape *Relapse Prevention with REBT* (Bishop 1993), available through the Albert Ellis Institute.

In addition to twelve-step self-help groups, the following self-help organizations may be helpful to clients:

- SMART® Recovery, www.smartrecovery.org, 216-292-0220, 24000 Mercantile Road, Suite 11, Beachwood, OH 44122.
- Women for Sobriety, 800-333-1605, P.O. Box 618, Quakertown, PA, 18951.
- Secular Organizations for Sobriety, 716-834-2992, P. O. Box 5, Buffalo, NY 14215-2922.

RESEARCH NOTE

In a study of 50 untreated former cocaine users (Toneatto et al. 1999), what was the major reason for quitting? "Cognitive evaluation," defined as "the conscious weighing of the pros and cons of cocaine use and deciding that continued use is

---

undesirable" (p. 264). A little under half of the subjects cited pressure or ultimatums from significant others. Fifty percent of the subjects said it was somewhat or extremely difficult to quit; 38 percent said it was somewhat or extremely easy. What helped them maintain their decision to quit? Ninety-two percent cited better self-esteem and more confidence and pride; 76 percent cited a change in friends; 70 percent cited a change in lifestyle; 65 percent cited support from a spouse; 58 percent cited help from a friend. Note that 56 percent cited an increase in marijuana and alcohol use. What helped them most to cope with urges? Cognitive coping strategies, including deliberately recalling the negative consequences of cocaine use, learning to accept the urges, deliberately recalling the positive consequences of not using, and distraction.

III

HELPING CLIENTS MANAGE THEIR EMOTIONAL LIFE

10 ANGER AND ADDICTIVE BEHAVIOR

Anyone can become angry—that is easy. But to be angry with the right person, to the right degree, at the right time, for the right purpose, and in the right way—that is not easy.

Aristotle, *Nicomachean Ethics*

IS THE CLIENT READY TO CHANGE?

Is the client abusing alcohol or drugs or engaging in other types of addictive behaviors (shopping? eating? gambling? sex?) to cope with anger? Does the client see that anger is a problem?

Both clinical experience and research (e.g., Project MATCH 1997b) suggest that anger contributes to many lapses and relapses. AA uses the acronym HALT to remind clients not to get hungry, angry, lonely, or tired. AA members learn that anger is one of the most frequent triggers. Clients can feel angry about many aspects of their lives, and at many people, including themselves. Consequently, helping people learn to better manage their anger often greatly reduces the frequency, duration, and intensity (FDI) of both their anger and their lapses and relapses to addictive behavior.

Clients often think about anger differently than they think about other emotions like depression and anxiety. They will often acknowledge feeling anxious and depressed but not angry. They want to be less anxious or less depressed, but they are ambivalent or in denial about anger. Clients may admit that getting explosively angry has caused them a lot of problems but still not be sure that it is a problem they want to work on. They may think their anger is justified or that it works for them. Or they may be vaguely aware that they are chronically angry at a deep level, but they have been so socialized against expressing any anger that the very thought of admitting they might be angry frightens them. They may deny they are angry or that anger is a problem, even when they are full of rage.

Consequently, clients are often in one stage of change regarding their addictive behavior and another regarding their anger. Clients go through the stages of change differently with each problem.

Jackson had a problem with heroin (snorting), shoplifting, anxiety attacks, angry outbursts, and depression, and he smoked over two packs of cigarettes a day. His life was a long series of miseries, according to him. He wanted to stop using heroin but not immediately. He wanted help with his anxiety, and he thought his doctor should change his antidepressant medicine. He did not see shoplifting as a problem, nor his angry outbursts. Over time, he made significant progress in each area. As we worked, however, it was important for me to remember that with each problem he needed time to move from stage to stage and that in each area, relapses would probably occur.

It may even be harder to get over feeling angry than it is to give up an addictive behavior. In addition, some clients may make themselves angry intentionally (although they may not be aware that that is what they are doing) in order to drink.

Ellis (1977) and Ellis and Tafrate (1997) argue persuasively that we make ourselves angry. It is not things that make us angry, although it often seems as if it is our boss or wife or teenage daughter who is causing the problem! But the idea that we make ourselves angry strikes many people as absurd. They will resist the idea, and thus it is important that the therapist intuit when to introduce it. Otherwise, many clients will make themselves angry at the therapist for proposing such a seemingly crazy idea. However, the idea has revolutionary power. When grasped, it puts considerable emotional control back into the client's hands.

As Ellis and other cognitive-behavioral therapists have pointed out, demandingness underlies most anger. Ellis asserts that people make themselves angry with three core beliefs: (1) "You should treat me differently (or should have treated me differently)"; (2) "The world should be different"; (3) "I should be different." People whip up even more anger by awfulizing and believing that they cannot stand what is happening. They may also add self-blaming and self-downing and other cognitive distortions to create a stew of emotional distress.

WHAT DOES THE RESEARCH SUGGEST?

- The Project MATCH study (1997a) found that clients high in anger had better outcomes when treated with motivational enhancement therapy (MET) than when treated with cognitive-behavioral coping skills therapy. MET may have worked better with clients high in anger because of its non-confrontative, motivational techniques (Project MATCH Research Group 1997b).
- The cognitive-behavioral approach used in the MATCH study may have been more directive than the MET approach, and angry clients may have resisted considering what may be their own contributions to their problems (Project MATCH Research Group 1997b).
- In a review of over 15 studies of persons with various impulse control disorders, most revealed a high incidence of substance use disorders (McElroy et al. 1998b); for example, one study found that 48 percent met the criteria for lifetime substance use disorder (McElroy et al. 1998a).

SELECTED CLINICAL TECHNIQUES

Session Goals

The goals in working with angry clients are as follows:

1. To reduce the FDI of lapses and relapses related to anger.
2. To reduce the FDI of anger.
3. To learn how to cool down without resorting to addictive behaviors.

Exploring the Problem

When working with clients who are in precontemplation about anger, therapists should watch for beliefs such as:

"Anger isn't my real problem. Drinking is."

"I'm not really angry. My wife just complains too much."

"I'm not angry all the time. She's just too sensitive."

"I'm not angry. I don't know why the therapist thinks I am."

Clients may also be holding on to a number of beliefs that are unstated and of which they are unaware, including:

"Anger works. It keeps people in line."

"Anger works for me. It keeps people away from me."

For clients who grew up in dysfunctional homes and, as a result, are extremely hesitant to trust anyone (often even themselves), such beliefs are not completely irrational. Anger may, in fact, keep people at bay. But that does not make the first belief—"It works for me"—necessarily valid, especially over the long run. Uncovering beliefs such as, "People frighten me. I must maintain distance because I couldn't cope if they got close to me" and bringing them out into the open and working on them often reduces their power to trigger a relapse.

In contrast to many clients who get angry about almost everything, some clients may be very averse to expressing anger. They may be thinking:

> "I don't like angry people, and I can't stand the idea that I might be angry."

> "If I ever started, I'd never stop."

> "I believe in the Gold Rule: Do unto others as you would want them to do unto you (or don't do unto others what you would not like them to do unto you). I don't like people being angry with me, so I feel uncomfortable expressing anger to them. And I hate feeling that kind of discomfort."

> "If I got angry, my friends would leave me, and I'd be all alone. I'd get so depressed, I'd have to drink again to cope."

> "If I show how angry I am, I'll get hurt."

When the client was 5 or 12 or 17, suppressing anger might have been very rational. Expressing anger might have led to psychological if not physical harm. So a policy of keeping one's mouth shut and just seething worked during those younger, vulnerable years. However, in adulthood those same beliefs may be undermining the client's efforts to change and to live a richer, fuller life.

Type II clients may be thinking:

> "If I gave up my anger, what would I feel?"

> "If I gave up being angry, I would not feel like a man."

> "If I don't act angrily, people will walk all over me. There isn't an alternative."

"You're not making any sense. How can I not be angry if someone does something like that to me?"

Therapists should also watch for other possibly unstated, hidden beliefs, such as:

"It's not fair."

"She can't speak to me like that. If I let her, it shows that I'm weak."

"I never express anger well. I always wind up looking foolish (and that's unbearable)."

"Feeling angry feels better than shame or guilt."

"If I start, I won't be able to stop."

Type III clients who are actively working to reduce the FDI of the anger outbursts may derail themselves with some typical irrational beliefs such as:

"This is too hard."

"These techniques don't work (as fast as alcohol or sex) (as they must). And I can't stand feeling angry any longer."

"A drink will help. I can't stand all this tension. Why put myself through this?"

"Other people moderate. Why can't I? It's not fair."

Here again, hidden, unstated beliefs may undermine the client's efforts; for example:

"A strong person can control him/herself. I'm such a weak-willed person."

"Forget 'em all. Who cares? It won't matter in the long run. I can get away with it."

Exploring Historical Roots

If the client seems always to blame others for his problems, what might be some of the roots of this cognitive-emotive-behavioral pattern? In the end, he will have to take responsibility for any change, but first he has to be motivated. The issue again is time. How much time does he want to spend getting angry over past events? It is akin to the question of how long someone thinks it is appropriate to mourn a death. Each person usually has his own answer, often influenced by his culture. But at some point it is time to move on, to look forward and not back. As I discussed in Chapter 7, there may be many reasons why the client does not want to give up his anger.

Uncovering the Client's Goals and Values

What does the client want, in the short, medium, and long term, that he is not getting? I usually start off with standard therapy questions: "Why are you so angry?" and "What's making you so angry?" Then when I think it won't make my client angry, I switch over to a more REBT-ish form of questioning: "How are you making yourself so angry?" and "What are you telling yourself to make yourself so angry?"

However, on a larger scale, as I wrote in Chapter 7, I am always looking for a "hook." What does (or did) the client really want in life that he is not getting (or has given up on getting)? Is (or was) his dream at all realistic? If so, how did he get derailed or how did he derail himself? Is it really too late to achieve his dream? If it is not, how is he convincing himself to give up? If it is too late, how can we work to help him accept that fact and what could he work toward instead? What kind of man—given the economic, social, and political realities he is living in—does he want to be? A value clarification exercise like asking him to write his obituary or a letter (which will not be sent) to a child (if he has one) may help bring this out.

Discussing Emotional Alternatives

Anger rarely rears its head alone. Usually clients feel a stew of emotions, any of which may act as a spur to use some form of addictive behavior. The client may walk around with a chip on his shoulder all day and periodically blow up at various people in his life. Or—and this seems especially true for women but for some men as well—the client may have been socialized against expressing anger. She may have been explicitly taught by her parents that expressing anger was bad, that expressing anger led to physical and psychological harm. As a result, she may report feeling anxious when she is very angry. She is afraid to express anger. She may also report feeling depressed. In fact, she feels trapped, unable to express her anger, and therefore she feels helpless and hopeless. To numb herself to this emotionally confusing state, she may drink or use drugs or engage in some other form of addictive behavior.

Emotional Vocabulary

In motivating a client to work on her anger, it may help to discuss with her the meaning of the terms she is using, and to give her a list of alternative terms she might try using instead. Instead of angry, the client could feel:

Aggravated

Determined

Concerned

Irritated

Very irritated

Mad

Annoyed

Very annoyed

"I'm an 8" (out of 10)

Healthy anger

What should the therapist and client call anger that seems appropriate, justified, or even helpful? Such anger, when expressed, may get people to take the action they want without significant negative consequences in the medium and long run.

What should the therapist and client call anger that has the opposite effect? It may work in the short run, but it has very negative medium- and long-run consequences. It often wrecks relationships (both personal and professional), and it causes far more problems than it solves.

Ellis and Tafrate (1997) argue that anger and irritation are not on the same continuum. Each is on a continuum of its own. The client will be mildly or extremely irritated as long as he sticks to *preferential* statements: "I really would prefer it if you had not yelled at me, but you did, and I am not going to react the way I usually do." However, if he slips into thinking, "You shouldn't have spoken to me that way and I can't stand it and someone should set you straight," then he will make himself angry or rageful. Ellis further argues that if the client does not change from demanding to preferential thinking, he will not really reduce his anger. It may just seem less, but it is simmering hotly underneath, ready to build up and explode. Changing to preferential thinking, however, will change anger into some less destructive emotion such as irritation or aggravation.

However, many clients object to the idea that irritation is somehow okay but anger is always bad. The word *irritation* does not seem strong enough for what they feel. And for a client who has been socialized not to express anger, it may be counterproductive to reinforce her irrational belief that "expressing anger is always bad." This may be especially true with women who are underemoting and drinking or drugging or overspending to cope with their repressed feelings.

The therapist and the client may decide that *rage* or *unhealthy anger*, or *toxic anger* (borrowing from Bradshaw's [1988] "toxic shame") is the phrase to use for the emotion that the client feels contributes to her addictive behavior or gives her irritable bowel syndrome or causes her insomnia. For what Ellis would call "strong irritation" (accompanied by strong, but preferential beliefs), *healthy anger* or *nontoxic anger* may work. But it may be simpler to call the first *rage* and the second *anger*. What is important is to try to discover what makes sense and feels right to the client and then use those terms.

In the beginning the client may feel that all anger is justified. Discussing what she means by various words will introduce the notion that she can choose which words to use, not only in therapy but also, more importantly, when she is trying to cope with a real-life situation.

Emotional Thermometer

The client can take her "anger temperature" periodically throughout the day, on a scale of 0 to 10 where 10 represents that she is about to explode. Some clients may exaggerate their anger while others consistently downplay it. The therapist and client will then be more aware of how the client is feeling periodically through the day. Some clients are "pressure cookers." They cook very quietly and then suddenly explode.

Brainstorming

With a client who has a long history of exploding in anger, brainstorming may help him recall what has and has not helped in the past. This is a useful technique when the therapist is clear that the client is not ready to work on his anger. In the process of brainstorming, the therapist may be able to introduce other ways of thinking, behaving, and feeling without directly working on his anger. A client who has a long history of repressing and denying anger may benefit from brainstorming because he is often stuck with a repertoire of avoidant and passive-aggressive behaviors that consistently undermine his goals. He will benefit from exploring other ways of talking to himself and to others, other ways of behaving, and even other emotions. This technique is especially fruitful in groups.

Evaluating the Time Effects of Anger

Over time, what are the positive and negative effects of getting angry? The client may not think he frequently reacts angrily. The therapist may have to come back to this question, gently and compassionately with some clients before they will be willing to look at what they get from being angry so often. From session to session, events in their life may provide opportunities to raise the possibility that getting angry is not the most effective response for them. It is also often an excellent opportunity to help clients think in terms of time: "What was your goal when you blew up?"

A client once said that he wanted justice, but it seemed to me that he wanted revenge. First, I tried a direct approach: "It sounds like you wanted revenge."

"No. That's not right," he said. "I just wanted my boss to admit that he was wrong and to give me my job back."

"Okay. Perhaps you're right," I said, although I was not convinced. "Did you get justice?" I asked. I knew he had not gotten his job back.

"No."

"Well, was it in your best interest to blow up?"

"I don't know."

"Well, how did it help?"

"Well, it helped to vent," he shouted at me.

"Yes, and I guess that felt good, in the short run. But that was not your goal—to feel good. What's your long-run goal?"

"I have to find another job."

"So I don't get it," I said as gently as I could. "How does blowing up at your old boss help that?"

"I don't know. But it felt good."

"Yes. That's like all addictive behavior. He feels good in the short run, but it hurts us in the medium and long run. He had hurt you, by firing you, and you got a chance to hurt him. And I am sure I would have wanted to hurt him, too, if I had been in your shoes. But that is revenge and I don't think revenge really helps in the long run, do you? According to an old Chinese saying: 'Man who goes on journey of revenge should dig two graves first.' Do you understand?"

After a few moments of silence, thinking, he said, "Yes, but I got it out of my system."

"But it also may have buried you. You didn't get your job back and now you may not get a good recommendation from your boss."

I then shifted tactics because there is usually no therapeutic value in getting into a debate with a client. He still thinks anger is worth it, and seems also to believe that he has to get something out of him, to vent. But I could come back to those issues another day. Instead, I decided to see if I could help him see how he got himself so angry in the first place. In other words, I did a pre-AB with C as his blow up.

A time-effect analysis is particularly effective with clients who are ambivalent. The therapist should focus on two aspects of the client's anger: (1) What are the benefits and costs in two minutes, two hours, two days, and so on, of getting angry? and (2) How does getting angry contribute to his addictive behaviors? The client is probably only looking at the short run.

Creating a "Loss List" with the Client

In session, the therapist and client can make a list of all of the things the client thinks he has lost because of his angry behavior, for example, jobs, his wife, the respect of his teenage son, and so on. Because anger is so often reinforcing for clients and because they so quickly forget (or deny) the negative consequences of anger, it may be helpful for a client to keep this list in his pocket. In that way, he can easily review it, reminding himself of the time effects of his anger outbursts.

Siding with the Client

If the client has a boss who, according to him, always picks on him, the therapist should try taking his side by asking him how he copes with such a difficult situation. It may open the door to working more directly on his anger. The therapist can explore what he has done in similar situations in the past. It may reveal a great deal about his thinking and provide another opportunity to explore the impact, over time, of getting angry so often or so much. It may bring to the surface just how ineffectively getting angry has worked for him in the medium and long run, even if in the short run it seemed to have gotten him what he wanted.

Doing an ABC on Someone Else's Anger

Just because the client does not think he gets angry in an unproductive manner does not mean that he won't quickly agree that someone else in his life gets angry for no reason. For example, his father may have frequently lost his temper. The therapist may be able to illustrate another way of responding by examining what his father might have been thinking when he flew into a rage and exploring what, hypothetically, his father might have told himself and felt and done instead. Or if the client's wife is frequently getting angry at him, the therapist can do the same thing using her anger as an example (as the C in a pre-AB analysis): "What was the activating event? How did she feel? What did she do? What do you think she was telling herself to make herself so angry at you? Was her thinking helpful at that moment? Why not? What could she have thought that might have worked better for her—and for you? What else could she have done instead? How else could she have felt instead of being furious with you?"

In working this way the therapist not only learns a great deal about how the client thinks, but also demonstrates how the therapist thinks and how the client could think (and feel and behave) in similar situations.

Teaching the ABC(DE)'s

Doing and teaching ABC's in session will help the client in two ways:

1. **It will help him figure out how he is making himself so angry.** Although therapists (and some clients) may think that the ABC technique oversimplifies complex psychological phenomena, it helps people sort out what is happening to them and what aspect of their own thinking may be contributing to the situation. This is especially true for angry clients who are often so incensed that they have difficulty doing anything else but rehashing what has happened to themselves and others—and for that reason, often turn to addictive behaviors to quiet the storm. Clients who are ambivalent about working on their anger will benefit from the therapist's help in identifying which aspects of their thinking contribute to increasing their anger and which do not.

2. **Working through the ABCDE's helps the client feel less out of control.** Teaching a client how to do an ABCDE gives him a tool. He has something practical that he can use, instead of chemicals (alcohol and drugs) and other addictive behaviors, to help him resolve the problem. Initially, he may not do it very well and he may not give up his belief that his anger is justified given what has happened. But even if he does an ABC badly, he will be focusing on something else than on the activating event. He will be looking at not only what someone else did to him but what he may have contributed in his thinking to heat up the situation. He has a method to use to help himself and to analyze the situation. It may also help him begin to take more responsibility for his emotional life without resorting to chemicals or other forms of addictive behaviors. As a result, he may feel less out of control.

Bruce, 35, had worked on and off over the past ten years as a construction worker, taxi driver, porter, and, lately, as a word processor. He had started drinking at 12 and then moved on to marijuana, and he occasionally used cocaine. But alcohol was his drug of choice. He had managed to get through college, but lost his first job after a year. He had also had periods of no work at all and a period of homelessness, both due to his drinking. Several times he had become so depressed that he had contemplated throwing himself in front of a subway train. He was not openly acknowledging how often he got angry or that he often drank to cope with anger. His goal was to stop drinking completely, but he relapsed often, and it seemed to me that he was usually angry about something right before he did so.

Bruce started out by saying, "My boss told me I wasn't going to get a promotion this year. When he hired me, he said I would get a promotion at the end of the year. It was company policy, and now they say they have to downsize, so I won't get it, or I'll get fired altogether." Bruce had gotten so angry that he had stormed out of the office and gone to a bar where he sat and drank until it closed. He also missed work the next day.

I considered several ways of working: Should we carefully review what he was telling himself before he stormed out of the office? That is, how had he convinced himself to drink? Or should we review how he had made himself so angry? I decided on the former.

"How did you convince yourself to drink?"

"I don't know. I just left my office."

"Well, what do you think you said to yourself very quickly to convince yourself to go to the bar?"

"I don't know."

"I don't think it was just a reaction like an eye blink. I think you thought something. But let's see if we can guess what you might have said. Certainly you didn't say, 'Well, this is not what I wanted, but I don't have to get so angry about it!' "

"No, I didn't say that."

"Then what do you think you said?"

" 'I'm going to say something that's going to get me fired. I better get out of here.' "

"But why did you go to the bar?"

"I don't know. Vodka works! That's for sure."

"Yup, it does, but, of course, only in the short run. So I guess you said: 'If I don't get a drink, I'll say something so foul that I'll get fired.' "

"Yes, so I figured, 'Why not?' "

"Because it doesn't work in the end."

"What do you mean?"

"The evidence from what you've told me says that every time in the past you've ended up without a job and homeless or practically homeless."

"But I was really about to pop him, I was so furious."

"So it may have been good that you left. I agree with that. But I think you also said to yourself, 'I can't stand these feelings. I just can't stand it. So I have to get a drink.' Why couldn't you stand it?"

"I don't know."

"And why couldn't you find another way to cool down? Right now you act as if you have only one way to cool down—chemicals. Meaning, alcohol. Perhaps you could learn how not to get so angry in the first place, and if you do, how to cool down. Do you want to work on that?"

"Well, yes, maybe, but I don't think it's possible."

"I can understand that. You're addicted to anger. It's the only thing you seem to know how to do—get angry—when things don't go your way. That's because you're sneakily telling yourself: 'People [this time your boss] should act differently.' And 'I can't stand it if they don't.' You keep applying 'Bruce's rule' to situations, and then you turn into the Old Testament God if they don't do as they must—in your mind. What would happen if you said to yourself, 'I don't like what he did, but he doesn't have to behave the way I want him to' and 'I don't like it, but I can stand it'?"

"I don't know."

"Do you think you could have said something like that to yourself?"

"I don't know. I don't think so because I deserved the promotion."

"Maybe you did according to company policy. But why should you always get what you deserve? I'm sorry you didn't get your promotion, but lots of people don't get what they have earned. Why do you think you should have gotten it?"

Bruce then went on to explain all of the things he had done in and for the company over the past year. In his eyes, he had been super-good. He had always helped out when he was asked. He had stayed late to finish projects. Compared to his behavior in the past, he had been an absolute angel!

"Yes, I'm assuming you're right. If the world were fair, you would have gotten the promotion. Could your boss have given you the promotion anyway despite the company's plans to downsize?"

"I don't know. Maybe."

"Well, what's your overall goal?"

"To keep my job."

"How did getting angry and drinking help? I'm not trying to make you feel bad, but if we just judge the *behavior*, not you, I don't think it helped. What could you have told yourself instead?"

"I don't know."

"Well, let's look first at how you got yourself so upset. Why did you get so angry?"

"Because it's not fair."

"Oh, I agree. It isn't. But you and I both agree that getting angry and drinking didn't help. Let's assume just for this session it *isn't* fair. Now what?"

"I don't know. You don't understand."

"Perhaps I don't. What made you so angry?"

"Because it's unfair. I have worked too hard to *not* get a raise."

"So this is very hard for you to accept."

"Yes."

"Why do you think it's so hard for you?"

"Because life sucks, and this is just one more pain-in-the-ass thing that has happened to me."

If I had not known Bruce fairly well, I might have asked him about the other bad things that had happened to him, partly to understand more about what had happened in his life, and partly to understand more about how he thinks. Instead, I went back to a functional (or practical) question: "Do you think holding onto your anger in this situation helps?"

"No. But I'm still pissed about it."

"I know, but does that help? If you were just mad, not rageful, what would happen? You seem to like holding onto your anger, and I just don't get it, at least in this case. Maybe I'm stupid or something."

"It's easy. I wanted that promotion."

"Yes, I know, but you seem to be saying 'I wanted that promotion and I have to have what I want.'"

"But it's unfair."

"We both agree on that. We are trying to figure out what's the best way to accept things when things are not fair. Should you fight? Drink? Get angry? What?"

"I don't know."

"I don't know what's right for you either. Certainly drinking and missing work don't seem to be good responses. If there were ten men like yourself in your shoes, what do you think they would do?"

"I don't know. Some would probably have accepted it."

"How do you think they would have felt?"

"I don't know. Pissed, I guess."

"Yes, and you could have felt pissed. Or perhaps some would have just felt very disappointed. What do you think they would've had to say to themselves to keep themselves from drowning their sorrow in booze?"

"I don't know."

"Come on. What do you think?"

"I guess, like, 'It's not the end of the world.'"

"Yes, probably so. But I don't think you think that makes sense. You think you *should* feel pissed, considering the injustice of it all."

"Yes."

"But then you have to learn to *stand* being pissed—maybe for a long time—without dissolving it in alcohol. Why can't you stand being really pissed? What's so bad about that?"

"It's not. I don't know what happened that day."

"Well, I think you have a habit of saying to yourself 'This is unfair' and then you know that alcohol will make you feel better. You don't actually hear yourself say, 'Alcohol will make me feel better,' but you or your brain knows it, so you just sort of go for it. It's kind of automatic."

"Maybe."

"Well, we have to end soon. Are we still clear about the goal here? The goal is to learn how to cope without drinking. It seems to me that anger often acts as a trigger for your drinking. Does that make sense to you?"

"Yes, maybe. But it's harder said than done. Especially when the world keeps fucking you."

"Yes, I agree totally. It is harder said than done. But if you could learn sometimes to accept the unfairness in the world—sometimes, not always—it might work better for you. Does that make sense?"

"Yes."

"Well, we can do that several ways. You could learn to stand angry feelings better so you don't have to drown them with alcohol. Or you could learn how not to get so angry in the first place. Or you could learn other ways to cool down. Does that make sense to you?"

"Yes."

"What could you do this week to help yourself?"

"Well, I met with my buddy, and that helped me cool down some. He's going to be staying with me, and he doesn't drink, so that may help."

"Well, here's a form to fill out if you want to. You don't have to fill it out, but if you do, then I will be able to understand better what is going on. Okay?"

"Okay."

At the beginning of the next session, I asked about the other things that Bruce had done to help himself cool down. He had gone to an AA meeting twice and had talked to his girlfriend. He had not filled in the form I gave him, but I did not really expect him to do that.

I was concerned that he might think I was suggesting that he accept every injustice in life. I knew that would not sit well with his idea of what it was to be a man. So we talked more about what a man could do on a job when things were clearly unfair. What could a man (or a woman) do that helped or made sense? How did drinking help?

Was his boss really being unfair or was he just hand-tied by the company's downsizing policies? How could he channel his anger in a way that would help him and perhaps help his coworkers as well?

The Anger Relapse Prevention Review Form

This form (Table 10–1) contains the critical questions for reviewing what happened during an anger-induced addictive episode. The therapist can give copies to the client and ask him to bring them into the next session or fax or mail them in. The form will help the therapist see how he is thinking in the heat of the moment. It will also give him something concrete and practical to do while he is angry, instead of continuing to rage and to drink or use drugs to cope.

Teaching Relaxation Techniques

Just because a client does not think anger is a problem, he may still be aware that he is very tense. He may look tense in therapy and thus give the therapist an opportunity to say, "You look very tense sometimes in my office, like right now. You look very uncomfortable. What do you do to help yourself other than drinking (or smoking pot, etc.)? Would you like to learn some quick ways to relax, ways you could use without people even knowing it?"

Again, my experience indicates that most of my clients will not accept anything that even hints at being Eastern or mystical. It has to be practical and easy to do, especially at the beginning (see Chapter 12).

Table 10–1.   The Anger Relapse Prevention Review Form

1. What happened? (What was the A, the activating event?)

2. How long did you stay angry?

3. How angry did you get, on a scale of 1 to 10?

4. How did you make yourself feel so angry? What did you tell yourself (the B's)?

5. What did you tell the other person?

6. What did you do? What were some of the behavioral consequences (the C's)?

7. What could you have told yourself instead?

8. What could you have told the other person instead?

9. What could you have tried to feel instead of rage?

10. What could you have done instead of repeating an addictive behavior?

Doing Rational Emotive Imagery

Rational emotive imagery (REI) is particularly effective with anger because it permits a person to work on his anger at various times of the day—walking to work, sitting on the subway, lying in bed—all at the level of imagery.

Michael had used a variety of drugs and alcohol throughout his life, partly it seemed to help him feel less angry at the world and at himself. He had been an only child in a single-parent household and had been "spoiled rotten," according to him, by his grandmother and his mother. Yet his mother was also very critical and demanding of him from the time he was very little. To help him work on managing his anger between sessions, I suggested that he use REI. He had recently become very angry at his mother because she had not understood why he had lost another job. He was particularly incensed because he was, he claimed, always understanding whenever *she* quit one of *her* many jobs. They had had a very bad fight, he had called her a bitch, and then he had come home and drunk two bottles of wine and some vodka before falling asleep.

I started by saying to him, "Sit back and get yourself really angry at your mother all over again. When you have really cranked it up, raise your finger so I will know when you are feeling angry. Do you understand?"

"Yes."

"Okay," I said.

After about fifteen seconds, he said, "I don't know whether I can get angry all over again."

"Well," I said. "Get as angry as you can, and then raise your finger."

He shut his eyes and tried again, and within about twenty seconds, he raised his finger.

"Now change your feelings to something not so destructive, something that won't contribute to your drinking again. And when you have done that, raise your finger."

About ten seconds later, he raised his finger again.

"Okay," I said, "Open your eyes. What did you do?"

"I calmed myself down," he answered.

"How did you do that?" I asked.

"I just said to myself, 'Look, she's always been like that. Why do you keep thinking she's going to be different? Why do you keep rising to her bait?'"

"Then how did you feel?"

"I don't know. A little . . . I don't know. Not as angry, I know that."

"Well you could feel disappointed and sad. You don't have the mother that you would like to have. That's too bad. You don't have to feel furious about it, but you could feel sad, regretful, resigned."

"Yes, I think I feel sad. She's really a bitch, you know."

"Maybe she is, but you are still hurting yourself because she is not as loving as you would like her to be. That's a hard thing to accept, but many people have to accept that one parent or both are not very loving. That's true, right?"

"Yup. I'm not the only one. But she sure pushes my buttons."

"Yes, but then you get angry very fast about a lot of things. If you practiced REI every day, a few times a day, for example, sitting on the subway, you might not lose it so often. Can you think of any reason that might motivate you to do that?" I asked.

"I don't know," he said.

"Well, think about it. What might get you to really work to control your anger?"

"I don't like Mikey [his 8-year-old son] to see me losing my temper all of the time. And I'd also not like to lose this job. He might not think much of me if I lose another job."

"Yeah, I think that might help. If you really want to be different for your son, then you might work on it."

Later, near the end of the session, we discussed the specific times and places he was going to practice REI so as to try to increase the odds that he would actually do it.

Testing Out a Possible New Plan

As with addictive behaviors, the client will not begin to change until he has a plan clearly outlining what he intends to try to do when he senses he is about to relapse. As I discussed in Chapter 2, he should decide on such a plan when he can think relatively rationally and perhaps in session. The trick then is to maintain the plan under difficult circumstances when he cannot think so rationally. The therapist can help him prepare for such circumstances. One way is to discuss and decide on a possible plan and then to try it out in real life. For example, when the client next starts to get angry, instead of yelling at and criticizing his teenage son, what would be more helpful? There are many possibilities. Perhaps when he feels himself getting very angry, his plan could be to say to his son, "Let's talk about this later" and then go talk the situation over with his friend who also has a difficult teenager. Or perhaps his plan might be to remain in the situation, telling himself, "I can stand this. I do not have to blow it up in my mind. I do not have to blow up at him. I do not have to respond to everything he says. Ask another question and listen. Judge later, after I have a chance to talk to [a friend, my wife]."

The client may still be ambivalent about working on his anger. So it is an experiment. He can test out and explore alternative ways of thinking, feeling, and behaving and then come back to therapy and discuss what he has found out.

A client of mine, Frank, frequently convinced himself that the way people were doing things in his office was not the right way, not the way he thought they should do things. He made himself so enraged that he often went immediately to a liquor store after work, bought a bottle, and then slowly drank himself to sleep. He was so convinced that his coworkers should work up to his professional standards that he decided to work on two plans at once: one related to his drinking and the other related to his anger. He decided to buy two small, airplane-size bottles of vodka instead of a fifth. And for his anger, he thought it would help to fill out an ABC homework sheet and bring it to the next session. I think he liked the idea that I would be looking at the way he was thinking, figuring that I would see that he was, in fact, right!

Practicing Role Playing (and Reverse Role Playing) in Session

With a client who is ambivalent about working on anger (or someone who will never fill out any kind of form), role playing and reverse role playing will enable the therapist to demonstrate other ways the client could have responded that might have worked equally as effectively as anger. Using role playing, the therapist may be able to "sell" the client on the idea that changing the way she responds may work better for her in the long run.

In role plays, the therapist can rehearse two kinds of dialogues: External dialogues between the client and someone else, such as a coworker or a waiter, and internal dialogues in her head. Clients who have habitually gotten angry and those who have habitually repressed or denied their anger need lots of practice to learn how to behave differently in future situations. Role playing provides that practice and, in reverse role playing, the opportunity for the therapist to model other responses.

Bruce and I had practiced role plays in the past, so Bruce initially played the role of his angry, unhelpful voice, and I played the healthy or rational voice.

"He should have given me that promotion," Bruce began.

"No. I *really* would have liked it. But it's just my bad luck that the company policy has changed."

"I always get screwed."

"That sounds like an overgeneralization, but maybe you have had a lot of bad luck. That's too bad, but what now?"

"I think I better look for another job."

"No," I said, looking at Bruce and changing my tone so that he knew that I had stopped role playing and was talking directly to him.

"I don't think that's what you said to yourself last Thursday. That *might* have been a good thing to say, but you must have said something much hotter than that. We're trying to role play so that you can learn how to talk to yourself in similar situations. Now what do you think you said?"

"I don't know."

"Well, then let's reverse roles, and I'll play the voice I think was in your head. Okay?"

"Yeah."

"Screw this," I said. "I've got to have a drink. This is it."

"That's how I felt," Bruce said.

"Okay, you take that line then."

"This is it. I need a drink," he said. "I'm going to get fired if I don't get out of here fast."

"That won't work," I said, playing his more helpful, rational voice. "He is pissing me off royally, but I can stand it. I am not going to die. I don't like it, but I'm not going to die."

"Oh, come on. This is ridiculous. One or two drinks won't matter," Bruce countered.

"That's good. That is probably what you said," I said to him. "So, let me continue. Let's see, 'One or two drinks won't matter.' Well, there's sure as hell no evidence for that. I have always gone on binges."

"But I didn't get promoted!"

"If I keep reciting that to myself, I'll just increase my anger."

"But he screwed me royally and you're not doing anything about it?"

"There may be things I can do, but not right now. I do not have to counterattack right now."

"Do you think you can reverse roles now?" I asked Bruce.

"Maybe."

"Okay, I'll start. He should have given me that promotion!" I said.

"I feel like agreeing with you," Bruce answered.

"Yeah, I know. That's why we're doing this, so you hear yourself saying: 'He should have promoted me,' and you feel your rage increasing. What could you say?"

"I didn't get what I want, but I don't have to throw a tantrum over it," Bruce responded.

"Oh, come on. This is a big deal," I said, continuing in a rageful voice.

"Yes, but I want to hold on to the job," he added.

"Having a drink won't cause you to lose your job," I said in a snide tone.

"It could."

"But he should have promoted you," I said.

"Yes, but he doesn't have to do what I think he should do," Bruce answered.

"Oh, come on," I said in as sarcastic and biting a tone as I could muster. "That's ridiculous. He screwed you!"

"No, that's not necessarily true. It may feel like that, but that may not be the case."

"Let's stop now," I said to Bruce. "What do you think? Do you think you could cool yourself down next time without alcohol?"

"I don't know. Maybe. But it's a lot harder at that time."

"Yes, of course it is. And you make matters worse by saying, 'I can't stand it.' Once you say that and convince yourself it's true, you feel you have to do something, and alcohol has always worked—at least over the short run."

Reviewing and Rehearsing

Once the client has decided on a plan, the therapist and the client will spend much of the time in the next few sessions reviewing how it is working and rehearsing for future difficult situations.

In general, they will begin each session by reviewing (1) the homework and (2) how successfully or unsuccessfully the client has maintained his plan during the previous week. With what situation and under what circumstances was the client able to follow his plan?

Then they will review when the client could not follow his plan, keeping the focus on the desired behavior and not on the client. It is helpful to work slowly so that both the therapist and client can visualize and sense where he was, who else was there, what he was telling himself, what he was feeling, and what he was doing just prior to lapsing.

To help the client maintain his plan, the therapist can prepare him for future difficult situations by doing pre-AB's both verbally and in writing (on paper, a chalk board, or flip chart), REIs, and a variety of role-play exercises.

SPECIAL PROBLEMS THE THERAPIST MAY ENCOUNTER

The Client Seems "Addicted" to Anger

Returning to our definition of an addiction, someone can be "addicted" to anger and may be very reluctant to change.

The Client Still Believes Getting Angry Pays Off

Anger does pay off sometimes. Not expressing anger may be a mistake, an example of avoidant behavior. Sometimes. The therapist should use functional questions. Does getting angry help? How? Do or review a time-effects analysis on anger.

It Is Unclear What the Client Is Feeling

Does what the client is saying make sense? Many people who drink do not realize how angry they are or how angry they are making themselves. In contrast, some clients, especially men, think they are angry when they are not. They are anxious or depressed but are so accustomed to expressing anger that they walk around all the time as "dry drunks," to use AA's term.

Tom had been drinking for over twenty years, but he was in therapy because he had begun to binge drink, two to three days in a row, something he had never done before. We spent twenty minutes carefully creating a "videotape" of the last episode. I wanted to be able to visualize and sense what might have occurred in terms of his feeling, thinking, and behavior every minute up to the start of his drinking—in a movie sense, frame by frame—and then through to its conclusion. His mother was going to visit that weekend.

"How do you feel about that?" I asked.

"Stressed," he said. "I always find her visits very difficult."

Later when we were examining the first few minutes of the binge, he told me that he had "gulped down" a few swallows of cognac. "I don't know how many," he said. "I just drank from the bottle."

"Gulped down" suggested that he certainly wanted to get rid of some kind of feeling fast.

We talked some more and then I asked, "Where were you feeling the stress? Can you point to the place in your body?"

He look at me blankly.

"Well, did you feel it in your big toe? Your knee?" I said with a smile. "Did you feel it throughout your body? In your stomach? In your hands? Where?"

He pointed to his chest.

"Generally," I said, "people who feel pain in their chest feel angry about something. We have an expression in English, 'I have something I want to get off my chest,' and it is usually not depression or anxiety. We are angry about something and we want to tell somebody what we think."

"Yes, I'm angry. Of course, I'm angry," he said.

"Why? What are you telling yourself about her?"

"She should have protected me against my father. She shouldn't have been so weak. She shouldn't be so critical."

"So you were not just feeling stressed before your mother came, you were feeling angry and guilty about feeling angry. Is that possible?"

"I guess so. She drives me nuts."

"Well, she may give you lots of things to use to drive yourself nuts, but many people would also feel angry. However, they wouldn't necessarily feel guilty about that, and they wouldn't necessarily think 'I can't stand these feelings' and try to drown them with wine. It *is* sad that your mother is so self-absorbed and still so critical, so most people would find it difficult to be around her—even if she *weren't* their mother. She is a hard person to be around, period. So it seems kind of unreasonable to try to feel lovey and warm around her. I know you would *like* to have such feelings for your mother—most people would—but that doesn't make sense given the kind of person she is. It makes more sense to feel sadness and regret, because she is not the kind of mother you would have liked to have had. Does that make sense to you?"

In subsequent sessions, it turned out that being able to feel annoyed and irritated (but not rageful) at his mother without feeling guilty on top of it was a revolutionary concept for Tom. Of course, we also worked to help him learn how to be with her without making himself so angry and to accept his mother as she was, which was difficult given the fact that she was still a very self-absorbed, critical, unloving person.

It Would Help If the Client Got Angry More Often, Not Less

This may be correct. Some people consistently avoid asserting themselves. Some even avoid confrontations so often that they cannot sustain good relationships and frequently stop themselves from obtaining their goals.

Emotive Rational Behavioral Therapy

I teach ERBT to some of my clients who cannot express anger or who cannot do so without totally losing control. They have to learn to behave more angrily and assertively without having a panic attack before, during, and after! They also have to learn how to cool down. If they don't learn how to cool down, they may refuse to consider starting to practice expressing their anger. They may be telling themselves, "If I start to express anger, I will explode. I don't know what I'd do. I might kill somebody. I might burn the house down. It's too scary to get angry." "My mother taught me never to express anger, and I must not violate that rule or I'll feel terribly anxious and guilty, and I won't be able to stand that."

The client can practice doing ABC's and rational emotive imagery. Then she can move on to assertiveness exercises, first in session and then outside of therapy, using role playing to help prepare. If the client will not act angrily in therapy, she may be willing to practice it in her bedroom or in her car. She may move back to being ambivalent about the whole exercise. For a long time, she may have held onto the belief that getting angry is a mistake. She may again forget the medium- and long-term consequences of such avoidant behavior. And alcohol, pot, or heroin provide faster relief, do not take practice, and always work!—at least in the short run.

Caution: With clients who rarely express anger, the therapist should try not to indicate his own discomfort with anger when clients start to emote. Looking away and crossing his arms may nonverbally communicate that he is uncomfortable with angry outbursts, especially in his office. Most therapists who are trained in Rogerian psychology or some form of psychodynamic psychology will not make that mistake, but those who lean more toward behavior therapy or cognitive therapy may. They may prematurely ask, "What are you telling yourself to make yourself so angry?" That is a "head question." It draws people's attention back to their thoughts, back into their head. If they are chronic underemoters, they need to stay with their feelings and learn that they will not break. They can express anger without someone crushing them or their crushing someone. The therapist does not want to move them from their body, their chest and heart where the anger is welling up, back to their head so fast that they shut off their anger prematurely.

ISSUES TO KEEP IN MIND

Frequency, Duration, and Intensity (FDI) of Anger

The client may not understand that even if he reduces the number of times he gets angry (the frequency) significantly, one intense episode may have serious consequences if he behaves violently. Family members may not care that he has made tremendous progress in therapy or that he doesn't get angry nearly so often or stay angry for so long or drink every time he gets angry. Getting hit simply wipes out those gains. Some clients have great difficulty accepting the way the world works, especially the way people respond over the long term to violence, lying, and cheating. The client may think this is unreasonable and unfair. Six months after the last incident, he may think that his family members should have forgiven and forgotten. But they may not, and he may make himself angry, thinking, "They should have forgiven me by now. They should trust me."

I find it helpful to ask my client, "If your girlfriend cheated on you, how soon would you forgive her?" Often, the answer is never. I sometimes follow this up with, "How soon would you forget?" But it is also helpful to explore what the client is thinking: "Why do you think they should forgive and forget? How would that be in their best interest?"

Is It a Psychotherapeutic Problem?

If the client thinks homicidal thoughts about her boss for half a minute, it may not be a psychotherapeutic problem no matter how much "shoulding" she may be doing. It is the consequences of that kind of thinking that counts. If she starts to drink heavily or develops irritable bowel syndrome (IBS) because she so frequently thinks such thoughts, those are psychotherapeutic problems (her thinking, her drinking, and her IBS). Similarly, blowing up may not be problematic. Again, the therapist can help the client to think through the consequences for her over time.

Frustration and Anger

God grant me the serenity to accept the things I cannot change, the courage to change the things I can, and the wisdom to know the difference.

—H. R. Niebuhr

Acceptance and change are central to both CBT/REBT and AA. AA strongly suggests looking to a higher power for help. CBT/REBT may emphasize developing one's own resources, but those resources often had better also be friends, a good psychotherapist, and perhaps membership in a club or a church. Learning how to accept and learning how to change usually require more than solely one's own resources. Of course, this is true of learning almost everything else whether that be something as complex as becoming a lawyer or a good auto mechanic or something as simple as learning how to scramble eggs. As noted throughout this book, REBT perhaps more than CBT places a great deal of emphasis on learning how to accept oneself (and others) with their imperfections and limitations.

How do we usually feel when we cannot change something that we think should be different? Or when people do not behave the way we think they should? Many clients will feel frustrated. But frustration stimulates many different emotions. Frustration occurs when we have a goal but we cannot reach it. Imagine a dog chained to a post. Someone places a bone in front of him but just out of reach. Some dogs will bark and pull on their chain all day. Others lie down and whimper.

It usually is best to explore how a client *feels* about being frustrated. How does he feel when he cannot get something that he thinks he deserves or must have? Some people feel hopeless, helpless, and depressed. Others are filled with rage.

Making Amends

If the client has hurt someone while in a rage, the therapist may want to explore whether he has apologized or wants to make amends. Making amends, the eighth step in AA, has therapeutic value in many ways (see Chapter 13).

Developmental Issues

Developmentally, a 20-year-old is often not angry about the same things as a 45-year-old. And for biological reasons, women between 38 and 43 are often angry about issues that do not exist for men. As I noted in Chapter 3, developmental issues affect people's underlying beliefs, which in turn influence their thinking, their feelings, and their actions. For example, Ken had underlying beliefs from his childhood that he should do everything well, avoid criticism at all cost, and be successful. When he was fired at 50, probably partly because of his age, he was furious: "It's not fair. I have given my life to that company. Who do they think they are?" If he had been fired at 26, he might have also been angry, but at 52 it was easier for him to think "I won't get another chance," and to feel trapped, helpless, and hopeless, turning to alcohol to help him cope. It is important to think about how age-related issues may be affecting what clients are thinking. It may help if the therapist asks herself, "If I were his age, what might I be feeling if I were in his situation? What might I be telling myself?" Then, if a client can't figure it out, the therapist can suggest what the client might be thinking.

Socioeconomic Issues

Ken's belief "I won't get another chance" may not be irrational given various socioeconomic and cultural factors. It is highly unlikely that another large corporation will hire a 50-year-old when they can hire a 26-year-old for half the salary. There are exceptions, of course, but it is not irrational to think "I probably won't ever get hired for such a high-level job again." It was certainly true that Ken had given a major part of his professional life to the company. However, it was clear that if he went on thinking "I have to get another chance. I can't accept never becoming a vice president," he was going to live miserably the rest of his life.

Familial/Genetic Issues

Is anger genetic? Are there other hotheads in the family? This line of questioning often surprises clients. But in fact, one or the other parent may also always be angry. The client may have observed a lot of anger-induced behavior and anger may also be something inherited. Pursuing this line of questioning may help in two ways:

1. **It may decrease the client's anger.** It may cause him to be less angry with himself for continually being angry and ruining his life. This can be especially true if a client thinks that he drank or used drugs throughout his life partly to cope with anger, and that it was all his fault, all his responsibility. In fact, his family and perhaps even his genetic background may have been partly responsible. And continuing to blame himself totally may simply fuel more relapses and more rage.

2. **It may motivate the client.** He may feel more determined to work on his problem. Clients from angry, dysfunctional households often do not want to be just like good old Dad, who beat them whenever he wanted to, but especially when he was drunk.

But won't that just give him an excuse? The choice is his. How will that help him in the short, medium, and long run?

Some clients make themselves angry at themselves and at others because they are so poor at arguing. Is that genetic? Are other members in the family really bad at arguing? Often a parent is equally poor at behaving assertively or equally good at avoidant behavior. Again, helping clients understand the "why" may help inspire them to work on the "how." Perhaps the client was born shy. She may have inherited a predisposition to feel anxious (see Chapter 12) and then developed a way of coping that, unfortunately, works only in the short run. Or in the face of a domineering, alcoholic father, she may have learned not to even try to argue. Therefore, she developed some deep-seated irrational beliefs: "Arguing never pays off. I always lose when I argue." These became coupled with feelings of helplessness and hopelessness. She may also have thought, "I might finally say what I feel and kill him," creating anxiety. In addition, she may be harboring deep rage at herself—for being so incompetent at arguing and for always backing off. It may be a long time before we understand the mechanisms involved, but careful, compassionate questioning may help people begin to stop blaming themselves. The client may have inherited it or learned it through years of conditioning. Given that reality, she needs to find a way to live that does not continually undermine her goals.

"What's wrong with getting angry? That's what I don't like about REBT. It teaches people not to get angry." REBT asserts that anger usually works against a client's best interests. *Irritation* and *concern* are suggested as less problematic alternatives. But earlier in this chapter, I noted that many of my clients, especially those with anger problems, have a lot of difficulty accepting such terms as appropriate. Consequently, we often find other terms that work better, such as *healthy anger* for a strong, negative emotion that does not usually lead to problems, and *rage*—or, as one client recently suggested, "escalating, aggressive, hostile anger"—for an emotion that *does* usually work against my client. REBT teaches people to figure out what works for them, given their goals and values.

REBT also proposes that we do not work most effectively when we are enraged. Although there may be exceptions, usually we do not think or behave in a way that furthers our goals when we are exploding. However, healthy anger may be very useful when we are trying to effect change—in oneself, another person, or a larger system.

Doesn't Venting Anger Help?

No research supports the idea that venting anger helps. In contrast, expressing "toxic" anger or rage does usually have several well-known effects:

1. Initially, the client gets himself even angrier. He may go quickly from being merely very angry to rageful to even violent.

2. After a while, he may feel completely wrung out, spent, exhausted—but in a pleasing, justified way. This reinforces the idea that venting is a good technique.
3. He may have been trained by his family or peers that expressing anger demonstrates manly behavior. He may feel pleased at or even proud of his anger.
4. After watching his wife or friend or coworker cower or cry, he may feel satisfied. He has effected a change in the other person's behavior, which is what he wanted to do in the first place: "She has to agree with me. He should behave the way I think people should behave."
5. But those whom he has cowered or caused to cry may learn to avoid him as much as possible. How many teenagers avoid going home because they know they are going to be yelled at or worse? Or they will avoid their parents by lying, telling them what they want to hear or not telling them what they don't want to hear.

Where did this venting theory come from? Writers often use the current cutting-edge technology as metaphors for complex psychological processes. Hence, we often talk about drugs altering people's "hard wiring," in addition to their "software," both allusions to computer technology. In Freud's time, pneumatics was the current rage, and to Freud it seemed that anger (and libido) built up inside people and had to be "vented," otherwise they would explode. It's a nice metaphor and many people will tell you that that is just the way they feel. But there is no research evidence that venting really helps, although, as mentioned in item 4 above, people may feel better in the short run and believe that acting angrily is always effective.

FIVE HOMEWORK ASSIGNMENTS

✓ **Practice REI:** The client can use spare moments of time, for example, while he is riding on the subway or stuck in traffic, to practice REI.

✓ **Do an ABC once a day:** The client can do at least one in writing (if that is something he will be willing or interested in doing), and bring it in to the next session or fax it to you.

✓ **Watch a funny video:** For reasons that I have never seen explained, humor can cut through anger faster than any other intervention. The client can recognize the therapeutic power of humor and use it.

✓ **Make an "A" list:** Normally we try to teach clients not to make themselves so angry about the various activating events (A's) in their life. But it can also help the therapist develop a better relationship with the client and to motivate him to do other forms of work on his anger if the therapist suggests working together to change some of his aggravating A's. Of course, as the Serenity Prayer (cited above) reminds us, there are things we cannot change. But there are also things that require courage to change. The therapist can get a list of the A's the client would like to change and begin to explore what can be changed and what cannot—and how he might develop "the wisdom to know the difference."

✓ **Write an obituary:** To motivate someone to work on better managing his anger, he has to become convinced that he is going to regret it in the future if he continues with his angry outbursts. Writing an obituary pulls a person's thinking out into the future, and gets him to focus on how he may want to be remembered by people. This may be a particularly powerful exercise if the client has children.

MEDICATIONS

Prozac and some of the other new selective serotonin reuptake inhibitors (SSRIs) appear to help people who report being on edge and irritable. Medications may help people while they are learning how not to make themselves so angry about so many things in their life. It may also help them to remain employed or to stay in a marriage until they have learned how to manage their emotional life to the point where they can think through more carefully what they want to do.

RESOURCES

Clients may find helpful:

- Ray DiGiuseppe's cassette tape *What Do I Do with My Anger: Hold It In or Let It Out?* (1990)
- Ellis and Tafrate's *How to Control Your Anger Before It Controls You* (1997)

11 | DEPRESSION AND ADDICTIVE BEHAVIOR

Is the client abusing alcohol or drugs or engaging in other types of addictive behaviors (shopping, overeating, gambling, risky sex) to cope with depression? As we know, depressed clients and those suffering from dysthymia often convince themselves that they are trapped, hopeless, and helpless, and that their life is out of control. To eliminate such disagreeable feelings, they may do something they can control, such as keeping themselves stimulated, excited, and distracted. Gambling, drinking to oblivion, or engaging in some other addictive behavior may do the trick, at least over the short run. As one client told me, speaking of her cocaine addiction, "That is one thing I know I can do. And when I do it, I know exactly what will happen and how I will feel." Talking in a very matter-of-fact tone, she continued to say, "I don't like doing coke, but it's better than sitting there feeling awful." When she felt in "awful pain" (her words), she knew she could help herself with a line of coke. Within one time frame (the very short run), she was right.

The only legal, fast-acting antidepressant (and antianxiety) "medication" on the market is alcohol. But, unfortunately, it becomes a depressant in about two hours. Nicotine may also ward off mild, short-term feelings of depression. (Heroin and cocaine are illegal fast-acting antidepressants both with clear negative medium- and long-run effects.)

Addictive disorders and depressive disorders have similar characteristics and may interact and intensify each other. Moreover, relapses into depression are quite similar to relapses to addictive behavior pattern. Most relapses to depression do not just come out of nowhere. This is true even if some relapses are kicked off by hormonal changes or other subtle chemical changes. Clients often contribute to their lapse.

One of my clients, Mike, knew that staying up very late Friday night channel surfing was dangerous behavior for him. However, he often arrived home late after working on an editing job and, because he was recently divorced, he found himself alone in a small cellar apartment that he had rented for himself. Saturday morning, instead of getting up and meeting friends to play baseball, he was "too tired to get out of bed." He then depressed himself further with thoughts, such as: "I always let my friends down. What's the point, anyway?" and slept late into the afternoon. Once finally up, he would usually start to watch television again, often continuing until late into Saturday night.

Mike is also ashamed of his behavior and of a recent hospitalization. He believes that it has stigmatized him for life. Despite the fact that society has become somewhat more accepting of depression, he does not think most people have really changed their way of thinking. Certainly, *he* has not changed his way of thinking. Moreover, when Mike does not eat all day, he feels more tired, lifeless, and hopeless. And on Monday he depresses himself further over what he has done (and has not done) all weekend. Is he addicted to depressive behaviors? He continually does what he says he knows hurts him, which he says he does not want to do.

Mike's cycle of lying around, doing nothing (other than watching one TV movie after another), eating only sporadically, and then sleeping all the next day was difficult to stop—as is true for binge drinkers. They slide into the same old behavioral patterns.

This often occurs as the result of a series of seemingly irrelevant decisions (as Marlatt [1985a] pointed out regarding relapses in drinking). Comments such as, "I'll just watch one hour more," "I'll just have one drink," "I'll just stay in bed until noon," are common to both problems, depression and drinking, and to many other addictive behaviors.

When a new client is reporting problems with alcohol and depression, it may be difficult to figure out what is contributing to what. Is the person's consumption of alcohol causing or contributing to the depression? Or is the person drinking to cope with depression? Is it some of both?

The treatment of alcohol and substance abuse had become separated from the treatment of psychological problems until relatively recently. It was the norm in the United States for people to be treated separately for their addictive disorder and for their other mental problems. Clients frequently got confused and frustrated by the mixed messages they were receiving. As a result, dual diagnosis units for mentally ill and chemically abusing clients have been set up in most hospitals, and ongoing efforts are being made to offer an integrated approach to such clients.

WHAT DOES THE RESEARCH SUGGEST?

- According to the Epidemiological Catchment Area Study, 5 percent of males and 19 percent of females dependent on or abusing alcohol also have a lifetime history of depression (Regier et al. 1990).
- For men, alcohol abuse preceded the depression in 78 percent of cases, but for women, depression preceded the alcohol abuse in 66 percent of cases (Helzer and Pryzbeck 1988).
- Even higher rates of comorbidity are seen in clients seeking treatment and in primary care settings (McGrath et al. 1996).

- The lifetime rate for major depression among opioid users was found to be 53.9 percent in one study (Rousaville et al. 1982, as cited in Brady et al. 1998); major depression was found in 15.8 percent of opioid users seeking methadone treatment in another study (Brooner et al. 1997). Rousaville and colleagues (1991) found that 61 percent of their sample of cocaine abusers had had a lifetime history of affective disorders; 30.5 percent had had at least one episode of major depression (as cited in Brady et al. 1998).
- Cocaine users who give up cocaine but who show high levels of depressive symptoms both prior to and during treatment have a greater likelihood of turning to alcohol abuse than ex-users who are not depressed (Brown et al. 1998).
- Antidepressants have helped people suffering from problems with alcohol and depression decrease their depression and lower their consumption of alcohol (Kranzler et al. 1995, Mason et al. 1996, McGrath et al. 1996).
- Cognitive-behavioral therapy was found to be as effective as antidepressant medication with severely depressed outpatients in a review of four major studies. According to DeRubeis and colleagues (1999), "Antidepressant medication should not be considered, on the basis of empirical evidence, to be superior to cognitive behavior therapy for the acute treatment of severely depressed outpatients" (p. 1007).

SELECTED CLINICAL STRATEGIES

Session Goals

The goals in treating these clients are the following:

1. To reduce the frequency, duration, and intensity (FDI) of lapses and relapses related to depression.
2. To reduce the FDI of depression itself.

As with other problems, what stage is the client in with regard to depression? He may not see depression as a problem. He may think that once he stops drinking his depression will lift, and he may be correct. But another client may see a lifelong link between his use of alcohol and his depression. He may not be able to ever remember feeling good. He may directly say that he started to drink to feel less depressed and hopeless. He may be very interested in working on his depression. A third client may be ambivalent about changing. Being depressed has been a part of his life for so long that changing would have a domino effect. If he were no longer depressed, he would have a much harder time rationalizing his drinking. Friends and family members might begin to expect different behaviors from him. Thus, contemplating change in either or both areas—depression and drinking—may be very frightening.

People who are on some form of social security or welfare disability because of depression will probably lose their medical benefits—the medication and therapy—if they improve and return to work. If the job is part-time, it will not come with medical benefits, but it will probably cause them to lose their disability benefits. Hence, for some clients it may be too dangerous to recover from depression under our present laws.

Clients often move back and forth between denial, ambivalence, and action on both problems, drinking and depression. What should the client work on in therapy sessions? Is there sufficient time to make some headway on both problems? I usually try to move forward on the addictive problem first. If the client feels as if he is not making any progress toward overcoming his addictive problems, that may further contribute to his depression.

Exploring the Problem

When working with depressed clients, here are some beliefs to watch for:

"I can't stand feeling depressed. I have to get some relief."

"If I drink or smoke (pot or a cigarette), it will help."

"When I gamble, the thoughts that usually bother me just aren't there."

"Life stinks. What's the point? (There is no point. Nothing I do will really change the situation.)"

"I am a failure. I have tried and tried and failed every time."

Other possible unstated beliefs include:

"I look like a fool. I can't stand looking like a fool."

"I have pushed away all my friends. No one can stand me anymore."

"Talking about depression is too uncomfortable. I can't stand it."

"It's depressing to be depressed again. What's wrong with me?"

Therapists must also be watchful that some of their own beliefs do not impede treatment, for example:

"This is a hopeless case."

"He's right. He'll never change."

"This is pointless."

"This person is too lazy to change."

"Why doesn't she just get over it?"

Many clients who are depressed are tortured by "should haves": "I should have done better in life. I should not have made so many mistakes. I should have taken that job . . . married Betty . . . gotten that promotion . . . not made a fool out of myself. . . ." An equal number of clients also seem to be suffering from "fortune telling" and overgeneralizing. Whenever they think about the future, they envision a repetition of their past behavior, replete with errors and failures. They think, "Nothing will ever change. Even if

I do decide to do X, I'll screw it up. Even if I get better, eventually I'll relapse." Thinking like this, they create waves of hopelessness and, in turn, begin to drown in helplessness. As a result, they remain inactive, and then put themselves down for that very inactivity: "I should never have gotten up today. What's wrong with me? I'm a failure. I never seem to be able to ever get things figured out and start *doing*. I continually question and requestion what I should do. I can't decide about anything important."

Awfulizing, demandingness, perfectionism, shame, and anxiety often interact with and generate even more depression, leading to what is sometimes called agitated depression. This in turn may produce rage toward the world and the self—"I should be different. The world should be different. In particular, you should be different"—compounded by I-can't-stand-it-itis, that is, low frustration tolerance (LFT). All of this may also leave a person wallowing in self-pity: "I never get what I want. The world (God) is against me. Everyone else gets breaks, but not me."

Exploring the Historical Roots

Depression, much more than anger, anxiety, or shame, provokes an intense desire to understand. "What is the meaning of life? Why am I like I am? What am I supposed to do with my life? How should I live? What's wrong with me?" are all questions that either lurk right below the surface or are explicitly voiced. The standard questions outlined in the chapter on assessment are useful for depression:

"When do you remember first feeling depressed?"

"What have you done that has helped in the past?"

"Why aren't you using the same techniques now?"

"What is stopping you? (Or . . . How are you stopping yourself?)"

"What makes this time different from the last?"

With clients who are familiar with CBT/REBT, the therapist can be much more direct and ask, "How are you depressing yourself right now?" However, clients who are unfamiliar with CBT/REBT will not only not understand the question, but also think that the therapist does not understand them. As a result, they may leave therapy. The question "How are you depressing yourself?" assumes that a client is responsible for at least some of her depressive feelings. This may be correct. But she may only conclude that the therapist is blaming her for her problem. The therapist must take the time to build a relationship with the client before taking such a direct approach. On the other hand, the very idea that the client's depression is to some extent a result of her way of thinking and her behaviors can be very therapeutic. It generates hope and may motivate her to learn ways to help herself become and remain undepressed.

Doing an ABC(DE)

CBT's (and REBT's) major advantage is that clients can use the techniques to help prevent both relapses into depression and relapses into addictive behaviors. For example, the client can learn to use the ABC to decrease the FDI of their depressive feelings. They can learn to identify and then question and challenge (dispute) the beliefs that contribute to their slides into depression and to their relapses into addictive behaviors.

Linking ("The Rating Game")

The most typical way clients initiate and worsen their depression is by rating their entire selves on the basis of their own behaviors or on the basis of how they think someone else is rating them. I call this "linking."

Sara has a knee-jerk, conditioned habit of linking how she feels about life and about herself with how she thinks her mother and her boss are thinking or feeling about her. If they are happy, she is happy. But if they are not, she is not. Consequently, her emotional life is, in effect, always out of her control. It is controlled by how she believes others feel and think about her. And she believes that she can control them only indirectly by working harder, being always nice, and never showing her irritation or disappointment. As a result, she feels trapped, helpless, hopeless, depressed, anxious, and angry (Hauck 1991).

Fortunately, she is aware of her "linking" habit and is much more watchful of her tendency to respond in such a dependent, knee-jerk fashion. She is ready to change. Unlike some depressed clients, she is not ambivalent about becoming less depressed. She now knows that she depresses herself when she thinks, "It's absolutely awful when my mother gets upset. She's never satisfied, and I can't stand it when she gets all unhappy and angry with me." As she has progressed, she has also worked on her tendency to engage in new forms of demandingness, self-condemnation, and LFT: "What's wrong with me? I'm such a hopeless case. Here I am 35 acting like a 5-year-old, wanting my Mommy's approval. I can't stand it any-more."

Sara also has a tendency to engage in all-or-nothing thinking. She veers from very much wanting her boss's approval ("He has to like what I've done.") to thinking that it was not worth concerning herself with it at all ("It's too much trouble. I can't stand being so needy. Who cares, anyway? He probably won't even look at it."). She and I have worked on helping her develop her own criteria for what she thinks is good performance at work and what she thinks is poor performance. I have encouraged her to rate her performance, but not, at the same time, herself. If she is not happy with her performance, we work to help her figure out how to make it better. At the same time, she has had to learn to savor her successes instead of always finding something she could have done better.

It was much more difficult for Sara to learn not to place her rating of her entire self on the line whenever she went into her boss's office. But, with practice, she learned not to be so concerned that she could not function effectively in meetings with him. Overall, the FDI of these changes varied over time, but, in general, she got much, much better at observing and changing her knee-jerk conditioned reactions. If she found herself beginning to feel depressed, she was able to reduce how intensely she felt depressed and how long she felt depressed. Instead of weeks and sometimes months, she managed to bring it down to hours.

Discussing Alternatives to Feeling Depressed

Having an emotional goal in mind (as well as behavioral goals)—one that the client thinks will be less problematic—may be extremely helpful. Instead of depressed, the client could feel:

Sad

Concerned

Accepting

Unhappy

Regretful

Resolved

Sorry

Irritated

Determined

Remorseful

Aggravated

Resigned

Teaching the Distinction Between Sadness and Depression

Many clients do not make a distinction between feeling sad and feeling depressed. Then, thinking that they feel depressed, they make themselves feel even more helpless, hopeless, and out of control, and relapse into both major depression and addictive behaviors may follow quickly. Rose Oliver, one of my supervisors at the Albert Ellis Institute when I was in training, pointed out that depression is sadness plus self-downing. Many clients benefit from talking and thinking about this distinction. If the client is depressed as well as sad over the death of her friend, what is appropriate? Sadness and grief? What does her cultural background suggest? If she insists she is depressed, is she downing herself over the death? Is she saying to herself, "I'm such a jerk. I should have gone to visit her before she died. I meant to visit her, but I just kept putting it off"?

It is always possible that her behavior was, in fact, not in line with her goals and values. Trying to help her feel better about herself may suggest that she should feel better about her behaviors. Perhaps she *did* convince herself that it was too much trouble or that she couldn't stand to see her friend in the hospital or that she was too tired to go and that she would go tomorrow.

In other words, the client may have good reasons to feel irritated with herself and aggravated by her behavior. Pointing out the discrepancy between the ways she says she wants to behave and the way she actually behaved may motivate her to work on behaving more in line with her goals and values in the future. At the same time, the therapist can point out that depressing herself (by linking her rating of her entire self with the rating of her behavior) will not help her behave differently in the future. In fact, the reverse is probably true. Depressing herself will cause her to continue to think that many things in life are too hard and, as a result, to procrastinate and make herself further unhappy.

Some clients do not want to feel any negative emotions like grief and sadness because they quickly slip from feeling bad about some event or person to feeling bad about themselves, thinking, "When I feel bad, I am bad." Such a powerful cognition will surely be accompanied by equally powerful feelings, possibly leading to addictive behaviors to get rid of both the thinking and the feelings.

Preparing for Future Trigger Situations

Developing a Specific Plan for the Client to Follow Whenever He Starts to Feel Depressed

Because a new bout of depression may trigger a relapse, it is important for the therapist and the client to decide on techniques that will help her manage her depression without resorting to addictive behaviors. The problem is that as depression sets in, a client's motivation to take any actions other than her well-known addictive behaviors often decreases significantly. Hence, a client may rapidly move from the action to the precontemplation stage regarding her depression. Nevertheless, it is useful to develop relapse prevention plans that are as specific as possible for both the depression and the addictive behavior(s). For example, the client and the therapist may agree that the client will do one or more of the following:

1. Call the therapist at a specific time during the day, for example, after work, at 5 P.M., or if he awakes feeling depressed, at 8 A.M. Perhaps an extra session would help. If the client knows, in advance, the specific time that he is going to take an action, he may feel less out of control and helpless. (Caution: With some clients, such a plan may only create an unhealthy level of dependency on the therapist. In addition, it may reinforce beliefs such as, "I cannot stand it." "Someone must help me." "My therapist has to solve my problems.")
2. Call his wife or girlfriend (assuming he has a supportive, understanding partner) at a similar, specific time of day. If he thinks he will be vulnerable at 5:30 P.M. at the end of the workday and that he might be tempted go to a bar to lift his spirits, would she be willing to meet him at his office, so they can go home together?
3. Go on-line and share his troubles with someone in a recovery chat room or on the SMART Recovery listserve.

4. Attend an on-line meeting.

5. Avoid being alone (one of the four bad situations in AA's mnemonic HALT). If he finds himself alone and feeling depressed and beginning to slip toward a relapse, what exactly is he going to do?

6. Go to an AA or SMART Recovery meeting.

7. Make an apple pie and share it with a friend.

8. Do an ABC and fax it or e-mail it to the therapist.

9. If the client is religious, call his religious leader, read certain scriptures, go to his place of worship to sit and meditate and pray, participate in a healing service, or take communion.

10. Read a self-help book (see Resources at the end of the chapter).

It is important to use the steps outlined in Chapter 8 for developing a plan, getting a commitment from the client, and exploring how she may derail her efforts to avoid relapse.

Doing an ABC on Another Person's Problem (see Chapter 7)

Frequently, a depressed client has grown up with a depressed mother or father. Although the client may not be able to see or cannot bring herself to admit how she contributes to her depression, she may be able analyze how another person in her life has depressed himself or herself. The therapist may be able to teach the ABC's to such a client using one of her parent's depressive problems.

Practicing Role Playing

Whether suffering from addiction or depression or both, the client may not be very good at disputing, questioning, or challenging his negative self-talk. His negative voice may be smooth and well practiced, and his healthier, more positive voice weak, confused, and ineffective. For one client I first role-played his negative, self-downing, self-condemning voice. He could not find any fault with what I said. So I reversed roles with him and modeled possible responses. Then we reversed again.

The client may not be very good at asserting himself in relationships with other people, leading to further negative self-rating (and more depressive feelings) based on his weak and addictive behaviors. Practicing in session what he might say to a waiter or a date or his boss, using reverse role playing as well, is extremely useful. Switching seats or standing up may make the exercise even more vivid.

The client may need a lot of practice to make up for years of avoidance and lack of practice. At the same time, he may undermine his attempt to change by being demanding in terms of how well he should perform, feeling he suddenly should be as assertive as he has always dreamed he could be. Despite having practically no practice most of his life, he feels he should behave as well as his friend or his boss or his coworker. This kind of demandingness may cause him to give up. At the same time he is probably evaluating his behavior in an overly critical and negative manner and convincing himself that it is too hard, as well. The therapist can work on all of these counterproductive beliefs from session to session, helping the client learn how to reprogram his conditioned, knee-jerk depressive responses.

Helping the Client Develop a More Balanced Lifestyle

Living a balanced lifestyle means developing ways to balance the conflicting wants (see Chapter 7) in the client's life. Clients who are depressed, like clients suffering from addictive disorders, often have a very dim view of their ability to affect any changes in the future. As a result, they focus most of their attention on trying to relieve their current suffering, either their depression or some other kind of emotional distress. They may have never thought about or studied how to intentionally manage their lives so as to get more overall pleasure and meaning out of life.

Some depressed and dysthymic clients have few if any ongoing projects, and it is often difficult for them, especially when they are depressed, to identify what they like and do not like. Even if they can identify their likes and dislikes, some clients (this seems especially true of women) feel uneasy or guilty doing what they like. Consequently, they may turn to addictive behaviors to quiet "the voice that will not just let me enjoy myself and relax," as one client put it. They also may have particular difficulty doing things for themselves. It is far easier for them to motivate themselves to do something for someone else. Also, they are continually anxious that they are not doing the right thing. As a result, they do nothing, or they do something that they do not want to do but feel that they should.

It is often difficult to get depressed clients to take steps to lead a more balanced life. Even the seemingly easy homework assignment, "Do something fun—other than your favorite addictive behavior," may lead to anguish. In addition, so much of their lives may have become entwined with activities and friends related to their addictive behaviors that developing a balanced life takes time, attention, and much practice. Alcoholics Anonymous and its many spinoffs are successful with some recovering clients because they provide a network of friends with similar goals and values. Without group support, many recovering individuals find cultivating balance in their lives very difficult, if not impossible.

SPECIAL PROBLEMS YOU MAY ENCOUNTER

Is It Depression or Dysthymia?

Many of the clients I see have been suffering from low-grade depression for a long time, sometimes all of their lives. Long-term, low-grade depression is called dysthymia and may, from time to time, turn into major depression. Not knowing what they were dealing with, many clients turned to a variety of addictive behaviors to manage and cope with their chronic low feelings.

Dysthymia is the "postnasal drip" of emotional disorders in that it is chronic and low grade. Most people can and do continue to go to work and to socialize, but they are frequently, if not always, "blue." They alternate between mild unhappiness, moderate depression, and major depression, or suffer from mild depression for years and years. Often a client suffering from dysthymia comes to therapy only after or during a crisis. The postnasal drip has turned into a major cold or perhaps pneumonia. Instead of being dysthymic, the client is feeling suicidal. Or perhaps a significant other, who has put up with the problem for years, finally says, "I can't stand it anymore. You're always so negative. You never seem to want to do anything. For God's sake, go talk to someone or I'm going to move out. This is just too much."

Bipolar I and II

It is increasingly common to encounter clients with bipolar I and II diagnoses. The National Comorbidity Study (Kessler et al. 1994) found bipolar I was the Axis I diagnosis most likely to co-occur with a substance use disorder. Bipolar I is defined in the *DSM-IV* as "characterized by the occurrence of one or more manic episodes or mixed episodes. . . . Often individuals have had one or more major depressive episodes" (p. 351). In contrast, bipolar II is "characterized by the occurrence of one or more major depressive episodes, accompanied by at least one hypomanic episode" (p. 359). A hypomanic episode is less severe than a manic episode in that it is "not severe enough to cause marked impairment in social and occupational functioning or necessitate hospitalization and there are no psychotic features" (p. 338). Given the fact that some clients do not reveal to psychiatrists that they are using drugs, the therapist should be careful to consider that the client may be suffering instead from a substance-induced mood disorder.

"Wonderfulizing" and "Awfulizing"

Perhaps many bipolar disorders have a chemical component, but my experience suggests that such a client is often desperately searching for a "fix," and not necessarily heroin. For months he goes through the day trying to figure out how to fix himself. He engages not only in linking but also in awfulizing.

Finally, he starts to formulate a plan, and he begins to develop hope. But then he starts to engage in "wonderfulizing." He starts to think: "This is going to work. This will really change my life. People won't think so ill of me if I do that. And I'll feel better." As he rolls these positive, hopeful thoughts through his mind, his thinking becomes increasingly positive, and the intensity of his elation increases. But no real plan can fix his constant negative rating of himself, and eventually the whole house of cards comes crashing down, and the cycle of self-condemnation begins again.

CBT-ers and REBT-ers teach clients not to awfulize, but with some clients, especially those who have a history of manic-depression, "wonderfulizing" is just as dangerous. It is often very difficult to get such a client to give up his deep-seated belief and feeling that there is something wrong with him, and the belief that something absolutely wonderful has to be found to fix him. The more that he feels is wrong, the bigger and better the fix has to be. Slowly changing some of his behaviors, adding some pleasurable activities to his life, and working through the roots of his desperately negative feeling about himself takes time, and in the meantime a down or an up cycle may lead to an addictive relapse.

Often such a client has resorted to chemicals (and sometimes gambling or sex) to cope with the extreme and painful ups and downs in his emotional life, often worsening the condition.

Forgiveness and Acceptance

Many depressed clients must be helped to forgive themselves and to accept that what they have done with their lives cannot be changed. (The issue of forgiveness is discussed in greater length in

Chapter 13.) Learning to stop demanding that things should have been different or that the client should have been different takes time. Using the ABC technique, the therapist can help the client begin to work on such difficult topics. At the same time, keeping the focus on the future, especially the next two weeks, often works effectively.

Depression and Procrastination: A Vicious Circle

Procrastination is, in essence, avoidant behavior and often addictive in itself. Because the client is frequently depressed (or suffering from dysthymia), he may also frequently procrastinate. He may then add to his depression by self-downing about his procrastination. So depression feeds into procrastination and procrastination feeds into depression. Moreover, the client may use another form of avoidant, addictive behavior such as drinking, gambling, sex, or shopping to avoid the distress created by his procrastination.

Although it is difficult to break these vicious cycles, getting something done that the client has been procrastinating on for months or years may have a surprisingly good effect on his feeling of self-efficacy. Of course, it is important to help the client select a goal that he can succeed at. Some goals are more easily achieved and will give the client more pleasure than others. When one of my clients finally bought himself an air conditioner, he had tangible, palpable evidence that he was beginning to change. And when he bought some new shirts, he felt even better. Because he is also addicted to "but . . . ing"—"But I should have bought these things a long time ago. I'm such a jerk." "But I should have gotten a new suit, too. I don't know why I didn't when I was right there in the store"—I spent considerable time in session ensuring that he was, in fact, learning to savor his accomplishments.

Low Frustration Tolerance

Procrastination may be caused by demandingness—"Life should be easier. I shouldn't have to do this"—and exaggerating the difficulty of doing something (awfulizing), but it is often due to LFT, an unwillingness to accept the discomfort and frustration that accompanies many daily activities. The client may consistently avoid doing things by telling herself, "It will be too hard. I won't be able to stand it" instead of, "This may be very hard, but I can probably get through it."

Helping the client identify her LFT and then practice working through it will significantly contribute to her recovery from depression. She will no longer be hit by the mess in her apartment and the mound of unpaid bills, and she will begin to recover some control in her life. Procrastination and avoidant behaviors have a lot in common with addictive behaviors. They are all self-control problems. What the client learns from overcoming one may help her overcome another.

ISSUES TO KEEP IN MIND

Working with a Psychiatrist or Psychopharmacologist

I am not a strong advocate of medication, but I am a strong advocate of risk or harm reduction. Many clients overestimate their ability, given renewed depressive feelings, to continue to moderate or abstain from destructive (sometimes potentially lethal) addictive behaviors. Consequently, I urge some clients to consult with a psychiatrist and to use various medications while they are learning how to live without engaging in addictive behaviors. I work with several good psychiatrists to help my clients, especially clients who have many difficult problems. I appreciate the insights and input I receive from another professional, and I like having someone else to consult with when emergencies occur. Moreover, I do not have the time to keep abreast of the information about various medications and their interactions with other medications. However, it may be difficult to find a good psychiatrist to work with. Many seem to spend little time with their patients and some may resent talking to another mental health care provider. Finding a good psychiatrist to work with the client while he or she is trying to cut down or stop is even more difficult.

The selective serotonin reuptake inhibitor (SSRI) antidepressants are especially effective with moderate depression and dysthymia, but the client may object for several reasons: he does not want to be on another drug, he is worried about the long-term effects, and he has heard about the side effects, especially sexual dysfunction. He may also have tried an antidepressant and had a bad reaction himself. Sometimes it is his internist who has prescribed it. Some internists do not have extensive experience with the variety of psychotropic medications now on the market. Consequently, he may not have urged the client to try different medication or a combination of medications.

Working with an Endocrinologist

There is evidence that some people are especially sensitive to changes in hormonal levels. Depression may be kicked off by such changes, postpartum depression being the clearest example. If the therapist suspects hormones may be playing a role, the client should consult an endocrinologist or a gynecologist who specializes in endocrinology as perimenopausal or early menopausal symptoms may trigger depression.

Depression About Depression

Many clients increase the intensity and duration of their depressed feelings by getting depressed about being depressed.

Wayne occasionally wakes up feeling as if the "black dog" of depression is back. He immediately begins to catastrophize and overgeneralize: "Oh, this is terrible. I'm going to be depressed again. How can I get through the day? What's wrong with me? I can't stand it anymore. I'm just no good—at anything." As a result of such of a combination of catastrophizing, overgeneralizing,

I-can't-stand-it-itis, and self-downing, he quickly increases his upsetness and the intensity of his depression.

Developmental Issues

What depresses a 25-year-old may not depress a 75-year-old and vice versa. On the other hand, they may both be thinking the same thing: "My life is finished. It's too late."

One of my 25-year-old clients, Alex, believed he had wasted the last ten years of his life smoking pot and playing around while his friends had gone to college and now were firmly established on a career path. Although many young people in their twenties have no idea where they are going, many people change markedly at 30, choosing and sticking to a path for a decade or so. However, from Alex's perspective, he was doomed.

Frank, a 55-year-old client, drank himself to sleep for similar reasons. He was always supposed to be a great architect, but it had not worked out that way. He had always had work as an architect, and he admitted that everyone he worked for valued his contributions tremendously (and he was well paid for his work), but he was by no means great. And it was too late, as far as he was concerned.

In both cases, I spent time exploring their criteria for a good life. In Frank's case, what was the measuring stick he was using to value life? Would his peers agree with him? Did his peers also feel like failures because they had not become great architects? It turned out that, to Frank, being average was intolerable. He had always set his sights on being exceptional. Fortunately, he was highly regarded by his peers and eventually he began to accept that although he had not become great, he was not a failure nor mediocre (something that in his mind was almost worse than a failure).

At the same time that Alex and I discussed the evidence that it was too late and he was doomed, I also helped him get over his low frustration tolerance regarding doing what he had to do to catch up.

That is, we worked hard not only to change the way he thought about his original A (activating event), having spent much of ten years of his life smoking pot and doing little else. He was, in fact, behind in his career development compared to many of his friends, so we also worked to help him change that A. That is, what was he saying and thinking and feeling that was getting in the way of his catching up, since that was what he said he wanted to do?

Stigma

People suffering from depression are embarrassed about it. They feel that other people are judging them and stigmatizing them for not being able to get over it, and they may be right. This may become especially true if the depression lasts for a long time or recurs frequently. The fact that some famous people have written books about their battles with depression has not changed the general public's stigmatizing mindset very much. The client's friends may begin to avoid him and his boss may try to find a reason to let him go. That makes depression similar to most addictions. Consequently, most clients who suffer from depression also suffer from shame and anxiety, and from depression about their depression. The therapist should address these feelings about the original problem. This is the rating game played at its most ferocious level: "I am no good. I deserve to die. I hate myself. I hate the world."

Familial/Genetic Issues

The client may beat himself up for being depressed as a result of agreeing with the people who he imagines are thinking, "You should be able to pull yourself together. For Pete's sake, get over it. Life is tough, but stop wallowing in it. Try harder." But usually he is not the only person suffering from depression in his family. Often a sibling and one or both parents have battled with it. The client must recognize that his problem may be due in part to inherited chemical differences, and it may have been worsened (or caused) by the family environment. His depressed parents may have found it difficult to attend to his emotional needs. His real problem is to learn how to compensate for the problem. What can he do to help himself?

Gender Issues

The client's gender will almost always contribute to her or his depression. For example, a 40-year-old woman may be very depressed by the idea that she will probably not have children. A 40-year-old man is not faced with the same dilemma. However, for some men, while they may treasure their children above everything else, they must succeed in their chosen career to feel good about themselves. To not succeed is to admit to being a failure as a person.

Social, Political, and Economic Issues

Some clients depress themselves over the state of the world— ethnic killings, huge disparities in wealth and power, political corruption, police brutality. Cognitive-behavioral therapy may emphasize working on oneself, but that does not negate the fact that aspects of the social, economic, and political reality often make life much more difficult for many people. The fact that race and gender may affect hiring and firing decisions are not imaginary problems. In Europe, therapists take into account the impact of political, social, and economic forces on an individual's problems, but American therapists may overemphasize the role of the individual over the system.

It is important to point out that depressing oneself is not the only possible emotional response to the impact of social, political, and economic forces. It may be the client's traditional, conditioned response to bad events. She may have learned or inherited it from her family. It may continue to be her initial, knee-jerk response. But that does not make it the only possible response. What do other people who are at times very upset by events in their city or state, country or world do? How do they think and feel?

Spiritual and Existential Issues

Depression and addictive behaviors are almost always affected by clients' underlying beliefs about life, whether they are aware of and can articulate these beliefs or not. All people have some ideas about what they should do with their lives, and many have ideas of what will happen after they die, often as a result of how closely they did what they should have done or not.

Because beliefs such as "What's the point?" "Life stinks" "The world stinks" are subscribed to be many people who are depressed, it is important to explore with clients what they think about life. What is the point? What do they believe a person should do with his life? What should one do at 30? At 45? At 75? How do you measure a life's worth or lack of worth? What seems to have influenced the lives of their parents? (Spiritual issues are addressed in Chapter 15.)

Rollo May (1969) has argued that all psychotherapy is existential. That is, therapists and clients inevitably wrestle with the most difficult questions of existence. Working on addictive behaviors inevitably draws us into discussing profound existential issues. What is the point of giving up an addictive behavior if the client has nothing meaningful in her life? As I mentioned in Chapter 2, it is the combination of broad, existential, sometimes spiritual discussions coupled with concrete, specific, frequently behavioral work that seems to appeal to many clients.

Caution: Some clients should avoid doing existential thinking ("What is the meaning of all this? Why should I bother? What's the point?") when they are depressed. Being depressed is like being drunk, but negatively. One's chemistry is off. When they feel better, they may begin to think about the answers to such difficult questions. But they must be careful because they are in a fragile state and could very easily depress themselves further. It may be safer to address these issues in therapy.

Exercise

For many people exercise constitutes the least expensive antidepressant available. Getting depressed clients to exercise is often as difficult as getting them to change their addictive behaviors. Even people who are not depressed have great difficulty exercising consistently. Using a stages of change approach and similar techniques (e.g., ABC's and trying out various specific plans) often ultimately effects an increase in exercise, which in turn, changes a client's thinking about himself and about his depression.

Nutrition

Poor nutrition affects our moods, but depressed clients are perhaps more susceptible to eating poorly than other clients. The underlying beliefs of depressed clients—"What's the point? Nothing will ever change. It's too much trouble"—cause them to take care of themselves less well than clients who primarily suffer from anger, shame, guilt, or anxiety. At some point, it may be helpful to find out exactly what the client eats for breakfast, lunch, dinner, and snacks. Sometimes, I say to a client with poor nutrition: "If I ate like you do, I would feel depressed, without energy, and probably anxious, too." I occasionally refer clients to a nutritionist because poor nutrition may contribute to lapses and relapses. However, my experience with nutritionists has not been good, as they are not psychologically oriented. They don't know about the stages of change and they act like everyone I refer is ready to make significant changes in their eating habits. Thus, nutritionists suggest major changes in diet and recommend massive doses of vitamins, and most of their recommendations are ignored, dismissed, or forgotten. Most of my clients are ambivalent about changing their diet, if they will even discuss the issue at all. They may be willing to swallow some vitamin pills—not much effort in that!—but even that they may do in only half-hearted attempts at the beginning and then, seeing no immediate result, quit. Changing the way they eat is even more difficult.

Sleep

Many clients are sleep deprived. From sleep research we know that as people become more sleep deprived they become irritable, lose the ability to concentrate, and feel sluggish. At work they become inefficient and feel hassled. Falling behind at work makes most people anxious and somewhat depressed: "What is wrong with me? I didn't get anything done today. My God, if the boss finds out how far behind on this project I am he's going to blow his top." Letting their home become a mess and failing to pay the bills contributes to awfulizing, LFT, self-condemnation, self-pity, and more procrastination and depression, which can lead some clients to drink or drug or hide under a pillow and sleep through the day, contributing further to their depressive thoughts. They also upset their chemistry and diurnal rhythms, making it even more difficult to get back on track. Conversely, some clients are so anxious and distraught that they cannot get to sleep, staying up all night watching TV. It is not difficult to understand why some clients resort to old, tried-and-true addictive behaviors to try to regain control over their wake–sleep cycle. Yet the research (Graham 1998, NIAAA 1998) is quite clear that alcohol in particular disrupts normal sleep patterns and contributes to sleep deprivation. Thus, the therapist should ask direct, pointed questions about the client's sleep patterns.

FIVE HOMEWORK ASSIGNMENTS

Homework assignments should focus on relapse prevention— of both depression and addictive behaviors. Here are a few suggestions:

✓ **Ongoing activities:** Client need help in developing more ongoing activities. Ongoing, enjoyable projects are extremely important for a client who suffers from dysthymia and/or recurrent depression. Once depressed, it is often impossible to start a new activity. If he puts all of his time and energy into only one or two areas, for example his job and his marriage, he makes himself vulnerable to relapse if one or both develop problems. However, if he is involved in ongoing activities, he may be able to help himself keep from getting depressed. Many people who enjoy such activities know that the annoyances and inconveniences in life that trouble others do not bother them as much. Motorcycle clubs, auto racing clubs, rock climbing, skiing clubs, choirs, hiking clubs, and political clubs all provide places where clients can enrich their lives and make friends.

Caution: Clients should avoid going to one-time-only events, like a walking tour or a hike. The people signing up for such events may be equally depressed, socially awkward, or lonely. The client may leave the event more convinced than ever that he is a loser and has made a fool of himself. Instead, he should join *ongoing* groups like those cited above.

The client may not acknowledge that it takes time for people to relax, open up, and greet him the way he wants to be greeted. He may be thinking, "People should be more friendly." Or he may think that he should be greeted when he enters a room when, in most cultures, it is the person entering who initiates the greeting. Or he may resist the fact that once having joined an organization, he often has to pay his "dues" in terms of work or attendance. He may be thinking: "I shouldn't have to make such an effort. People ought to be able to see what kind of a person I am from the beginning." He wants (demands?) people to welcome and embrace him as if he were an old member from the beginning, and he never attends enough meetings to discover that they would if he gave them enough time. He quits too soon.

The client should learn the "rule of three." The first time he attends a meeting, he may think he is going to die. The second time he may feel almost as bad. But the third time he will feel much better. Most importantly, after four or five meetings, some people will begin to welcome him with, "Hi, Joe. How's it going? Nice to see you."

Gardening and cooking are two other activities that can be ongoing. Gardens grow each year, and weeds need to be pulled. If something fails to grow, you can try again next year. You do not ever want to weed, but if you want to get another of your "wants," a nice garden, you know you have to. In cooking, new

dishes can be tried, and if they fail, the client can learn to shrug
it off rather than feeling foolish, ashamed, rageful, or depressed.

   Language classes, art classes, t'ai chi classes, yoga classes, and
meditation all provide the same kind of ongoing interactions,
provided they meet for at least ten or twelve sessions during a
term. Again, developing a skill and/or cultivating relationships
takes time. The client may also find it difficult to accept that
people never quite seem to act the way she thinks they should:
"They're so stupid/insincere/judgmental, as they shouldn't
be. I can't stand it." The therapist can help her develop the
skills—both cognitive and behavioral—that will help her build
new relationships.

✓ **Exercise** is difficult to do and to continue, but it is an
inexpensive antidepressant.

✓ **Regularize sleeping:** The client should figure out how much
sleep she needs and then try to get it. At the same time, she
should not become obsessive about sleep. Thoughts like, "I
have to get enough sleep" will probably only contribute to the
problem. Many people who have trouble with alcohol have
trouble sleeping. Which came first, the sleep problem or the
drinking problem? That is often difficult to answer, although we
know that taking a drink before going to sleep contributes to
poor sleeping in the second half of the night. Sleeping too little
or eating very irregularly may exacerbate the problems.

✓ **Depression as a virus:** The client can try to treat depression like
a mild virus: "Get up. Shower. Go to work. Tell yourself that
you will not strain to do anything today. You will just do what
has to be done and nothing more, because you are sick." Many
clients find that by eleven o'clock the "virus" has passed. Instead
of awfulizing and depressing themselves about their depressed
feelings, moving their body, going to work (as opposed to
staying inactive in the apparent safety of their bed) eliminates
the problem.

To get her blood sugar up and her metabolism going, the client can start her day slowly in bed by wiggling her toes. She can try not to think. Then she can move to the bathroom, shifting her focus of attention away from herself, her feelings, and her preoccupations to something that she has to do outside of herself, like going to the bathroom. The physical movement and engagement in the world may be far more effective than any cognitive disputing.

✓ **Reading non-CBT/REBT books:** Men and women have grappled with the meaning of life since time began. Clients can read Bertrand Russell's *Unpopular Essays* (1950) or *The Conquest of Happiness* (1930), Victor Frankl's *Man's Search for Meaning* (1959), Tillich's *The Courage to Be* (1952), Rollo May's *Love and Will* (1969), or the Bible, the Koran, or some other religious book.

MEDICATIONS

Antidepressants

Only two years ago I called a psychiatrist and asked him if he would see one of my clients who was depressed and had a drinking problem. "No. I don't see patients who have a substance abuse problem. But if you get him off the alcohol, I'll be happy to see him." Even in a sophisticated city like New York, this is not an unusual response.

The SSRI drugs may help the client prevent lapses and relapses for several reasons. First, he may not feel as low and hopeless and helpless. Any of these negative affect states may have precipitated a relapse in the past. Second, some of the SSRIs seem to help people be less obsessive-compulsive. It is possible, therefore, that they will also be less obsessive about getting whatever it is they want— alcohol, cigarettes, heroin, a new pair of shoes. Third, the same drugs that help with depression also seem to be effective on a variety of chronic anxiety disorders, including social anxiety. Finally, some SSRI drugs also seem to be helpful in decreasing the anger and hostility that some clients chronically feel through most days and that in the past they drank to cover up.

Certainly it is preferable to stop drinking alcohol, a known depressant, before taking an SSRI antidepressant such as Prozac, Zoloft, or Effexor, but there is no research evidence that I know of that they interact with negative effects. (However, clients using the older monoamine oxidase (MAO) inhibitor antidepressants can kill themselves if they drink wine.) Alcohol may cancel out the effects of the antidepressant, but, again, I know of no research that indicates this. While clients may not recover from depression while they are taking ethanol and SSRI antidepressants, they may not get more depressed and they may not drink as much or as frequently.

RESOURCES

The following books can serve as further resources for clients:

- Burn's *Feeling Good* (1981)
- Ellis and Harper's *A New Guide to Rational Living* (1975) and Ellis's *How to Make Yourself Happy and Remarkably Less Disturbable* (1999)
- Ellis and Becker's *A Guide to Personal Happiness* (1982)
- Ellis & Hauck's *Overcoming Procrastination* (1977)
- Peck's *A Road Less Traveled* (1978)

12 ANXIETY AND ADDICTIVE BEHAVIOR

It is not death that man should fear, but he should fear never beginning to live.

—Marcus Aurelius

The mental health movement, in promising a freedom from anxiety that is not possible, may have had a significant role in the current belief that it is a right to feel good, thus contributing to the burgeoning consumption of alcohol and the almost universal prescription of the tranquilizer by physicians.

—N. A. Cummings

Is the client abusing alcohol or drugs or engaging in other types of addictive behaviors (shopping, overeating, gambling, risky sex) to cope with anxiety? Anxiety is a part of the human condition, and humans have developed thousands of ways to calm down, including chemicals, medications, herbs, teas, meditation, yoga, sex, fishing, listening to music, baths, spas, gambling, shopping, cleaning, reading, and working. Unfortunately, some people get into trouble by overusing one or more of these techniques, which work well in the short run but create problems in the medium and long run. It is not surprising, therefore, that anxiety disorders and addictive disorders often interact and contribute to each other.

WHAT DOES THE RESEARCH SUGGEST?

- Carey and colleagues (1999) report that 14.6% of persons with anxiety disorders also meet the lifetime criteria for an alcohol or drug disorder.
- In a seven-year, follow-up study of 454 freshmen at a midwestern university, participants with a anxiety disorder in the first and fourth year of the study showed a four times greater likelihood of having being diagnosed with alcohol dependence in the seventh year. Those with alcohol dependence in years one or four were three to five times more likely to be diagnosed with an anxiety disorder in the seventh year. In fact, initially, anxiety disorders were more prevalent in participants who came from families with an alcohol use disorder than from families without such a disorder. Either disorder may precede—and probably contribute to—the other (Kushner et al. 1999).
- In laboratory-induced panic and state anxiety, alcohol consumption significantly reduced the reported state anxiety and the number of panic attacks (Kushner et al. 1996).
- Positron emission tomography (PET) scan research suggests that some people become "stuck" in an anxious, hypervigilant state. Related blood flow patterns in the brain remain even when the fear-producing factor has been removed (Rauch et al. 1994, 1995).
- Kagan (1989) and Kagan and Snidman (1991) found that some people are born with more reactive nervous systems than others. Coping with such a nervous system can be a lifelong problem. Shyness and, in extreme cases, social phobia may result. However, supportive, gentle parenting may help children overcome the effects (Dadds et al. 1999).
- Research suggests that nicotine is angiogenic—that is, it causes an increase in anxiety—rather than anxiolytic, causing a decrease in anxiety. Smokers may find that hard to believe.

However, while the act of smoking may relax a smoker, West and Hajek's (1997) research suggests that nicotine actually contributes to an overall greater feeling of anxiety. In a carefully designed study of seventy subjects who stopped smoking and did not smoke at all during the first four weeks, anxiety decreased significantly from the first week of abstinence.

SELECTED CLINICAL STRATEGIES

Session Goals

The goals with these clients are the following:

1. To reduce the frequency, duration, and intensity (FDI) of lapses and relapses related to anxiety by reducing the FDI of anxiety itself.
2. To help the client learn how to reduce his or her anxiety without resorting to addictive behaviors.

As with other emotions that may contribute to addictive behaviors, the client may be in one stage regarding changing her addictive behaviors but in another stage regarding working on her anxiety. Drinking or pot use may be a Type III problem. She has already decided that she wants to stop or reduce her use. However, she may or may not see that anxiety plays a significant role in lapses and relapses. Consequently, she may not be interested in learning ways to better manage her anxiety. Conversely, she may openly acknowledge her problems with anxiety but deny that she has serious problems with alcohol or marijuana. She has come to therapy because she is having panic attacks, and if the therapist does not carefully question her about possible addictive behaviors, she won't report them.

Exploring the Problem

The therapist should listen carefully to the client, especially while exploring what was happening just prior to her last addictive episode and while doing a pre-AB (see Chapter 2). Here are some typical beliefs to watch for:

I must not lose control in this social situation of how I behave or of my bodily functions.

I must behave in a socially acceptable manner at all times.

I must never make a fool of myself in front of other people. If I did, it would be terrible and I couldn't stand it.

When I'm anxious, people can tell—and that mustn't happen. I can't stand it if I think they can see I'm anxious.

Anxiety isn't my real problem. Drinking is.

If I drink or smoke (pot or a cigarette), it helps (and I must help myself).

If I smoke (pot or a cigarette), I can work better—concentrate better, sit longer, and produce more (with less discomfort anxiety).

The last belief is not necessarily irrational or dysfunctional. In moderate quantities, alcohol works quite effectively as an antianxiety medication. Many people smoke pot for similar reasons, and some appear not to run into serious problems. For that reason, the client may resist giving up such a widely accepted anxiolytic.

The very fact that alcohol and pot are used so widely may contribute to other, often even more potent and dangerous, irrational beliefs, such as "It's not fair. Others can drink. I should be able to drink when I want to, too." These beliefs may add anger and self-pity to the emotional mix.

Here are some other possible unstated, hidden beliefs:

Talking about anxiety is too uncomfortable. I can't stand it.

I'm ashamed to be so anxious. Real men aren't so anxious.

I'll never get over my anxiety.

I always make mistakes (and I shouldn't—it upsets people when I do, and I hate it when people get upset). Even thinking about making mistakes makes me anxious.

If I drink something (anything) it will help, and the caffeine in this Coke (or coffee) really won't affect me.

One cigarette won't matter, and it will help me calm down.

Again, it is important to help the client see what parts of the above sentences/beliefs are true, for example, "It will help me calm down" and what part may be completely irrational, "One cigarette won't matter." "It won't matter" may be true for some people, but it is not true for someone trying to quit. It is especially not true for someone who has quit in the past year or so.

Using Inference Chaining

Inference chaining is one of the most powerful cognitive techniques to use when a client is suffering from anxiety, especially when he is deeply confused about his anxiety reactions. He knows rationally that nothing terrible will happen, but he feels deeply that it will. In the example below, Marty simply could not understand why he continued to resist making cold calls even after his boss had warned him that he might lose his job. It just didn't make sense to him. He knew, he said, that nothing terrible was going to happen, but he felt terribly anxious even when he thought about making such calls.

Marty, a 43-year-old client, had been a stockbroker for over ten years with the same firm. He used to get plenty of business through old friends and a few family member, but for a variety of reasons outside of Marty's control, that business started to drop off a year ago. His boss had warned him that he had to generate more business and that meant making cold calls. For the past four months he had been trying to make such calls, but usually he managed only one or two a month, and even these were usually to old customers. He had also begun to drink heavily after work. His wife was complaining, and recently his boss called him into her office because she could smell alcohol on his breath. She told him that he had to get his drinking under control and he had to generate more business if he was going to stay with the firm.

Marty was very anxious about his situation. He feared that he might get fired and he could not see how he could maintain his lifestyle if that happened. At the same time, it was also possible that Marty simply did not like his job anymore. It had always been extremely stressful, and the need to generate new business was making it worse. It appeared to have turned an enjoyable job into a dreaded one. Perhaps Marty was going through a mid-life crisis, assessing and evaluating what he had done with his life up to that point. The added pressure to find business was making it very difficult for him to think in an even-handed manner about such important issues. At the same time, the thought that he actually might quit and do something else may also have been adding to his anxiety.

On the other hand, as I looked at him sitting in my office, I reflected that he was actually not in such a bad position. If he lost his job, he could get another one relatively easily. The stock market was doing well, and firms were looking for experienced traders. He had been married ten years and he and his wife still seemed to love each other. They had two children and lived in a good neighborhood in New York, in an apartment that they owned. He had friends with whom he went regularly to Knick and Ranger games, and he loved to play golf. Neither he nor his wife seemed to be extravagant spenders, and his wife's work as an attorney brought in almost as much income as Marty's.

In the second session, after some preliminary chitchat, I asked, "What would you like to work on? How did the cold calling go?"

"Not very well. I don't know what's the matter with me. I just don't do it. I do everything else. I did call a few old clients, but those are not really cold calls."

"Well," I said, "Let's imagine you're just about to pick up the phone and you feel your anxiety rising up in you. Close your eyes and imagine yourself sitting at your desk about to make a cold call. When you have yourself really worked up and anxious, raise your finger. (After Marty signaled with his finger): Okay. Now what are you thinking?"

"He may not accept my call. Or if he takes the call, he'll tell me he's not interested."

"Well, let's suppose he tells you he's not interested, then what?"

"Then I'll hang up and feel awful."

"Well, let's assume you hang up and feel awful. Then what?"

"I'll do something else instead of making any more calls."

"Well, let's assume you don't make any more calls. Then what?"

"Well, then Pam will fire me. She's already warned me."

"Okay, let's assume Pam fires you. I don't think that would happen, but just for this exercise, let's assume it did. Now, I don't want to seem callous. Remember, this is just an exercise to try to understand what is so frightening to you. What would be so terrible about that?"

"Well, actually, not that much, to be honest with you. I probably should have changed firms a long time ago. Getting the boot would probably be just the thing I need to get myself moving."

"Yes, I know. That might be correct, but let's keep on the irrational track today. We are trying to find out what you are telling yourself that is scaring you so much. So we want to listen to the really irrational thoughts. I am hypothesizing that there is a whole string of really irrational thoughts—I call them 'really wacky' when I am thinking of myself. Does 'wacky' bother you?"

"No."

"Okay, so let's listen to your really wacky thoughts today so that we can get a better idea of how you are making yourself so anxious. I think there is a whole chain of thoughts. Later we can go back and examine the reasonableness or rationality of each link, but for now, let's give your wacky thoughts their day in court. It's like they never get a chance to be heard. You quash them down so fast that you have no idea of what you are really thinking. So try to stay on the irrational side for now. Okay?"

"Okay."

"So, let's assume that you get fired, what's so terrible about that? What frightens you about that?"

"Well, then I might not be able to pay my bills. I might lose my house."

"Yes, you might. I don't think that would happen, but for this exercise, let's assume you can't pay your bills and you lose your house. Then what?"

"Well, my wife would leave me."

"Perhaps. I don't think so, but let's assume you're right, so she leaves you. Then what?"

"Well, I know it's wacky, but I see myself as some kind of bum on the street."

"Right. And then?"

"I don't know. What's worse than that?"

"I don't know. What is? Let's assume that you're a bum on the street."

"That would be terrible."

"Why?"

"I don't know. That would mean I was a complete failure."

"Well, let's go along with that for a while. So you're a complete failure and a bum on the street, then what would happen?"

"I don't know. That's the end of the line."

"Well, what do you look like? Where are you? Can you see yourself?"

"Yeah, I'm lying on the sidewalk with a blanket over me."

"Anything else?"

"I'm filthy. I haven't had a bath for who knows how long?"

Looking at Marty, who was always very well dressed, I realized that that could be his worst fear. On the other hand, having done inference chains with lots of clients, I thought that it was more likely that this was only another link in the chain. I suspected he probably feared something much worse than winding up a bum in the streets. Another client, a cell phone salesman, 28, equally well dressed—he looked like he really wanted to be an investment banker—feared that he would eventually wind up lying in the gutter, then the police would take him to a hospital. There someone would give him too many drugs. He told me, "Then I'll wind up in one of those insane asylums. You know, I'll be one of those guys that they gave so many drugs to that he can't speak." When I asked him what he looked like, he said, "I'm on the floor slobbering all over myself." That was his worst fear.

Continuing with Marty, I asked, "And what does that mean?"

"That I'm a complete failure, like I told you."

"So you're lying on the sidewalk, filthy and a complete failure. What would happen then?"

"I don't know. That's it."

"Nothing more?"

"No."

"Okay, perhaps it is. So my hypothesis is that when you reach for the phone, you're putting your entire life at risk. You are not just risking that someone will reject your call or tell you they're not interested. You're really thinking that you'd lose your job and then your house and then your wife would leave you and then you'd be all alone, by yourself, filthy, on the sidewalk. Everything you've ever wanted or dreamed of would be gone. You'd be, to use your words, a complete failure. Is that right?"

"Yes. Maybe."

"That's why you're so scared. There *is* a lot at stake."

"But I don't really think all those things will happen."

"Well, part of you doesn't, but part of you does—at least, that's what it seems. That's why you're so anxious and why it doesn't make sense to you. You aren't really aware of everything you're thinking."

"Well, now what do I do?"

"Well, we can work in three different ways—cognitively, emotively, and behaviorally. Cognitively, you and I can look at your beliefs. We can examine each link in the chain. You are thinking that if you lost your house, then your wife would leave you."

"But that's crazy. I know she wouldn't do that."

"Well, what would happen if you couldn't afford to keep up your payments on your house?"

"Well, she sure wouldn't be happy. That would put a lot of strain on our marriage, but the truth is she's always stood by me, and I know she wouldn't dump me for that. I don't know what we'd do, but that's not what's going to happen."

"Well, what might happen?"

"I guess we'd have to move into a smaller house, or she might have to go to work. I don't know."

"Right. But now at least a part of you is thinking, although you don't realize it, if you lose your house, you'd also lose your wife. But that's just one link. We have to examine all of them. You can take this piece of paper home. I've written down what you said. When you bring beliefs to the surface, you can kind of air them out. You can see how much they make sense or not. And the more you acknowledge them, sometimes even with a sense of humor, rather than denying their existence and pushing them down, the less powerful they become. At the same time, behaviorally, you can try to make a call tomorrow and focus simply on succeeding or failing at that one call. You can try saying something to yourself like: 'I won't die. And I'm not going to become a bum if this guy isn't interested. It's just a call, not my whole life.' Do you think you could do that one time each day?"

"Yes."

"At what time of the day? I recommend 9:30 or 10 in the morning so that you get it done and then you can savor having done it all day. Otherwise you may infect the whole day with anxiety over doing it. What do you think?"

"Okay. I think I can do that."

"How confident are you that you'll do it at 10 A.M. every day for a week?"

"100%."

"Okay. We'll see how that goes."

Discussion

Inference chaining hypothesizes that the things people really fear are hidden behind a long chain of inferences, many of which do not on their surface make sense to the client. Inference chaining is a way of bringing to consciousness the dreaded events that they anticipate subconsciously will happen if they give up drinking or smoking or using benzodiazepines, or make a presentation, or fly on a plane.

Marty has a number of beliefs, each more dreadful than the previous one, leading all the way back to his fear that he will wind up a bum on the street. Each belief constitutes a link in this chain of fears. Uncovering the links in this chain of inferences has three therapeutic effects: (1) It helps Marty understand why he is feeling so anxious when what he is trying to do, on the surface, does not seem so terrifying. (2) That, in turns, helps him begin to accept himself with the problem. (3) Then he can begin to examine the rationality of each link.

Points to Keep in Mind

1. **The therapist should usually keep his responses to a minimum.** After asking, "What do you think will happen if you made a cold call?" and the client has answered, the therapist simply says: "And then?" "And then what would happen?" "And what would that mean?" "What would be so terrible about that?" "What's the worst-case scenario?"
2. **The therapist should keep a record,** writing down what the client says so that each link will be remembered, along with the client's way of phrasing it.
3. **The therapist can facilitate uncovering the links.** If the client has a hard time coming up with or uncovering the

next link, the therapist can repeat the most dreadful part of what he has just implied will happen: "Okay, so then your wife will leave you. Then what?"

4. **The therapist must reassure the client.** If the client seems anxious during this process, the therapist can add some reassurance that what he is hypothesizing probably won't actually occur: "Okay, so let's assume that your wife leaves you. I don't think that's very probable, but let's assume just for this exercise that she leaves you, then what?"

5. **The therapist should stay with the "irrational."** Keep the client expressing his fears. He may suddenly switch to a more rational comment: "Well, then I might lose my job, but that might be great because I've needed to leave this rotten job for a long time. I'd probably get a better one if I would just get out there and look."

The therapist replies: "Yes, that may be true. But that is not what is making you so anxious. Let's give your irrational side its day in court. Let's listen to your not-so-rational side. It may seem so terrifying to you that you keep pushing it down and denying it. That way, you never really find out what you are thinking. Try to stay on the irrational side for the time being. So let's assume you lost your job, then what? What would be so terrible about that? What's the worst-case scenario?"

Using Graduated In Vivo Exposure

Gaining insight into possible reasons why the client feels anxious so much of the time may help a great deal. It may cause him to take a more compassionate, accepting attitude toward himself and his problem. As a result, he may be more motivated to work directly, that is, behaviorally, on his problem. However, insight is usually not sufficient. Behavioral exercises designed to help the client work on his fears are critically important.

Behavioral exercises are most effective when they are planned, graduated in difficulty, and repeated a sufficient number of times to change the client's conditioning and thinking.

Planning permits the client to feel that he has some control over his anxiety reactions. At least, he can sometimes choose when they occur. But, many clients may be very reluctant to intentionally bring on their terribly scary and uncomfortable anxiety symptoms. Clients must be motivated to move from precontemplation to contemplation to action.

Graduated refers to the fact that most people have a hierarchy of fears in their mind. For example, it is less frightening to go out with three good friends than to go to a party. It is less frightening to go to a party where you know all of the people than a party where you know only one or two people. Therefore, the client should do a series of exercises that gradually become more anxiety producing.

Many clients do not want to accept that they probably will have to repeat the exercise several times before they feel any significant reduction in anxiety. I tell them that a "rule of three" seems to be true. The first time you feel like you're going to die. The second time you feel slightly better. And the third time you feel substantially less anxious.

As Craske and Barlow (1994) point out in their *Client Workbook*, clients may feel that they have already tried in vivo desensitization and that it hasn't worked. Craske and Barlow propose several reasons why it may not have worked. For example, the client may not have repeated the exercise enough times. Or he may have "white knuckled" himself through the experience. That is, he did not really change the way he was thinking, he just forced himself to stand the anxiety. That is why simply taking a behavioral approach will often not work. Clients must also work on their irrational beliefs at the same time.

Some clients use objects or people or other behaviors to keep themselves safe, in the belief that these objects, people, or behaviors will prevent the feared reactions. For example, one client, Andreas, always had at least three drinks before he went to a party, "to make sure I won't feel anxious." He also always stood near the door so that if he started to feel panicky, he could leave without anyone noticing him. Clearly, Andreas had not given up his irrational beliefs ("I must never appear anxious in front of people, and, most important, I must never lose control or have a panic attack").

The client may have spent so much time trying to distract himself, that, again, he never confronted his real fears. He still feels that he would die of shame if he were to exhibit any anxiety symptoms in front of a group of people.

The guidelines for helping a client work through a series of exercises are similar to those used for shame attacks (see Chapter 13).

Exploring Alternatives to Anxiety

What Are the Client's Emotional Goals?

What does the client *want* to feel? I often ask that in my office. Many people don't know how to answer the question. They may know that they don't want to feel anxious, but they don't know what they would like to feel instead. Some people say "calm," "peaceful," or "serene." I often smile and suggest that not many people feel that way. In fact, many people prefer to feel energized and stimulated. They don't want to be "calm" and "serene." That would feel boring to them. However, the demands of their job or difficulties in their relationships may push them over the top. And some drink coffee all day to keep going, partly because they are chronically sleep deprived.

Eventually, they cannot cope with the energizing challenges of their jobs, the caffeine, and the lack of sleep without becoming uncomfortably anxious. They may suddenly begin to have panic attacks or develop phobias to bridges, tunnels, planes, crowds, presentations, meetings, and even elevators. So what can they reasonably expect to feel during the day? Most of us do not expect to be happy at work or to have fun much or all of the time, but we do hope to be engaged and challenged.

I have found it very useful to discuss with my clients what they would like to feel. What is their emotional goal? What do they think other people feel when they are at work or at home, or when their spouse wants them to do something on Saturday that they don't want to do? Many clients have difficulty answering such questions. They have so consistently tried to avoid or to change both uncomfortable feelings and anticipated uncomfortable feelings that they have no idea how they might feel instead or how other people feel.

Emotional Vocabulary Builder

Many people use only a very few words to describe how they feel: *upset, bad, angry, frustrated, depressed, anxious.* They know other words, but they do not use them. Part of cognitive-behavioral therapy involves helping people be more careful about how they talk to themselves.

Some clients may benefit from the following exercise:

"In three minutes, see how many emotional vocabulary words you can write down on a piece of paper. Do this exercise once a day during the next week and keep a record of the number of words you can think of in three minutes."

Possibly, Marty could learn to be alert, challenged, determined, interested, and concerned rather than anxious when he makes a cold call. Of course, such a change will not occur overnight. He will have to make many calls (that is, do behavioral work) so that he learns at a deep level that the awful things he imagines will happen don't happen. But besides talking to himself and examining his chains of beliefs (the cognitive component) and making calls (the behavioral component), he can also try to feel differently. Telling him to calm down may not make sense. It is important to him to succeed at getting some new customers. On the telephone, it may be more appropriate for him to be "on" rather than "calm," that is, alert and ready to use all of the skills that have made him a great salesperson in the past.

Instead of anxious, the client can feel:

Concerned

Vigilant

Engaged

Peaceful

Excited

Relieved

Interested

Amused

Cautious

Calm

Stimulated

Happy

Alert

Challenged

Enthused

Relaxed

Emotional Thermometer

It may also be useful to have the client note how he feels during different times of the day and during different activities. I suggested that Marty check his "emotional temperature" every time he was waiting at the elevator (something that happened about five times a day). He was to name how he felt—all of the feelings he could identify—and give them a number, for example, anxious, 8; tired, 6; angry, 9. I knew he loved to go to basketball games and that he was a good cook. So I asked him to take his "temperature" during those recreational activities, as well. Not surprisingly, it turned out that he was almost always anxious. It was a chronic condition that he carried with him no matter what he was doing. As a result, it was easier to understand why he turned so frequently to alcohol. It shut off his constantly worrying voice and eliminated his nagging tense/alert state. It was the only way he could really relax.

Practicing REI in Session

REI is especially useful for working on anxiety, and the client can do it without people knowing what she is doing, for example, while she is waiting for an elevator or a meeting to start or while she is quietly sitting at her desk, or just before she gets up in the morning. (See Chapter 10.)

Doing Pre-AB's on the Anxiety

It is important to try to get at what happens and what the client says to herself *before* she gets anxious. Like urges, blushing, and vertigo, feelings of anxiety usually rise up in a client all of a sudden. With the therapist's help, the client can rewind the videotape, that is, go back in time a bit and try to figure out what preceded the feelings of anxiety. What was happening? (She was in a meeting.) Or what was she thinking about that was *going* to happen? (She realized she was going to have to speak to her boss about something that had gotten fouled up.)

Once the therapist and client have a better idea about the possible activating events (A's) and the things she was telling herself (B's), they can begin to figure out together how she cranked up legitimate concern (it *is* appropriate to be concerned if you have to talk to your boss about something that is fouled up) into full-blown anxiety. Then they can move on to figuring out what kind of cognitive, emotive, and/or behavioral intervention might be most helpful.

Things to Keep in Mind

Philosophical vs. Empirical Questioning

In doing an ABC, it is important to note that many people who are anxious are not affected by the evidence. Hence, empirical questioning or disputing often will not have much effect. Clients may never have had a panic attack on an elevator, but they will not ride on one because it would be intolerable to them if such an attack were to occur in a confined space in front of other people. (Hence, one client would only ride the elevator early in the morning and late at night when he calculated that no people would get on between the lobby and his floor or vice versa.)

It is very important to use what has been called philosophical questioning or disputing. That is, the therapist must examine what the client fears is the worst-case scenario. That is why inference chaining as discussed above is so valuable. A client who is afraid of flying is usually not interested in the empirical statistics. That is, the fact that 99.9 percent of plane flights do not end up in a crash is not going to have much, if any, impact on her. To help her, the therapist must try to get at what she believes will happen when and if she is on the plane. What are her worst fears?

One colleague described the difference between a CBT and an REBT therapist with the following story: A client walked into a CBT therapist and said, "My mother hates me." The therapist responded: "What is the evidence that your mother hates you?" using an empirical approach. The unhappy client then went to an REBT therapist. "My mother hates me," he told the therapist. The REBT therapist responded, "Well, let's assume you're correct. Why is that so terrible?" This is a joke, of course, because if a therapist started a session with that kind of seemingly callous question, most clients would never come back. But if we want to work effectively on anxiety problems, we must be sure to explore the worst-case scenario with the client.

Functional Questioning

It may also help to use functional questioning, which examines the practical consequences of the client's thinking. Taking a very concrete, practical approach—"How does it help to think that way? What do you think might be some positive consequences of thinking that way?"—may motivate some clients to take a more direct approach to solving the problem. Others, however, may simply respond, with a bit of exasperation in their voice, "I *know* it doesn't help. But I can't seem to do anything about it. That's why I came to see you."

Empathetic Questioning

The therapist's saying, "That must be very difficult to be that anxious all of the time. How do you cope?" or "What do you do that helps?" or "What has worked well in the past?" may not help a client examine or dispute the thinking that is contributing to his anxiety, but it may reassure him that the therapist appreciates the anguish that he is experiencing. It may uncover practical ways the client has used in the past, like t'ai chi or visualization, but is not using now. The ABC format can uncover why he is not doing so.

Teaching Behavioral Relaxation Techniques

Many clients complain of anxiety-related problems but do not use any behavioral techniques to help themselves during the day. Often, they just get another cup of coffee or a Coke. Convincing them of the ineffectiveness of such "techniques" and of the importance of practicing some kind of effective relaxation techniques is often difficult. Many are accustomed to putting something in their mouth to get relief, or they believe that just talking about their problems may help.

It is useful to think of our nervous system as one very large interconnected, interactive system with several very important nodes, the most important being the brain. But the brain is not separate from the nervous system. In fact, none of our various organs and systems is completely separate. They all affect and are affected by each other to a greater or lesser degree.

Many clients think of nerves as those tiny hairline things we see in illustrations in textbooks. They do not realize these are illustrations of dendrites, some of the smallest parts of the system. The system also includes cables running down our back that are as large as our thumb and the sciatic nerve, as large as our middle finger, running down our leg.

Some of these cables are constructed of relatively enormous nerve cells, some over a yard long. The whole system then is made up of hundreds and hundreds of cells of varying sizes. When this system of cells becomes excited or agitated, perhaps by caffeine or by thinking about some anticipated event, it is not an easy thing to calm it down quickly. Chemicals often work quite well, of course. Xanax and Ativan are popular today because they are very effective. Vodka also works quite effectively for millions of people. Unfortunately, however, Xanax, Ativan, and vodka work quite badly for millions, as well. What are some nonchemical ways the client could use to calm down this large conglomeration of nerve cells?

All of the following are important to teach in therapy. (Referring clients to a biofeedback specialist may also help.) Many clients resist using such techniques when they are feeling anxious. In many cases, they may start to try one of the techniques but then quit because (1) they are uncomfortable doing something that seems very foreign to them; (2) they fear the techniques won't work or work well enough; (3) they fear they will not be able to stand the anxiety or another panic attack; and (4) they know chemicals or certain behaviors like shopping, sex, or gambling *will* work and work quickly.

Deep Diaphragmatic Breathing

As the client walks around during the day, he may gradually tighten his diaphragm. It makes good sense to be aware of who is around us and whether or not our boss is in a good mood. Tightening one's stomach muscles (and diaphragm) in response to danger, real or imagined, is a common human response.

Most of the time we breathe automatically. Those who suffer from anxiety and especially from panic attacks are known to breathe in a very shallow manner. That is, the diaphragm is held in a very tense, tight manner. However, we can intervene. We can change the way we breathe so as to loosen the diaphragm. The brain picks this up and interprets it. Such a tight, vigilant, ready-to-flee-or-fight stance is not required. As a result, it may respond with other chemicals that further reduce the tension level in the body.

Clients do not need to do deep diaphragmatic breathing in some sort of special setting or at some sort of special time. One minute of deep breathing while sitting at their desk or riding in the elevator can help to reduce the level of tension in the thick network of cables called the nervous system. Of course, 20 minutes would probably do even more good, but many people will not do it, and on-the-spot decompressing, for example just before making another phone call, can have a significant impact. In particular, it can prevent them from becoming even more tense, pushing the threshold toward a full-blown panic attack.

Teaching Deep Diaphragmatic Breathing

Teaching and Practicing It in Therapy

Therapists may also have a few irrational beliefs about deep diaphragmatic breathing: "It really doesn't work. My client will think it's stupid. It's too much trouble. Listening and empathizing with clients is easier and less bother." But it is very worthwhile taking some time to teach this technique.

Once they are excited, clients may not calm down immediately, so they may not think a technique is helping even though it is. And if it is not making them feel calmer, the therapist can point out that it may be helping them not feel even worse. Without doing a little deep breathing, they might continue to stimulate their nervous system even further. Moreover, concentrating on their breathing will take their mind off of other troubles, at least temporarily.

Using the Technique

The therapist tells the client: "Put your right hand on your chest and your left hand on your gut, on top of your belly button. Now take a slow, deep breath."

Usually the person's right hand, over his chest, rises, but the left hand does not move.

"Now take a long breath in such a way that your right hand does not move. Only your left hand moves." If he cannot do it, then the therapist demonstrates with his own hands, breathing in slowly and out slowly. The hand on the chest should move only very slightly while the hand on the stomach should rise and fall very clearly.

This takes a few tries before someone can do it. Wearing loose-fitting clothing helps. It may also help to count out loud slowly, one, two, three, four, as the therapist raises his hand, palm up, and the client inhales, and then palm down, counting again slowly, one, two, three, four. The therapist should do three or four breaths together with the client with hands on the belly and chest so that the client can watch.

If he has difficulty doing it, he can practice at home. In addition, suggest that he lie on a bed, put a book on his belly, and practice breathing so that the book goes up and down but not his chest.

Checking for Progress in the Next Session

Most clients will not continue doing deep breathing without considerable encouragement. They are not used to using behavioral techniques to reduce their anxiety. Coming back to it in subsequent sessions will help.

Progressive Muscle Relaxation

Telling someone to calm down doesn't help. They do not know how. Progressive muscle relaxation, initially developed by Jacobson (1929), is designed to take advantage of the fact that the client may not be able to relax, but he can tense up his muscles even further. He can use a tape (see Suggested Resources at the end of this chapter) or the therapist can teach him to tighten one set of muscles at a time. Once he has tightened it as much as he can, when he lets go or relaxes, that muscle tends to relax to a less tense level than it was before being tensed. Over twenty years ago, Arnold Lazarus (1981, 1997), the founder of multimodal therapy, made a tape guiding the listener through an entire progressive muscle relaxation session and it remains one of the best available. Once the client learns the technique, he can do parts or all of it at his office or while waiting in an airport or even while sitting in a plane. Again, the goal is to work directly on the nervous system while at the same time perhaps also using ABC's, self-talk, and imagery to become less anxious.

Visualization and Muscle Relaxation

Visualization combined with muscle relaxation is one of the most potent relaxation techniques. It is also particularly useful because we can do it without other people realizing what we are doing.

It takes approximately five minutes for me to demonstrate it with a client, but it consistently relaxes people right there in my office. Nevertheless, despite its efficacy, it is usually difficult to convince people to practice. Perhaps it is because they often still subscribe to the traditional medical model: They want a cure without having to work on themselves on an ongoing basis. Or they want a pill that will take away their distress without any effort at all. The therapist may have to spend quite a bit of time "selling" the client on the idea that he will only do better when he starts to learn and practice techniques that have shown to be effective. Benson's (1975) research, for example, shows that people's autonomic nervous system remains at a less excited state for several hours after only 20 minutes of meditation.

In this exercise, the therapist asks the client to think of a place where she has been relaxed and calm, the way she would like to be without the benefit of chemicals. Unfortunately, some clients cannot think of a single time in their lives when they have been calm and relaxed. During every moment of their existence, as they remember it, they have been vigilant or, worse, hypervigilant, tense, anxious, and uneasy. In such cases, they will have to imagine a place. But with a little pushing, most clients can remember at least one time and place where they were genuinely relaxed.

The client picks a moment in that place and describes it in some detail. Then she sits back in her chair and visualizes being there. But this is much more than a visualization exercise. The therapist is trying to help her learn a way to calm down her entire body without chemicals.

In a quiet voice, the therapist says, "Okay, can you see yourself sitting there that Saturday afternoon? It is warm and you can look down over the lake. You have nothing that you have to do. You can just sit there if you like. Can you imagine the way your feet felt that day when you were just sitting there calm and content, the way you would like to feel more of the time. Can you make your feet feel the way they felt that day, calm and relaxed, from the inside? Work from the inside, and try to get your cells in your feet to be and feel like they were that day.

"Now move to your legs. Get your legs to feel—from the inside—how they felt that day when you were calm and relaxed and content sitting in your chair, just sitting. Try to get your feet and legs to feel the way they did that day.

"Now go to your arms. Get your arms to feel the same way they felt that day, from the inside, all of the cells and muscles, relaxed and calm, like they were that day.

"Now go to your shoulders. Working from the inside, make them feel the same way they felt that day.

"Now let's go back to your feet and your legs. Make sure they are relaxed like they were that day, and your arms, and your shoulders, and now let's move up your neck and relax your neck and the top of your head. Get them to feel the way they felt that day, sitting overlooking the lake.

"And now move down into your face. Get your forehead, especially right between your eyes, to be and feel the way it felt that day, and move into your cheeks and then into your jaw, down to your chin, and up to near your ears, and get them to feel relaxed and calm the way they felt that day when you were sitting in the mountains looking over the lake, peaceful, not having to do anything that day, you could just enjoy the air and the scenery and the temperature.

"Now move down into your chest and get your chest to feel the way it did that day and now move down into your stomach. Now try to get your whole body to be and feel, from the inside, all of the cells and muscles, relaxed and calm, the way they were that day. You can see yourself sitting there and you can feel the way you felt that day. Check your legs and arms. Make them relaxed the way they were that day."

After a half a minute or so, the therapist asks the client to look up. "How successful were you at getting to feel the way you felt that day? 50 percent? 85 percent? 90 percent?"

Many clients will answer 75 to 80 percent, even on the first time. The more clients practice this technique, the faster they can obtain the relaxed state—the relaxation response. Hence, it becomes a powerful tool and one that can be used even in the midst of a meeting, that is, in front of people, without their being aware of it.

RESEARCH NOTE

Based on a theory of social anxiety, Wells (1997) advocates a "symptom-induction" exposure and "assertive" cognitive approach. First, a therapist should carefully assess (1) a client's protective safety behaviors, (2) her theory about how these behaviors protect her, and (3) her specific predictions about what will happen and how she will behave in an anxiety-producing situation. Then Wells advocates "counter-intuitive interventions." The client is encouraged to think the thoughts that she fears and to engage in "symptom-induction" exposure that will purposefully provoke the symptoms, similar to Ellis's (1969, Ellis and Velten 1992) "shame attack" exercises.

SPECIAL PROBLEMS THE THERAPIST MAY ENCOUNTER

Procrastination and Its Role in Anxiety and Addictive Behaviors

Many people procrastinate in order to avoid the anxiety that they anticipate feeling if they were to do the task. This is ironic, because they then create even more anxiety as they worry all day about the consequences of having not done what they think they should have done or should be doing. Procrastination may also be fueled by combining discomfort anxiety with ego anxiety, and in that way increasing the risk of what is at stake.

Sheila frequently procrastinated at home and in the office. She hated to feel the slightest bit uncomfortable or frustrated. When she thought about paying bills, she knew she would be uncomfortable, having to face, again, the fact that she had put off budgeting her expenses and had, again, spent more than she had earned. She also felt uncomfortable when she thought about writing the memo her boss had asked her for last week. Because she systematically avoided discomfort, she consistently fell behind at home and at work. At the same time, she went through the day making herself anxious, worrying that her boss might ask her for the memo or that she might have to pay a late fee on her credit card.

She also downed herself for procrastinating and then got angry at the world for being so hard. Thus, most of the time she was quite miserable, except when she made herself feel better by shopping, which she did frequently, including shopping at night on QVC.

But she also felt uncomfortable, especially at work, because she continually put her ego on the line when she wrote a memo or talked on the telephone or met with her coworkers. If her boss liked a memo, she felt good. If she asked her to revise it, she felt miserable. If she thought she made a good impression in a meeting, she felt good. If not, she felt depressed. Making a presentation was pure torture. She could not just rate her performance. Her entire self, her entire identity was at risk. So it was not surprising that she procrastinated. Some Saturdays she stayed in bed reading most of the day. She felt better there. And that was understandable given what she put at risk when she went out with friends. If she thought someone thought ill of her, she would get panicky and, ultimately, very depressed.

The more the therapist can help a client rate only her behavior and not her self, the more she will be able to take her emotional life out of the hands of others. The less anxious she is, the less likely she will be to avoid tasks.

Anxiety about Anxiety

Most people who suffer from anxiety are anxious about being anxious. This is particularly true for people with social anxiety, who fear they will appear anxious to other people and they cannot accept that happening, and people who suffer from panic attacks, who panic if they sense they may have a panic attack. To ward off any possibility that they might start to feel anxious, they may "medicate" themselves in advance. Even people with only mild anxiety problems may take a drink or smoke some pot before they go to a party.

Anxiety and Dysthymia

Some clients cannot accept themselves with their anxiety. As a result, they create or contribute to chronic low-grade depression.

A client of mine has grappled with this for years, continually putting himself down for being anxious. "A real man shouldn't feel so anxious. What is the matter with me?" He feels like a "defective human being," he says, despite the fact that he has a successful marriage, has two teenage children, and has been successful (although not to the extent he thinks he should have been) in his career. His considering that he may have inherited his tendency to feel anxious has helped him a bit. He has begun to see his anxiety as a problem, like diabetes, that he can work on. In role plays, he practiced being more assertive with his wife and at work. This led to his wife returning to work and lessened his and the family's financial burdens. Recently, he started using Paxil and we shall see how that helps. We also explored what he might be gaining from being so demanding on himself, thereby creating some of his anxiety. This led to his admitting that he felt compelled to do especially well in order to "fix" himself. That is, the worse he felt about himself, the more he felt he had to do. And because there was always the possibility of failing, confirming his belief that he was, in fact, "defective," he became even more anxious.

Emotional Numbness

Many people who drink or use drugs on a regular basis do not realize how anxious they are. They are careful to drink or use enough to avoid any discomfort anxiety they might feel if they were to slow down or stop entirely. They might also feel angry, depressed, ashamed, or guilty! Some of their anxiety may stem from their beliefs, such as, "If I ever told people how I felt (i.e., if I ever expressed my true angry feelings), they'd all leave me." So they may feel trapped. They cannot dare express how they feel. This leads them to feel helpless and hopeless and even more angry and depressed. This stew of pent-up emotions may lead to what is called agitated depression, and many people use alcohol, drugs, and other addictive behaviors to smother such intense, conflicting, confusing emotions.

Trauma, Hypervigilance, and Chronic Anxiety

Trauma and posttraumatic stress disorder (PTSD) are beyond the limits of this book, but there is ample evidence that both significantly contribute to addictive behavior. The client's anxiety may be partly due to the effect that trauma has on parts of the brain, especially the amygdala. Traumatic events appear to get etched deeply into the amygdala and are never forgotten. In our prehistoric past, this may have had considerable survival value. We did not forget what had almost killed us. But in modern society, while it may help us to survive, it makes it difficult to thrive.

If the client has never talked to anyone about the traumatic events in her life, then the therapist will want to spend some time listening. Some research suggests that working through specific instances of trauma moment to moment may help alleviate the client's suffering. But other experts disagree, arguing that this just causes a client to retraumatize herself.

Many clients, however, have been talking about their trauma with therapists for some time. They may have even been encouraged in the belief that talking will eventually eliminate the problem. Unfortunately, there is no research to support such a view. In contrast, such clients may want a guarantee that nothing like that will ever happen to them again, while knowing at some level that that is impossible. That is, they think not only, "That shouldn't have happened to me" but also "That must never happen to me again" and "I couldn't stand it if it did." While perfectly understandable, these beliefs may increase their hypervigilance and heighten their anxiety. The therapist can help them see that while they cannot have a guarantee about anything in life, they *can* have considerable control over their emotions—and without addictive behaviors. Learning and practicing assertive behavior, relaxation techniques, and ABC's can contribute significantly to their sense of emotional control. The more they can learn to think in a preferential rather than a demanding manner—"I wish that had not happened, but it did. Insisting that it shouldn't, won't help me"—the more they will not only feel better but also do better.

Some clients hold themselves responsible. Often the evidence that they really could not have done anything is crystal clear. For example, when Betsy's uncle raped her, she was 5 and her uncle was often drunk and known for his fits of rage and violence. The problem is that thinking there is nothing she could have done can make a client feel even more helpless, anxious, and depressed. So if there was, in fact, anything that she could have done, it may have great therapeutic value if she can discover it. The tricky part is helping her, at the same time, not blame herself because she didn't realize what to do at the time or couldn't see how to do it. For example, maybe there really was someone in Betsy's family or at her kindergarten who could have helped her, but she was too embarrassed or too frightened to say anything. Now, being older, she can work on her ability to handle her embarrassment and to speak up. If she also sees that the therapist takes very seriously any current threats to her well-being and moves quickly and decisively to help her take appropriate practical steps, this will relieve some of her anxiety, as well.

ISSUES TO KEEP IN MIND

Familial/Genetic Issues

When someone who suffers from snake phobia is asked to think of a snake or touch a rubber snake, PET scans (Rauch et al. 1994) clearly show dramatic changes in blood flow in the brain. More important, however, is the fact that these changes do not immediately disappear once the feared item is removed. The person appears to be "stuck" with the new blood flow pattern, sometimes for up to several hours. But this is exactly what many clients report. Once they become anxious or hypervigilant or begin to have flashbacks, they get stuck. They have great difficulty becoming calm again.

Kagan's (1989) research shows that people are born with more or less reactive nervous systems. When I sense that one of my clients may have been born a high reactive, I propose to him that he was born with an "overreactive nervous system" and that he has been struggling to cope with that neurological reality ever since. Many people stumbled on alcohol or marijuana when they were as young as 10 or 12 and found, not surprisingly, that it helped immensely, which is in line with Khantzian's (1985) "self-medication" hypothesis. This possibility often helps a client, especially a male client, a great deal. He may have been damning himself all his life for being so anxious. As a result, he had two reasons to drink: to cope with his jumpy nervous system, and to silence his condemning voices— "Why are you always so nervous? You're such a wimp. What's wrong with you?" Many such clients have also avoided potentially anxiety-producing situations much of their lives, and have put themselves down for doing so. The overreactive nervous system hypothesis makes sense to them, given their lifelong struggles with fear and anxiety.

Social phobia, in contrast to shyness, is so debilitating that those afflicted have great difficulty leaving their house and find it almost impossible to go to parties or job interviews. The environment appears to have an important impact on whether shy children become withdrawn and socially reclusive or, in contrast, outgoing and socially comfortable. So it appears that children raised by supportive, gentle, and patient parents may be able to learn how to cope with their reactive nervous systems. No one has yet researched what happens to high-reactive children who were raised in a household with parents afflicted with addictive problems. Hence, we do not know what the impact of such a household might be. However, I often find that clients remember being especially anxious at a young age. Like Kagan's subjects, they had many fears, for example, of loud noises, the dark, the "boogie" man under the bed or in the closets, and they are often still suffering from fears about, for example, riding in the subway or crossing long bridges. They also often grew up in chaotic, dangerous, abusive families.

RESEARCH NOTE

Dadds and colleagues (1999) suggest that a brief intervention with 7- to 14-year-olds can reduce the number experiencing problems with anxiety over a two-year period. Using Kendall's (1990) FEAR program, each child develops his or her own plan for gradually approaching and working through a feared situation. The F in the acronym FEAR stands for *f*eeling good by learning to relax, the E for *e*xpecting good things to happen through positive self-talk, the A for *a*ctions to take facing up to fear stimuli, and the R for *r*ewarding oneself for efforts to overcome fear or worry.

Caffeine

Clients with anxiety and panic attacks often drink five or more cups of coffee a day. Most people can drink up to 200 grams per day without problems, but individual nervous systems vary greatly. Some people may be able to drink a cup or two a day, and some people cannot tolerate caffeine at all.

Many people will cut down their consumption of coffee quite rapidly within a week with only a little encouragement from the therapist. Practical suggestions will help: buy a smaller cup; use more milk; fill the cup with half caffeinated and half decaffeinated coffee; buy a richer roast, but decaffeinated; fill only half the cup; immediately dump out half. Clients should be warned against stopping completely in one day. Most people suffer headaches, sometimes severe headaches, if they come off caffeine too rapidly.

Other Nutritional Issues

Although nutritional factors sometimes affect anxiety levels and, in turn, lapses and relapses, nutritional changes alone will not solve the problem. Some foods, such as pasta, appear to be calming to some people, whereas protein has the opposite effect. So far, however, the research is unclear in this area.

Low Blood Pressure and Panic Attacks

A client may have low blood pressure. At times, her blood pressure may drop so low that she begins to feel dizzy and may even pass out. The feelings (or actually passing out) may become so frightening that she develops a full-blown panic attack disorder. Teaching her to relax will worsen her problem. She needs to learn to keep her blood pressure up. Fortunately, it is relatively easy to increase her blood pressure. Any movement—talking, laughing, walking, crossing her legs, gripping the steering wheel more tightly—will increase her heart beat and her blood pressure. Tightening her leg muscles, thereby forcing blood up into her upper body, will also help. Increasing her salt intake will cause her to retain more water, also increasing her blood pressure. She should avoid diuretics, and alcohol is a major diuretic, as is caffeine. As one colleague put it, "Urinating a lot has the same effect on the blood pressure that children opening a lot of hydrants in the summer has on the city's water pressure." Some prescription and over-the-counter medications, such as ibuprofen, are also diuretics.

Being able to exercise some control over her symptoms naturally has a very therapeutic effect. At the same time, standard cognitive techniques may also help her overcome her beliefs about her symptoms that may not be rational: "It would be absolutely horrible and humiliating if I ever passed out in front of people. I must always be in control. I cannot accept that my body seems to have a mind of its on. I must always behave well, no matter what."

Gender Issues

It is particularly difficult for some men to accept, let alone admit, that they are anxious. They may believe, "It is unmanly to feel anxious. It is also unmanly to admit that you are anxious." Various addictive behaviors—gambling, drinking, drugging—silence this negative inner voice.

Anxiety in women—and some men—is frequently related to a fear of expressing their anger. They have been well socialized against expressing anger. Moreover, they believe that they are so full of boiling rage that they dare not even begin to say how they feel. If they did, there is nothing that could stop it from destroying all of their relationships. The effect of this repression is twofold. First, such clients have had little practice at expressing anger. As a result, they are, in fact, not good at it. They *do* sometimes behave foolishly, as they fear they will. Second, when they get into a disagreement, because they fear that their anger may show, they can only respond in a weak, ineffectual manner. Moreover, they know that by being weak at arguing, they allow themselves to be pushed around and taken advantage of, so they often wind up loathing themselves, as well.

FIVE HOMEWORK ASSIGNMENTS

✓ **Low frustration tolerance (LFT) exercise:** The therapist suggests that the client do something that will help her reduce her LFT, something that is related to how anxiety has a negative impact on her life. The best anti-LFT exercises will most likely be related to her addictive problem(s). But she might also benefit from working on her LFT in other areas of her life. If she procrastinates a lot, she can pay three bills each night or clean up one small portion of her apartment.

✓ **Do an ABC sheet.** The client can bring it to the next therapy session or fax it.

✓ **Listen to a** self-help tape or some other kind of tape.

✓ **Practice progressive muscle relaxation** or visualization combined with muscle relaxation or taking three deep diaphragmatic breaths five times a day.

✓ **Body time:** The client can ask her body what it wants at any particular time during the day. This is an exercise that Marlatt (1985b) describes and can help teach the client to take better care of herself throughout the day. It encourages clients to learn how to enjoy pleasuring themselves in non-addictive ways.

MEDICATIONS

Many clients are suffering because they are using one particular chemical or a variety of chemicals—alcohol, marijuana, heroin, cocaine—to help manage their emotional life. The problem is that the time effects of these particular chemicals are negative. Unfortunately, the same can be said for many of the legal prescription drugs such as Valium and Ativan. Although many people can use them occasionally and without problems, some people consistently become dependent on them.

Nevertheless, when a therapist is working with clients for whom anxiety is a major, chronic, ongoing problem, a psychiatrist may be able to help them find other chemical solutions to their problem, it may be unprofessional solutions that will work better over the medium and long run. A recent client who complained of chronic low-grade anxiety started on Paxil and immediately found that his obsessive habit of going over and over anything disagreeable that had happened at work or at home simply stopped. He did not find that his ability to express his emotions in other ways was negatively effected. He simply did not worry and obsess as much as he had before, and his low-grade anxiety disappeared. We had also been working on a number of his irrational beliefs, including their roots in his early childhood, so this may have been the reason that the Paxil was so effective, but it is impossible to know. The placebo effect (Kirsch and Lynn 1999) may have been operating in this case. But even this study suggests that 25 percent of the impact may be due to the medication.

Some readers may think that substituting one chemical for another does not constitute a gain. The issue comes down to which chemical contributes the least negative effects over time. If the new chemical creates as many problems as the old one, then nothing has been gained. However, using a prescription medication, in some cases simply because it is legal or socially accepted, may constitute a positive move.

The client may resist suggestions to try prescription medication for his anxiety problems because he has tried one in the past and he either did not think it worked or did not like the side effects. But people react differently to different chemicals. Moreover, there are at least five groups of medications that have been shown to be effective with some kinds of anxiety disorders, including benzo-diazepines (e.g., Valium, Ativan, and Xanax), beta blockers (e.g., Inderal), monoamine oxidase (MAO) inhibitors (e.g., Nardil and Parnate), selective serotonin reuptake inhibitors (SSRIs, e.g., Paxil), and the tricyclic antidepressants (TCAs, e.g., Elavil, Anafranil). Consequently, while one medication may not have helped, it may be worth trying another. The client may prefer a solely CBT/REBT approach. However, when he is in danger of harming himself and others as the result of addictive behaviors, a combined approach of CBT/REBT with medication may be better.

RESOURCES

- Craske and Barlow (1994) have developed a highly effective program to help clients overcome social anxiety, including panic attacks and agoraphobia. The program is cognitive-behavioral and stresses the importance of in vivo exposure.
- Arnold Lazarus's tape *Learning to Relax* teaches how to do progressive muscle relaxation. It is available through the Albert Ellis Institute.

- *Twenty-one Ways to Stop Worrying* presents Albert Ellis's approach to reducing worry. It places particular emphasis on changing the way one thinks as opposed to what he sees as only palliative approaches.
- Other helpful books include David Burns' *Feeling Good Handbook* (1990), Albert Ellis's *How to Control Your Anxiety Before It Controls You* (1998), and Ed Nottingham's *It's Not As Bad As It Seems* (1994).

13 SHAME AND GUILT AND ADDICTIVE BEHAVIOR

Is the client abusing alcohol or drugs or engaging in other types of addictive behaviors (shopping, overeating, gambling, risky sex) to cope with shame and guilt?

"Why didn't you call earlier?" I asked, sensing that I already knew the answer.

"I don't know. I just felt so awful, so I kept on drinking."

I have worked with Nancy for about ten years. She is an artist and most of the time she manages to stay away from alcohol, but occasionally she starts drinking again, usually sneaking sips on the sly or when no one is home. She had relapsed only three months before, and I had managed to get her into an outpatient group. But then she had started to drink again two weeks ago, and we were meeting after she had called asking for an appointment.

"Did you go to group?"

"No."

"How come?"

"I don't know. I just couldn't face them last week."

"It sounds as if you were ashamed of what had happened."

"I don't know. You know how I get. I just started to feel like such a horrible person all over again. I have deceived everyone and let down everyone—again. They thought I had quit completely, when I hadn't. I didn't want to go and lie to them again."

"Most people feel shame when they violate a rule, such as not deceiving people they care about. Were you too ashamed to call me or go to group?"

"It's hard to face people when I've screwed up again. So I just continued to drink."

Shame and guilt may dramatically affect the frequency, duration, and intensity (FDI) of lapses and relapses. One objective of therapy is to get a client to call soon after a lapse or relapse so the therapist can help her get back on track. Another objective is to reduce the extent to which shame and guilt contribute to her addictive behaviors. Initially, the client may feel too ashamed or too guilty to call anyone (including the therapist) and admit that she has started drinking or using (or gambling or overspending) again. Even thinking about it may make her feel painfully ashamed, so she drinks more (or takes more drugs or gambles more) to stop the thoughts and numb the pain.

Having run many workshops and worked with many clients, I have learned that the terms *shame, guilt, feeling ashamed,* and *feeling guilty* have different meanings for different clients. Some feel guilty if they break a societal rule or law, but feel ashamed if they break one of their own rules or do not meet one of their own standards. For other people, the reverse is true. They feel ashamed if others know what they have done, but guilty if they violate one of their own standards. Since our standards, goals, and values usually reflect our society's standards, goals, and values, it is not surprising that these terms are sometimes used interchangeably.

WHAT IS THE CLIENT'S RATING STYLE?

Global shame involves a client's whole self, rather than limited shame over a specific act. Global shame has a self-denigrating, self-downing, self-demeaning quality. It is this global sense of shame that Bradshaw (1988) aptly labeled "toxic shame." It poisons every aspect of a client's thoughts, feelings, and behavior. Almost everything she does or may do is pervaded with a sense of shame and/or anticipated shame. She may wake up in the morning dreading going to work or socializing with friends, thinking she will inevitably make a fool of herself before the day is done. It is global shaming of the entire self that appears to be so destructive and debilitating.

We do not all rate ourselves so globally. We may behave stupidly and, as a result, feel embarrassed. Or worse, we may do something more serious and feel ashamed, and perhaps even say to ourselves or others, "I felt ashamed of myself." But more often, we manage to be ashamed of what we have done but not of our total selves. We manage to limit the extent to which our feelings of shame about what we have done affect our feelings about our entire self. But some of our clients consistently experience global shame, a shame about their entire selves that is difficult if not impossible to push down or obliterate.

It is not surprising that some clients so consistently rate their selves at the same time that they rate every behavior and what they think other people are thinking about their behaviors. We traditionally use linguistic shortcuts—"He's a liar" "He's a slimeball" "He's an asshole" "He's a really good person" "She's an angel" "He's a hunk"—to quickly communicate how we feel about someone to another person. These shortcuts (often metaphors) ignore the myriad other qualities that person may possess.

In a similar fashion, however, we may also use linguistic shortcuts to assess our entire selves on the basis of one piece of data. After saying the wrong thing to someone at a party, we may think to ourselves, I'm such a jerk. When a recent client's girlfriend left him, for weeks he totally ignored all of his other good qualities and behaviors, fixating solely on rating himself badly on the basis of one fact: Sara had left him. He linked his feelings about himself to that one fact. He was totally devastated, worthless, and without hope. He was consumed with shame—for gambling and for losing his girlfriend. He could not see any good in any aspect of his self. As the existential psychoanalyst R. D. Laing (1970) points out in *Knots* (p. 38):

I want it
I get it
therefore I am good

I want it
I don't get it
therefore I am bad

I am bad
    because I didn't get it

I am bad
    because I wanted what I didn't get

I must take care
    to get what I want
    and want what I get
    and not get what I don't want

In contrast to chronic, global, "toxic" shame, feeling moderately ashamed or guilty about a specific behavior—having done something wrong that may have hurt or injured someone else or been against one's values, standards, or rules—may be a sign of psychological health. It certainly may not be a psychotherapeutic problem. But when the client chronically feels ashamed and engages in addictive behaviors to cover such feelings, that is a psychotherapeutic problem. Conversely, some clients appear to feel little or no shame, even when they have frequently done things that many people would feel guilty and ashamed about. Such clients may be very difficult to work with (see Special Problems the Therapist May Encounter, page 395).

ATTRIBUTIONAL STYLE AND SHAME: WHO'S RESPONSIBLE?

To feel shame, ashamed, or guilty, a client must believe she has broken a rule or not measured up to a standard that she accepts. However, as Lewis (1993, 1998) points out, the more she thinks she has responsibility for what happened, the more she blames and shames herself. Again, this is in line with societal beliefs. People who have a disease like a physical disability or who abuse drugs or have AIDS are all somewhat stigmatized in our society. But people suffering from drug use or AIDS are more stigmatized because they are thought to have been responsible for their condition. Similarly, if a woman gives birth to a retarded child, she blames and shames herself and feels guilty if she believes it is her responsibility, for example, if she thinks that the retardation occurred because she continued to smoke during her pregnancy or she drank a glass of wine during the first trimester. But if she sees the retardation as resulting from a chance event, she does not blame or shame herself or feel guilty. Many clients are particularly ashamed of their addictive behaviors and will not bring them up in therapy unless specifically asked. They almost always believe that they are entirely responsible (and to blame) for what they have done and may be too shamed to address the topic unless the therapist does so.

The sense of responsibility and desire to remain in control frequently causes people to continue addictive behaviors for years. But at some point they may no longer be able to pretend, even to themselves that their gambling or drinking or sexual behavior is not a problem. They may deny it to others, but slowly they start to realize that their ability to control their behavior is lessening or lost. They are consistently doing things that they would call stupid and that they sense are against their best interests. Yet they continue. Shame and /or guilt often arise as a result of this disparity between what they think they ought to be doing and what they see themselves doing.

Many clients then behave even more rashly, attempting to prove that what they sense is not true. They *can* control their behavior.

But the more they cannot, the more ashamed and distressed they become. Lewis (1998) states, "The idea of responsibility and perceived responsibility is central to . . . shame" (p. 127). He further notes, "Violation of standards, rules, and goals is insufficient to elicit shame unless responsibility can be placed on the self" (p. 128). The client may have lived for years pretending he could stop or slow down when he wanted to, "in denial," to use the popular term, and attempting to avoid the shame he would feel if he admitted his problem.

As a result, the client may appear resistant to treatment. But in reality it is difficult to function when he feels intensely ashamed and that there is nothing he can do about it. So he may continue to try to maintain control over his emotional life by engaging in addictive behaviors, setting up a vicious cycle of drinking and blaming and shaming, and drinking more to cope with the blame and shame.

WHAT DOES THE RESEARCH SUGGEST?

There are no studies that directly relate shame to substance abuse or shame to the FDI of lapses and relapses. Researchers tend to focus on disorders that are categorized in the *DSM*, and unlike anxiety and depression (but like anger), shame and guilt are not *DSM-IV* disorders. Consequently, there are only a few recent studies linking sexual and physical abuse with shame, depression, and "negative attribution style," that is, the tendency to blame oneself for everything that goes wrong in one's life. None looks directly at the impact of shame and guilt on addictive behaviors.

- Lewis (1992) notes that the extent to which victims of sexual abuse suffer depends on how they attribute the blame. If they blame something internal and global about their selves, then they suffer more. If they attribute it to other factors—"My uncle was sick"—they suffer less. Wyatt and Mickey's (1988) study suggests that more severe abuse leads to stronger self-blaming attribution styles. Feiring and colleagues (as cited in Lewis 1998), in a study of eighty-two known sexually abused children, also found that more abuse was associated with more shame and negative attribution style, which in turn were both linked to more depression. People who have suffered sexual abuse often hide what has occurred and only reluctantly talk about it, even to a professional.

- The research by Andrews (1995, 1997) indicates a link between shame and depression and shame and bulimia.
- Physically maltreated preschool girls (who wound up in protective services) showed more shame when they failed a task and less pride when they succeeded as compared with non-maltreated preschool girls. In contrast, maltreated preschool boys showed both less shame and less pride under the same circumstances, as if their emotional responses to both success and failure had become muted (Alessandri and Lewis 1996).

These few studies suggest fertile ground for research. Shame appears to have an impact on attributional style (and vice versa), which in turn may have an impact on depression, and all three taken together may affect the extent to which people engage in addictive behaviors.

SELECTED CLINICAL TECHNIQUES

Session Goals

The goals with these clients are the following:

1. To reduce the frequency, duration, and intensity (FDI) of lapses and relapses related to shame and guilt.
2. To help the client feel less shameful and guilty in a global sense without resorting to addictive behaviors.

Exploring the Problem

Regarding shame and the role it plays in addictive behavior, the client may be in precontemplation, a Type I client. He may be unaware that shame is contributing to his addictive behavior. In contrast, he may be fully aware and wanting to work on it (a Type III client) or somewhere in between, that is, ambivalent (a Type II client).

Therapists should watch for beliefs such as:

"I cannot talk about what I have done (even to my therapist) because it is too shameful."

"Really terrible things have been done to me, and I cannot stand thinking about it. I could never tell someone else."

"It's too embarrassing to call my therapist now that I've failed again (especially after all his work)."

"It's too embarrassing to go back to group now that I've relapsed."

"If I drink or smoke (pot or a cigarette), it will help."

"When I gamble, the thoughts that usually bother me just aren't there."

Shame and guilt may also be difficult to work on, because clients hold a variety of unstated, hidden beliefs, for example:

"Talking about shame is too uncomfortable. I can't stand it."

"I'm ashamed to be so ashamed. Only children feel ashamed like I do. What's wrong with me?"

"I have done some really terrible things, and I cannot talk about them to anyone."

"I would go crazy if I talked about what happened."

"I would be too ashamed to talk about my problems in a group."

"I am bad because I did bad things. I am bad because I allowed someone to do bad things to me."

Testing Out Hypotheses

If the therapist hypothesizes that shame and guilt play a significant role in fueling addictive behaviors but the client seems unaware of their impact, the therapist should discuss the hypothesis with the client. What does she think? Does she often fear that she will in some other way make a fool of herself and then feel terrible later? What kind of terrible feeling does she fear she might feel? Humiliation? Guilt? Shame? Does she think she would have a physical reaction that she couldn't stand? Does she think shame and guilt contribute to her addictive behaviors?

Waiting for More Evidence

If the client answers no to the above questions, the next addictive behavior episode may provide more information. The evidence may suggest that the original hypothesis was wrong, or the therapist may be strengthened in his belief that shame and guilt play a significant role, especially in increasing the duration and intensity of a lapse or relapse.

Looking for Historical Roots

Where did the client learn these beliefs? Who in her family might have taught them to her? Who shares these beliefs, perhaps to this day? What may have happened in her youth to contribute to these feelings? Perhaps despite the fact that her parents did not believe in shaming her, she came to feel this way on her own or through peers. She may even have thought that her parents were dumb. In her mind, they just did not understand when they told her not to be so concerned about what other people think.

If the evidence continues to strongly suggest that shame plays a role, the therapist can come back to it when the client might be more receptive. (But avoid engaging in thug therapy; see Chapter 2.) A phone session where the client does not have to face the therapist might help. Or can she write down some of the things that happened in the past and leave them for the therapist to read.

Ongoing Assessment of Shame

Once the client has begun to acknowledge the possible role of shame and/or guilt, she can watch and record how often she feels ashamed or guilty during her daily life. How often does she feel the beginnings of a shamed or guilty response when she is only thinking about doing something? That is, how often does she stimulate anticipated shame or guilt in herself?

Assessing the Positive and Negative Effects of Shame and Guilt

If the client acknowledges that she often feels embarrassed, ashamed, or guilty, or fears feeling embarrassed, ashamed, or guilty but does not see how that may affect her addictive behavior, at least three paths can be explored:

1. **Has shame and/or guilt prevented her from reaching out for help?** In the past, when she drank too much or overspent on her credit cards, was it shame that prevented her from talking about her predicament with someone else, even a therapist? Has she sometimes continued drinking partly because she was ashamed of how much she had drunk so far?

2. **How has shame and guilt affected the rest of her life?** Has she never discussed something with a counselor or therapist because she would have felt too ashamed or too guilty to do so? Are there things she wishes she had done but hasn't because she would feel too ashamed if she failed? Has she had sex sometimes because she was too ashamed to appear "cold" or uninterested?

On the other hand, she may believe shame and guilt or the fear of being embarrassed have been very valuable in her life. For example, she may think (and may be correct in thinking) that it helped her not get pregnant—she would have been too ashamed! Or it may have helped her study very hard in school. She would have been too ashamed to have received less than a B (or an A) in a course. So in her mind, shame and guilt may have been important inhibitors and are not something to be given up lightly.

She may be confusing global shame with shame about a particular behavior that violates her values, rules, and standards. Being ashamed of accidentally getting pregnant is not necessarily a serious problem. Shaming her entire self and seeing getting pregnant as further evidence that she is not a worthwhile human being, however, is a different matter.

3. **How has it affected (or how is it affecting) her sense of herself?**

This is a critically important area to explore. As I discussed in the introduction to this chapter, often people see themselves as somehow inferior products or damaged goods. They may say, "I don't know what's wrong with me" or, more directly, "I'm evil" or "I'm a failure and I don't see anything changing." They have a global negative opinion about themselves and low self-esteem. They ignore all their other good qualities, focusing only on the consequences of one of their many behaviors, for example, gambling.

Discussing Alternatives to Feeling Ashamed or Guilty

It is the global rating, the shaming of the entire self, that destroys and debilitates so completely. But how are people to feel when they really do act badly? What can therapists teach clients to feel instead of global shame or global guilt?

When the focus is on a specific behavior and not on the behaver, Lewis (1992) opts for guilt. But in my work with clients, I do not find that that distinction makes sense to them. They often use both terms—*shame* and *guilt*—globally. A client who can not help his parents as much as he had thought he would when they got older told me, "I feel terribly guilty that I cannot help them more. I feel so ashamed. I had always thought I would have enough money to help them, but I can't be responsible for my family and help them, too. I feel like a total failure."

Again, we return to the question of alternative emotional states and the words we use to label them. What alternatives might one feel instead of global shame or global guilt? Instead of guilty and/or ashamed, the client could feel:

Sad

Concerned

Embarrassed

Apologetic

Regret

Annoyed

Sorry

Amused

Angry

Irritated

Resigned

Determined

Remorseful

Contrite

Relieved

With many clients, it would probably be more appropriate if they felt irritated or annoyed (or even angry) instead of ashamed. If they want to not drink or not spend any more money on clothes, but they do drink or purchase a new dress, they have not done what they wanted. Normally, when we do not do what we want, we feel irritated, annoyed, aggravated, or angry, especially if we have worked hard at it.

If clients ski, I often ask, "How do you feel when you fall?" Some will admit that they feel embarrassed, especially if other people are watching. But most are mildly irritated. They do not want to fall. They want to make the whole run without a fall. If they try again and fall again, they may feel even more irritated. Rarely do they feel ashamed.

I also ask them how they would feel if they invited four friends for dinner, and then somehow managed to burn the main dish. The answers are revealing. Some people would be very embarrassed. Others would be irritated but would make do. One person said that she would shrug and announce that she was ordering in Chinese.

The therapist can help clients by reminding them that in most cases in their lives when they try to change behaviors and fail, they feel irritated, concerned, and determined to get it right the next time. Changing addictive behaviors is no different.

Global shame and guilt are often deeply conditioned responses, so progress toward feeling a less debilitating emotion will often be slow. Moreover, as with other types of change, clients first have to acknowledge that shame (or guilt) is a problem before they can begin to work on it, and they must be sufficiently convinced that it is having a serious negative impact on their lives to be sufficiently motivated to work on it. Learning what other feelings they might feel (and words they might use for those feelings) is obviously only part of the process, but it is an important part.

Doing an ABC(DE)

The therapist can explore with the client what may be some of the underlying beliefs that contribute to or are associated with his shame reaction. What is he thinking when he anticipates feeling ashamed or guilty?

When he engages in an addictive behavior to cope with, suppress, or distract himself from his shameful feelings, what is he telling himself? He can examine, question, challenge, and dispute those beliefs with the therapist's help, using a variety of approaches: functional, empirical, philosophical, didactic, and Socratic. The therapist should focus especially on two probable underlying beliefs: (1) The client is responsible for everything that has happened to him and everything that he has done. (2) He is equal to his behavior. He believes that if he has behaved badly or even if he has allowed someone else to behave badly toward him, this means he *is* bad.

Case Example

From my previous work with Fred, one of my hypotheses was that he continued to drink because he felt so ashamed of starting once again. In this part of the session, in an attempt to understand what contributed to the relapse, we could have focused on what happened before he relapsed. However, I was interested in helping Fred focus on how shame prolonged the relapse. I was also concerned that Fred was still shaming himself and might start drinking again in a short time.

"Let's use the ABC format to see if we can get a better handle on what happened," I said. "We'll first look at what happened after you started drinking. We'll call your relapse A. Once you started drinking, then what were the C's, the consequences?"

"Well, of course, I felt great for a while," Fred responded. "And then I started to feel awful, so I just kept drinking. I drank on and off all day and practically through the night."

"And why didn't you call Jack [the person running his group at the outpatient clinic] or me?"

"I just felt so rotten," he said.

"Do you think you felt ashamed about starting again?"

"Yes, of course. My parents were really furious."

"What do you think you were telling yourself before you called?" I asked.

"I don't know."

"I mean that stopped you from calling," I continued.

"Oh, I suppose something like, 'I've screwed up again.'"

"And you thought Jack or I would think ill of you?" I said.

"Maybe. And I felt so bad I just kept drinking," he responded.

"Okay, so you felt awful, felt ashamed, kept drinking, and didn't call anyone for help. Is that about right?"

"Yes."

"Now let's look for the B's. What were you telling yourself or thinking that made you feel ashamed?" I asked.

"I don't know," Fred answered. "I'm such a screw-up. I really did it this time."

"And I think you were thinking, 'Jack will think I'm a screw-up,' and you felt bad about that, specifically, ashamed," I suggested.

"Yes, I really felt bad, especially about facing the group. I don't know if I can ever go back there."

"How did you make yourself feel so bad?"

"I don't know. I'm such a failure. I don't know what's wrong with me," he answered.

"It sounds like you were saying more than that. It sounds like you're saying something like: 'I'm such a failure, as I'll always be.' 'They'll think ill of me.' 'I can't stand that.' And you felt ashamed. If you had cancer and you felt ill again and thought it was the cancer coming back, how would you feel then? Ashamed?"

"No."

"Why not?"

"Because it's not my fault."

"Is your drinking behavior all your fault?"

"Well, yeah."

"I don't think so, but how does shaming your entire self help? That's your knee-jerk reaction—shame. We've talked about that before. You always feel that you've done something dreadful and that it's all your fault, and you always feel terribly ashamed. But what else could you feel? How would you feel if you had cancer and it came back?"

"Scared," he answered.

"Why?"

"Because I might die."

"Well, why couldn't you feel scared when you were drinking?" The last time you got very drunk you were talking about committing suicide. So you could die. I think it's because you feel responsible for the drinking, but you wouldn't feel responsible for the cancer."

"Yes, I think that's right," Fred said.

"But feeling concerned, even scared, wouldn't be crazy, would it?"

"No."

"And I think you think your problem with alcohol is partly, not totally, a disease. I don't get it. How are you totally responsible for one disease but not the other?"

"I don't know. [He laughs.] Maybe I got lung cancer because of my smoking."

"I agree. And you would probably feel terrible if that happened, but I still don't understand how shaming yourself helps."

"I don't know. I just feel that way."

"I agree. You do, and then you drink even more to drown it. But that's your old conditioning. Why should you feel ashamed? I'm suggesting that you feel scared and concerned instead, even though I know you will first feel ashamed because that is your normal knee-jerk reaction whenever you make a mistake or even think you're going to make a mistake. But you could feel scared and concerned, because you are in real danger. Then you would have to tell yourself, 'I did screw up. But lots of people make mistakes as they're learning to control their drinking. This is scary and danger-ous. I'm sick of always feeling ashamed when I make a mistake. And it doesn't help me learn how to behave differently.' Do you think you could say something like that?"

"I don't know."

"Well, let's write it out. The A is the relapse. Then what did you say to yourself?"

"I'm such a screw-up."

"Yes, that was one of the thoughts that probably went through your head. But there were more. That wouldn't have created so much shame. What else?"

"I always screw up—and my father used to yell at me, 'You should be ashamed of yourself. You're such a disaster.'"

"Yes, he labeled you and told you how to feel. So is that what you might have been thinking even though a part of you knows it's not true?"

"Yes, maybe."

"Okay, so you thought to yourself, 'I'm such a screw-up' and you felt ashamed, and then you drank more to drown all of that out, right?"

"Yup."

"So those were the consequences of your drinking and thinking. Let's move on to the D's. How could you have questioned that thinking and what could you have done instead of continuing to drink?"

"Well, just because my father said I was a disaster—well, it wasn't always true. *He* was certainly a disaster. He was practically always drunk. But as you said to me last week, I don't have to agree with his assessment of me. In fact, it makes me angry to think about agreeing. I drink too much, I know that. But I have not wrecked the rest of my life, and I have a good relationship with my son."

"Right, at least so far. That was one of the things you have always told me you want—a good relationship with your son. You don't want to follow in your father's footsteps. Remember Glasser's three questions: What do you want? What are you doing? How do you like it?"

"Yup."

"Well, what are you doing? And how do you like it?"

"I drank again and I don't like it—now, at least."

"And shaming yourself is another thing you are doing. How does that help get you what you want?"

"Maybe it will keep me from drinking again."

"Maybe. If you limit yourself to being ashamed of that aspect of your behavior—your drinking—and don't go and put your entire self down, then it might help. But you always go overboard and make yourself feel completely rotten. Maybe you do that in order to feel so rotten that you can drink again?"

[Thinks a moment] "Maybe. Do you think I could be that manipulative?"

"Sure. Why not? You forget what you want in the medium and long run, the good relationship with your son, being a man who doesn't drink, unlike your dad. People are very clever, underhanded, sneaky when they want to stimulate in themselves the urge to drink."

"Hmmm. Jeez, I hope I'm not that bad."

"You don't have to label yourself as 'bad' just because you act badly. But now you know that that is a possibility, so you can be on guard against it."

"My father really fucked me up. He should have been ashamed of his behavior, not me."

"Well, maybe, but maybe not. Let's focus for the time being on what you could feel and do in the future. We can come back to your father later if we want to. I think you felt too ashamed to call. How did that help? What could you do next time? What could you have tried to feel instead of your knee-jerk, father-taught shame?"

"Scared, I guess. But that would be hard to feel when I'm drunk."

"Yes, I agree, but that doesn't mean it's impossible to think or feel differently. And perhaps shame plays a role in getting you started. We can look at that next time. And if you didn't feel so ashamed, don't you think you could return to group?"

"Yes."

"Well, can you go back?"

"I guess they will understand. After all, half of them have relapsed lots of times."

"Right. So you can feel aggravated about what you did, and determined to change your behavior. Between sessions, how do you feel about doing an ABC to help you understand how you convinced yourself to relapse in the first place?"

"Okay. You want me to bring it in next time?"

"Yes, please. Thanks. See you then."

Using Shame-Attack Exercises

When a client is clear that his addictive behavior may often be spurred on by shame or when he realizes that he has often felt inappropriately ashamed in many situations or has stopped himself from doing many things that might have enriched his life, he may want to work more directly on shame. Ellis's shame-attack exercises can be extremely helpful—not necessarily in the same form that Ellis suggests.

Shame attack exercises very effectively evoke shame; hence, they are emotive exercises. But to be effective, they must be done. That is, clients must be willing to go out into the real world and do the exercises. So I see them also as behavioral exercises.

Setting the Goals

As the term implies, a shame-attack exercise is designed to actively attack and reduce the frequency, duration, and intensity (FDI) of the conditioned shame response, changing not only the way the client thinks but also the way he feels. It provides him with an opportunity to work directly on his problematic emotional response when and where he wants to.

Like a blush, shame often wells up in people in social situations. It is very difficult to work on it at that moment. And to many people it is shameful to feel so ashamed. Working on it at that moment often makes matters worse—the same thing that happens if you concentrate on the fact that you are blushing. So an exercise that permits a client to work on shame in a planful manner is very useful.

Although it is unlikely that people will ever completely eliminate their first knee-jerk reaction to feel shame, they can learn to short circuit that reaction, replacing shame with some other less undermining emotion. To do so, they will have to change the way they think. But that will probably not be sufficient. They will also have to behaviorally go through shame experiences several times before they begin to respond differently.

Targeting the Activating Event

The client can choose to work on shame related to addictive behavior or shame as a frequent conditioned reaction to many situations. One client thought he would be too embarrassed to ask for a soda when others were drinking cocktails or wine. His beliefs? "People must not find out that I have a drinking problem. It would be too embarrassing. I should drink with everyone else. It may bother people that I have a problem—and I shouldn't bother people, especially when they are trying to relax and have a good time. I cannot stand the idea that they would be uncomfortable (I cannot stand the discomfort of their being uncomfortable)." He chose asking for soda as a shame attack exercise. Another client did not always admit that he had drank during the past week when he went to his AA meeting. His belief? "It's too embarrassing to admit that I screwed up." He also thought: "It's none of their business. I do not want to have to start all over (and I should always get what I want). I couldn't stand listening to my sponsor." He worked on being more honest in his meetings. Finally, one client always left his meeting early, trying to avoid having to speak to anyone. As his shame attack exercise, he chose to stay and to speak to at least one person. His beliefs: "I am too embarrassed by my problem to speak to someone. It is embarrassing to speak to someone I don't know. I am always awkward talking to someone new, and being awkward (because they can see it) is embarrassing." His other beliefs: "I can't stand being uncomfortable, and I shouldn't have to stand what I don't like. Someone might want to be my sponsor, and I don't want anyone else butting in my life—and I should not get what I don't want."

The client may prefer to work on shame in other settings unrelated to his addictive problems. One client went to a department store, spent fifteen minutes looking at lingerie, and then left without making a purchase—something he felt was embarrassing. His beliefs? "The sales clerks may think I'm a pervert. I don't think I could stand that." A workshop group member decided to go to a fancy store, ask to look at various articles, and then leave without purchasing anything. His beliefs? "I am really not 'good enough' to enter such upscale stores. I would look foolish, especially if ultimately I don't buy something. The sales help will see that I can't, in fact, afford such products. I couldn't stand it if they knew that, especially if the sales clerk was a woman. I should not take a salesperson's time without buying something." He committed himself to doing the assignment over lunch, but he bought a wallet, the least expensive item in the store, because he felt too ashamed to leave without purchasing anything. The group sent him back to return the wallet, and that time he succeeded.

Another client got on a bus without the exact change required and asked people on the bus to change a five-dollar bill. His beliefs: "People should always be ready in life for what is required of them. They should never inconvenience or delay other people. They should not have to ask for help."

Setting the Rules

The client can do anything that may evoke the feelings of shame in him except something that will (1) hurt other people, (2) get him fired, or (3) get him in trouble with the law. Ellis often suggests standing on the subway in New York City and announcing the stops in a loud, clear voice, and then staying on the train. But one does not have to do something as outlandish as that, and it may be more therapeutic to do something related to the client's interests and concerns. Planning for the first time to decline a drink at a family function when no one (supposedly) knows about the client's problem can be a strong shame-attacking exercise. Or doing something that might enrich his life, like singing in a choir, may involve a shame-producing activity, in this case, auditioning. Helping him prepare for the audition and seeing it as a shame-attacking exercise may help him take the necessary steps to do something that he will ultimately really enjoy.

Planning the Activity

Shame-attack exercises are valuable at several points in time. The therapist plays an important role in planning the activity, an activating event, in advance of its occurring. The therapist can discuss with the client what he thinks might be helpful and provide him with some examples to choose from if he cannot come up with an idea himself.

Preparing the Exercise

Then, in that session, the therapist can go through the shame attack, exploring with the client what he anticipates thinking and feeling, what he expects might happen, and especially what he might tell himself to stop himself from doing the exercise at all.

Reviewing the Exercise

At the beginning of the next session, the therapist asks what happened. What was the client thinking and feeling before he did the exercise? What was he thinking and feeling while he did the exercise? What was he thinking and feeling after he did the exercise? Did he think it was worthwhile? What did he learn? Would it be good to do it again? What would he do differently, if anything?

Preparing for Future Trigger Situations

Because shame often plays such a powerful role in lapses and relapses, discussing future troublesome situations may help the therapist meet several important therapeutic goals:

Openness and Honesty

It is better therapeutically when clients are open and honest about their return to addictive behaviors. But despite their desire and intent to be honest, shame may prevent them from doing so.

The therapist can ask the client: "Suppose you relapsed? Do you think you would feel ashamed to tell me? Do you think you could call me even if you were very drunk? What do you think I would think about you?" The therapist should demonstrate that his aim is practical and should be careful to judge the behavior, not the client. It is the behavior that is dangerous.

The therapist also can ask the client: "What do you think I would feel? Angry? Irritated? Disappointed?" If the therapist feels disappointed when the client relapses, he may be caring too much. We care to some degree about clients and hope that they will be able to help themselves change. But when we get irritated or disappointed, it is evidence, I think, that we have invested in *our* treatment goals. In addition, we risk being seen as just one more authority figure with an agenda against which the client can rebel. Alternatively, we can feel concerned that (1) the client may hurt himself or others, and (2) he is not meeting his therapeutic goals. We are interested in finding out what might help or work more effectively in the future.

The therapist should take the opportunity to demonstrate that his aim is practical. How can he be helpful? If he were recovering from an operation and started to bleed, he would call the doctor because he would be concerned. Most people would not feel too ashamed to do so. Like post-operative bleeding, a relapse represents a serious problem.

Decrease the FDI of a Lapse or Relapse

A major treatment goal is to reduce the FDI of lapses and relapses. In the past, clients often spent years in a relapse before they returned for treatment. The therapist can ask the client: "If you relapse, what could you feel instead of shame—concerned, disappointed, irritated, determined to get back on track? How would you have to think about what happened to feel hopeful instead of hopeless and helpless? What would you have to tell yourself in order to learn from what happened?"

Making Amends

Suppose the client got drunk and abused or hit his wife, or gambled away all of the family's money. Or worse, he engaged in unsafe sex while high on cocaine, contracted HIV, and gave it to his spouse. Feeling guilty or full of shame won't help his wife and family very much. Even if he learns not to feel "toxic shame" or "global shame" and instead feels and expresses remorse, regret, and contrition, he may still benefit by doing something concrete to make up for what he has done. In addition, making amends shifts the focus to the future and away from the past and what cannot be undone. It also inevitably stimulates a discussion about values and goals, both important elements of successful therapy.

The therapist can follow the same steps to plan and process making amends as for a shame attack. But the people the client has injured must want him to make amends. Some clients want to make amends more to feel better themselves than to help someone they have injured to feel better (see below).

Reframing

There may be times when it is best to attempt to reframe what has occurred as a tragedy. That is, what occurred may have hurt many people, including the client, but attempting to assign responsibility and blame may be impossible. There are too many complex, interacting factors that contributed to the event. For example, what happened to many people in Vietnam was tragic. Many factors conspired to place people in situations that they were unprepared or untrained to handle. Having an alcoholic father who in turn was raised in an alcoholic family may also have tragic consequences. Blaming the father—and his father—may not have any therapeutic value. But acknowledging that the circumstances were (and perhaps continue to be) tragic may help a client respond more appropriately, for example, by feeling sad and resigned rather than ashamed, depressed, and enraged.

Practicing Role Plays in Session

By role-playing the various voices in her head, the client can do an ABC or talk to herself more effectively when she feels ashamed or guilty (or anticipates feeling ashamed or guilty). In this way, she learns how to reprogram her conditioned shame response.

Doing REI

Rational emotive imagery (REI) is always effective when people are trying to learn how to feel differently in various situations. It may also be very valuable in preparing to do a shame-attack exercise.

SPECIAL PROBLEMS THE THERAPIST MAY ENCOUNTER

Shame about Shame

Many clients may feel ashamed about feeling ashamed. Therefore, they may be hesitant to admit that they feel ashamed, or they are so ashamed that they cannot accept how much shame may be contributing to their problems. Shame about shame is another secondary problem, and it should often be addressed first.

Guilt and Shame over Serious Events

A client who served in the military in wartime may have done things that were against his most deeply felt values, such as killing women and children. He may feel terribly guilty and ashamed of his behavior. Another client may have gotten drunk and, while driving, crashed into another car and killed all of the occupants. He also may be drinking or drugging to cope with his feelings of guilt and shame. How can the therapist help such clients?

Many cultural, ethnic, and religious factors will probably affect how therapy proceeds. The therapist should find out more about the client's beliefs, especially regarding religion. What does his religion suggest someone who has sinned should do? Has he followed that advice? Has he talked with his religious leader? What did his leader suggest? If that didn't help, why not?

What is the therapist's role? As Kellogg and Triffleman (1998) point out, "Therapists cannot grant spiritual forgiveness or dispense judicial pardons" (p. 409). Ellis's position is that the therapist can acknowledge the badness of the act and the client can feel ashamed and guilty about it whenever he thinks about it. He may also choose to make amends for his act. But to judge and feel guilty about and ashamed of his *self* serves little purpose. It will not undo the act, and it may cause him to continue to drink and thus increase the probability that he will commit some other harmful act. Most religions suggest that it is not for us to judge, as that is God's work.

But what should the therapist do if the client has done some very serious things and does not seem to feel guilty, ashamed, or concerned? Will that affect how the therapist judges her? Surely, it should affect how thearpy proceeds because a client who feels no remorse is clearly very different from one who is continually drowning in guilt and shame. However, the key factor may be the client's self-perceived stage of change. Does she think she has a problem? Is she ambivalent? Ready to take some action? What are her goals? To forget about it? To make amends?

Caution: Telling a client that he need not feel globally ashamed of or guilty about what he has done may not be understood the way the therapist intends. He may hear something very different: "Get over it. It wasn't so bad. Forget it." He may even begin to get angry at other people because they are not following the therapist's advice and forgetting and forgiving him! Why should they want to remember something bad he has done? How does that help?

A friend of mine who works in prisons says that he feels he has made some progress when some of his clients begin to feel shame. However, again we return to whether we mean ashamed of what they have *done*, that is, their behavior, or of their *selves*.

Forgiveness

How can we help people get over their guilt and shame when that seems appropriate? How can we help them forgive themselves and get on with their lives?

Case Vignette: Helping Claire Accept Herself with Her Errors and Problems

Claire had physically beaten her daughter when her daughter was a child. She could not forgive herself and still relapsed into heavy drinking periodically, due partly to her shame over her past behavior. It turned out that her daughter, now 24, has no ill feelings toward her mother; in fact, she is very fond of her, calls her frequently, and gets together with her at least twice a month for dinner. We discussed how Claire might forgive herself. Initially, she said that she did not believe she could ever forgive herself. We discussed the fact that traditionally, if one commits a crime, society's laws set the punishment. Because she has such a good sense of humor, and given the fact that she had already apologized to her daughter and that her daughter felt so positively toward her, I suggested that we could decide on a punishment to fit the crime. Then she could self-administer the punishment and when done, come back to see me. She was amused, but then I asked her, "Seriously, what do you want to do? Maintaining your shame over your past behavior is also maintaining your addictive behavior. What form and how much punishment do you think you should give yourself?"

She looked back at me with a smile. Perhaps because she goes to AA meetings, she proposed making amends to her daughter. Initially, that sounded like a possible path. But upon examination, it turned out that her daughter did not want to discuss the matter any longer. For her it was over. Making amends might have made Claire feel better, but it would have made her daughter feel worse, so that was not as good a solution as it had appeared to be.

Claire is Christian, so we discussed the story of Mary Magdalene in the Bible. Although most people know the first part of the story—"He who has not sinned, cast the first stone"—they forget the ending, which is equally important for our purposes. According to the Bible, after all of the men who were about to stone Mary Magdalene for adultery (or perhaps prostitution, the term is interpreted in various ways) left, Christ went over to her, extended His hand to help her up, and said, "Neither do I condemn thee. Go and sin no more." It seems clear that Christ is telling her two important things: I am also not judging you, and change your behavior.

As I often point out to my clients, He did not say, "You're a really bad sinner [judging and labeling her]. You should be ashamed of yourself and feel very guilty. Go to a nunnery, and for six months eat only bread and water and sleep on the stone floor." In other words, He did not tell her to go punish herself and feel bad for six months. That is not the point of the story. Behavior change seems to be the point of the story, not self-condemnation, shame, guilt, and punishment.

Sometimes the client may still feel she should punish herself and feel bad. It may help to suggest that she appears to be saying that she knows better than Christ. That has helped many Christians and even some non-Christians start to reassess their thinking.

If the client still feels ashamed and guilty, the therapist could discuss and decide on some "punishment". After all, in society, if we do wrong, we are expected to pay for it, but usually not forever, which is the point that many clients miss. The punishment is supposed to fit the crime. Usually this type of discussion will not actually lead the therapist and client to decide on a punishment—partly because the client has already been punishing himself for years—but the discussion itself is frequently very therapeutic. It may also help clarify what may be and may not be appropriate shame and guilt.

The therapist can also encourage the client to make amends. At times, making amends may be very therapeutic (see below). The therapist can also encourage the client to change his life so as to do as little harm as possible to others and to himself in the future.

ISSUES TO KEEP IN MIND

The Connection Between Shame, Anxiety, and Depression

If the client habitually rates his entire self every time he does anything well or poorly, the potential for feeling ashamed may already exist prior to doing anything, because he puts his entire self on the line in each instance and at every moment. Thus, the potential for making mistakes and then blaming and shaming his entire self looms as a very real threat. As a result, he may feel hypervigilant and anxious practically all of the time, unless he uses chemicals or engages in some other consciousness-changing addictive behavior.

In addition, because he knows he will come down on his entire self if he makes an error—that is, he will not limit his negative evaluation to his behavior but will negatively and powerfully evaluate his self, as well—he anticipates feeling ashamed and depressed eventually. He knows that eventually he will make a mistake. This state of anticipated failure and dread contributes powerfully to a chronic state of felt, anticipated, low-grade depression, that is, dysthymia.

Discomfort anxiety is often connected with shame. The client may relapse because he feels too ashamed to not have a drink: "It would have made me too uncomfortable not to order a drink when everybody else was ordering a drink. I couldn't stand it." Or someone may relapse into addictive sexual behavior, thinking, "I don't want him to think I'm cold or uninterested."

When the Medical Model Breaks Down

Kellogg and Trifleman (1998) point out that many therapists operate from the perspective of a medical model and clients are seen as having some sort of mental health disorder. They are sick in some sense of the term. They are also seen as victims, either of a disease or of past events. However, when a client brings up something especially violent, the therapist may no longer see such behavior as evidence of mental illness. Suddenly, the client may be perceived as evil and a perpetrator, not a victim. The problem is that therapists are not generally trained to deal with evil or with perpetrators. Hence, they are at sea professionally. Again, the solution may be to focus on the behaviors that the client wants to change, focusing on past events only to the extent that they impact on the client's current efforts to change, while refraining from judging (globalizing and labeling) him. When the therapist finds this impossible, he can consult with a supervisor or a peer.

Developmental Issues

People feel ashamed about different things as they grow older. A 14-year-old boy may be ashamed that he seems developmentally far behind his peers, perhaps socially as well as physically, and may begin to smoke pot to compensate and look "cool." A 17-year-old may be drinking excessively because he would be ashamed if it seemed that he was not keeping up with his peers. A man in his forties may start steadily drinking because he is ashamed that he has not achieved what he expected to achieve by that time in his life. An elderly person may begin to drink heavily because, after the death of his wife, he is too ashamed to admit that he wants to commit suicide.

Familial/Genetic Issues

Clients may frequently shame themselves for behaving in what they consider shameful ways. But their family members may be shy, easily feel ashamed, be isolated, have few friends, and engage in a variety of addictive behaviors. Thus, genetic and other family/ environmental factors may have contributed to some of the client's feelings and behaviors—feeling ashamed, drinking too much, impulsivity, gambling. That is, she may stop spending so much time and energy blaming and shaming herself, and come to see that her problems result partly from genetic factors coupled with many conditioning trials, that is, a lot of learning and overlearning in the family environment. Many clients begin to feel and behave better when they accept and try to figure out better ways to compensate for familial and genetic factors.

Socioeconomic Issues

Socioeconomic issues may contribute to feelings of shame, and they may also interact with developmental factors. Our consumer-oriented society affects our goals and values in both subtle and not-so-subtle ways. Clients who have always wanted to succeed but have not been able to do as well as they had hoped may be very ashamed that they cannot afford to live where their peers live, drive the kind of car they think they should, or belong to the right club. A client who has been let go after a merger may be ashamed because he or she was fired while other coworkers were retained.

Gender Issues

Patricia, a client I have seen off and on for over ten years, occasionally has new bouts of shame. She has decided not to have children. She prefers to pursue her artistic career, and she did not think she could do both. But with the explosion of babies on the streets of her city and babies in practically every television comedy, she is occasionally overcome with doubt and shame. Although she has read of older women having babies, at 44 she thinks it would be too risky, and she still does not think she can pursue her art and have a child. A man at 44 is not faced with the same biological limitations. Moreover, few men feel ashamed about not having children.

Gender may contribute to shame in other issues, as well. Some men, for example, may feel too ashamed to stay home and take care of their children. Other men may feel shame if their spouse or partner makes more money than they do.

Questions Related to Making Amends

How Does Making Amends Benefit a Client?

To make amends, one must focus on what another person wants. Many people who suffer from addictive behaviors are self-absorbed. They are so concerned with their needs and their pain that they have great difficulty taking into account the effect of their actions on other people. Activities that take themselves outside of themselves and shift their focus from self-concern to concern for others often challenge many of their strongly held irrational beliefs.

Should the Therapist Encourage a Client to Make Amends?

Perhaps, just as the therapist may encourage clients to do many other types of cognitive-behavioral homework.

Suppose He Cannot Make Amends Because the People He Has Injured Will Not Permit It?

People who have been injured by the client may prefer now to be left alone. They may have no desire to help the client recover or feel less bad about what he has done. What happened is in the past, and they have no desire to open old wounds. The client may think this is unfair, telling himself: "They should be willing to help me recover. They shouldn't think irrationally, telling themselves that they can't stand it. I can stand it. It's not that bad anyway." It is critically important to explore with the client why he wants to make amends. Is it only to help himself recover?

If someone who has been injured by the client does not want any contact with him, there are many other ways the client can make amends. For example, if he injured a child, he may want to help raise money for a child-oriented fund or hospital. Or he may want to help a niece or nephew go to college.

Doesn't Making Amends Reinforce the Idea that the Client Should Feel Guilty and Ashamed?

It may be psychologically healthy for the client to feel ashamed and/or feel guilty about the act. There is nothing wrong with feeling guilty about killing another person while the client was drunk or high on drugs. The therapist and client can judge that the act was very bad and decide to do something to make up for it, if only partly. This may be true even if the client is in jail as one of the consequences of his behavior. Again, feeling guilty or ashamed about something bad is not necessarily a psychotherapeutic problem.

FIVE HOMEWORK ASSIGNMENTS

✓ **Shame attacks:** Initially most clients will not be willing to work directly on their shame reactions. But if they are encouraged to start off with small exercises, they will begin to see their value. The client may even be too ashamed to go into a fancy store or to cook dinner for a friend. The therapist may make more progress by zeroing in on something the client has wanted to do for a long time.

✓ **Making amends:** This is a somewhat tricky assignment (see above).

✓ **Ongoing projects:** The client may be able to build his confidence and work on his tendency to feel shame by involving himself in projects with other people, such as community projects, helping produce a play, and working in a shelter once a week.

✓ **Writing out a role play:** The client can write out an imagined interaction between herself and someone else, a situation in which she now feels she would be too ashamed to be able to express herself effectively. She can practice it in therapy and write out new responses.

✓ **Having a Phone Session:** Initially a client may find it easier to tell the therapist something over the telephone rather than in session. She may think—and she may be right—that not being able to see the therapist's reaction and vice versa will help. (This is one possible reason that teenagers spend hours talking on the phone with their peers—peers they see every day and may have just seen an hour before!) In the next session, the therapist can work on what the client was telling herself prior to the phone session, during it, and after it.

MEDICATIONS

If global shaming is a frequent problem or if the client cannot stop shaming himself once he starts, a psychiatric consult may be helpful. Drugs like Prozac may reduce obsessive-compulsive thinking. Therefore, they may also help the client stop thinking so much about how shamefully he behaved.

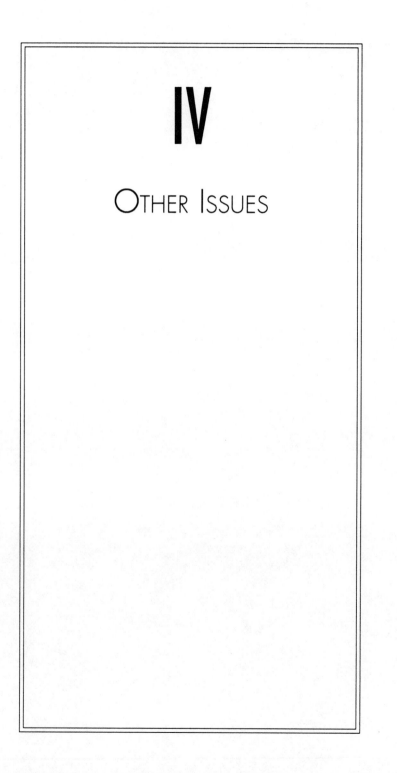

IV

OTHER ISSUES

14 WORKING WITH CLIENTS WITH SEVERE PSYCHOLOGICAL PROBLEMS

Most clients who have an addictive problem also have some other kind of psychological problem (and many clients who have psychological problems also have addictive problems). However, some clients have more serious, ongoing, chronic psychological problems, including personality disorders.

Historically, clients who had an addictive problem along with another psychological problem were treated in separate units by separate teams of mental health workers. The teams had their own treatment philosophy and techniques, which did not always mesh well with each other. But as the recognition that underlying psychological problems often interact with addictive problems grew, dual diagnosis and MICA (mentally ill, chemically abusing) programs sprang up around the country.

CBT and REBT are particularly well suited for working with clients who have two or more diagnoses (cf. Olevitch 1995). What clients learn in order to manage one problem may help them manage other problems as well. Consequently, many dual-diagnosis treatment centers are incorporating various forms of CBT/REBT into their programs.

WHAT DOES THE RESEARCH SUGGEST?

- In a study of 716 opioid users who sought methadone treatment (47 percent were women and 60 percent were Caucasian), 34.8 percent were diagnosed with an axis II disorder (25.1 percent met the criteria for an antisocial personality disorder) (Brooner et al. 1997). Of 30 pathological gamblers (23 percent women) recruited through an advertisement in Iowa, 33 percent met the criteria for antisocial personality disorder, 23 percent also engaged in compulsive shopping, 17 percent engaged in compulsive sexual behavior, and 13 percent met the criteria for intermittent explosive disorder (Black and Moyer 1998).
- Forty-seven percent of people suffering from schizophrenia also have a substance use disorder during their lifetime; 70 to 90 percent are dependent on nicotine (Ziedonis and Wyatt 1998).
- Of 295 clients diagnosed with schizophrenia and substance use disorder who were evaluated for their stage of change regarding alcohol abuse, 53 percent were assessed in the precontemplation and contemplation stages (Ziedonis and Wyatt 1998).
- Of those diagnosed with a bipolar disorder in the Epidemiological Catchment Area study (Regier et al. 1990), 60.7 percent had an addictive disorder, 46.2 percent had an alcohol use disorder, and 40.7 percent had a drug use disorder. Bipolar I was the most likely co-diagnosis with a substance use disorder.

HOW DOES A PERSONALITY DISORDER DIAGNOSIS AFFECT THERAPY?

In working with people with more serious problems, what the therapist believes about personality disorders will affect therapy. If the client has been diagnosed as having an antisocial personality disorder, can he change his functioning sufficiently? Or is antisocial behavior a trait that he cannot change? If the therapist believes the client cannot change his underlying personality disorder, then what *is* possible? An underlying assumption of this book is that such a client, even a client who has psychotic problems, can learn techniques to help him cope with and manage his disorder. He can learn ways to reduce the frequency, duration, and intensity (FDI) of his problematic behavioral patterns. He can also learn ways to reduce the harm that he might do to himself and to others.

THE ROLE OF THE STAGES OF CHANGE MODEL IN HELPING CLIENTS WITH SERIOUS PSYCHOLOGICAL PROBLEMS

A dually or multiply diagnosed client needs help changing and/or managing many behavioral patterns. Clients may have problems with substance abuse and other addictive behaviors, problems with intense anxiety and depression, including parasuicidal and suicidal behaviors, problems with rapid mood swings, problems in relationships, problems with work or the lack of work, and the challenge of finding meaningful, life-fulfilling ways to fill the day. For each problem, the therapist should be mindful of what stage the client is in. Each behavioral change will probably move through the various stages of change. As usual, those patterns of change will not always move in a positive direction. The client may relapse back into depression as well as relapse back into an addictive behavior pattern. If the client's problems are chronic, it is even more important to keep in mind the stages of change model.

Moreover, clients with multiple problems are often the least able to manage them. They have difficulty accepting who they are, what they are doing with their life, how other people act, and how the world works in general. Specifically, they tend to "awfulize" moods swings, thoughts that pop into their head (intrusive thoughts), times when they have difficulty concentrating, and various physical ailments. They rarely exercise, eat poorly and irregularly, and sleep irregularly and often too much or too little. They often use addictive behaviors to cope, and then they create more problems in their lives as a result of opting for these short-term solutions.

To work with such complex clients, therapists need to focus on the key points for building a good therapeutic relationship (outlined in Chapter 5): unconditional acceptance, respect, empathy and support, reducing the harm, doing effective therapy, sharing, using humor, and remaining client-centered. However, with a client who has severe psychological problems, the therapist should be especially cautious about sharing. Clients who are delusional may easily misinterpret information about the therapist's private life. Similarly, some clients will consistently misinterpret the therapist's use of humor as a way of making fun of them or trivializing their problems. On the other hand, it is important to remain client-centered, focused on what the client has identified as important. But at the same time the therapist can bring up a problem that he thinks the client would benefit from working on. The client may protest, but eventually, if he sees that the therapist is client-centered, he may listen.

SELECTED CLINICAL STRATEGIES

Session Goals

The goals with these patients are the following:

1. To reduce the FDI of lapses and relapses of various behaviors as the result of the client's many psychological problems.
2. To help the client learn to better manage her psychological problems without the help of addictive behaviors.

Exploring the Problem

Where Is the Client in Terms of the Stages of Change?

A client with several problems cannot work on them all at once. That is, he cannot be in the action stage on all of his problems at the same time.

Jane was one of the angriest people I had ever seen in therapy. She seemed angry at the entire world. I could see it on her face, a face with deep lines and blood-shot eyes. But her wry, Irish sense of humor was also immediately evident. She had several serious problems: a tendency to become rageful at herself, others, and the world; a tendency to get very anxious in many situations; a tendency to get very depressed; and a tendency to drink too much on a daily basis and to binge drink on the weekend.

Jane had been married twice and had one teenage girl, Jennifer, by the second marriage. Jennifer had a spotty record at school. She had done well in the past, but once she went to high school her grades started to fall off and she started to hang out with "the wrong crowd of kids," according to her mother.

Jane has three sisters and four brothers. She gets along with some of them, but cannot stand some of the others.

In the first session, Jane seemed to want to get rid of her anxiety and depression. I say "seemed" because there may have been secondary gains to remaining depressed or anxious. Some clients may lose their Medicare benefits if they become undepressed. Other clients, especially women, may be anxious because they are afraid they might explode—a very bad thing to do if you have been raised to be a good little girl. So they may be conflicted about getting over their anxiety, that is, ambivalent or in Stage II. In Jane's case, she did not see her contribution to making herself anxious or depressed. Consequently, she was not interested in working on her anxiety and depression. She hoped that with some talking, and perhaps some medications, those problems would go away.

Jane was not ready to accept that her anger was not fully justified. "After what Jennifer said to me? No way!" she told me in one session. Her father and mother were also "impossible," as they had always been. They were never there for her. So she was not about to stop being angry at them. Regarding anger, Jane was in Stage I, precontemplation.

She said she wanted to stop drinking, but she was ambivalent. She had been to some AA meetings but she did not like them. She tried some SMART® Recovery meetings, but she did not like them either. Her mother had gone to Recovery, Inc. meetings on and off throughout her life, but Jane was repulsed by the idea. "I'm not as crazy as my mother," she said. As I noted above, she said she wanted to stop, but she shared with me that she did not think she could stop for long. She had never been able to in the past.

Despite all of her difficulties, Jane had managed to keep her job at a printing firm. In fact, her boss is very pleased with her work. That is not surprising because Jane is a very demanding, exacting person, not only on herself. She knows when to push suppliers and subcontractors for deliveries and better service, and, at all times, she is relentlessly driving herself.

Here are some typical beliefs to watch for:

"I can't stand the way I am."

"I can't stand this world."

"You don't understand (as you must)."

"I have to explain. (It's very hard for me to stand it if I think you don't understand.)"

"You have to validate me—what I feel, what I did, what I said."

Here are some other hidden beliefs to watch for:

"I'm crazy. I'm hopeless."

"I can't change the way I feel."

"Only medication will help me."

The therapist's beliefs may interfere with the therapy. Similar to the stigma associated with addictions, there are stigmas associated with multiple psychological problems. The therapist may be telling himself:

She'll never change.

I've seen hundreds of clients like this before. None of them has ever changed very much, and she won't either.

Without intensive group therapy and at least two individual sessions a week, we won't make any progress.

Given the limited resources in many facilities today, some of the above beliefs may not be incorrect or irrational. However, they may undermine the therapy.

Practicing Unconditional Acceptance

These clients can benefit from learning to be accepting of themselves and others and life in general. Their multiple problems may be due to factors over which they have had little control (their genetic makeup, the environment of their upbringing, their current environment, their family members and friends, their inability to work without losing their Medicare benefits, etc.). In addition, they have difficulty thinking straight and thinking problems through. They have few skills to work with and are often incapable of using those they have. They often have no employment or any other activity to fill their day or provide them with a focus outside of themselves. Without such an outlet, they become self-absorbed and focus on their various ailments and practical difficulties.

In addition, many clients with multiple problems have few friends and are often shunned by old friends and even family. As a result, they wind up making friends with other people who also have problems. In fact, the person the client chooses to try to develop a relationship with may be unable to be in a relationship or even in a friendship. Consequently, the very people who are least able to question and challenge and dispute irrational thinking are confronted with the most difficult activating events—being alone and having difficult, often demanding friends.

As Rogers (1961) pointed out, unconditional regard has immense therapeutic value. But it is even better if the client can begin to give unconditional acceptance—despite and in the face of his many problems—to himself. At the same time, he also needs help to become more accepting of others and of the world.

When the client is angry at a specific person in his life, why is he condemning the person? He is probably thinking in a demanding way: "He shouldn't have behaved that way." How does being demanding help? Does it change the person? Does it help the client? Can he condemn the behavior without condemning the person at the same time? Does that make any sense to him? What would be the payoff for him if he adopted such a philosophy?

Practice Zen Caring

When the client lapses or relapses, the therapist will have a perfect opportunity to show how she cares without caring too much. That is, she cares to be of help. She cares about helping the client do what she wants to do with his life. But it is his life, and the therapist is careful not to care to the extent of becoming another parental or authority figure for him to rebel and act out against and to lie to. However, the therapist may be clear that she thinks the client's behavior is dangerous and that it will not help him fulfill his goals.

Using Traditional REBT to Help the Client Accept Things She Cannot Change

Using the ABC(DE) technique, the therapist can help the client think through situations when life confronts her with circumstances that are, given her goals and values, difficult to accept.

When the client is having a hard time accepting something, she is usually engaging in a poisonous cycle of demandness, awfulizing, low frustration tolerance (LFT), and self-downing.

Jane would think to herself about her daughter, "She shouldn't have spoken to me in that tone of voice. I'm losing control of her. She's going to become an addict. I don't know what to do (as I should)."

Then Jane usually increased her emotional upset by "awfulizing." That is, she rated what had happened or was happening as very, very bad or very, very unacceptable (an 8 or 9 on a 10-point scale, where 10 is atrocious). This was easy for Jane to do because she had only one daughter, and she was close to very few other people. However, usually what had occurred was a 4 or a 5. It was not catastrophic. Her daughter had not died. They were not caught in a war.

Next Jane usually added the belief, "I can't stand this anymore." She could tolerate high levels of frustration at work, but once she had elevated her distress over her daughter to a high level, she convinced herself that she could not stand what had occurred and what she thought was going to occur.

Finally, she always added some form of self-downing or self-pity to the mix: "What's wrong with me? How did I get into this mess (as I shouldn't be)? I'm such a basket case (as I shouldn't be). I'm acting just like my mother (and I can't stand that). Why is life so difficult for me?"

To help her begin to accept her problems and to move toward effectively solving some of them, I tried to help her see how to break the links in this vicious circle. It was quite easy to empathize with her. I would not have wanted to be in her situation. I would especially not have wanted my daughter going to the high school where her daughter went. It was a tough school and there were lots of children who would eventually end up in jail, on drugs, or dead. But I tried to help Jane see that thinking in a demanding way caused her to get so upset that she could not think straight. I tried to help her see that while it might be very scary and very confusing, she had not lost her daughter. She was in a very difficult situation, and she needed to be able to think straight to solve it. I alluded to her solution-based approach at work, and we talked about how and why she did not get so upset there. I also pointed out that when she thought to herself, "I can't stand it," she quickly added, "I'm trapped, hopeless, helpless, doomed." Finally, I used a variety of approaches to try to get her to see how self-downing only made her feel less able and less willing to deal with her problems. To further help her accept herself *with* her problems, we discussed forgiveness from a New Testament standpoint.

Reducing the Harm

As I am listening to a client, I am always wondering, What is the riskiest thing she is doing? How could I help her reduce the harm she might do to herself or to someone else this week? The answers to these simple questions often guide what I do in the session. It also helps my client and me stay focused on *how*—how she can help herself feel and do better—instead of on *why* this is happening.

We have continually worked together to prevent relapses, and when they occur, to reduce their length and severity and, especially, the risk involved. Jane usually does not drink alone at home, so by going to bars she increases the risks significantly, and she must also get home safely. We not only wrote out a time-effect sheet (and she has a copy in her purse), but also tried to figure out ways that she could get home safely if she went out drinking. The problem is that she is usually so enraged by the time she arrives at a bar that she hates everything and everybody, most of all herself. So we had a hard time coming up with an effective plan. The last time, the police found her sitting on the curb and, luckily, brought her home.

Exploring Possible Plans

Despite the fact that the client may have a multiplicity of interacting problems, it is important to be watchful for opportunities to encourage him to try out a plan for dealing with a problem, especially an addictive problem that contributes to his other problems. Therapy should initially focus on those behaviors that are most dangerous. Such behaviors take precedence over all other problems and should almost always be addressed first.

Teaching Corsini's Four R's of Parenting for Self-Parenting

Corsini and Painter (1989) proposed the four R's of parenting: respect (including self-respect), responsibility, resourcefulness, and responsiveness. These are a good guide for some clients, especially those who were never parented very well. It is also a very useful guide for some disturbed clients who are also parents.

When clients have serious, ongoing psychological problems, and especially when addictive behaviors are involved, it is difficult to teach them how to respect themselves and to take responsibility for their choices in life. However, teaching self-respect and respect for others and teaching responsibility for one's choices may be even more important with such clients, because they have so little respect for themselves, and because they probably have had more than a few instances when they have not been treated with respect in their dealings with mental health professionals.

Roger's (1961) client-centered therapy and Glasser's (1965, 1989) reality therapy both dovetail easily with these concepts, as do CBT and REBT. By listening to clients and working on what they want to work on, therapists not only respect their goals and values but also teach them to respect their sense of what is of value to them and what is not.

Respect. Jane was highly disrespectful of most other people. She did not always show it, but she clearly thought most people were beneath contempt. She was overtly disrespectful of her daughter. She raised her voice and swore at her and called her names. Although she never did it to her face, she called her own mother a "fucking bitch" and referred to some of her siblings in a similar fashion. At times, she saved the most searing contempt for herself.

However, in her marriages she had not insisted on being treated with respect. She had stayed in both relationships despite the fact that both husbands verbally abused and one physically abused her. She had also stayed with the second husband despite the fact that she knew he was cheating on her. Eventually he left her. So she was not used to treating herself or others respectfully, unless they were figures of authority, such as her boss and me. To me, she was respectful, polite, and funny. I suspect she treats her boss the same way.

Responsibility: Jane appeared to be too responsible at her job, but she was not sufficiently responsible at home. She could not responsibly take care of her daughter when she was drinking. I knew that she was Catholic, and that she tried to be ethical, so I tried to use those two elements as my motivational levers. I tried to help her begin to act more responsibly while teaching her how blaming and shaming did not help. I repeatedly reminded her of the Mary Magdalene story, stressing that it was her responsibility to learn to change her behavior without judging herself as she was learning. I knew she wanted to act responsibly with respect to her daughter, so that was my handle, but I had to use it without judging her and while trying to keep her from judging herself.

Resourcefulness: Jane would sometimes ask me what I thought she should do. I knew that she could think straight and that she was very effective at solving problems at work. I did not want her to look to me as some guru with the answers, especially as I did not always have them. So I was always careful to reframe the conversation to make it a conversation between two parents who were raising children and sending them to public school. We discussed her options (e.g., sending her daughter to a Catholic school, changing high schools, sending her away to a Catholic boarding school if her daughter could get a scholarship, turning her over to the guardianship of the state), and developed ways she could work more effectively helping her daughter grow up. At the same time, we always took time to work on her drinking problem, to help her learn better not to build up her anger during the week and then drink it off Saturday night.

Responsiveness: Jane was frequently so angry that she could not give to anyone. She would do her job well because she believed she should, but she frequently could not be responsive to her sisters and brothers or her mother or even her daughter. We looked at what she was telling herself when she neglected to prepare a meal. Usually she was full of anger: "She's such a pain (as she mustn't be). She probably cut class again today. I can't stand her anymore." We carefully looked at the rationality, the helpfulness, and the ethics of each idea. I also pointed out that I thought she was also slipping into "I can't be bothered. It's too hard. I'm too tired." Because she was so angry, she would not override her fatigue and LFT and cook a meal for her daughter. However, I suggested that she could do it even if she felt angry and that it might make her feel better, less angry at her daughter, less angry at herself, and less angry at the world. Slowly she began to cook again, and she and her daughter had more dinners together.

Being a Coach

Much of what I do with many of my clients can be called coaching. A coach teaches things and gives tips. Clients may benefit from this practical advice. The problem is to know when to give it and especially to prevent therapy from turning into advice giving. At one point I directly suggested that Jane never discuss upsetting topics with her daughter at mealtime, which should be a time and a place where her daughter can enjoy herself eating and talking to her mother and feel safe. I advised her to pick a place in some other part of the house to have heart-to-heart conversations. I also advised her to try as much as possible to think out what she wanted to say in advance. This was in an attempt to stop the hurtful fights that could flare up at any moment.

Exploring Secondary Problems

Clients with many complex problems often make problems out of problems. That is, if they feel depressed, they begin to get upset and anxious about feeling depressed. Then they may get angry that they are suffering so much from so many emotional problems. Then they often turn to a mixture of chemicals to alleviate their distress. It is important to help them become more aware of how they escalate their emotional reactions to full-blown emotional storms.

The problem is to do this without sounding unsympathetic. If the therapist appears to be trying to help the client change the way he thinks about many admittedly fairly negative aspects of his life, the client may stop listening. He will only think the therapist is trying to help him pretend that everything is okay, not great, but not awful either. He may have to work toward thinking that way—toward accepting that a lot of the things in his life aren't great—but he will not be motivated to stay in therapy if that is all it offers. How will he benefit if he tries to be more accepting, if he tries to not upset himself so much? What will he get? That is why it is equally important to look at the larger issues, perhaps spiritual, perhaps existential, in his life. Even with all of his problems, how can he build a more satisfying, more meaningful life? On a more concrete level, how can he change some of the A's as he is working on changing his B's?

Helping the Client Become Less Reactive

Some clients, regardless of their mental capacities, dislike doing ABC's. Perhaps it is too complex or suggests taking on too much responsibility. However, they may like giving one or more of their problematic thinking styles a name.

Jerry, a heavyset, burly man, worked as an auto mechanic. He was drinking too much, getting into fights, and thus thinking about quitting drinking. His boss, Sam, often lost his temper, and Jerry and Sam had almost come to blows several times. Jerry could sometimes see that his boss's ranting and raving had nothing to do with him, but he got upset anyway. He would think to himself, "He's such an asshole." One time he said, "I feel like killing him." I stopped to warn him of what I might have to do (in terms of breaking confidentiality) if he made such statements in my office. He acknowledged that he would not really do anything like that although he felt like it. We discussed it a little more, and I decided he had not meant it as a real threat, and we continued on.

Jerry realized that thinking in such a "hot" manner got him into trouble. He could see that if someone called him an asshole, it was not true. It was just a label that often worked as a weapon. It got people very angry, very fast, which was its whole point. I taught him that when someone called him an asshole they were labeling him and probably trying to make him lose his temper. Labeling was just a technique like a good feint, and it was up to him to decide how to respond. He could take it personally and get upset, or he could see it for what it was and not get tricked.

Because I also knew Jerry liked to fish, I suggested that he did not always have to take the bait. Older, wiser, bigger fish do not get fooled as easily and he did not have to get suckered in as easily either. He could watch the fishing plug go by. That seemed to help him a lot. He understood immediately what I was saying.

When he seemed open to it, I pointed out to Jerry that he also seemed to think in a black-and-white, all-or-nothing manner. He immediately agreed. "I know I do that," he said. It surprised me how quickly he agreed, but that has happened in the past sometimes. The next session he told me, "On Tuesday, I started to think, 'I'm just going to quit. This is it.' but then I said to myself, 'Calm down. You're just thinking in your old black-and-white stinking way.'" I suggested that he did not have to put his way of thinking down by calling it stinking, and then we went on again.

Another client, Brad, had had a series of very serious psychotic episodes twenty years ago. According to him, the FBI had forced him to eat too many candies, which had caused him to lose his hair. This had all occurred near Madison Square Garden. He would get very anxious whenever he was afraid he had made a mistake, especially if he was making some connection between his current behavior and what had occurred many years before. He was, however, able to learn to identify these connections, and I decided to label them as such. As we worked together over the next few months, he would sometimes come into my office and say, "I wanted to go to a Knicks' game [at Madison Square Garden], but then I thought I wouldn't be allowed to go because of what happened before, but then I said to myself, 'I'm just making a connection.' That's right, right?"

"Yes," I would say.

"So I decided I could go. That was right, right? That was just a connection, right?"

"Yes," I would say.

Brad was able to help himself tremendously with that simple device. To the immense surprise of his managed care case manager, he began to take less medication for his back pain, kept his job, controlled his tendency to talk to himself out loud when he was walking on the street, and reduced his smoking.

Role Playing (and Reverse Role Playing)

Disturbed clients can often benefit from learning how to more effectively talk to the other people in their lives. Role playing demonstrates what they might say (instead of what they usually say) and helps them practice.

ISSUES TO KEEP IN MIND

Rent-a-Friend

Some clients may feel desperately that they have to tell the therapist everything that has happened in the last twenty-four hours or the last week. This may be because they see therapy as a place where they talk about the past. However, some clients may truly have no other person they can talk to or trust. They have no dependable, stable friendships, and their family members are less than helpful. Consequently, they want to share what has happened and what is happening with the therapist. Sometimes I spend the entire session listening because I realize that my client is not open to working on something. But I often strive for a balance between what has happened in the past week or two and what we could do to make the next week or two better. I also strive for a balance between the why and the how: why something may have happened and how he could have responded differently and could respond differently in the future.

Addictive Problems First, Emotional Problems Second

If the client has many overlapping, interacting problems, he may be in so much distress that he only wants to talk about how angry or how depressed he is and why. These are important issues, but the therapist's effort to cut down or stop an addictive behavior may get lost in the turmoil. It is also possible that the client is talking fast because he feels uneasy or ashamed about his failure to modify or stop his addictive behavior. Consciously or unconsciously, he is attempting to steer the session away from a topic he does not want to touch. Therefore, gently, near the beginning or at the beginning of the session, the therapist can ask how he is doing in terms of his addictive behavior. If he is clearly uncomfortable discussing what has happened, it provides a wonderful opportunity for the therapist to demonstrate that he is not judging the client for his failure to do what he had set out to do. If he is berating himself, the therapist can ask him to explain why the therapist should join him in berating him. This should help him into another direction.

FIVE HOMEWORK ASSIGNMENTS

Even disturbed clients can benefit from homework assignments, if they seem interested in having something to do between sessions.

✓ **Doing an ABC:** Even some very disturbed clients can do ABC's in writing. Having a form to fill in may help, and it can be reviewed in the next session. ABC exercises also prevent them from going on and on about the A's (activating events, i.e., aggravating events) in their lives, which simple journal writing may encourage. In fact, if the therapist just asks them to write how they feel, they may rehearse all of their dysfunctional thinking.

✓ **Changing some A's:** There may be many benefits in helping clients work to change some of the aggravating events in their lives, for example, poor housing and abusive relationships.

✓ **Practicing relaxation techniques:** Clients can do various techniques in therapy and then also between sessions.

✓ **Baking an apple pie:** Some clients who have many serious problems still have little to do during the day. In addition, much of what they do is inactive. They spend hours watching television, on the Web, on the telephone, or sleeping. They often wonder what to do. They can bake an apple pie! It will get them on their feet and doing something. They can give it to someone else to help them become a bit less self-absorbed and a bit more other-directed. The apple pie is a metaphor for doing something active that they might enjoy and that might take them out of their preoccupation with their problems.

✓ **Going to a Meeting**—a twelve-step meeting, a SMART® meeting, or a Recovery, Inc. meeting.

MEDICATIONS

I find it very helpful to work with a psychiatrist or a psychopharmacologist when I am working with a very disturbed person. I can benefit from my colleague's insights and expertise, and he or she can help me help my client manage his many and often difficult problems.

RESOURCES

- Recovery Inc.
- National Alliance for Mental Health
- TIP number 9, "Treatment Improvement Protocol on Co-Existing Mental Illness and Substance Abuse," from the National Clearinghouse on Alcohol and Drug Information (NCADI), 1-800-729-6686. All NCADI documents are free.

15 THE ROLE OF SPIRITUALITY

We were trained to talk to our clients comfortably on just about any other topic, no matter how personal: emotions, sex, money, family relationships, drug use, whatever. Yet we were never taught how to talk to our clients about what is often, to them, the most important aspect of their lives.

W. R. Miller (1998)

Faith . . . the substance of things hoped for, the evidence of things not seen.

Hebrews 11:1

I work with clients of diverse ethnicity, class, and religion—the successful, agnostic lawyer with a cocaine addiction; the orthodox Jewish computer expert with a sexual addiction; the marathon-running, vegetarian videographer with an alcohol abuse problem; and the professor who has been, according to his belief system, married fifteen times to the same woman in past lives.

Most of my clients are religious in varying degrees, and many of them find CBT/REBT techniques helpful and combine them easily with their religious practices. There is no reason to take a position for or against integrating traditional spiritual techniques with traditional CBT/REBT techniques. I can work with my clients to find the techniques that are most helpful to them.

Historically, most religious practices included various techniques to help people further their spiritual growth, and many of these techniques were and are cognitive-behavioral in nature. Fasting, repeating sayings, visualization, prayer, pilgrimages, and many other practices change the way people think, feel, and behave. They are used by religious believers to cope better with the difficulties in life, as well as to further their spiritual development.

All religions have a variety of prayers and sayings that believers use to help themselves cope and get through the day. Ellis (1962, 1994) has argued that sayings are only palliative. Repeating them does not alter the client's underlying problematic way of thinking. But he also often explicitly tells clients coping statements: "It's a hassle, not a horror." "It's not awful. It's only inconvenient." "What's the worst thing that can happen? You won't die." When I ask clients what has helped most in therapy, it is often something that I have said that they have remembered and repeated to themselves that they think has helped most. (This is, I think, a researchable topic: What helps most? Learning to do ABC's or simple coping statements? Perhaps coping statements are especially helpful to people who cannot or do not want to work more directly on their underlying belief. Moreover, such statements may benefit from being suggested by an authority.)

Most followers of religions also use and repeat sayings in order to quickly remind themselves of their faith's teachings, such as "Judge not, that ye not be judged" (Matthew 7:1) and "Love thy enemy as thyself" (Matthew 22:39). These and other helpful sayings are collected in Hank Robb's (1988) pamphlet, "How to Stop Driving Yourself Crazy with Help from the Bible."

AA also has many sayings that are CBT/REBT-like in character (Velten 1996, p. 108):

First things first.
There but for the grace of God . . .
Take time but take steps.
Think, think, think.
Do it for yourself.

90 meetings in 90 days.
Avoid slippery places.
Let go, let God.
Easy does it, but do it.
Live and let live.
Get off the pity pot.
Go to a meeting.
Get a sponsor.
Fake it till you make it.
Get your feet to a meeting and your mind will follow.

In the above list only two sayings cite God. Most of the rest could be standard CBT coping statements.

WHAT IS THE MEANING OF "SPIRITUAL"?

The word "spiritual" is derived from the Latin *spiritus*, meaning breath or breath of a god. Interestingly, it is related to several key concepts underlying change. When one is *inspired*, there is a feeling of available energy, accompanied by a desire to do something. *Inspired to change* and *motivated to change* are clearly similar in meaning. In contrast, *expire* means to die, and a client who has no inspiration in his or her life may well want to commit suicide, either in a once-and-for-all effort or little by little with addictive behaviors.

It is the deity-focused, transpersonal meaning of "spiritual" that appears to most trouble those opposed to including spiritual concepts and techniques in psychotherapy. The idea that god or spirits may exist who, despite their invisibility, are ready to help humans simply does not make sense to them. They may even see such concepts as harmful. In their opinion, attributing change to an outside agent reduces a client's sense of self-efficacy by denying the fact that it is the individual who has caused the change to occur.

Another source of tension (sometimes acrimony) may be the fact that during the past thirty or so years, the treatment of addictions has been dominated in the United States by programs devoted to the twelve-step, spiritual approach to recovery. While there may be some debate as to whether such an approach is religious or not, there is no debate as to whether it is a spiritual program. Advocates are clear that unless people afflicted with addictions make a spiritual change in their life, their lives will remain unmanageable.

In addition, a part of our society's approach to the treatment of addictions has been the acceptance of mandating clients to treatment. We do not use such an approach with any other form of disease or biopsychosocial phenomenon. In most cases, this has meant that people have been forced to go to a twelve-step treatment program. Inevitably, they have met zealous believers in the twelve-step approach. Sometimes they have been told that if they do not acknowledge that they are alcoholics, it only proves that they are in denial and that they *are* alcoholics—something that reminds some of the Salem witch trials. Such a confrontational approach, especially considering that the research shows it to be generally ineffective, has offended, angered, alienated, and traumatized some people. As a result, there are those in the field who adamantly oppose using any CBT/REBT approaches and others who just as strongly oppose integrating any spiritual techniques.

A National Institute for Healthcare Research report (Larson et al. 1998, as quoted in McCrady 1998) proposed that spirituality includes "the feelings, thoughts, experiences, and behaviors that arise from the search for the sacred" where sacred means a "divine being or Ultimate Reality or Ultimate Truth as perceived by the individual" (p. 6). Shafranske (1995, as quoted in Shafranske 1996) used six statements representing a continuum of spiritual beliefs to survey a random sample of American Psychological Association (APA) members listing degrees in clinical or counseling psychology. The numbers represent the percentages of respondents who subscribed to each statement.

1. There is a personal God of transcendent existence and power whose purposes will ultimately be worked out in human history (23.9 percent).

2. There is a transcendent aspect of human experience which some persons call God but who is not immanently involved in the events of the world and human history (13.6 percent).
3. There is a transcendent or divine dimension which is unique and specific to the human self (6.8 percent).
4. There is a transcendent or divine dimension found in all manifestations of nature (31.1 percent).
5. The notions of God or the transcendent are illusory products of human imagination; however, they are meaningful aspects of human existence (23.5 percent).
6. The notions of God or the transcendent are illusory products of human imagination; therefore, they are irrelevant to the real world (1.2 percent).

In 1988, Miller and Martin suggested a working definition of spirituality: "The acknowledgment of a transcendent being, power, or reality greater than ourselves." He added, "From a spiritual perspective, the individual or collective humanity is not the measure of all things, but instead ultimate concern is vested in a transcendent reality, a higher power, a spirit" (p. 514). In 1998 Miller broadened that definition, suggesting that "variables or phenomena [could possibly] be defined as spiritual by virtue of their reference to the transpersonal, that which transcends material reality" (p. 21). Approximately three-fourths of the respondents to Shafranske's survey, that is, those who chose either statements 1, 2, 3, or 4, appear to subscribe to such a transpersonal definition.

Dunn (1998) suggests a broader definition that even people subscribing to statements 5 and 6 might be able to accept—that for people in recovery, a useful definition of spirituality might be "a lifestyle of thinking and behaving that continually improves one's relationships with people, places, and things" (p. 16). Several participants in a National Institute of Drug Addiction (NIDA) grant studying the role of spirituality in recovery defined spirituality as "being the best that we can be" (Laudet 1998, p. 19). Others defined it as "the feeling of belonging, of being part of something with other group members who share the same experiences that I have had" (p. 19).

THREE TYPES OF SPIRITUAL TECHNIQUES

Deity-Focused, Transpersonal Techniques

Prior to the development of psychology and psychiatry, people attributed their afflictions to a god's anger, evil spirits, or curses. Hence, it was logical that they would turn to their priests and other religious and spiritual teachers for solace and "treatment." As a result, a wide variety of techniques were developed to win the intervention of various deities and to placate them, as a well as to further one's spiritual development. Praying, pilgrimages, and offerings, including animal sacrifices (and until fairly recently, human sacrifices) are common deity-focused techniques.

Praying

Should therapists encourage clients to pray? Internists usually do not ask patients to pray with them, because the practice of healing has become so separate from the practice of religion, and most people no longer believe that their physical ailments are due to spiritual causes, curses, or God's anger.

However, if the client prays, it is often helpful for the therapist to find out something about how and what he prays for to provide insight into the client's beliefs, not just his spiritual beliefs. If someone reports that, for her, prayer helps, why would we not encourage her to pray? Some readers may object that there is no scientific evidence that prayer helps. They may also feel that praying encourages clients to place the source of their change outside of themselves. However, for some clients it does not make sense to see themselves as solely responsible for change. They see their efforts to change as part of a larger schema. Even atheist clients may benefit from working with a therapist because the working *with* someone makes change more likely. Most therapists and researchers would probably agree that it is not just the techniques that help people change, it is also their relationship with a therapist. A religious person has a relationship with God. Doing a major project like changing an addictive behavior without God's help makes no sense to him or her.

Pilgrimages

For hundreds of years, pilgrims from all over Europe made their way under the sign of the scallop shell—the sign of St. James—to Santiago de Compostela in northwestern Spain, the place where tradition has it St. James, one of Christ's most beloved disciples, died. Before the advent of psychoanalysis and Prozac, there was perhaps no more formidable way to affect one's thinking, feeling, and behavior. Many went in the hope of influencing God to grant their requests. But others went as a way of working on themselves and their own spiritual development.

I remember as a young boy going to the Oratory of St. Joseph, a great cathedral-like structure on a hill overlooking Montreal. As we climbed up the hundreds of steps leading to the great carved wooden doors, we passed several people on their knees praying. My mother explained (although not sharing in their faith) that they were climbing up on their knees, praying on each step, slowly making their way to the altar in the massive cathedral.

On entering the cathedral, in the portals on either side, stacked on top of each other, old and musty and covered with dust, were hundreds and hundreds of crutches, sticks, braces, wheelchairs, and other support devices. The guide explained that these had been left behind by people who had come to the cathedral in hopes of being healed. I was skeptical. However, I remember thinking, even if they were not cured by God, because I was not sure God existed, certainly their belief in God or something "cured" them. Even if they were not organically, physiologically crippled, they were changed after mounting those steps to this building. The same can be said of many other shrines in the world and of many therapy offices and clinics. Anyone interested in psychology and particularly on how the mind affects the body cannot help but be intrigued.

Offerings

People who have lit a candle or dropped a dollar into an offering box or left a flower at an altar know the effect such a simple act may have on one's thoughts, feelings, and subsequent behaviors. Making an offering also joins one with a community of people who have done the same thing. It increases hope, and the act of lighting a candle and making an offering reconfirms one's belief in something more than oneself. Whether any of it makes sense from a scientific standpoint is a matter for research to investigate.

RESEARCH NOTE

According to a 1990 survey conducted by Shafranske and Malony, 57 percent of Division 12 (Clinical Psychology) APA members "use religious language or concepts," 32 percent "use or recommend religious or spiritual books," 36 percent "recommend participation in religion," and 7 percent "pray with a client" (as cited in Shafranske 1996).

Non–Deity-Focused, Transpersonal Techniques

Non–deity-focused transpersonal definitions include the notion that all reality, including human reality, is interconnected in some way, a view that is particularly prevalent in Eastern religious and spiritual thought. With the rise of Buddhism, many non–deity-focused techniques, in particular, many forms of meditation, were developed. Buddhism was initially not a religion. It was a guide to a way of living, albeit along a spiritual path that might encompass many thousands of lives. In the approximately 45 years from the time of his enlightenment under a pipal tree to his death, Buddha spent his time traveling throughout the Ganges region of India spreading his teachings based on the four noble truths and the eightfold path, including right views, right resolve, right speech, right action, right livelihood, right effort, right mindfulness, and right concentration. There was no deity in early Buddhism to placate or to pray to for intervention.

Meditation

There is ample research evidence that meditation helps with many psychological and physiological conditions (Benson 1975), and a few research studies showing that one form of meditation, transcendental meditation (TM), improves outcomes in smoking cessation (Royer 1994) and abstinence rates in the treatment of alcohol problems (Taub et al. 1994).

Fasting

Fasting has a profound effect on how one thinks and feels. As a person tries to maintain a fast, he is forced to think through why he is engaging in such behavior. Why is he trying to say no to his natural, biological urge to eat? If his reasons are spiritual, then he will almost certainly begin to review his beliefs about his relationship to God and, in this way, begin to leave some aspects of his self-absorption behind. As a behavioral technique, fasting may also help a person develop more tolerance for discomfort. Because we know making behavioral change almost always involves enduring some discomfort, developing high frustration tolerance (HFT) may have value.

If the client engages in fasting because he hates his body, because his body represents everything that is base and evil, the therapist should ask him to explain his beliefs. Such a belief has had many hundreds of thousands of adherents over the centuries. Therapists have no right to say that such beliefs are false or inferior. However, nothing prevents them from asking, in a genuine attempt to learn and to understand the client's beliefs and ways of thinking, how such beliefs help him fulfill his goals.

Testifying and Testimonials

Many religions, as well as AA and REBT, use testimonials. They demonstrate to others that there is a way to work on their problems. Theoretically, if they work as hard as the testifiers have worked and are working, they, too, will feel better or begin to live a better life. REBT does not make this an explicit part of therapy, but REBT-ers share stories of how one or another REBT technique worked. Ellis's talks are popular partly as a result of his own personal stories attesting to the effectiveness of REBT techniques on his own problems. Case studies are essentially testimonials hypothetically designed to help others understand how the theory and techniques of a particular school of psychotherapy or psychoanalysis works in practice. However, they seem designed equally as much to attract new converts.

AA urges members to share in meetings and, in the twelfth step, "to carry this message to alcoholics." The latter is based on the Christian technique of building one's faith and knowledge through proselytizing. Ellis also often advises his clients to teach REBT to their spouses and children as a way of learning it better themselves.

Non—Deity-Focused, Non-Transpersonal Techniques

Most CBT/REBT techniques were initially developed to help individuals better manage their lives and to self-actualize. Lazarus's (1981) book, *The Practice of Multimodal Therapy*, contains an appendix with a glossary of thirty-eight principal techniques, including anger expression, anti–future shock imagery, behavioral rehearsal, bibliotherapy, biofeedback, contingency contracting, Ellis's ABC(DE) technique, friendship training, graded sexual approaches, hypnosis, meditation, problem solving, recording and self-monitoring, relaxation training, the empty chair, thought-blocking, and tracking. Most of the techniques, with the possible exception of meditation, are not transpersonal. They are designed to help people behave differently and better manage their thoughts and emotions.

Studying/Bibliotherapy

Many CBT/REBT therapists suggests that clients read books and listen to tapes that they have found have helped other clients. Bibliotherapy, however, is nothing new. For generations, students of various religions and spiritual leaders have assiduously read and reread texts, seeking for the truths that would help them live better lives.

Teaching Stories

Many religions and most parents use stories to teach. Buddhism, Judaism, Christianity, and Islam make frequent use of teaching stories (parables). Such stories usually have several levels of meaning and, as a result, are both amusing and thought-provoking. In Chapter 13, I discussed my use of the Mary Magdalene story to help clients examine and work through forgiveness of themselves and others. Sufis, sometimes called the mystical part of Islam but probably predating Christianity, have a more complex theory about teaching stories: What you have to learn cannot be taught. You cannot hear what you most need to know. The only way you may be able to learn what you need to learn is through stories. Sufi tradition suggests that if you like a story, you should learn it and retell it to others. In that way, you may gradually learn what you need to learn. Such a theory recognizes that one's thinking and behavior are often affected by forces outside of one's awareness, although it does not suggest what may be at work—conditioning, neurochemistry, the subconscious, or genetic givens.

Rehearsing a Set of Beliefs

Many clients who have been in psychoanalysis or some other form of psychotherapy use similar terms and expressions to explain someone else's behavior or their own. The same is often true for AA members. Such people may not set aside a certain time each day to say a "creed," but they clearly adopt a set of beliefs that they use to interpret the world and their own responses to it. This is as true for people who have found psychotherapy helpful as it is for religious people. Only the beliefs differ and not always by that much. Each group of believers believes it has found a way to help itself and to make sense out of the world.

Dream Interpretation

Although Western clergy rarely engage in dream interpretation, in many ethnic groups believers routinely seek out their spiritual guides for such interpretations. Therapists who use CBT and REBT may also find it helpful to inquire about their clients' dreams. In Freudian psychoanalysis, the underlying theory suggests that the important, potent factors affecting the way we think, feel, and behave are not directly accessible to us. They are repressed and defended against; hence, psychoanalysts must rely on slips of the tongues and dreams to gain insight into the patterns of thinking underlying a person's conscious life. Although we may subscribe to a very different theory, CBT/REBT therapists may still gain considerable insight into the underlying belief patterns that often and repeatedly affect the way that clients feel, think, and behave.

Trance States

Trances are used by many types of healers. Given the beneficial effects of placebos, often equaling the impact of selective serotonin reuptake inhibitors (SSRIs) (Kirsch and Lynn 1999), it is not surprising that as dramatic an intervention as a trance, either on the part of the healer or the client, would produce some desired effects. Future research may begin to uncover how trances affect underlying neurochemical functioning, perhaps in a similar way to electroconvulsive therapy (ECT), which is also used with little understanding of how or why it works. It is often employed for the sole reason that it sometimes works after other less intrusive, anti-depressive methods have been tried and have failed. Eye movement desensitization and reprocessing (EMDR), believed in by some and severely criticized by others, may also function along similar lines.

We cannot know what helps most, the REBT/CBT techniques or their religious practices, and we cannot know if we are correct in our attributions.

One client had a recurring, serious problem with alcohol and had struggled with fits of rage, anxiety, and depression for several years. In the computer animation company where he worked, he had been learning rapidly and moving up in his field, but he knew (or knew of) others who had been part of dot-com startups and were now reportedly millionaires. He would drink heavily at night and then get into work late. Occasionally at work, he would sneak out for a joint, which he asserted helped him work for longer, uninterrupted periods of time. He was not convinced, however, that anyone noticed or cared, but this habit caused him to hesitate in asserting himself or asking to work on the more challenging projects. He feared someone knew and would use it against him. His relationships with a series of girlfriends were stormy and unsatisfying.

Nevertheless, he persisted in his attempts to manage his problems better, and after three years, when it was clear that he was on his feet and doing much better, I asked him what he thought had helped. He was not sure. He had gone to AA meetings quite regularly throughout most of the period, and he thought that they had helped. AA had certainly helped him develop a set of friends who didn't drink or use drugs, and that had been very helpful. He had come to therapy once a week and had struggled to learn how to think, feel, and act differently when he was confronted with problems. According to him, REBT helped him "work the steps" and do what he set out to do, whether that meant going to meetings, listening to a sponsor, or getting to work on time. He thought Prozac, which he had been on for a year, had been particularly helpful with his raging. He had also spent quite a number of weekends at a Zen monastery that runs retreats for AA. Getting up at 5 A.M. and sitting, just sitting, for an hour, was one of the most difficult things he had ever done. But he felt that had been extremely worthwhile. It had taught him, he said, a great deal about his lack of ability to control his emotions and physical well-being. It had also taught him how to sit with himself and accept what is, even when he didn't like it. He was not sure, but he thought that had helped the most. Neither of us could know for sure what each part had played in his recovery. To my mind, each piece had played a part and he had taken from each experience what he needed and had slowly but surely learned to live differently.

Is an AA meeting non-transpersonal or transpersonal? Non–deity-focused or deity-focused? Does it matter? To whom does it matter? To many people, the references to God in the twelve-step are clearly deity-oriented. Those who argue that AA is not religious are no doubt emphasizing the non–deity-focused aspects of twelve-step groups: meeting together with other people who are struggling with similar problems, listening to testimonials, sharing and learning from others, working the steps with a sponsor. To some, these may all have transpersonal aspects, but that is a matter of opinion. However, ending a meeting with the Lord's Prayer, a practice that is far more widespread in the United States than in other countries, suggests a deity-focused orientation to a meeting and may offend some participants.

I have worked with both religious and nonreligious people, even people who assert they are not spiritual, and many of them believe strongly that AA has been of great help to them. I have also worked with people who combine deity-focused techniques such as praying with REBT technique. Ultimately, whether a technique is deity-focused or not, or transpersonal or not, may only matter to therapist, counselors, and researchers.

GOD'S ROLE? THE CLIENT'S ROLE?

Cognitive-behavioral therapists focus on helping people see themselves as agents of self-change, while at the same time accepting that only some things can be changed, and sometimes by only a little. It may be very useful to ask a client what he believes he is supposed to do. How might therapy help him fulfill his responsibilities? How does he feel when he does not fulfill his responsibilities? How does that help or hurt his efforts? What gives life meaning and how can therapy help him develop into the kind of person he thinks God wants him to be?

The third phrase of the Lord's Prayer states, "Thy will be done." The client may interpret this phrase to mean that he has no will or that his will has no role. Part of the problem may be in the translation. If "will" is thought to mean wish or command, it may be difficult to see what role a human might have. If two humans have two distinctly different wishes, often we can work out a compromise. But working out a compromise with God seems out of the question. On the other hand, if "will" is interpreted to mean plan or goals—resulting in "Thy plan be carried out" or "Thy goals be accomplished"—it may be easier for the client to see that he may have a role.

The client may be a concrete thinker. If so, it is especially important to help him figure out what he is supposed to do. To what extent does he think God will help him resolve his problems? And if God will help him, what is his role? What is his responsibility? I have never met an AA-attending client who thought God would completely solve his problems for him. Almost all clients who believe in God also believe that "God helps those who help themselves."

THE ADVANTAGES OF INCLUDING SPIRITUAL TECHNIQUES IN THERAPY

Most Americans see themselves as religious. Thus, therapy cannot ignore their beliefs, especially since beliefs have impact on feelings and behaviors, and vice versa. According to a 1992 Gallup Poll, 91 percent of the people surveyed reported an "explicit religious preference," 87 percent said religion is fairly or very important in their life, 71 percent were members of a church or synagogue, 66 percent had an active prayer life, and 75 percent believed in an afterlife (quoted in Johnson and Nielsen 1998). In addition, 62 percent of those who had been involved with AA or in some sort of treatment plus AA, found religion helpful, but only 37 percent of the participants with no treatment history or involvement with AA found religion helpful (Murphy et al. 1998).

Changes in addictive behavior often require changes in fundamental beliefs about life. In one study, 54 percent of the people surveyed reported that religious experiences or involvement had "greatly helped" in their recovery (Murphy et al. 1998). (Seventy percent also checked "a change in personal will-power or self-control," 65 percent a "change in social life or social activities," and 55 percent changes in physical health.)

The large-scale, federally funded Project MATCH study (1997a) found that all three programs—twelve-step facilitation, cognitive-behavior, and motivational enhancement—reduced drinking. In addition, in a naturalistic, multisite study including over 3,000 clients, the effectiveness of a CBT, twelve-step, and combined program were all approximately the same (Ouimette et al. 1997). Abstinence rates were higher in the twelve-step group, but the other measures—related problems, employment, arrests, and homelessness—did not differ.

CBT/REBT techniques may not be sufficient to overcome some clients' pervasive, interacting existential/spiritual problems. "What should I do with my life? What's the point? Who cares? Why bother?" Learning how to stop drinking may dramatically improve how a client feels, but to sustain such a change, she may have to change some of her underlying beliefs about how to live.

CBT techniques have roots in both behavior change research and in the medical model (both Aaron T. Beck and David Burns are M.D.s). They were designed to help people overcome problems with depression or anxiety, and more recently, personality problems. For the most part, they were never designed to help people grapple with larger, philosophical issues that were always the focus of existential psychotherapy (May 1953, 1969, Yalom 1980).

REBT differs from CBT primarily in its emphasis on the importance of making philosophical changes and, as Velten (1996) notes, "in its open promotion of humanistic values and its detailed methodology for constructing a satisfying philosophy of life" (p. 111). Ellis especially advocates developing ongoing interests in life in order to better prepare oneself to handle serious emotional upsets, and he and others in the CBT/REBT school have written many books designed to go beyond simply removing the source of psychological anguish (e.g., Ellis and Becker's [1982] *A Guide to Personal Happiness*, and Ellis's [1999] *How to Make Yourself Happy and Remarkably Less Disturbable*, and Seligman's [1994] *What You Can Change and What You Can't*).

There are many ways to lead a meaningful life. A person might decide to try to become the best in her field or to be as good a lawyer or a computer programmer or a receptionist as possible. Or she might decide to make as much money as possible. Or she might decide to devote her life to a particular religious path and to try to become a good Muslim. Some of my clients benefit from learning a few simple techniques or by making relatively minor adjustments in their thinking. But others seek coaching and encouragement to find a more fulfilling philosophy of life and to develop a more satisfying lifestyle. A few find it in AA. Some find it in traditional Western religions. Some find it in Buddhism. Some find it in a fuller, richer life of relationships, career involvement, and recreational activities. Tens of thousands of books have been written designed to help people figure out how to lead happier, fuller lives including Russell's *The Conquest of Happiness*, Frankl's *Man's Search for Meaning*, Mays's *Psychology and the Human Dilemma*, Peck's *A Road Less Traveled*, Covey's *Seven Habits of Highly Successful People*, Tillich's *The Courage to Be*, Ellis and Harper's *A Guide to Rational Living*, and more esoteric books such as Krishnamurti's *The Impossible Question* and Ouspensky's *In Search of the Miraculous*.

CBT/REBT techniques may help clients pursue or fulfill their religious and spiritual goals. Like all humans, religious and spiritual people often have difficulty following the path they have chosen. A client may think he should take time each morning to meditate, but he consistently finds himself running off to work without doing so "because I have so much to do." Another client may think that he should go to church every Sunday, but does not do so. In essence, each client wants to better manage his behavior. Each client, like clients who are struggling with addictive problems, wants to do X but winds up doing Y. The underlying beliefs that derail his attempts at spiritual growth may be similar to those that derail his attempts to change his addictive behaviors.

In many ways, AA and REBT/CBT overlap. For example, AA, REBT, and increasingly other forms of CBT focus on the importance of acceptance. Both also stress the importance of taking action. They diverge in that AA strongly urges its members to "turn over" the problem to God, while REBT and CBT stress self-efficacy (DiGiuseppe et al. 1990, McCrady 1994, Velten 1996).

POTENTIAL DANGERS?

Some practitioners who truly believe that their way is the one true way will attempt to impose that set of beliefs and teach their techniques to clients. It is this that worries some people about opening the door to spiritual techniques in the practice of psychotherapy. But something like this occurs in medicine. If you injure your back, a surgeon will often suggest an operation, a massage therapist will recommend massage, a chiropractor will suggest manipulation, a physiatrist will recommend physical therapy, an acupuncturist will recommend needles. Similarly, if you are feeling depressed, a cognitive-behavioral psychologist will explore the way you are thinking, a psychiatrist will prescribe a pill, and a psychoanalyst will ask you about your childhood and your dreams. That this occurs does not make it correct, but we need to acknowledge that consumers make many decisions between alternative treatments every day.

However, until very recently, almost all addicted clients were told that they had to abstain and that they had to enter some form of twelve-step program. In the field of addictions treatment, few alternatives are currently available, and some practitioners go beyond simply strongly suggesting what they think will be the best treatment. They are also disdainful of any other approach and may go as far as to predict that a client will die unless she or he follows their advice.

IS THERE A SCIENTIFICALLY "BEST WAY"?

Several researchers (Finney and Monahan 1996, Finney and Moos 1998, Hester 1994, Nathan and Gorman 1998) have developed a variety of criteria to explore this question. The extensive MATCH study indicated that twelve-step approaches are at least as effective as cognitive-behavioral approaches. Smith (1999) notes that the APA Division 12 Task Force on Psychological Interventions endorses treatment, not theories. He further asserts that it is not really important whether a set of techniques are "cognitive-behavioral" but rather whether "they accomplish what you want them to accomplish" (p. 8), and whether something else might accomplish it better.

To decide whether or not a spiritual technique is helpful, we do not necessarily have to know how it works. Several techniques currently in vogue today are used without any understanding of how they work, for example, ECT and EMDR. ECT is becoming more popular again despite no clear understanding of why or how it works. Empirical studies of EMDR have shown mixed results and have aroused considerable controversy (Lipke 1999, Lohr et al. 1998). And even though we have a theory for the way the new SSRI drugs like Prozac may work, it still appears from careful research studies (Kirsch and Lynn 1999) that approximately 50 percent of the impact results from an expectancy effect. Only 25 percent may be attributable to the chemical itself. The other 25 percent seems to be due to the fact that people recover even if they do nothing.

All of the techniques discussed above could be the focus of research to determine if and how they might help clients, because all of them affect the way people think, feel, and behave. For

example, we could explore whether or not fasting improves outcomes. Does praying by clients who believe in a deity help? Does
reciting sayings from the Bible help?

However, we can never expect to prove that God has lent a
hand or not, that it was God's will or not—in scientific vernacular,
that God was an intervening variable. In fact, as John Allen (quoted
in McCrady 1998) has pointed out, God may not play by our rules.
He could decide to help the very people who were in the nonprayer
group for some reason (e.g., they were more in need of help). We
can know that praying helps, but we cannot know why. It may be
because focusing our attention on a problem helps. It may be that
removing our ego function from an addictive problem helps—by
giving up, we get control. It may be that a belief that we are not
alone may help.

To learn how to manage a serious problem like an addiction,
clients have to have good reasons for spending so much time and
effort and for standing the discomfort that often accompanies their
efforts. Knowing *how* to change is critical and sometimes sufficient,
but not always. We may be most effective in motivating and helping
clients change when we focus on issues central to their lives, issues
that some might call existential and others might call spiritual.

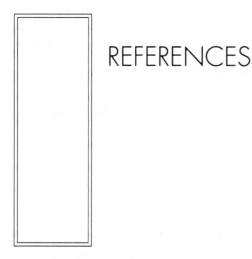

REFERENCES

Albee, G. W. (1982). Preventing psychopathology and promoting human potential. *American Psychologist* 37:1043–1050.

——— (1996). Revolutions and counterrevolutions in prevention. *American Psychologist* 51:1130–1133.

Alessandri, S. A., and Lewis, M. (1996). Differences in pride and shame in maltreated and nonmaltreated preschoolers. *Child Development* 67:1857–1869.

American Psychiatric Association (1994). *Diagnostic and Statistical Manual of Mental Disorders.* Washington, DC: APA.

American Society of Addiction Medicine (ASAM) (1998). Appendix B, section 1: screening instruments. In *Principles of Addiction Medicine*, ed. A. W. Graham and T. K. Schultz, 2nd ed., pp. 1283–1286. Chevy Chase, MD: American Society of Addiction Medicine.

Andrews, B. (1995). Bodily shame as a mediator between abusive experiences and depression. *Journal of Abnormal Psychology* 104:277–285.

——— (1997). Bodily shame in relation to abuse in childhood and bulimia: a preliminary investigation. *British Journal of Clinical Psychology* 36:41–49.

Anthenelli, R. M., and Schuckit, M. A. (1998). Genetic influences in addiction. In *Principles of Addiction Medicine*, ed. A. W.

Graham and T. K. Schultz, 2nd ed., pp. 17–35. Chevy Chase, MD: American Society of Addiction Medicine.

Bandura, A. (1997). *Self-Efficacy: The Exercise of Control.* New York: W. H. Freeman.

Bargh, J. A., and Chartrand, T. L. (1999). The unbearable automaticity of being. *American Psychologist* 54(7):462–479.

Bateson, G. (1994). The cybernetics of "self": a theory of alcoholism. In *The Dynamics and Treatment of Alcoholism: Essential Papers,* ed. J. D. Levin and R. H. Weiss, pp. 313–332. Northvale, NJ: Jason Aronson.

Baumeister, R. F., Bratslavsky, E., Muraven, M., and Tice, D. M. (1998). Ego depletion: Is the active self a limited resourse? *Journal of Personality and Social Psychology* 74:1252–1265.

Beck, A. T. (1976). *Cognitive Therapy and the Emotional Disorders.* New York: International Universities Press.

Beck, A. T., Wright, F. D., Newman, C. F., and Liese, B. S. (1993). *Cognitive Therapy of Substance Abuse.* New York: Guilford.

Benson, H. (1975). *The Relaxation Response.* New York: William Morrow.

Berridge, K. C., and Robinson, T. E. (1995). The mind of an addicted brain: neural sensitization of wanting versus liking. *Current Directions in Psychological Science* 4:71–76.

Bien, T. H., Miller, W. R., and Boroughs, J. M. (1993). Brief interventions for alcohol problems: a review. *Addiction* 88:315–336.

Bishop, F. M. (1993). Relapse prevention with REBT. Audiotape. New York: Albert Ellis Institute.

——— (1995). Rational emotive behavior therapy and two self-help alternatives to the 12–step models. In *Psychotherapy and Substance Abuse: A Practitioner's Handbook,* ed. A. M. Washton, pp. 141–160. New York: Guilford.

Black, D. W., and Moyer, T. (1998). Clinical features and psychiatric comorbidity of subjects with pathological gambling behavior. *Psychiatric Services* 49:1134–1139.

Blume, S. A. (1998). Addictive disorders in women. In *Clinical Textbook of Addictive Disorders,* ed. R. J. Frances and S. I. Miller, 2nd ed., pp. 413–429. New York: Guilford.

Bohn, M. J., Babor, T. F., and Kransler, H. R. (1995). The Alcohol Use Disorders Identification Test (AUDIT): validation of a screening instrument for use in medical settings. *Journal of Studies on Alcohol* 56:423–432.

Bradshaw, J. (1988). *Healing the Shame that Binds You*. Deerfield Beach, FL: Health Communications.

Brady, K. T., Myrick, H., and Sonne, S. (1998). Co-morbid addictions and affective disorders. In *Principles of Addiction Medicine*, ed. A. W. Graham and T. K. Schultz, 2nd ed., pp. 983–992. Chevy Chase, MD: American Society of Addiction Medicine.

Brooner, R. K., King, V. L., Kidorf, M., et al. (1997). Psychiatric and substance abuse use comorbidity among treatment-seeking opioid abusers. *Archives of General Psychiatry* 54:71–80.

Brown, R. A., Monti, P. M., Mark, G., et al. Depression among cocaine abusers in treatment: relation to cocaine and alcohol use and treatment outcome. *American Journal of Psychiatry* 155:220–225.

Brownell, K. D., Marlatt, G. A., Lichtenstein, E., and Wilson, G. T. (1986). Understanding and preventing relapse. *American Psychologist* 41:765–782.

Bruner, J. (1983). *In Search of Mind: Essays in Autobiography*. New York: Harper Colophon.

Burns, D. (1981). *Feeling Good*. New York: Signet.

——— (1990). *The Feeling Good Handbook*. New York: Plume.

Carey, K. B., Bradizza, C. M., and Stasiewicz, P. R. (1999). The case for enhanced addictions training in graduate school. *Behavior Therapist* 22(2):27–31.

Castro, F. G., Proescholdbell, R. J., Abeita, L., and Rodriques, D. (1999). Ethnic and cultural minority groups. In *Addictions: A Comprehensive Textbook*, ed. B. S. McCrady and E. E. Epstein, pp. 499–526. New York: Oxford.

Chen, M., and Bargh, J. A. (1999). Nonconscious approach and avoidance behavioral consequences of the automatic evaluation effect. *Personality and Social Psychology Bulletin* 25:215–224.

Corsini, R. J., and Painter, G. (1989). *Parenting Tapes* (cassette recording). Muncie, IN: Accelerated Development.

Covey, S. R. (1989). *The Seven Habits of Highly Successful People.* New York: Simon and Schuster.

Craske, M. G., and Barlow, D. H. (1994). *Mastery of Your Anxiety and Panic II: Agoraphobia Supplement—Client Workbook.* San Antonio: Psychological Corporation, Harcourt Brace.

Cummings, N. A. (1979). Turning bread into stones: our modern antimiracle. *American Psychologist* 34:1119–1129.

Curry, S. J., Grothaus, L. C., McAfee, T., and Pabniak, C. (1998). Use and cost effectiveness of smoking-cessation services under four insurance plans in a health maintenance organization. *New England Journal of Medicine* 339:673–679.

Dadds, M. R., Holland, D. E., Laurens, K. R., et al. (1999). Early intervention and prevention of anxiety disorders in children: results at 2-year follow-up. *Journal of Counseling and Clinical Psychology* 67(1):145–150.

DATA, Brown University *Digest of Addiction Theory and Application.* Newsletter. Providence, RI: Manissess Communications Group.

DeRubeis, R. J., Gelfand, L. A., Tang, T. Z., and Simons, A. D. (1999). Medications versus cognitive behavior therapy for severely depressed outpatients: mega-analysis of four randomized comparisons. *American Journal of Psychiatry* 156:1007–1013.

DiGiuseppe, R. (1990). *What Do I Do with My Anger: Hold It In or Let It Out?* (Cassette recording). New York: Institute for Rational-Emotive Therapy.

DiGiuseppe, R., Robin, M., and Dryden, W. (1990). On the compatibility of RET and Judeo-Christian philosophy: a focus on clinical strategies. *Journal of Cognitive Psychotherapy: An International Quarterly* 4(4):355–367.

Dimeff, L. A., Baer, J. S., Kivlahan, D. R., and Marlatt, G. A. (1999). *Brief Alcohol Screening and Intervention for College Students (BASICS): A Harm Reduction Approach.* New York: Guilford.

Dimeff, L. A., Comtois, K. A., and Linehan, M. M. (1998). Borderline personality disorder. In *Principles of Addictive Medicine*, ed. A. W. Graham and T. K. Schultz, 2nd. ed., pp. 1063–1079. Chevy Chase, MD: American Society of Addiction Medicine.

Donovan, D. M. (1999). Assessment strategies and measures in addictive behaviors. In *Addictions: A Comprehensive Textbook*, ed. B. S. McCrady and E. E. Epstein, pp. 187–215. New York: Oxford University Press.

Dryden, W., and Still, A. (1998). REBT and rationality: philosophical approaches. *Journal of Rational-Emotive and Cognitive-Behavior Therapy* 16(2):77–100.

Dunn, C. (1998). Letter to the editor. *The Addictions Newsletter* 6(1):16–17.

Edelstein, M. R., and Steele, D. R. (1997). *Three Minute Therapy: Change Your Thinking, Change Your Life*. Lakewood, CO: Glenbridge.

Ellis, A. (1962). *Reason and Emotion in Psychotherapy*. Secaucus, NJ: Citadel. (Rev. ed., Secaucus, NJ: Carol Publishing Group, 1994.)

——— (1969). A weekend of rational encounter. In *Encounter*, ed. A. Burton, pp. 112–127. San Francisco, CA: Jossey-Bass.

——— (1973a). *How to Stubbornly Refuse to be Ashamed of Anything* (cassette recording). New York: Institute for Rational-Emotive Therapy.

——— (1973b). *Twenty-One Ways to Stop Worrying* (cassette recording). New York: Institute for Rational-Emotive Therapy.

——— (1977). *Anger—How to Live with It and Without It*. Secausus, NJ: Citadel.

——— (1978–1979). Discomfort anxiety: a new cognitive behavioral construct. Parts I and II. *Rational Living* 14(2):3–8; 15(1):25–30.

——— (1992). My current views on rational-emotive therapy and religiousness. *Journal of Rational-Emotive and Cognitive-Behavior Therapy* 10:37–40.

———— (1993). Changing rational-emotive therapy (RET) to rational emotive behavior therapy (REBT). *Behavior Therapist* 16:257–258.

———— (1994). My response to "Don't throw the therapeutic baby out with the holy water": helpful and hurtful elements in religion. *Journal of Psychotherapy and Christianity* 13:323–326.

———— (1996). *Better, Deeper, and More Enduring Brief Therapy: The Rational Emotive Behavior Therapy Approach.* New York: Brunner/Mazel.

———— (1998). *How to Control Your Anxiety Before It Controls You.* Secausus, NJ: Birch Lane Press.

———— (1999). *How to Make Yourself Happy and Remarkably Less Disturbable.* Atascadero, CA: Impact.

Ellis, A., and Becker, I. (1982). *A Guide to Personal Happiness.* North Hollywood, CA: Wilshire.

Ellis, A., and Dryden, W. (1997). *The Practice of Rational Emotive Behavior Therapy.* New York: Springer.

Ellis, A., and Harper, R. A. (1997). *A Guide to Rational Living.* North Hollywood, CA: Wilshire.

Ellis, A., and Hauck, P. A. (1977). *Overcoming Procrastination.* New York: Signet.

Ellis, A., and MacLaren, C. (1998). *Rational Emotive Behavior Therapy: A Therapist's Guide.* San Luis Obispo, CA: Impact.

Ellis, A., McInerney, J. F., DiGiuseppe, R., and Yeager, R. J. (1988). *Rational-Emotive Therapy with Alcoholics and Substance Abusers.* New York: Pergamon.

Ellis, A., and Tafrate, R. C. (1997). *How to Control Your Anger Before It Controls You.* Secaucus, NJ: Birch Lane Press.

Ellis, A., and Velten, E. (1992). *When AA Doesn't Work for You: Rational Steps to Quitting Alcohol.* Fort Lee, NJ: Barricade.

Emrick, C. D. (1994). Alcoholics anonymous and other 12-step groups: establishing an empirically based approach for the health care provider. In *Textbook of Substance Abuse Treatment*, ed. M. Galanter and H. Kleber, pp. 351–358. Washington, DC: American Psychiatric Press.

Fillmore, K. M. (1988). *Alcohol use across the life course.* Toronto: University of Toronto Press.

Finney, J. W., and Monahan, S. C. (1996). The cost-effectiveness of treatment for alcoholism: a second approximation. *Journal of Studies on Alcohol* 57:229–243.

Finney, J. W., and Moos, R. H. (1998). Psychosocial treatments for alcohol use disorders. In *A Guide to Treatments that Work*, ed. P. E. Nathan and J. M. Gorman, pp. 156–166. New York: Oxford University Press.

Fleming, M. F., and Bary, K. L. (1997). Brief physician advice for problem alcohol drinkers: a randomized controlled trial in community-based primary care practices. *Journal of the American Medical Association* 277:1039–1045.

Frankl, V. E. (1959). *Man's Search for Meaning.* New York: Pocket Books, 1984.

Fritsch, J. (1999). 95% regain lost weight. Or do they? *The New York Times*, May 25, D7.

Gerstein, J. (1998). Rational recovery, SMART Recovery and non-twelve step recovery programs. In *Principles of Addiction Medicine*, ed. A. W. Graham and T. K. Schultz, 2nd ed., pp. 717–723. Chevy Chase, MD: American Society of Addiction Medicine.

Glasser, W. (1965). *Reality Therapy.* New York: Harper & Row.

────── (1989). Control theory. In *Control Theory in the Practice of Reality Therapy*, ed. N. Glasser, pp. 1–15. New York: Harper & Row.

Goleman, D. (1994). *Emotional Intelligence.* New York: Bantam.

Gollwitzer, P. M. (1999). Implementation intentions: strong effects of simple plans. *American Psychologist* 54(7):493–503.

Goode, E. (2000). Sharp rise found in psychiatric drugs for the very young. *The New York Times*, February 23, pp. A1, A14.

Graham, A. W. (1998). Sleep disorders. In *Principles of Addiction Medicine*, 2nd. ed., ed. A. W. Graham and T. K. Schultz, pp. 793–808. Chevy Chase, MD: American Society of Addiction Medicine.

Greenwald, M., and Young, J. (1998). Schema-focused therapy: an integrative approach to psychotherapy supervision. *Journal of Cognitive Psychotherapy* 12(2):109–126.

Harrison, P. A., and Hoffman, N. G. (1989). *SUDDS, Substance Use Disorder Diagnosis Schedule manual*. Ramsey Clinic, St. Paul, MN.

Hauck, P. A. (1991). *Overcoming the Rating Game: Beyond Self-Love—Beyond Self-Esteem*. Louisville, KY: Westminster/John Knox.

Hays, P. A. (1995). Multicultural applications of cognitive-behavior therapy. *Professional Psychology: Research and Practice* 26(3): 309–315.

Hazelden Foundation (1998). *National Survey Shows It Takes Smokers an Average 11 Attempts Before They Quit for Good*. Center City, MN: Hazelden.

Heather, N. (1995). Brief intervention strategies. In *Handbook of Alcoholism Treatment Approaches*, ed. R. K. Hester and W. R. Miller, 2nd ed., pp. 105–122. Boston: Allyn & Bacon.

Heather, N., Miller, W. R., and Greeley, J. (1991). *Self-Control and the Addictive Behaviors*. Botany, Australia: Maxwell Macmillan.

Hester, R. K. (1994). Outcome research: alcoholism. In *Textbook of Substance Abuse Treatment*, ed. M. Galanter and H. Kleber, pp. 35–43. Washington, DC: American Psychiatric Association Press.

——— (1995). Behavioral self-control training. In *Handbook of Alcoholism Treatment Approaches*, ed. R. K. Hester and W. R. Miller, 2nd ed., pp. 89–104. Boston: Allyn & Bacon.

Hester, R. K., and Delaney, H. D. (1997). Behavioral self-control program for Windows: results of a controlled clinical trial. *Journal of Consulting and Clinical Psychology* 65:686–693.

Hester, R. K., and Miller, W. R., eds. (1995). *Handbook of Alcoholism Treatment Approaches: Effective Alternatives*, 2nd. ed. Boston: Allyn & Bacon.

Horvath, A. T. (1994). Comorbidity of addictive behavior and mental disorder: outpatient practice guidelines (for those who prefer not to treat addictive behavior). *Cognitive and Behavioral Practice* 1:93–110.

—— (1998). *Sex, Drugs, Gambling, and Chocolate.* San Luis Obispo, CA: Impact.

Hubbard, R. L., Craddock, S. G., Flynn, P. M., et al. (1997). Overview of 1-year follow-up outcomes in the Drug Abuse Treatment Outcome Study (DATOS). *Psychology of Addictive Behavior* 11:261–278.

Hughes, J. R., Goldstein, M. G., Hurt, R. D., and Shiffman, S. (1999). Recent advances in the pharmacotherapy of smoking. *Journal of the American Medical Association* 281:72–76.

Hutchinson, G. T., Patock-Peckham, J. A., Cheong, J., and Nagoshi, C. T. (1998). Irrational beliefs and behavioral misregulation in the role of alcohol abuse among college students. *Journal of Rational-Emotive and Cognitive-Behavior Therapy* 16:61–74.

International Buddhist Information and Research Center (1993). *The Path to Inner Peace and Happiness: Selected Verses from the Dhammapada and Other Sayings of the Buddha.* Toronto, Canada: Buddhist Centre Toronto Maravihara.

Jacobson, E. (1929). *Progressive Relaxation.* Chicago: University of Chicago Press.

Jacobson, G. R. (1989). A comprehensive approach to pretreatment evaluation: I. Detection, assessment, and diagnosis of alcoholism. In *Handbook of Alcoholism Treatment Approaches: Effective Alternatives,* ed. R. K. Hester and W. R. Miller, pp. 17–53. New York: Pergamon.

James, W. (1958). *Talks to Teachers on Psychology.* New York: Norton.

Jaycox, L. H., Reivich, K. J., Gillham, J., and Seligman, M. E. P. (1994). Prevention of depressive symptoms in school children. *Behavior Research Therapy* 32(8):801–816.

Johnson, W. B., and Nielsen, S. L. (1998). Rational-emotive assessment with religious clients. *Journal of Rational-Emotive and Cognitive-Behavior Therapy* 16(2):101–122.

Jorenby, D. E., Leischow, S. J., Nides, M. A., et al. (1999). A controlled trial of sustained-release bupropion, a nicotine patch, or both for smoking cessation. *New England Journal of Medicine* 340:685–691.

Kagan, J. (1989). Temperamental contributions to social behavior. *American Psychologist* 44:668–674.

Kagan, J., and Snidman, N. (1991). Temperamental factors in human development. *American Psychologist* 46:856–862.

Karniol, R., and Ross, M. (1996). The motivational impact of temporal focus: thinking about the future and the past. *Annual Review of Psychology* 47:593–620.

Kasl, C. D. (1992). *Many Roads, One Journey: Moving Beyond the Twelve Steps.* New York: Harper Perennial.

Kellogg, S., and Triffleman, E. (1998). Treating substance-abuse patients with histories of violence: reactions, perspectives, and interventions. *Psychotherapy* 35(3):405–414.

Kempis, T. à. (c. 1413). *The Imitation of Christ.* New York: Penguin, 1952.

Kendall, P. C. (1990). *The Coping Cat Workbook.* Ardmore: PA: Workbook Publishing.

Kessler, R. C., McGonagle, K. A., Zhao, S., et al. (1994). Lifetime and 12-month prevalence of DSM-III-R psychiatric disorders in the United States. *Archives of General Psychiatry* 51:8–19.

Khantzian, E. J. (1985). The self-medication hypothesis of addictive disorders: focus on heroin and cocaine dependence. *American Journal of Psychiatry* 142:1259–1264.

Khrisnamurti, J. (1989). *The Future Is Now.* New York: Harper & Row.

King, M. P., and Tucker, J. A. (2000). Behavior change patterns and strategies distinguishing moderation drinking and abstinence during the natural resolution of alcohol problems without treatment. *Psychology of Addictive Behaviors* 14:48–55.

Kirsch, I., and Lynn, S. J. (1999). Automaticity in clinical psychology. *American Psychologist* 54:504–515.

Kishline, A. (1994). *Moderate Drinking: The New Option for Problem Drinkers.* San Francisco, CA: SeeSharp.

Koss, M. P., Gidycz, C. A., and Wisniewski, N. (1987). The scope of rape: Incidence and prevalence of sexual aggression and victimization in a natural sample of higher education students. *Journal of Clinical and Consulting Psychology* 53:162–170.

Koumans, A. J. R., and Muller, J. J. (1965). Use of letters to increase motivatiton in alcoholics. *Psychological Reports* 16:1152.

Koumans, A. J. R., Muller, J. J., and Miller, C. F. (1967). Use of telephone calls to increase motivation in alcoholics. *Psychological Reports* 21:327–328.

Kranzler, H. R., Burleson, J. A., Korner, P., et al. (1995). Placebo-controlled trial of fluoxetine as an adjunct to relapse prevention in alcoholics. *American Journal of Psychiatry* 152:391–397.

Krishnamurti, J. (1972). *The Impossible Question*. New York: Harper & Row.

Kushner, M. G., Mackenzie, T. B., Fiszdon, J., et al. (1996). The effects of alcohol consumption on laboratory-induced panic and state anxiety. *Archives of General Psychiatry* 53:264–270.

Kushner, M. G., Sher, K. J., and Erickson, D. J. (1999). Prospective analysis of the relationship between DSM-III anxiety disorders and alcohol use disorders. *American Journal of Psychiatry* 156:723–732.

Kwee, M. G. T., and Ellis, A. (1998). The interface between rational emotive behavior therapy (REBT) and Zen. *Journal of Rational-Emotive and Cognitive-Behavior Therapy* 16(1):5–43.

Laing, R. D. (1970). *Knots*. New York: Vintage.

Lamb, R. J., Preston, K. L., Schindler, C. W., et al. (1991). The reinforcing and subjective effects of morphine in post-addicts. *Journal of Pharmacology and Experimental Therapeutics* 259:1156–1173.

Larimer, M. E., Irvine, D. L., Kilmer, J. R., Marlatt, G. A. (1997). College drinking and the Greek System: Examining the role of perceived norms for high-risk behavior. *Journal of College Student Development* 38:587–598.

Larson, D. B., Swyers, J. P., and McCullough, M. E. (1998). *Scientific research on spirituality and health: A consensus report*. Rockport, MD: National Institute for Healthcare Research.

Laudet, A. B. (1998). Letter to the editor. *The Addictions Newsletter* 6(1):18–19.

Lazarus, A. A. (1981). *The Practice of Multimodal Therapy*. New York: McGraw-Hill.

——— (1997). *Brief but Comprehensive Psychotherapy*. New York: Springer.

Leake, G. J., and King, A. S. (1977). Effect of counselor expectations on alcoholic recovery. *Alcohol Health and Research World*, 11:16–22.

Lee, S. (1996). Cultures in psychiatric nosology: The CCMD-2-R and international classification of mental disorders. *Culture, Medicine, and Psychiatry* 20:421–472.

Lerner, A. G., Gelkopf, M., Sigal, M., and Oyffe, I. (1997). Indicators of good prognosis in naltrexone treatment: a five year prospective study. *Addictions Research* 4:385–391.

Leshner, A. I. (1997). Addiction is a brain disease, and it matters. *Science* 278:45–47.

Levin, F. R., Evans, S. M., McDowell, D. M., and Kleber, H. D. (1998). Methylphenidate treatment for cocaine abusers with adult attention-deficit/hyperactivity disorder: a pilot study. *Journal of Clinical Psychiatry* 59:300–305.

Lewis, M. (1992). *Shame: The Exposed Self*. New York: Free Press.

——— (1993). Self-conscious emotions: embarrassment, pride, shame, and guilt. In *Handbook of Emotions*, ed. M. Lewis and J. M. Haviland, pp. 563–573. New York: Guilford.

——— (1998). Shame and stigma. In *Shame: Interpersonal, Psychopathology, and Culture*, ed. P. Gilbert and B. Andrews, pp. 126–140. New York: Oxford University Press.

Linehan, M. M. (1993a). *Cognitive-Behavioral Treatment of Borderline Personality Disorder*. New York: Guilford.

——— (1993b). *Skills Treatment Manual for Treating Borderline Personality Disorder*. New York: Guilford.

Lipke, H. (1999). Comments on "Thirty years of behavior therapy . . ." and the promise of the application of scientific principles. *Behavior Therapist* 22(1):11–14.

Lohr, J. M., Tolin, D. F., and Lilienfeld, S. O. (1998). Efficacy of eye movement desensitization and reprocessing: implications for behavior therapy. *Behavior Therapy* 29:123–156.

MacCoun, R. J. (1998). Toward a psychology of harm reduction. *American Psychologist* 11:1199–1210.

Mahoney, M. J. (1991). *Human Change Process*. New York: Basic Books.

Marlatt, G. A. (1985a). Relapse prevention: theoretical rationale and overview of the model. In *Relapse Prevention*, ed. G. A. Marlatt and J. R. Gordon, pp. 3–70. New York: Guilford.

——— (1985b). Lifestyle modification. In *Relapse Prevention*, ed. G. A. Marlatt and J. R. Gordon, pp. 280–344. New York: Guilford.

———, ed. (1998). *Harm Reduction: Pragmatic Strategies for Managing High-Risk Behaviors*. New York: Guilford.

Marlatt, G. A., and Gordon, J. R., eds. (1985). *Relapse Prevention*. New York: Guilford.

Marlatt, G. A., Larimer, M. E., Baer, J. S., and Quigley, L. A. (1993). Harm reduction for alcohol problems: moving beyond the controlled drinking controversy. *Behavior Therapy* 24:461–504.

Mason, B. J., Kocsis, J. H., Rutvi, E. C., and Cutler, R. B. (1996). A double-blind, placebo-controlled trial of desipramine for primary alcohol dependence stratified on the presence or absence of major depression. *Journal of the American Medical Association* 275:761–767.

May, R. (1953). *Man's Search for Himself*. New York: Dell.

——— (1969). *Love and Will*. New York: W. W. Norton.

——— (1979). *Psychology and the Human Dilemma*. New York: W. W. Norton.

McCrady, B. S. (1994). Alcoholics anonymous and behavior therapy: Can habits be treated as diseases? Can diseases be treated as habits? *Journal of Consulting and Clinical Psychology* 62(6):1159–1166.

——— (1998). Some meditations on spirituality. *The Addictions Newsletter* 6(6):25–26.

McCurrin, M. C. (1992). *Pathological Gambling: Conceptual, Diagnostic and Treatment Issues*. Sarasota, FL: Professional Resource Press.

McElroy, S. L., Soutullo, C. A., Beckman, D., et al. (1998a). *DSM-IV* intermittent explosive disorder: a report of 27 cases. *Journal of Clinical Psychiatry* 59:203–210.

McElroy, S. L., Soutullo, C. A., and Goldsmith, R. J. (1998b). Other impulse control disorders. In *Principles of Addiction Medicine*, ed. A. W. Graham and T. K. Schultz, 2nd ed., pp. 1047–1061. Chevy Chase, MD: American Society of Addiction Medicine.

McGrath, P. J., Nunes, E. V., Stewart, J. W., et al. (1996). Imipramine treatment of alcoholics with primary depression. *Archives of General Psychiatry* 53:232–240.

McGue, M. (1999). Behavioral genetic models of alcoholism and drinking. In *Psychological Theories of Drinking and Alcoholism*, ed. K. E. Leonard and H. T. Blane, 2nd ed., pp. 372–421. New York: Guilford.

Meichenbaum, D. (1977). *Cognitive-Behavior Modification*. New York: Plenum.

Miller, W. R. (1985). Motivation for treatment: a review with special emphasis on alcoholism. *Psychological Bulletin* 98:84–107.

——— (1988). Including client's spiritual perspectives in cognitive-behavior therapy. In *Behavior Therapy and Religion: Integrating Spiritual and Behavioral Approaches to Change*, ed. W. R. Miller and J. E. Marten, pp. 43–56. Newbury Park, CA: Sage.

——— (1995). Increasing motivation for change. In *Handbook of Alcoholism Treatment Approaches: Effective Alternatives*, ed. R. K. Hester and W. R. Miller, 2nd ed., pp. 89–104. Boston: Allyn & Bacon.

——— (1998). Can we study spirituality? *The Addictions Newsletter* 6(1):4, 21.

Miller, W. R., Brown, J. M., Tracy, L. S., et al. (1995). What works? A methodological analysis of the alcohol treatment outcome literature. In *Handbook of Alcoholism Treatment Approaches:*

Effective Alternatives, ed. R. K. Hester and W. R. Miller, 2nd ed., pp. 12–44. Boston: Allyn & Bacon.

Miller, W. R., and Hester, R. K. (1995). Treatment for alcohol problems: toward and informed eclecticism. In *Handbook of Alcoholism Treatment Approaches: Effective Alternatives,* ed. R. K. Hester and W. R. Miller, 2nd ed., pp. 1–11. Boston: Allyn & Bacon.

Miller, W. R., Leckman, A. L., Delaney, H. D., and Tinkcom, M. (1992). Long-term follow-up of behavioral self-control training. *Journal of Studies on Alcohol* 53:249–261.

Miller, W. R., and Martin, J. E. (1988). Spirituality and behavioral psychology. In *Behavior Therapy and Religion: Integrating Spiritual and Behavioral Approaches to Change,* ed. W. R. Miller and J. E. Martin, pp. 13–23. Newbury Park: CA: Sage.

Miller, W. R., and Munoz, R. F. (1982). *How to Control Your Drinking.* Albuquerque, NM: University of New Mexico Press.

Miller, W. R., and Rollnick, S. (1991). *Motivational Interviewing: Preparing People to Change Addictive Behavior.* New York: Guilford.

Miller, W. R., Zweben, A., DiClemente, C. C., and Rychtarik, R. G. (1992). *Motivational Enhancement Therapy Manual.* Rockville, MD: National Institute on Alcohol Abuse and Alcoholism.

Mozes, A. (1999). Poverty has greater impact than cocaine on young brain. *Reuters HealtheLine,* December 6.

Murphy, J. G., Lawyer, S. R., Vuchinich, R. E., and Tucker, J. A. (1998). *The influence of religion on recovery from alcohol problems.* Poster presented at the Annual Conference of the Association for the Advancement of Behavior Therapy, Washington, D.C.

Nathan, P. E., and Gorman, J. M. (1998). Treatments that work—and what convinces us they do. In *A Guide to Treatments that Work,* ed. P. E. Nathan and J. M. Gorman, pp. 3–25. New York: Oxford University Press.

National Institute on Alcohol Abuse and Alcoholism (1998). Alcohol and sleep. *Alcohol Alert* 41:1–4.

National Institute on Drug Abuse (1999). Pain medications. Infofax 13553. Bethesda, MD: National Institute of Health.

Noble, H. B. (1998). Adult brain cells said to reproduce. *The New York Times*, October 30, pp. A1, A29.

Nottingham, E. (1994). *It's Not as Bad as It Seems*. Memphis, TN: Castle.

O'Brien, C. P., and McLellan, A. T. (1998). Myths about the treatment of addiction. In *Principles of Addiction Medicine*, ed. A. W. Graham and T. K. Schultz, 2nd ed., pp. 309–314. Chevy Chase, MD: American Society of Addiction Medicine.

Olevitch, B. A. (1995). *Using Cognitive Approaches with the Seriously Mentally Ill*. Westport, CN: Praeger.

O'Malley, S. S., Jaffe, A. J., Chang, G., et al. (1996). Six-month follow-up of naltrexone and psychotherapy for alcohol dependence. *Archives of General Psychiatry* 53:217–224.

Oppenheimer, E., Tobutt, D., Taylor, C., and Andrew, T. (1994). Death and survival in a cohort of heroin addicts from London clinics: a 22-year follow-up study. *Addictions* 89:1299–1308.

Ouimette, P. C., Finney, J. W., and Moos, R. H. (1997). Twelve-step and cognitive-behavioral treatment for substance abuse: a comparison of treatment effectiveness. *Journal of Consulting and Clinical Psychology* 65:230–240.

Ouspensky, P. D. (1949). *In search of the miraculous*. New York: Harcourt, Brace & World.

Panepinto, W. C., and Higgins, M. J. (1969). Keeping alcoholics in treatment: Effective follow-through procedures. *Quarterly Journal of Studies on Alcohol* 30:414–419.

Peck, M. S. (1978). *The Road Less Traveled*. New York: Simon and Schuster.

Perls, F. S. (1969). *Gestalt Therapy Verbatim*. New York: Delta.

Pettinati, H. M., Pierce, J. D., Wolf, A. L., et al. (1997). Gender differences in comorbidly depressed alcohol-dependent outpatients. *Alcoholism: Clinical and Experimental Research* 21:1742–1746.

Prochaska, J. O., and DiClemente, C. C. (1982). Transtheoretical therapy: toward a more integrative model of change. *Psychotherapy* 20:161–173.

Prochaska, J. O., DiClemente, C. C., and Norcross, J. C. (1992). In search of how people change: applications to addictive behaviors. *American Psychologist* 47:1102–1114.

——— (1994). *Changing for Good*. New York: Avon.

Project MATCH Research Group (1997a). Matching alcoholism treatments to client heterogeneity: Project MATCH posttreatment drinking outcomes. *Journal of Studies on Alcohol* 58:7–29.

——— (1997b). Project MATCH secondary *a priori* hypotheses. *Addictions* 92:1655–1682.

Rauch, S. L., Jenike, M. A., Alpert, N. M., et al. (1994). Regional cerebral blood flow measured during symptom provocation in obsessive-compulsive disorder using oxygen 15–labeled carbon dioxide and positron emission tomography. *Archives of General Psychiatry* 51:62–70.

Rauch, S. L., Savage, C. R., Alpert, N. M., et al. (1995). A positron emission tomographic study of simple phobic symptom provocation. *Archives of General Psychiatry* 52:20–28.

Regier, D. A., Farmer, M. E., Rae, D. S., et al. (1990). Comorbidity of mental disorders with alcohol and other drug abuse: results from the Epidemiological Catchment Area (ECA) study. *Journal of the American Medical Association* 264:2511–2518.

Robb, H. (1988). *How to Stop Driving Yourself Crazy with Help from the Bible*. Lake Oswego, OR: Author.

Robins, C. J. (1999). A dialectical behavior therapy perspective on the case of Anna. *Cognitive and Behavioral Practice* 6:60–67.

Robitschek, C., and Kashubeck, S. (1999). A structural model of parenting alcholism, family functioning, and psychological health: the mediating effects of hardiness and personal growth orientation. *Journal of Counseling Psychology* 46:159–172.

Rogers, C. R. (1961). *On Becoming a Person*. Boston: Houghton-Mifflin.

Rosenberg, H. (1993). Prediction of controlled drinking by alcoholics and problem drinkers. *Psychological Bulletin* 113:129–139.

Rosenberg, H., and Davis, L. (1993). *Acceptance of controlled drinking by alcohol treatment services in the United States.* Poster presentation, Sixth International Conference on Treatment of Addictions.

――― (1994). Acceptance of moderate drinking by alcohol treatment services in the Unites States. *Journal of Studies on Alcohol* 55:167–172.

Rosencrance, J. (1989). Controlled gambling: A promising future. In H. J. Shaffer, S. A. Stein, B. Gambino, and T. N. Cummings (Eds.), *Compuslive Gambling* (pp. 147–160). Lexington, MA: D. C. Health & Co.

Rousaville, B. J., Anton, S. F., Carroll, K., et al. (1991). Psychiatric diagnoses of treatment-seeking cocaine abusers. *Archives of General Psychiatry* 48(1):43–51.

Rousaville, B. J., Wiessman, M. M., Kleber, H., et al. (1982). Heterogeneity of psychiatric diagnoses in treated opiate addicts. *Archives of General Psychiatry* 39(2):162–168.

Royer, A. (1994). The role of the transcendental meditation technique in promoting smoking cessation: a longitudinal study. *Alcoholism Treatment Quarterly* 11:221–239.

Russell, B. (1930). *The Conquest of Happiness.* New York: Liveright.

――― (1945). *A History of Western Philosophy.* New York: Simon and Schuster.

――― (1950). *Unpopular Essays.* New York: Simon and Schuster.

Sanchez-Craig, M. (1993). *Saying When: How to Quit Drinking or Cut Down.* Toronto: Addictions Research Foundation.

Sanchez-Craig, M., Annis, H. M., Bornet, A. R., and MacDonald, K. H. (1984). Random assignment to abstinence and controlled drinking: evaluation of a cognitive-behavioral program for problem drinkers. *Journal of Consulting and Clinical Psychology* 52:390–403.

Schuckit, M. A., and Smith, T. L. (1996). An 8-year follow-up of 450 sons of alcoholic and control subjects. *Archives of General Psychiatry* 54(2):202–210.

Seligman, M. E. P. (1994). *What You Can Change and What You Can't.* New York: Knopf.

————— (1998). Work, love and play. *APA Monitor* 29(9):2.

Shaffer, H. J. (1996). Understanding the means and objects of addiction: Technology, the internet, and gambling. *Journal of Gambling Studies* 12:461–469.

Shaffer, H. J., Hall, M. N., and Vanderbilt, J. (1997). *Estimating the Prevalence of Disordered Gambling Behavior in the United States and Canada: A Meta-Analysis.* Boston, MA: Harvard Medical School, Division on Addictions.

Shafranske, E. P. (1996). Religious beliefs, affiliations, and practices of clinical psychologists. In *Religion and the Clinical Practice of Psychology,* ed. E. P. Shafranke, pp. 149–164. Washington, DC: American Psychological Association.

Shafranske, E. P., and Malony, H. N. (1990). Clinical psychologists' religious and spiritual orientations and their practice of psychotheray. *Psychotherapy.* 27:72–78.

Sharkey, J. (1997). You're not bad, you're sick. It's in the book. *The New York Times,* September 28, section 4, pp. 1, 5.

Simon, S. B., Howe, L. W., and Kirschenbaum, H. (1972). *Values Clarification: A Handbook of Practical Strategies for Teachers and Students.* New York: Hart.

Smith, D. A. (1999). Stuart Smalley syndrome: what is *not* cognitive-behavioral psychotherapy. *Behavior Therapist* 22:5–8.

Sobell, L. C., Cunningham, J. A., and Sobell, M. B. (1996). Recovery from alcohol problems with and without treatment: Prevalence in two population surveys. *American Journal of Public Health* 86:966–972.

Sobell, L. C., Ellingstad, T. P., and Sobell, M. B. (2000). Natural recovery from alcohol and drug problems: methodological review of the research with suggestions for future directions. *Addiction* 95:749–764.

Sobell, M. B., and Sobell, L.C. (1993). *Problem Drinkers: Guided Self-Change Treatment.* New York: Guilford.

Sternberg, R. J. (1986). A triangular theory of love. *Psychological Review* 93(2):119–135.

Strang, J., Bacchus, L., Howes, S., and Watson, P. (1997). Turned away from treatment: maintenance-seeking follow-up. *Addictions Research* 6:71–81.

Tatarsky, A. (1998). An integrative approach to harm reduction psychotherapy: a case of problem drinking secondary to depression. *In Session: Psychotherapy in Practice* 4:9–24.

Tate, P. (1993). *Alcohol: How to Give It Up and Be Glad You Did.* Altamonte Springs, FL: Rational Self-Help Press.

Taub, E., Steiner, S. S., Wengarten, E., and Walton, K. (1994). Effectiveness of broad spectrum approaches to relapse prevention in severe alcoholism: a long-term, randomized, controlled trial of transcendental meditation, EMG, biofeedback and electronic neurotherapy. *Alcoholism Treatment Quarterly* 11: 187–220.

Thomas, A. T., Chess, S., and Birch, H. G. (1968). *Temperament and Behavior Disorders in Children.* New York: New York University Press.

Thomas, E., Plansky, N., and Kounin, J. (1955). The expected behavior of a potentially helpful person. *Human Relations* 8:165–174.

Tillich, P. (1952). *The Courage to Be.* New Haven: Yale University Press.

Toneatto, T., Sobell, L. C., Sobell, M. B., and Rubel, E. (1999). Natural recovery from cocaine dependence. *Psychology of Addictive Behaviors* 13:259–268.

Torrey, E. F. (1986). *Witchdoctors and Psychiatrists.* New York: Harper & Row.

Trimpey, J. (1992). *The Small Book: A Revolutionary Alternative for Overcoming Alcohol and Drug Dependence.* New York: Delacorte.

Tucker, J. A., and King, M. P. (1999). Resolving alcohol and drug problems: influences on addictive behavior change and help-seeking processes. In *Changing Addictive Behavior*, ed. J. A. Tucker, D. M. Donovan, and G. A. Marlatt, pp. 97–126. New York: Guilford.

Vaillant, G. E. (1996). A long-term follow-up of male alcohol abuse. *Archives of General Psychiatry* 53:243–249.

Velten, E. (1996). The rationality of Alcoholics Anonymous and the spirituality of rational emotive behavior therapy. *Journal of Humanistic Education and Development* 35:105–116.

Wager, The (1997a). Memory of wins and losses. Vol. 2, no. 33, August 19.

———— (1997b). Pathological gambling as a reflection of cultural norms. Vol. 2, no. 40, October 28.

Watkins, K. E., Well, K. B., and McLellan, A. T. (1999). Termination of social security benefits among Los Angeles recipients disabled by substance abuse. *Psychiatric Services* 50:914–918.

Wegner, D. M., and Wheatley, T. (1999). Apparent mental causation: sources of the experience of will. *American Psychologist* 54:480–492.

Wells, A. (1997). *Cognitive Therapy of Anxiety Disorders: A Practice Manual and Conceptual Guide*. New York: Wiley.

West, R., and Hajek, P. (1997). What happens to anxiety levels on giving up smoking? *American Journal of Psychiatry* 154:1589–1592.

Wilsnack, S. C., Vogeltanz, N. D., Klassen, A. D., and Harris, T. R. (1997). Childhood sexual abuse and women's substance abuse: national survey findings. *Journal of Studies on Alcohol* 58:264–271.

Wilson, G. T., and Fairburn, C. G. (1998). Treatments for eating disorders. In *A Guide to Treatments that Work*, ed. P. E. Nathan and J. M. Gorman. New York: Oxford University Press.

Wodak, A. (1995). Harm reduction: Australia as a case study. *Bulletin of the New York Academy of Medicine* 72(2):339–347.

———— (1998). Harm reduction as an approach to treatment. In *Principles of Addiction Medicine*, ed. A. W. Graham and T. K. Schultz, 2nd ed., pp. 395–405. Chevy Chase, MD: American Society of Addiction Medicine.

Wyatt, G. E., and Mickey, M. R. (1988). The support of parents and others as it mediates the effects of child sexual abuse: An exploratory study. In *Lasting Effects of Child Sexual Abuse*, ed. G. E. Wyatt and G. J. Powell, pp. 211–225. Newbury Park, CA: Sage.

Yalom, I. D. (1980). *Existential Psychology*. New York: Norton.

Yochelson, S., and Samenow, S. E. (1986). *The Criminal Personality, Vol. 3: The Drug User*. Northvale, NJ: Jason Aronson.

Young, H. (1984). Practicing RET with bible-belt Christians. *British Journal of Cognitive Psychotherapy* 2:60–76.

Young, J. E. (1994). *Cognitive Therapy for Personality Disorders: A Schema-Focused Approach*, rev. ed. Sarasota, FL: Professional Resource Press.

Ziedonis, D., and Wyatt, S. (1998). Psychotic disorders. pp. 1007–1027. In *Principles of Addiction Medicine*, ed. A. W. Graham and T. K. Schultz, 2nd ed., pp. 1007–1027. Chevy Chase, MD: American Society of Addiction Medicine.

Zinberg, N. E., and Jacobson, R. C. (1976). The natural history of "chipping." *American Journal of Psychiatry* 133:33–40.

Zweben, A., and Fleming, M. F. (1999). Brief interventions for alcohol and drug problems. In J. A. Tucker, D. M. Donovan, and G. A. Marlatt (Eds.), *Changing Addictive Behaviors* (pp. 251–282). New York: Guilford Press.

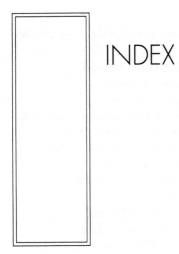

INDEX

ABC model. *See also* CBT/REBT techniques; Client engage-ment; Moderation/abstinence issue; Stages of change model
addition applications, 18–24
enhanced models, 16–18
issues in, 30–36
research in, 36–38
spiral interactions, 24–29
stages of change model, 9–15
Abstinence. *See* Moderation/abstinence issue
Abstinence violation effect (AVE)
additions and, 22
type III clients, 254
Acceptance, forgiveness and, depression, 319–320
à Kempis, T., 237–238
Albee, G., 85
Alcoholics Anonymous (AA), recovering term, 5
Alcohol Use Disorders Identifica-tion Test (AUDIT), 132
Alessandri, S. A., 377
Allen, J., 446

American Psychiatric Association (APA), 76, 111, 112
American Society of Addiction Medicine (ASAM), 132
"Anchors" and "spin doctors" metaphor, CBT/REBT techniques, 72–74
Andrews, B., 377
Anger management, 263–301
change readiness, 263–265
clinical techniques, 266–290
ABC(DE) teaching, 276–282
ABC on other's anger, 275
brainstorming, 272–273
emotional alternatives, 270–272
goals and values, 269
historical roots, 269
new plan testing, 286–287
problem exploration, 266–268
rational emotive imagery, 284–285
relaxation techniques, 282

Anger management (*continued*)
    reviewing and rehearsing,
        289–290
    role playing and reverse role
        playing, 287–289
    session goals, 266
    time effects, 273–275
    homework, 299–300
    issues, 293–299
        amends, 295
        developmental factors,
            295–296
        family and genetics, 296–298
        frequency, duration, and in-
            tensity (FDI), 293–294
        frustration, 294–295
        psychotherapy, 294
        socioeconomic factors, 296
        venting, 298–299
    medications, 300–301
    problems, 290–293
    resources listed, 301
Anger relapse prevention review,
    282, 283
Antabuse, type III clients, 257
Anthenelli, R. M., 91, 100, 102
Antidepressants, depression,
    331–332
Anxiety, 333–369
    clinical strategies, 335–358
        alternatives, 346–349
        behavioral relaxation tech-
            niques, 351–357
        graduated in vivo exposure,
            344–346
        inference chaining, 337–344
        pre-AB's, 349–350
        problem exploration,
            336–337
        questioning, 350–351
        rational emotive imagery, 349
        session goals, 335
    homework, 366–367
    issues, 362–366
        caffeine, 364
        family and genetics, 362–364
        gender differences, 366
        low blood pressure, 365
        nutrition, 365
    medications, 367–368
    overview, 333
    problems, 358–362
        anxiety about anxiety,
            359–360
        dysthymia, 360
        emotional numbness,
            360–361
        procrastination, 358–359
        trauma, hypervigilance, and
            chronic anxiety,
            361–362
    research in, 334–335
    resources listed, 368–369
    shame and guilt, 399
Aristotle, 263
Assessment, 107–135
    behavior patterns, 120–123
    client's goals, 116–117
    client's knowledge, 124–127
    client's motivation, 130
    client's resources, 127–128
    client's stage of change, 116
    definitions, 108–110
    DSM-IV, 110–114
        other behaviors, 113–114
        substance abuse, 110–111
        substance dependence,
            111–113
    first session, 114–115
    handout of behavior change,
        130, 131

homework, 130
instruments for, 130, 132–135
overview, 107–108
problem seriousness, 118–120
risk, 128–129
shame and guilt, 380–381
treatability issue, 120
type I clients, 170
Attributional style, shame and
guilt, 375–376
Automatized behavior, CBT/
REBT techniques, 61–68

Balanced lifestyle
depression, 316–317
type III clients, 246–247
Bandura, A., 17
Bargh, J. A., 62, 63, 65, 68, 70,
71, 93, 97
Barlow, D. H., 345, 368
Bateson, G., 67
Baumeister, R. F., 65
Beck, A. T., 10, 16, 22, 24, 25, 58,
70, 442
Becker, I., 332, 443
Behavioral relaxation techniques.
See Relaxation techniques
Behavior patterns, assessment,
120–123
Beliefs, rehearsal of, 437–438
Benson, H., 356, 435
Berridge, K. C., 35
Bibliotherapy, 437
Bien, T. H., 114
Bipolar clients, depression,
318–319
Bishop, F. M., 254, 259
Bishop, M., ix
Black, D. W., 408
Blume, S. A., 100

Bohn, M. J., 132
Boredom, type II clients, 230
Bradshaw, J., 272, 373
Brady, K. T., 306
Brainstorming
anger management, 272–273
CBT/REBT techniques, 51–53
Brief Sexual Behaviors Survey
(BSBS), 133
Brooner, R. K., 306, 408
Brown, R. A., 306
Brownell, K. D., 17
Bruner, J., 96
Buddha, 10, 53, 434–435
Bupropion, smoking cessation,
258–259
Burn, D., 58, 332, 369, 442

Caffeine, anxiety, 364
CAGE test, 132
Carey, K. B., 37, 107, 334
Castro, F. G., 103, 104
Catastrophizing, depression,
322–323
CBT/REBT techniques, 39–74.
See also ABC model; Client
engagement; Moderation/
abstinence issue; Stages of
change model; Type I clients;
Type II clients; Type III
clients
ABC(DE) teaching, 41–50
additions and, 19
aspects in, 53–60
emotions, 58
enlightened hedonism, 53–54
irrational thinking, 56–58,
59, 60
unconditional self-acceptance,
54–55
brainstorming, 51–53

CBT/REBT techniques (*continued*)
  issues, 61–74
    "anchors" and "spin doctors"
      metaphor, 72–74
    automatized behavior, 61–68
    difficult clients and difficult
      problems, 61
    "mind" as committee meta-
      phor, 68–70
    "voices" metaphor, 70–71
  overview, 39
  plan development, 40–41
  role playing, 51
  stages of change model integra-
    tion, 9–15
  time-effect analysis, 50–51
Change readiness, anger, 263–265
Chartrand, T. L., 62, 63, 65, 68,
  70, 71, 93, 97
Chen, M., 63
Chronic anxiety, 361–362
Client-centered stance, client
  engagement, 144–145
Client engagement, 139–151
  client-centered stance, 144–145
  empathy and support, 141
  harm reduction, 141–142
  information sharing, 142–144
  problems, 145–151
    client's substance use, 150
    difficulty of change, 151
    lying and denial, 148–149
    multiple diagnoses, 149–150
    professional enabling, 149
    therapist's negative feelings,
      145–148
  respect, 141
  unconditional acceptance,
    139–140
Client types, stages of change
  model, 8–9

Coaching, severely disturbed
  clients, 419
Common ground, type II clients,
  207
Compassion, type II clients, 207
Conflicts
  type I clients, 174–176
  type II clients, 208–210
Confrontation, type I clients, 168
Contemplation stage, change
  model, 4
Controlled drinking. *See*
  Moderation/abstinence issue
Corsini, R. J., 417
Countertransference, therapist's
  negative feelings, client
  engagement, 145–148
Covey, S. R., 443
Craske, M. G., 345, 368
Cultural factors, problem etiology,
  103–104
Cummings, N. A., 333
Curry, S. J., 104

Dadds, M. R., 334, 364
Davis, L, 156
Deep diaphragmatic breathing,
  anxiety, 353–355
Deity-focused, transpersonal tech-
  niques, 432–434
Delaney, H. D., 163
Denial, lying and, client engage-
  ment problems, 148–149
Depression, 303–332
  clinical strategies, 306–317
    ABC(DE), 310–312
    ABC on other's problem, 315
    alternatives, 312–313
    balanced lifestyle, 316–317
    historical roots, 309–310

problem exploration,
307–309
role playing, 315–316
session goals, 306–307
trigger situations, 314–315
homework, 328–331
issues, 321–328
catastrophizing, 322–323
developmental factors,
323–324
endocrinology, 322
exercise, 326–327
family and genetics, 324–325
gender differences, 325
nutrition, 327
psychiatry and medications,
321–322
sleep, 327–328
social, political, and economic
factors, 325
spirituality and existential
issues, 326
stigma, 324
medications, 331–332
overview, 303–305
research in, 305–306
shame and guilt, 399
special problems, 317–321
bipolar clients, 318–319
dysthymia, 317–318
forgiveness and acceptance,
319–320
low frustration tolerance,
320–321
procrastination, 320
DeRubeis, R. J., 306
Developmental factors
anger management, 295–296
depression, 323–324
problem etiology, 98–99
shame and guilt, 400

type I patient problems,
198–199
*Diagnostic and Statistical Manual
of Mental Disorders (DSM-IV)*
bipolar clients, 318
disease concept, 76–81, 83, 85
other behaviors, 113–114
shame and guilt, 376
substance abuse, 109, 110–111
substance dependence, 111–113
Diaphragmatic breathing, anxiety,
353–355
DiClemente, C. C., 6
Difficult clients and problems,
CBT/REBT techniques, 61
DiGiuseppe, R., 301, 444
Dimeff, L. A., 82, 99, 100, 132,
133, 155, 199
Disease concept, problem etiology,
76–90. *See also* Problem
etiology
Disputing, types of, 45–47
Donovan, D. M., 132
Dreams, 201, 438
Drinkers Inventory of Conse-
quences, 133
Drug therapy. *See* Medications
Dryden, W., 9, 10, 48, 54
Dunn, C., 431
Dysthymia
anxiety, 360
depression, 317–318
type II clients, 229–230

Eating disorders, *DSM-IV,*
113–114
Economic factors
anger management, 296
depression, 325
problem etiology, 104–105
shame and guilt, 401

Edelstein, M. R., 50
Ellis, A., 9, 16, 18, 19, 20, 41, 48,
    50, 52, 54, 58, 70, 123, 139,
    159, 246, 250, 259, 264, 265,
    271, 301, 332, 358, 369, 391,
    396, 428, 443
Emotional numbness, anxiety,
    360–361
Emotions, CBT/REBT techniques,
    58. *See also* Anger manage-
    ment; Anxiety; Depression;
    Shame and guilt
Emotive rational behavior therapy
    (ERBT), anger management,
    292–293
Empathic questioning, anxiety, 351
Empathy
    support and, client engagement,
        141
    type II clients, 207
Empirical questioning, anxiety,
    350–351
Employment, client's resources,
    124
Emrick, C. D., 154, 155
Endocrinology, depression, 322
Enlightened hedonism, CBT/
    REBT techniques, 53–54
Ethnic factors, problem etiology,
    103–104
Etiology. *See* Problem etiology
Exercise, depression, 326–327
Existentialism
    depression, 326
    problem etiology, 102–103
Experimental plan, type II clients,
    210–217

Fairburn, C. G., 158
Family factors
    anger management, 296–298

anxiety, 362–364
client's resources, 124
depression, 324–325
problem etiology, 102
shame and guilt, 400–401
Fasting, 435–436
FEAR program, 364
Fillmore, K. M., 155
Finney, J. W., 114, 445
First session, assessment, 114–115
Fleming, M. F., 114
Forgiveness
    acceptance and, depression,
        319–320
    shame and guilt, 397–398
Four R's of parenting for self-
    parenting, severely disturbed
    clients, 417–419
Frankl, V., 331, 443
Frequency, duration, and intensity
    (FDI)
    anger management, 293–294
    shame and guilt, 372, 389, 393
Freud, S., 68, 92, 93, 299
Fritsch, J., 158
Frustration, anger management,
    294–295
Functional questioning, anxiety,
    351

Gambling, *DSM-IV,* 113–114
Gender differences
    anxiety, 366
    depression, 325
    problem etiology, 99–101
    shame and guilt, 401
Genetics
    anger management, 296–298
    anxiety, 362–364
    depression, 324–325

problem etiology, 91–92
shame and guilt, 400–401
Gerstein, J., 254
Glasser, W., 131, 159, 184, 417
Gollwitzer, P. M., 62, 96, 97, 210, 212
Goode, E., 258
Gordon, J., 23, 236
Gorman, J. M., 445
Graduated in vivo exposure, anxiety, 344–346
Graham, A. W., 328
Greenwald, M., 16
Guilt. *See* Shame and guilt

Hajek, P., 335
HALT acronym, 263
Harm reduction
client engagement, 141–142
moderation/abstinence issue, 161
risk, assessment, 128–129
severely disturbed clients, 416
Harper, R. A., 54, 332, 443
Hauck, P. A., 53, 311, 332
Hays, P. A., 103
Hazelden Foundation, 239
Heather, N., 153
Hedonism, enlightened, CBT/REBT techniques, 53–54
Helzer, J. E., 154, 305
Heredity. *See* Genetics
Hester, R. K., 5, 145, 153, 156, 163, 168, 445
High frustration tolerance (HFT). *See also* Low frustration tolerance (LFT)
spirituality, 435
type III clients, 255
Hobbies, client's resources, 125

Homework
anger management, 299–300
anxiety, 366–367
assessment, 130
depression, 328–331
severely disturbed clients, 423–424
shame and guilt, 403–404
type I clients, 199–201
type II clients, 233–234
type III clients, 254–255
Horvath, A. T., 259
Hubbard, R. L., 37
Hughes, J. R., 258
Hurt, H., 104–105
Hutchinson, G. T., 29

Inference chaining, anxiety, 337–344
Information sharing
client engagement, 142–144
type I clients, 174
Institutional issues, type I patient problems, 199
Insurance reimbursements, cautionary note on, 110
In vivo exposure, graduated, anxiety, 344–346
Irrational beliefs, ABC model, 11–15
Irrational thinking, CBT/REBT techniques, 56–58, 59, 60

Jacobson, E., 355
Jacobson, G. R., 133
Jacobson, R. C., 157
James, W., 65–66
Jaycox, L. H., 42
Johnson, W. B., 442
Jorenby, D. E., 258

Kagan, J., 334, 363, 364
Karniol, R., 35
Kashubeck, S., 102
Kasl, C. D., 95
Kellogg, S., 185, 396, 399
Kendall, P. C., 364
Kessler, R. C., 37
Khantzian, E. J., 84, 363
Khrisnamurti, J., 10, 443
King, M. P., 157, 173
Kirsch, I., 368, 438, 445
KISS acronym, ABC model, 16–18
Koss, M. P., 82
Koumans, A. J. R., 169
Kranzler, H. R., 306
Kushner, M. G., 334
Kwee, M. G. T., 246

Laing, R. D., 374
Lamb, R. J., 35
Lapse. *See also* Relapse
  relapse compared, type III
    clients, 236–239
  shame and guilt, 393
  stages of change model, 6
  techniques, 49–50
Larimer, M. E., 99
Larson, D. B., 430
Laudet, A. B., 431
Lazarus, A. A., 135, 207, 355, 368,
  436
Leake, G. J., 173
Lee, S., 103
Lerner, A. G., 257
Leshner, A. I., 77, 83
Levin, F. R., 256
Lewis, M., 375, 376, 377, 381
Lifestyle, balanced
  depression, 316–317
  type III clients, 246–247
Linehan, M. M., 16

Linking, depression, 310–312
Lipke, H., 445
Lohr, J. M., 445
Loss list, anger management, 274
Love, client engagement, 143–144
Low blood pressure, anxiety, 365
Low frustration tolerance (LFT).
  See also High frustration
    tolerance (HFT)
  additions and, 20, 21
  anxiety, 366
  depression, 309, 320–321
  severely disturbed clients, 409,
    415
  type III clients, 249–250
Lying, denial and, client engage-
  ment problems, 148–149
Lynn, S. J., 368, 438, 445

MacCoun, R. J., 156
MacLaren, C., 54
Mahoney, M. J., 10, 16
Maintenance stage, change model,
  5
Malony, H. N., 434
Marcus Aurelius, 333
Marlatt, G. A., 20–21, 22, 23, 121,
  142, 153, 156, 199, 222–
  223, 234, 236, 246, 254,
  305, 367
Martin, J. E., 431
Mason, B. J., 306
May, R., 92, 103, 326, 331, 442,
  443
McCrady, B. S., 430, 444, 446
McCurrin, M. C., 157
McElroy, S. L., 113, 265
McGrath, P. J., 305, 306
McGue, M., 91
McLellan, A. T., 17, 204

Medications
  anger management, 300–301
  anxiety, 367–368
  depression, 321–322, 331–332
  political factors, 105–106
  severely disturbed clients, 424
  shame and guilt, 404
  type I clients, 201–202
  type III clients, 255–259
    Antabuse, 257
    methadone, 257–258
    naltrexone, 256–257
    smoking cessation, 258–259
Meditation, 435
Meichenbaum, D., 10
Mencken, H. L., 75
Methadone, type III clients,
  257–258
Michigan Alcoholism Screening
  Test (MAST), 132–133
Mickey, M. R., 376
Miller, W. R., 5, 48, 145, 155, 156,
  158, 160, 163, 166, 168,
  169, 173, 427, 431
"Mind" as committee metaphor,
  CBT/REBT techniques,
  68–70
Mirror-in-the-morning technique,
  information sharing, 143
Moderation/abstinence issue,
  153–163
  discussion of, 161–162
  overview, 153
  predictors, 158
  research findings, 154–158
  resources listed, 162–163
  therapist/client relationship,
  159–161
  type I patient problems, 199
Monahan, S. C., 445

Moos, R. H., 114
Motivation
  assessment, 130
  first session, 114–115
  research in, 259–260
  stages of change model, 5
  type I clients, 169
Moyer, T., 408
Mozes, A, 105
Muller, J. J., 169
Multiple diagnoses, client engage-
  ment problems, 149–150
Munoz, R. F., 163
Murphy, G., 39
Murphy, J. G., 442
Muscle relaxation, anxiety,
  355–357

Naltrexone, type III clients,
  256–257
Nathan, P. E., 445
National Institute of Drug
  Addiction (NIDA), 431
National Institute on Alcohol
  Abuse and Alcoholism
  (NIAAA), 328
National Institute on Drug Abuse,
  90
Niebuhr, H. R., 294
Nielsen, S. L., 442
Noble, H. B., 87
Non-deity-focused
  non-transpersonal techniques,
  436–440
  transpersonal techniques,
  434–436
Nottingham, E., 50, 369
Nutrition
  anxiety, 365
  depression, 327

O'Brien, C. P., 17, 204
Offerings, 434
Olevitch, B. A., 407
Oliver, R., 313
O'Malley, S. S., 256
Oppenheimer, E., 157
Ouimette, P. C., 442
Ouspensky, P. D., 443
Ovid, 139

Painter, G., 417
Panic attacks. See Anxiety
Peck, M. S., 332, 443
Perls, F., 201
Personality disorders, severely dis-
    turbed clients, 408–409
Pettinati, H. M., 100
Pharmacology. See Medications
Philosophical questioning, anxiety,
    350–351
Pilgrimages, 433–434
Polansky, T., 169
Political factors. See also Economic
    factors; Social factors
    depression, 325
    problem etiology, 105–106
Posttraumatic stress disorder,
    anxiety, 361–362
Praying, 432–433
Precontemplation stage, change
    model, 3
Predictors, moderation/abstinence
    issue, 158
Preparation stage, change model, 4
Problem etiology, 75–106
    cultural and ethnic factors,
        103–104
    developmental factors, 98–99
    disease concept, 76–90
        beliefs impeding treatment,
            81–83

brain disease hypothesis,
    83–88
case vignette, 88–90
DSM-IV, 76–81, 83
familial factors, 102
gender differences, 99–101
genetics, 91–92
overview, 75–76
political factors, 105–106
social and economic factors,
    104–105
spirituality, 102–103
temperament, 101–102
unconscious processes, 97–98
willpower, 92–96
Prochaska, J. O., 6, 134
Procrastination
    anxiety, 358–359
    depression, 320
Professional burnout, prevention
    of, stages of change model, 7
Professional enabling, client engage-
    ment problems, 149
Progressive muscle relaxation,
    anxiety, 355–357
Project MATCH Research Group,
    17, 30, 38, 166, 263, 265,
    442, 445
Pryzbeck, T. R., 305
Psychiatry, depression, 321–322
Psychopharmacology. See
    Medications
Psychotherapy, third mode of, first
    session, 115

Questioning, anxiety, 350–351

Rating game, depression, 310–312
Rating style, of client, shame and
    guilt, 372–374

Rational emotive imagery (REI)
  anger management, 284–285
  anxiety, 349
  shame and guilt, 395
Rauch, S. L., 334, 362
REBT techniques. *See* CBT/
  REBT techniques
Recreational activities
  client's resources, 125
  type I clients, 200
Reframing, shame and guilt, 394
Regier, D. A., 305, 408
Rehearsal, anger management,
  289–290
Relapse. *See also* Lapse
  anger relapse prevention review,
    282, 283
  lapse compared, type III clients,
    236–239
  shame and guilt, 393
  stages of change model, 6
  techniques, 49–50
Relaxation techniques
  anger management, 282
  anxiety, 351–357
Religion. *See also* Spirituality
  client's resources, 124–125
  problem etiology, 102–103
Resistance, type I clients,
  170–172
Respect
  client engagement, 141
  type II clients, 206
Reverse role playing
  anger management, 287–289
  CBT/REBT techniques, 51
  severely disturbed clients, 422
  type III clients, 242–246
Review, anger management,
  289–290

Risks
  assessment, 128–129
  type II clients, 230–231
Robb, H., 428
Robins, C. J., 16
Robinson, T. E., 35
Robitschek, C., 102
Rogers, C., 116, 144, 414, 417
Role playing
  anger management, 287–289
  CBT/REBT techniques, 51
  depression, 315–316
  severely disturbed clients, 422
  shame and guilt, 395
  type III clients, 242–246
Rollnick, S., 160, 166
Rosenberg, H., 153, 156, 158
Rosencrance, J., 157
Ross, M., 35
Rousaville, B. J., 306
Royer, A., 435
Russell, B., 246, 331, 443
Rutgers Alcohol Problems
  Inventory, 133

Sadness, depression contrasted,
  312–313
Samenow, S. E., 250
Sanchez-Craig, M., 153
Schuckit, M. A., 91, 100, 102
Self-assessment, 134–135
Self-parenting, four R's of parenting
  for, severely disturbed clients,
  417–419
Seligman, M. E. P., 42, 443
Seneca, 165
Severely disturbed clients,
  407–425
  clinical strategies, 410–422
  coaching, 419

Severely disturbed clients (*continued*)
four R's of parenting for self-
parenting, 417–419
harm reduction, 416
plan exploration, 416–417
problem exploration,
411–413
reactivity, 420–422
REBT, 414–416
role playing and reverse role
playing, 422
secondary problem exploration,
419–420
session goals, 410
unconditional acceptance,
413–414
homework, 423–424
issues, 422–423
medications, 424
overview, 407
personality disorders, 408–409
research in, 408
resources listed, 425
stages of change model,
409–410
Sex differences. *See* Gender
differences
Sexuality, client's resources, 125
Shaffer, H. J., 98
Shafranske, E. P., 430, 434
Shame and guilt, 371–404
attributional style, 375–376
clinical issues, 377–395
ABC(DE), 383–388
alternatives, 381–383
amends, 394
assessment, 380–381
historical roots, 379–380
problem exploration,
378–379
rational emotive imagery, 395

reframing, 394
role playing, 395
session goals, 377
shame-attack exercises,
389–392
trigger situations, 392–393
homework, 403–404
issues, 399–403
amends, 402–403
anxiety and depression, 399
developmental factors, 400
family and genetics, 400–401
gender differences, 401
medical model limitations,
399–400
social and economic factors,
401
medications, 404
overview, 371–372
problems, 395–398
rating style of client, 372–374
research in, 376–377
Shame-attack exercises, 389–392
Sharkey, J., 76
Simon, S. B., 194
Skill teaching, client engagement,
142
Sleep, depression, 327–328
Smith, D. A., 445
Smith, T. L., 102
Smoking cessation, medications,
258–259
Snidman, N., 334
Sobell, L. C., 163
Sobell, M. B., 163
Social anxiety, 358
Social factors
anger management, 296
depression, 325
problem etiology, 104–105
shame and guilt, 401

Social networks, client's resources, 124

Sophocles, 203

"Spin doctors" and "anchors" metaphor, CBT/REBT techniques, 72–74

Spirituality, 427–446
advantages of, 441–444
client's resources, 124–125
dangers of, 444–445
depression, 326
God's role, 440–441
meaning of, 429–432
overview, 427–429
problem etiology, 102–103
science and, 445–446
techniques, 432–440
deity-focused, transpersonal, 432–434
non-deity-focused
non-transpersonal, 436–440
transpersonal, 434–436
type I clients, 201

Stages of change model, 3–38. *See also* ABC model;
Moderation/abstinence issue; Type I clients; Type II clients; Type III clients
I - precontemplation, 3
II - contemplation, 4
III- preparation, 4
IV - preparation, 4
V - maintenance, 5
VI - termination, 5
ABC model, 9–15
advantages of, 5–8
assessment, 116
client types, 8–9
severely disturbed clients, 409–410 (*See also* Severely disturbed clients)

Steele, D. R., 50

Sternberg, R. J., 143

Stigma
depression, 324
shame and guilt, 375

Strang, J., 157

Stress, addictions and, 29

Substance abuse, *DSM-IV*, 110–111

Substance dependence, *DSM-IV*, 111–113

Support
empathy and, client engagement, 141
type II clients, 207

Tafrate, R. C., 264, 271, 301

Tatarsky, A., 142, 156, 199

Tate, P., 50, 259

Taub, E., 435

Teaching stories, 437

Temperament, problem etiology, 101–102

Termination, change model, 5

Testimonials, 436

Therapeutic approach, stages of change model, 6–7

Therapist-avoidance behavior, type III clients, 250

Therapist self-disclosure, common ground, type II clients, 207

Therapist's negative feelings, client engagement, 145–148

Third mode of psychotherapy, first session, 115

Thomas, A. T., 101, 169

Three-column technique, type III clients, 248–249

Three-peers technique, information sharing, 143

Tillich, P., 331, 443

Time effects
  anger management, 273–275
  CBT/REBT techniques, 50–51
  type II clients, 222–223
Toneatto, T., 157, 259–260
Torrey, E. F., 82, 107
Toxic shame, 373, 374
Trance states, 438–439
Trauma, anxiety, 361–362
Treatability issue, assessment, 120
Triffleman, E., 185, 396, 399
Triggers
  assessment, behavior patterns,
    120–123
  shame and guilt, 392–393
Trimpey, J., 71
Tucker, J. A., 157
Type I clients, 165–202
  clinical strategies, 169–197
    ABC on another's problem,
      186–191
    ABC on other problem,
      191–193
    assessment, 170
    conflicting goals, 174–176
    explorations, 176–185
    goals and values, 193–197
    hook, 172–174
    information sharing, 174
    resistance, 170–172
    session goals, 169
  confrontation, 168
  homework, 199–201
  medication, 201–202
  motivation research, 169
  overview, 165–168
  problems, 197–199
  resources listed, 202
Type II clients, 203–234
  anger management, 267–268
  clinical strategies, 205–223

    common ground, 207
    conflicts, 208–210
    empathy, support, and
      compassion, 207
    experimental plan, 210–217
    historical roots, 208
    information, 207–208
    life goals and values review,
      223
    problem exploration,
      205–206
    respect, 206
    reviews, 217–220
    session goals, 205
    time-effect analysis, 222–223
    urges, 220–222, 224–225
  homework assignments,
    233–234
  issues, 229–233
    altered states of consciousness,
      232–233
    boredom, 230
    dysthymia, 229–230
    pleasure, 231–232
    risk taking, 230–231
  overview, 203–204
  problems, 223, 226–229
    ambivalence, 223, 226
    reframing, 226–228
    relapse understanding,
      228–229
Type III clients, 235–260
  anger management, 268
  clinical strategies, 239–250
    balanced lifestyle, 246–247
    low frustration tolerance,
      249–250
    plan development, 239–241
    reviews, 241–242
    role plays and reverse role
      plays, 242–246

session goals, 239
therapist-avoidance behavior,
    250
three-column technique,
    248–249
homework, 254–255
issues, 253–254
lapse and relapse, 236–239
medications, 255–259
    antabuse, 257
    methadone, 257–258
    naltrexone, 256–257
    smoking cessation, 258–259
overview, 235–236
problems, 251–253
resources listed, 259

Unconditional acceptance
    CBT/REBT techniques, 54–55
    client engagement, 139–140
    severely disturbed clients,
        413–414
Unconscious processes, problem
    etiology, 97–98
University of Rhode Island
    Change Assessment
    (URICA), 134

Vaillant, G. E., 98, 154, 199, 238
Values
    anger management, 269
    type I clients, 193–197
    type II clients, 223

Velten, E., 48, 50, 259, 358, 428,
    443, 444
Venting, anger management,
    298–299
Visualization, muscle relaxation
    and, anxiety, 355–357
"Voices" metaphor, CBT/REBT
    techniques, 70–71

Wegner, D. M., 62, 97
Wells, A., 358
West, R., 335
Wheatley, T., 62, 97
Wilde, O., 153
Willpower, problem etiology,
    92–96
Wilsnack, S. C., 100
Wilson, G. T., 158
Wodak, A., 129, 142, 156
Wyatt, G. E., 376
Wyatt, S., 408

Yalom, I. D., 442
Yochelson, S., 250
Young, C., 16
Young, H., 160
Young, J., 16

Zen Buddhism, 16, 414
Ziedonis, D., 408
Zinberg, N. E., 157

About the Author

F. Michler Bishop, Ph.D., CAS, is Director of Alcohol and Substance Abuse Services at the Albert Ellis Institute and an associate professor at the State University of New York, College at Old Westbury. He is also a past president of the New York State Psychological Association's Division on Addictions and national vice president of SMART Recovery, a cognitive-behavioral self-help organization. In the last ten years, he has primarily focused on prevention and expanding the availability and variety of treatment. He has specifically reached out to individuals who are engaging in addictive behaviors but do not know what they want to do or can do. In numerous workshops in this country, Spain, and Peru, Dr. Bishop has trained hundreds of practitioners in the cognitive-behavioral treatment of addictions.